r

The Advanced Nikon System

Laterna magica

Magic Lantern Guide to
The Advanced Nikon System

A Laterna magica® book

First English Language Edition January,1994
Published in the United States of America by

The Saunders Group
21 Jet View Drive
Rochester, NY 14624

From the original German edition by Michael Huber
Edited by Joseph Meehan
Translated by Hayley Ohlig
Production Coordinator, Marti Saltzman

Printed in Germany by Kösel GmbH, Kempten

ISBN 1-883403-03-0

Contents

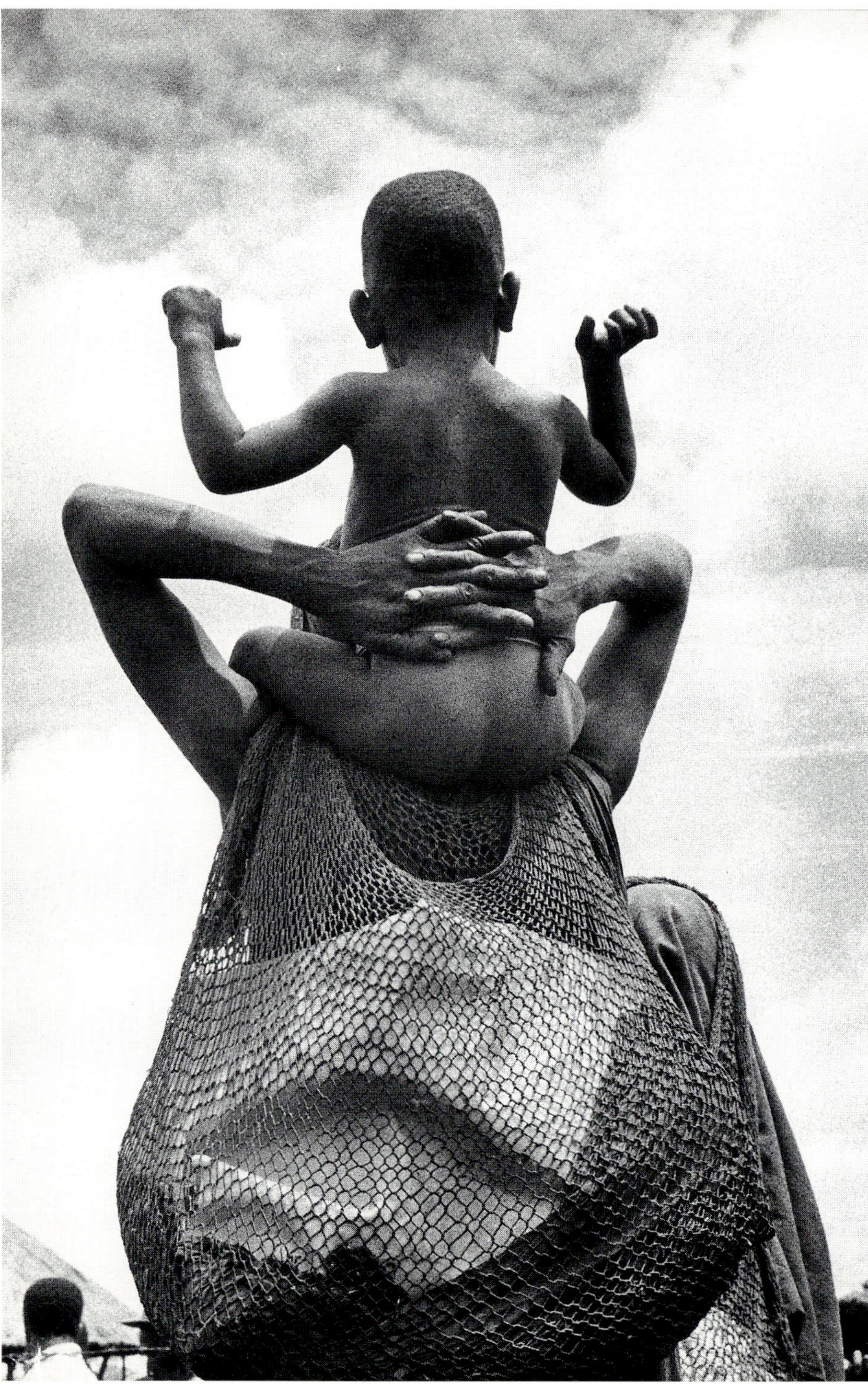

Purpose and Scope of This Book

The main purpose of this book is to provide extensive technical information about Nikon cameras, lenses and accessories to those readers who are interested in the Nikon system of photographic equipment. This information is presented in a comparative format to provide the reader with the kind of information that is very helpful, if not essential, when trying to decide which camera, lens, or accessory would best fit their purpose. In that sense, this book is not just a computation of specifications and procedures as is typically found in the instructional manuals and other informational sheets that accompany new equipment. On the contrary, this book goes beyond such approaches to provide the kind of insights about the equipment that one would expect to hear from a discussion between a group of knowledgeable photographers comparing the important features of various equipment.

Typically then, this book prepares the way for answers to questions such as: "which lens should I buy, X or Y?" "What is the difference between the program and auto metering mode and what difference will it make in my work?" "Is it really worth paying the higher price for the F4 rather than the N8008/F801?" Answers to such questions are, of course, based to a large degree on the individual photographer's needs. But more often, the answers are a lot easier to work out when the photographer has a grasp of the whole system of photography that the camera or lens is part of, rather than just the narrow view offered by an instructional manual. This is particularly true of the Nikon system because it is the most complete 35mm Single Lens Reflex system presently being offered. It is our view then that the photographer is better served by presenting both a technical description and a certain amount of insight into the comparative qualities of the equipment under discussion. Furthermore, by covering the entire range of equipment the reader should understand something of the whole approach to photography represented by the Nikon system. That, in turn, should give them more of an appreciation of the potential uses of the equipment they own, as well as what is available to help them expand their photographic horizons.

It should also be said at the outset, that while this book attempts to provide solutions to the photographer's needs with Nikon equipment, it is not a book written to praise Nikon cameras and equipment. Nor has this text been commissioned or supported by Nikon in any special way. There was important help provided by Nikon Germany, whose PR department supplied a great deal of technical information and some of the illustrations, and their customer service department answered many questions during the preparation of the technical material. Other than this type of support, this book represents the views of its authors and those professionals who have served as resources.

Also, while a major effort has gone into providing as much technical information as necessary to understand the design and function of a particular piece of equipment, this book is not a substitute for the more detailed specifications that accompany individual equipment, or is available from Nikon's various technical services. Thus, this book does

An example of the type of documentary photography that earned Nikon its reputation for ruggedness and reliability while "on the road." Photo: Rudolf Dietrich

not claim to cover every last technical detail. Rather, the guiding principle has been to provide all that is necessary to understand what the equipment does as well as how it may relate to other, similar equipment. For example, noting that "the MB-21 battery pack for the F4 comes in two sections and that the hand grip must be connected, versus the MB-23 which comes in one piece," is the kind of detail that is of limited value to a reader and prohibitively expensive in terms of space in a book of this size. It is, in fact, the kind of detail expected from individual equipment manuals.

Sources

The information contained in this book is based on personal experiences with the cameras, lenses and accessories as well as the valuable input of many other professional photographers. Written sources include original Nikon publications such as instructional manuals, brochures and, especially, the "Nikon Sales Program," which is published in Switzerland, Germany and France, approximately once every two years. A detailed bibliography can be found at the end of the book. A special thanks is also extended to Nikon, Germany for the help they provided as previously cited.

Notes on Phraseology

In the interest of clarity, and to avoid unnecessarily long citations, complete specification of model names and numbers used in both Europe and the United States generally occurs only in the chapter on cameras along with the notations for the later variants. Throughout the rest of the book, just the main model numbers are used unless there is a need to make some point of differentiation particular to the variant. Consequently, a statement about the "F4" generally applies to all F4 models, unless an explicit reference is made to the special features of the different models. This also applies when referring to the US/European designations as in N4004/F-401, N6006/F-601 and N8008/F-801, in conjunction with their variants; N4004s/F-401s, N5005/F-401x, N6000/F-601m, N8008s/F-801s respectively.

Suggestions Welcome

Although this book has taken more than a year to complete with careful attention to details, the odd "misprint" may have slipped in and any criticism of this fact will be gratefully accepted. Moreover, any suggestions concerning how to improve a future edition would be equally well received.

Nikon - A Brief History of A Highly Successful Camera Company

This short chapter is intended to highlight the extensive and interesting history of Nippon Kogaku, the company that produces Nikon photographic cameras, lenses and accessories. The purpose here is to briefly illustrate the development of the company's philosophy and not to serve as a substitute for the more extensive readings available in the collector's literature.

How it all Began

Nikon was founded in 1917, as "Nippon Kogaku" (The Japanese Optical Company), in Tokyo, Japan. Since Japan had no optical industry to speak of at the time, Nippon Kogaku first had to build its own complete glassworks and glass-grinding workshop with the aid of technicians from Germany which was the leading nation in the field of optics and glass manufacture at that time. Although a fledgling company breaking new ground, Nippon Kogaku had certain key factors in their favor from the beginning, not the least of which was, what we would probably call today, an aggressive management team. But there was also the early and strong commitment to research and development (which continues to this day) and the availability of high-quality reserves of practically all the raw materials needed for the manufacture of optical glasses.

Nippon Kogaku, or "Nikon" for short, eventually became an international leader in camera optics through their development of "Nikkor" lenses. By the beginning of the 1950s, not only had Nikon developed and produced over 200 different lenses, but one of their creations, the 85mm f/2.0 appearing on the market in 1949, was arguably the best lens in 35mm photography. This early and remarkable success was shortly paralleled by innovations in the production of 35mm cameras.

From Copier to Leader

While the ground work was being laid for the eventual leadership role that Nikon would play in 35mm SLR photography, the earliest products were basically copies of established models. But by the beginning of the 1950s, this began to change. While their remarkable 85mm f/2.0 was helping to make their optic reputation, the Nikon I 35mm viewfinder camera was also changing minds. The heavy brass body, milled "from the block", and mechanical details, which were simple in comparison to the Contax II original, were regarded with smug disdain by German competitors. But these disadvantages quickly became desirable advantages as the camera proved itself to be virtually indestructible when used by American reporters during the Korean War. Furthermore, some of the Nikkor lenses were considered by many as at least equal to their German competitors Zeiss or Leitz in terms of speed and sharpness and were, in some respects, actually superior. So, some photographers exchanged their Leica or Contax for the Nikon rangefinder cameras, in some cases for the sake of the 85mm f/2.0 lens.

Following the Korean war, the improved Nikon S rangefinder camera became, with sales of over 36,000, one of the first worldwide successes of the Japanese camera industry. This was followed by different S versions, including the Nikon SP, produced from 1957 to 1965. Featuring a titanium slit shutter with a top speed of 1/1000 seconds, it emerged as the main competitor to Leica cameras with worldwide sales of over 20,000. But, in contrast to Leitz, Nikon was quick to recognize the limitations of the 35mm viewfinder camera. Thus, they concentrated their energies on the development of the 35mm SLR camera.

The Nikon SLR

Nikon brought out their first SLR, the Nikon F, in 1959. The groundbreaking feature of this camera was that it was designed as a system camera with interchangeable viewfinders and viewfinder screens, as well as a back that could take motor drives with normal or bulk film magazines. This versatile camera system intended to meet the requirements of the professional photographer.

In addition to the interchangeable features, Nikon also opted for a single-twist bayonet lens mount from the start. The durable titanium slit shutter, the 100% viewfinder image, and the particularly bright and clear focusing screens of the Nikon F were also features which the professional considered desirable and were only offered by Nikon.

Within a few years, when a complete range of lenses became available, Nikon had become a leader in SLR photography. But while the 35mm format had been widely accepted in the field of photojournalism and among many non-professionals, the quality and speed of black-and-white and color films left something to be desired. That meant a technological improvement in emulsions would be necessary before the 24mm x 36mm "miniature format" of 35mm could be more widely accepted. While improvement in emulsion technology progressed and the 35mm format grew in acceptance, the potential for automation in the SLR design was evolving with Nikon at the forefront. The major areas of development were in simplifying exposure metering and reducing the setting of the aperture and shutter speed to a single operation rather than the sequence of steps as it had been.

In 1965, a first step down the road to the types of automation we are used to having in our modern SLRs was taken with the Nikon F with a Photomic T metered prism. This meter arrangement featured an interchangeable viewfinder with integrated internal metering, or "Through The Lens" ("TTL") metering as it was eventually called.

Emergence of the 35mm SLR Camera Line

Paralleling the success of the professional F series was the Nikkormat line, aimed at a more general market. Its interchangeable nature was limited to use of different lenses, but with the later FT models, it also provided the highly desirable TTL metering feature along with "wide open metering." That is, readings could be taken with the lens wide open instead of "stop down metering" in which light readings had to be taken by literally stopping down the aperture. In wide open metering, the view remains bright as the aperture remains physically wide open. The meter reads the light coming through the lens and makes adjustments in the readings as the aperture (and shutter speeds) are changed. In order to achieve wide open metering on the F cameras, Nikon designed a meter-to-lens linkage based on each lens having to be keyed into the meter prism. This was done by giving the aperture ring a quick turn immediately after mounting the lens to the body. Through this action, the aperture setting was automatically transmitted to a cam in the camera.

With the appropriate meter head on an "F" body and with the FT Nikkormat series, this wide open form of automatic metering became standard with the Nikon SLR line. Thus, the term "automatic" on lenses at this time meant that they could be used in a wide open, but manual metering approach. The next step came in the Nikkormat series with the Nikkormat EL, the first automatic aperture priority camera from Nikon. Thus, Nikon showed early on its tendency to introduce its most advanced features in cameras considered to be just below their top of the line "F" series, as was again done just recently with the Nikon N90 and the new "D" or Distance Technology.

While wide open aperture metering became a standard feature of the "F" series, it was the unique interchangeable prism which gave it, a specific design advantage. Specifically, it meant you could upgrade the metering system as well as offer other prisms for different uses, without having to build a whole new camera body for each option. Nikon's F2 (from 1971) really refined this design advantage providing for advances in the metering system right up to the 1976 Nikon F2SB.

With the appearance of the Nikon F2A and F2AS, additional metering possibilities opened up thanks to the new AI (automatic indexing) generation of lenses. The speed of lens mounting was thus made quicker as the lens could be placed on the camera with one movement which mounted the lens, and automatically transmitted its minimum aperture to the camera by means of a simple control pin. The arrival of the F2AS made Nikon the undisputed leader in photojournalism as 35mm photography itself was being made more "respectable" because of improved film stocks. In addition, as all this was occurring, the whole consumer photography market entered its greatest boom to date.

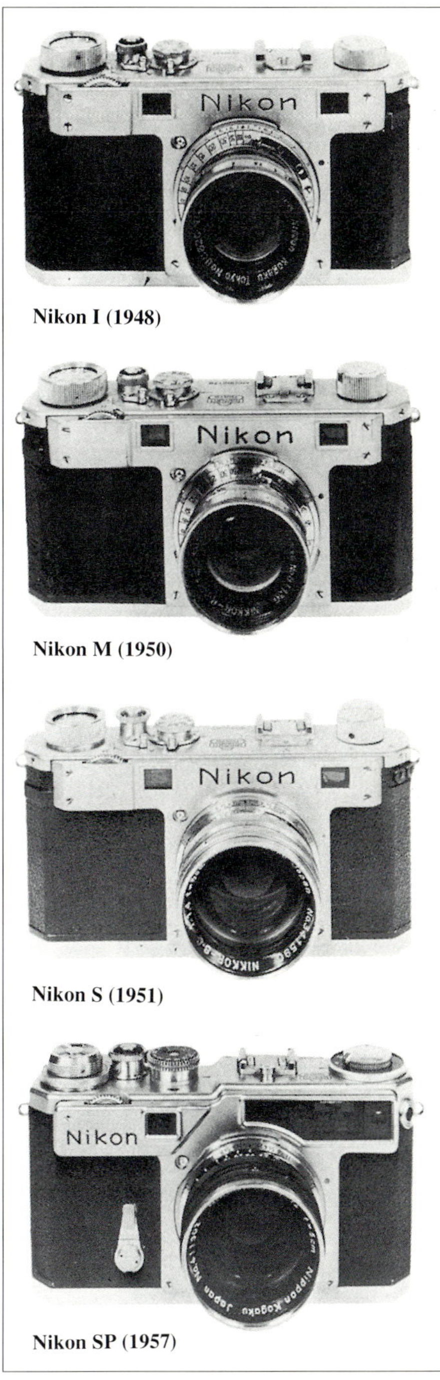

Nikon I (1948)

Nikon M (1950)

Nikon S (1951)

Nikon SP (1957)

Nikon Goes Electronic

While the Nikon "F" and Nikkormat lines had such undeniable advantages as a brighter viewfinder, a huge range of excellent lenses and a well deserved reputation for robustness, they were large and somewhat bulky cameras. Nikon could not ignore the advances in compactness and ease of operation that were occurring in non-professional SLRs. The appearance of the Olympus compact OM line of cameras and their quick acceptance by a significant number of photographers, pointed to the desire to have a smaller, compact, but still fully professional camera. The "F" camera had provided versatility unmatched at the time, but it was a bulky camera when compared to the new SLR compact models.

Thus, Nikon released the Nikon FM in

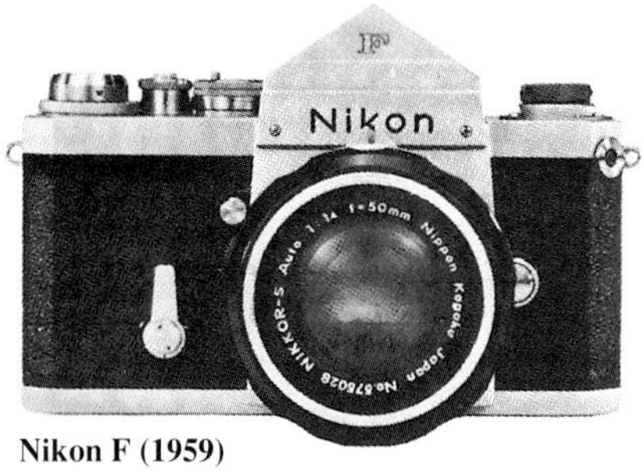

Nikon F (1959)

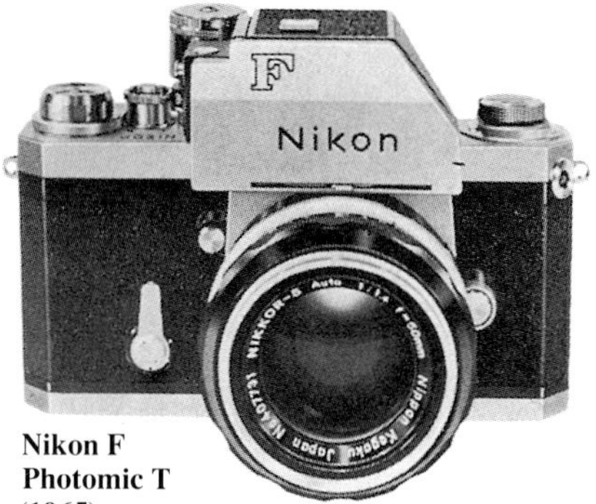

Nikon F Photomic T (1965)

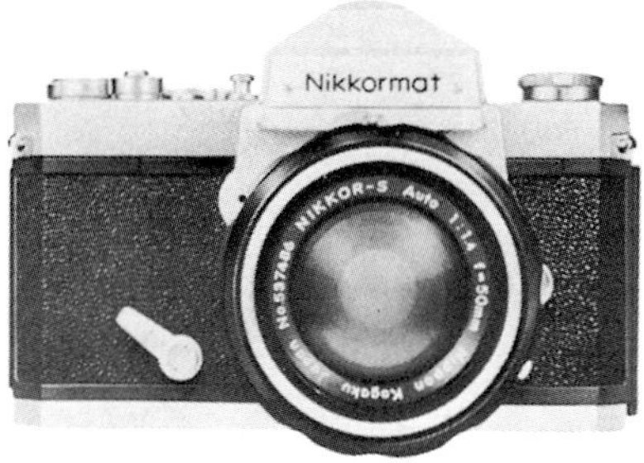

Nikkormat FT (1965)

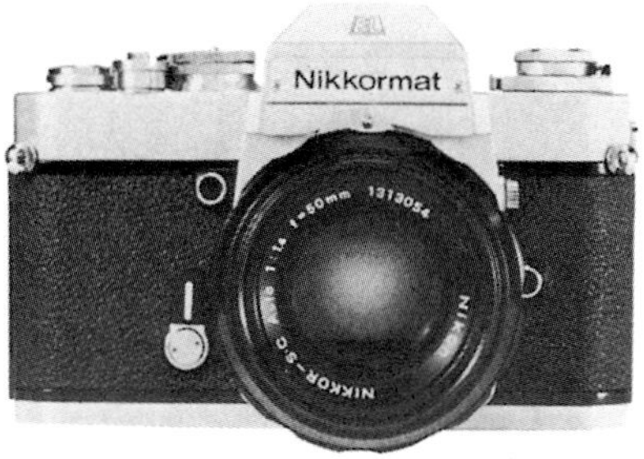

Nikkormat EL (1972)

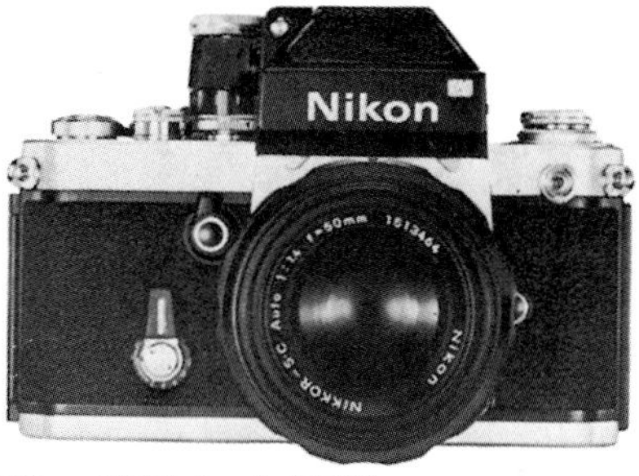

Nikon F2 Photomic (1971)

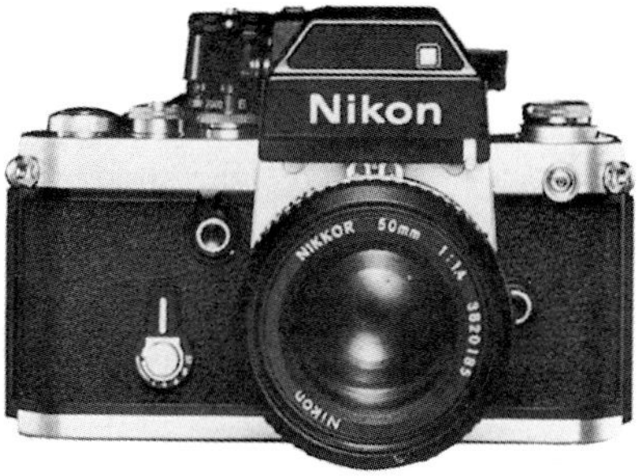

Nikon F2SB Photomic (1976)

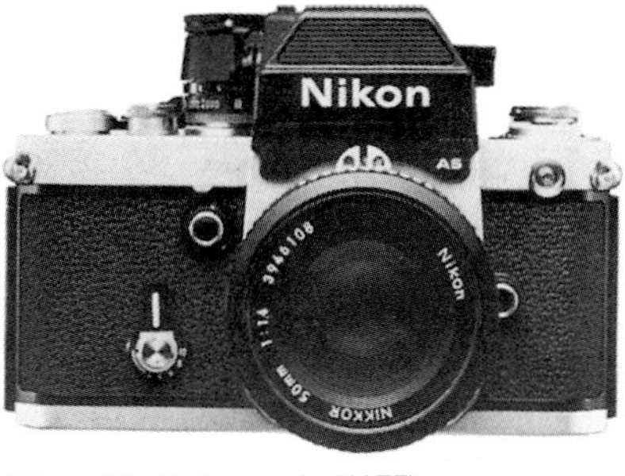

Nikon F2AS Photomic (1977)

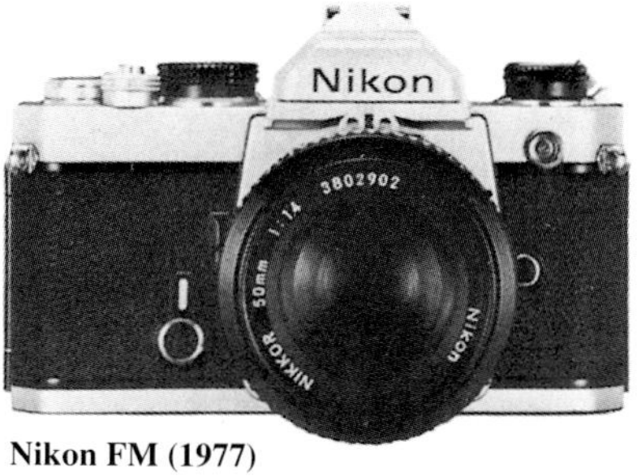

Nikon FM (1977)

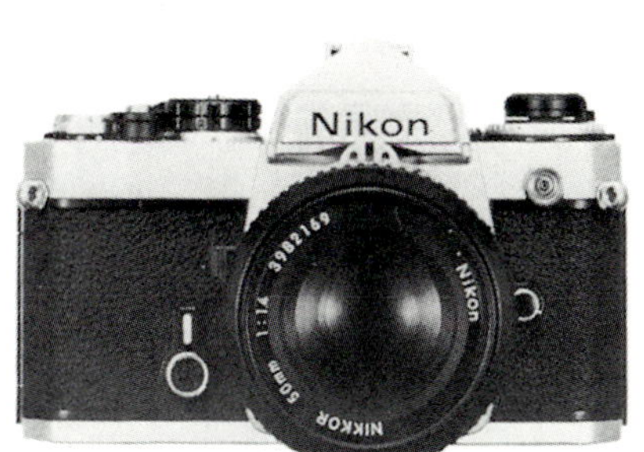

Nikon FE (1978)

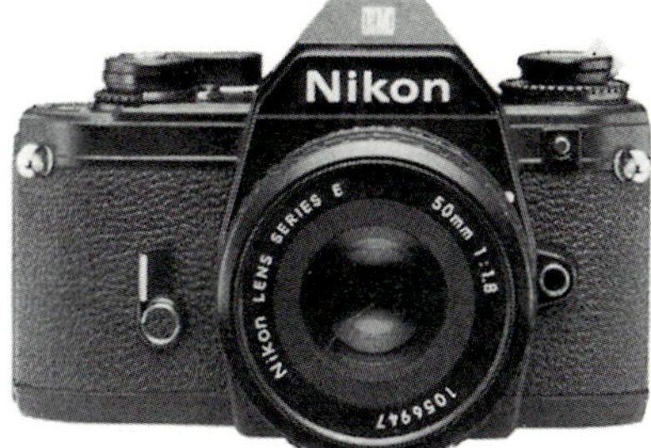

Nikon EM (1979)

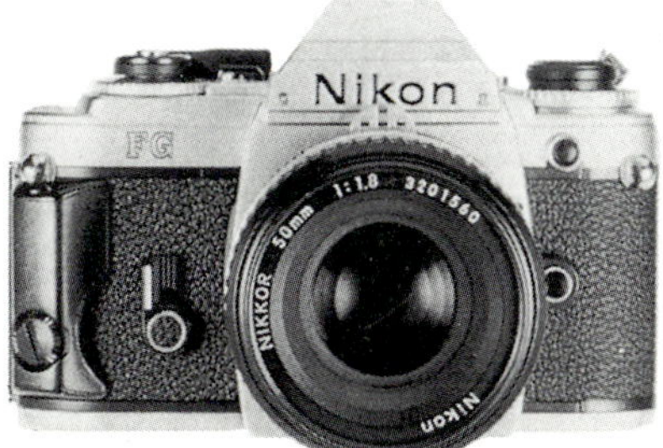

Nikon FG (1982)

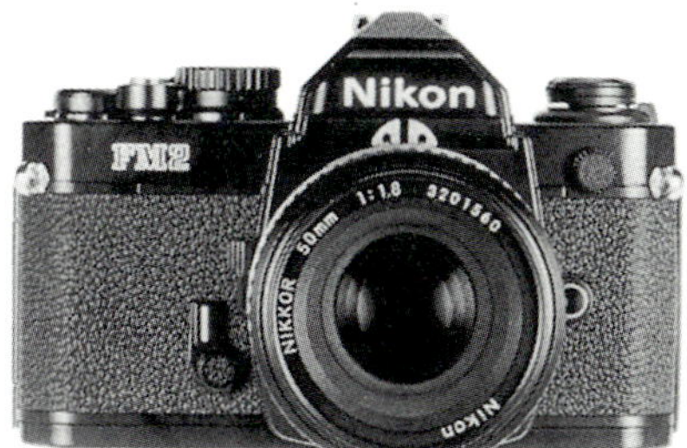

Nikon FM-2 (1982)

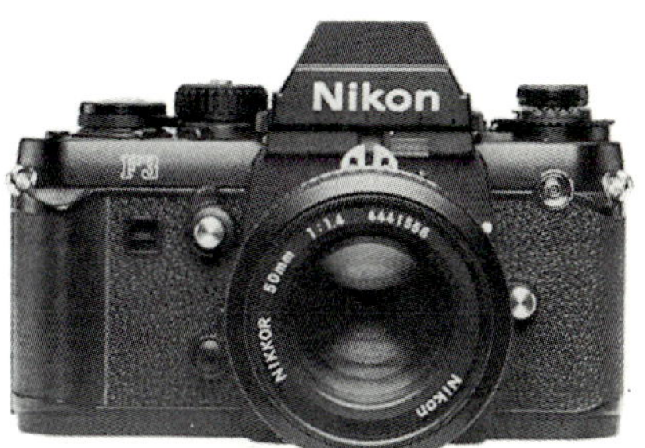

Nikon F3 (1980)

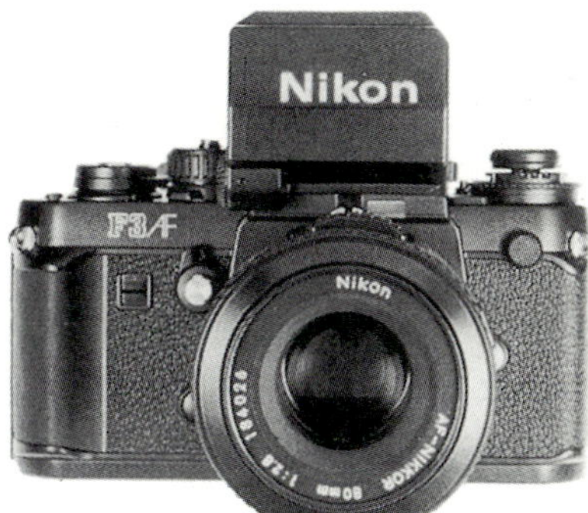

Nikon F3 AF (1983)

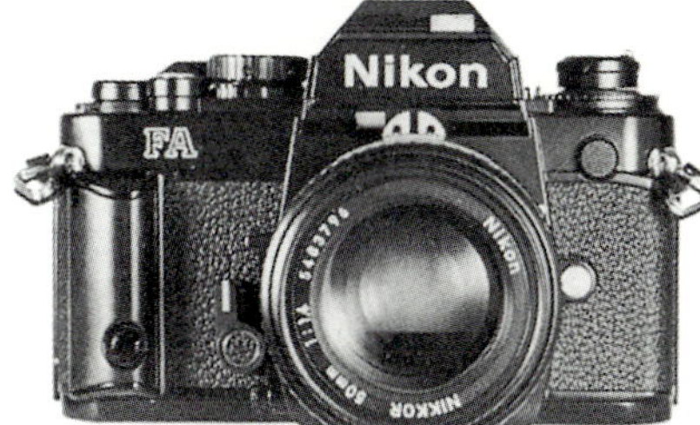

Nikon FA (1983)

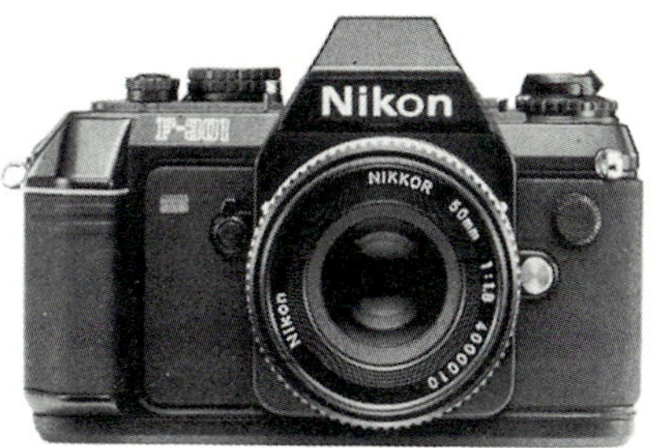

Nikon N2002/F-301 (1985)

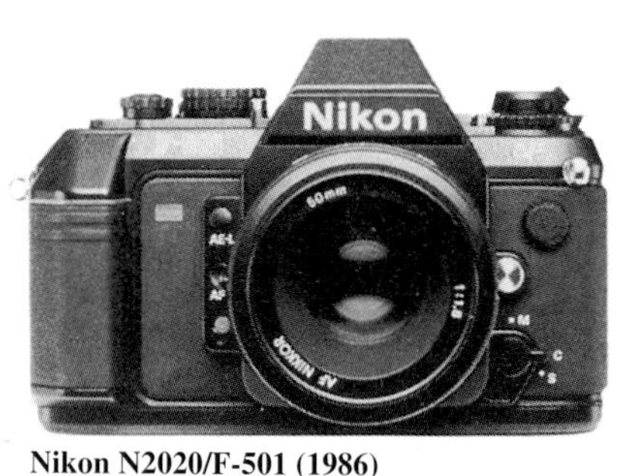

Nikon N2020/F-501 (1986)

Nikon N4004/F-401 (1987)

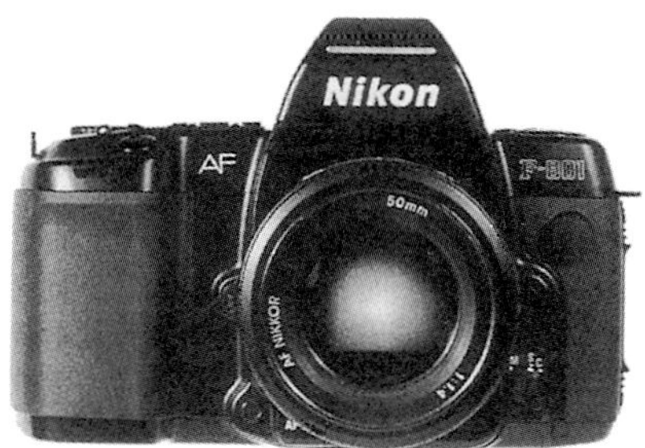

Nikon N8008/F-801 (1988)

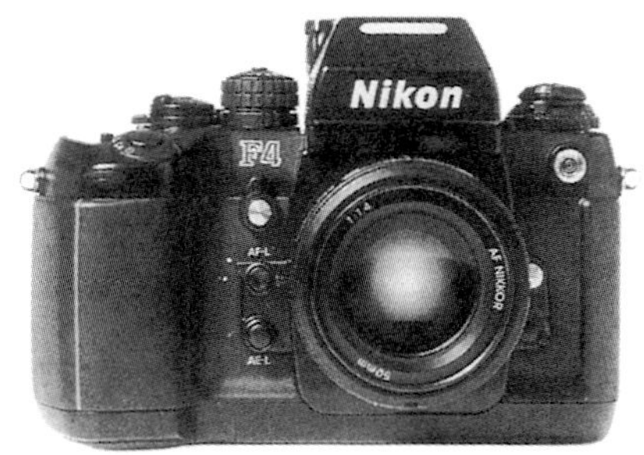

Nikon F4 (1988)

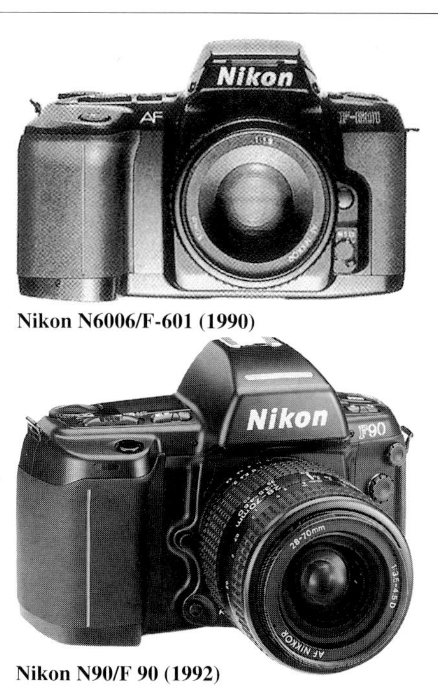

Nikon N6006/F-601 (1990)

Nikon N90/F 90 (1992)

1977, a relatively compact, but still essentially fully-mechanical camera. This was meant to be a backup camera for the professional and the ideal mechanical camera for those who were put off by the increasing use of electronics. Its improved versions, the FM-2 (from 1982) and FM-2n (from 1983) all proved to be durable machines that met a very definite market need. The original FM was followed in 1978 by the Nikon FE, an up-to-date, aperture priority automatic camera in virtually the same body configuration as the FM.

The automatic only, Nikon EM (or "plastic Nikon" as its detractors called it), was introduced in 1979. It did not fair nearly as well in terms of sales to the consumer market. The same low sales fate greeted the less expensive "E" series lenses that came with the EM and (later FG line) even though at least one of these lenses, the 75-150mm, has become a favorite, almost a "cult lens," among serious photographers because of its excellent performance and light weight.

The lack of enthusiasm for the Nikon EM was made up for by the release of the FG which appeared in 1982 becoming, like the simpler model, the FG-20 (from 1984), an extremely popular model worldwide in the so-called amateur market. Despite its non-professional delineation, the FG was the first fully-automatic Nikon camera to feature shutter priority, aperture priority, and automatic program exposure control. This advance in automation brought with it the need for a new generation of lenses, the AIS series. In aperture-priority metering, it was only necessary to transmit the pre-selected aperture setting from the lens to the camera and "shut down" the aperture to this "working value" by means of a spring lever when the shutter was released. But in the case of shutter-speed priority or program exposure metering, the aperture had to be precisely closed to a setting calculated in advance by the camera and that function meant new lenses.

Nikon was also making major strides with its professional models. The next top of the line "F" camera rolled off the line in 1980 in the form of the Nikon F3. While it did not garner the same initial acclaim as the F2, it has emerged as one of the real all-time workhorses for professional photographers throughout the world. The aperture-priority exposure, the TTL automatic flash exposure, and the Liquid Crystal viewfinder display, together with AIS lenses made taking pictures quicker, more reliable, and easier. At the same time, the new F3 could use virtually all the lenses in the "F" line, albeit with some minor modification of the oldest lenses. This is, again true of the recent "D" lenses that fit on virtually any Nikon, as well as the N90/F90 without, of course, the benefit of Distance Technology. In terms of accessories such as interchangeable viewfinders, focusing screens, motor drives, etc., the F3 was more technically advanced than the old F2 and, therefore, these were not interchangeable.

In 1983, Nikon introduced the Nikon FA, the first SLR camera in the world to feature automatic exposure compensation through multi-field exposure metering. This was the precursor to the Matrix Metering configurations of today's cameras. In addition to this, it also had: a compact construction, an LC (Liquid Crystal) viewfinder display, an efficient film motordrive, aperture priority, shutter speed priority and automatic program exposure control, as well as a top shutter speed of 1/4000 seconds. All this made the FA popular with both professionals and serious amateur photographers alike and, in hindsight, it was a harbinger of what was still to come on the professional level. It should be said, however, that in practice, the FA's multi-field metering did not entirely live up to expectations. Nevertheless, it demonstrated, once again, a market need among serious and professional photographers for a a camera that had advanced features and could use all the Nikkor lenses, but was not a "built like a tank, one hundred rolls a day" top-of-the-line camera.

In 1985 the Nikon N2000/F-301, the first Nikon with a built-in motor drive, signaled the start of a new direction and ushered in a new physical look to Nikon's cameras. Not all of this was well received initially. For example, its high proportion of plastic like materials caused some Nikon purists to shudder. On the the other hand, there were some changes that would prove to be standard features for the next generation of cameras, such as the first really error free automatic film threading system with simultaneous checking of the film transport. Functionally, this camera proved to be extremely versatile and easy to operate, thanks to the practical manner of using exposure options which included: manual, aperture program and the automatic program. The N2000 proved itself to be an ideal camera for those taking their first steps in serious photography or in the amateur field. It became one of the best-selling SLRs worldwide and would probably have continued to sell well after production was discontinued in 1991. But by this time Nikon was already concentrating fully on autofocus cameras and a new generation of AF lenses.

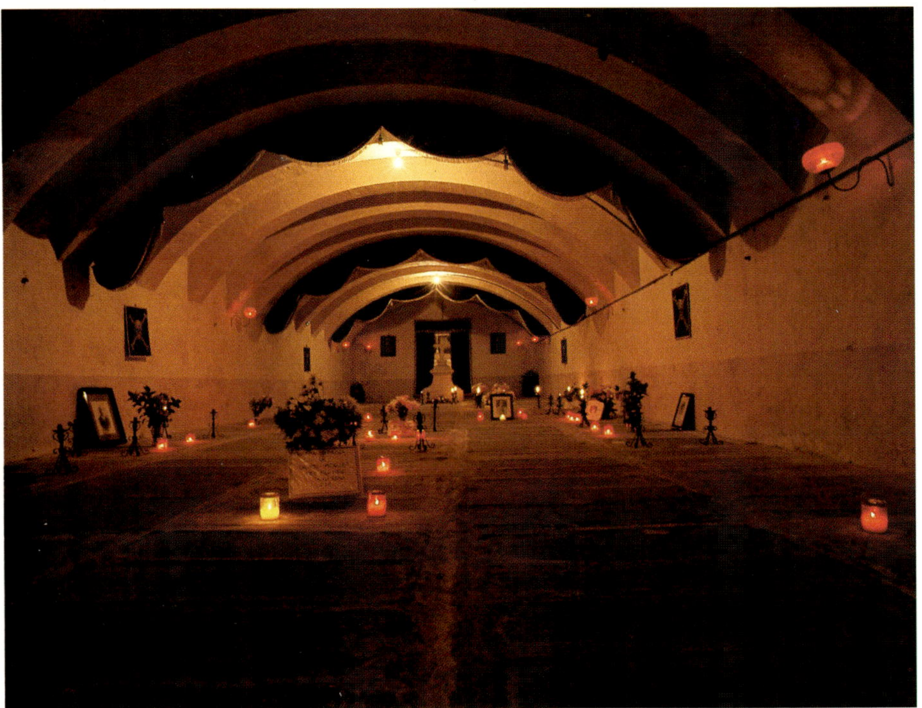

This vault was shot by "available" candlelight with the camera resting on the floor in aperture priority automatic mode (20mm f/5.6 at about 30 sec. using the self-timer). In order to improve sharpness, the aperture was not opened wider and focus was made first in the automatic mode, locked in and then the camera switched to manual focus.

Nikon Autofocus Cameras

During the first half of the 1980s, several manufacturers experimented with automatically-focusing cameras, including Nikon with its modified F3, designated as the F3AF. However, Nikon's efforts in this field actually date back to 1971, when the prototype of an AF lens was presented. The AF "intelligence hardware" was integrated in a special AF viewfinder and there were two AF lenses and an AF converter. Another feature was the "passive" focusing of the viewfinder image in a relatively simple variant of "phase detection." Looking back, this innovative approach probably failed partly because this AF system was relatively slow and somewhat unreliable; it was also expensive and there was no real ground swell of support for this level of autofocus technology among professionals. The course of development of autofocus technology, as well as the continued perfection of automated exposure systems, were changing the way camera manufacturers had to think about new productions as never before. With the beginning of the "AF Revolution" it was now becoming clear that Nikon was confronted with the same hard facts that had reduced the market share of the major German camera manufacturers such as Zeiss, Rollei and Leitz earlier on: that is, technological advances were no longer principally developed through professional market segments, but from the mass market made up of a diverse range of non-professional photographers.

So while the professionals ran thousands of rolls through their cameras, the ever-growing category of non-professionals was demanding features that made picture taking easier but with better results. Thus, as technology permitted the manufacture of "dream equipment," the reality of economics was obvious; without a

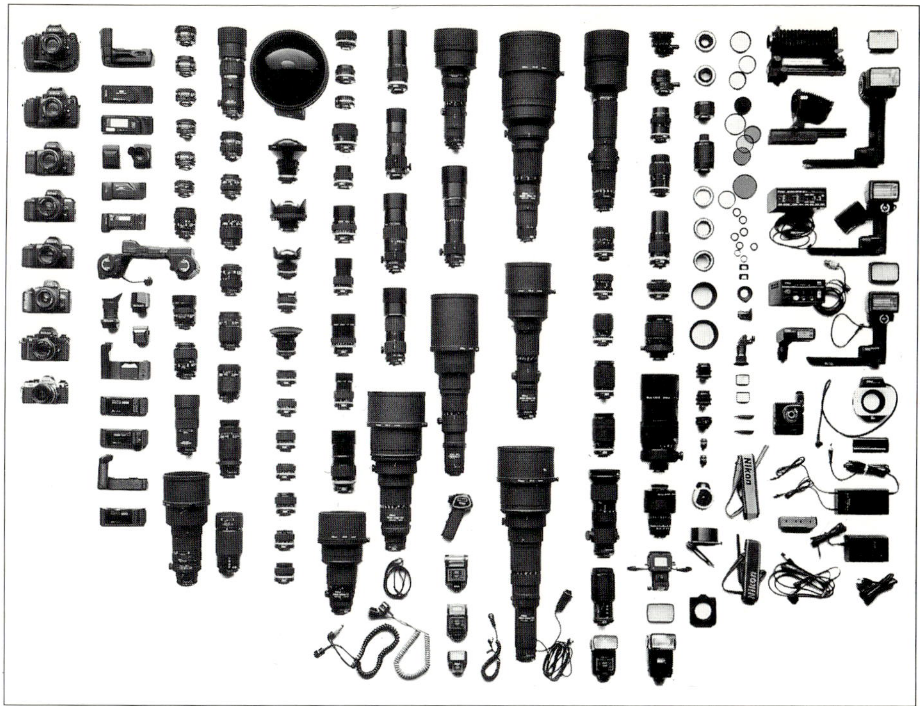

Nikon equipment represents the most complete line of compatible 35mm cameras, lenses, flash units and other accessories available for the demanding amateur and the professional photographer to use in every conceivable application.

reasonable market to recoup the substantial capital required to build advanced equipment, there would be little or no return on investments. What is the point, for example, of developing a top quality, super fast, and very expensive telephoto lens if only a few thousand can be sold worldwide to professionals? Such realities would not, in some cases, even pay for developmental or manufacturing costs. Whereas a telephoto lens of similar quality which is not quite so fast, costing less than one fifth the amount, will find tens of thousands of buyers around the world within a matter of months.

The dynamic effect of this mass market sales reality is even more extreme when considering the specifics of electronics. Whether it be picture sensors or microcomputer chips, any small-scale production in this area is extremely expensive and involves high reject quotas. Only mass production of chips provides consistent quality at an affordable price. In the very early days of AF photography, Nikon was probably unwilling to risk this basic investment in modern electronics and so Minolta, with their Minolta 7000 camera, produced the first all electronic AF-SLR bestseller. This brought Minolta a lot of new customers, but their switch to a new bayonet mount made the old non-AF lenses obsolete. Canon followed Minolta's lead to produce the EOS series which had its own lenses.

In 1986 Nikon did finally release their first mass-produced AF SLR, the Nikon N2020/F-501. This camera was recently replaced by the N6006/F-601 AF which now occupies the market segment between the N5005/F-401x and the N8008/F-801. The AF qualities of the N2020/F-501 were impressive at the time, but seem rather deficient by today's standards. In glaring contrast to its competitors, however, the Nikon N2020 had two features which were typical of Nikon: compatibility with the old non-AF lenses and the use of classic Nikon operating controls as opposed to the complete reliance on dial-in video display controls of Minolta and Canon. It was quite well received by serious photographers and some professionals invested in the N2020 as a relatively economical second body and thus made their first attempts at AF photography without risking any excessive investment.

Naturally, a new generation of AF lenses accompanied the first AF Nikon. These Nikkors have the classic Nikon bayonet mount but, in addition, each lens contains a small microcomputer which transmits the necessary information on the focusing movements to the camera and also provides digital electronic data on the effective aperture value, lens speed and focal length. In a sense, the N2020/F-501 and the first AF lenses fulfilled a pilot function during which Nikon had enough market presence and time to develop a completely new generation of AF cameras and AF lenses. The N4004/F-401, which appeared in 1987, with its "total automatic exposure" principally covered the amateur end of the market.

It was in 1988 that Nikon introduced its real competitors in the growing AF market; the Nikon N8008/F-801 and the Nikon F4. The N8008 was aimed, primarily, at that diverse market just below the working professional. With its multi-field metering, in the tradition of the FA, it is also Nikon's first truly fully-electronic camera. However, in contrast to many other modern electronic cameras, the operating controls of the N8008 are ergonomically efficient and very easy to learn. So it is not surprising that it very quickly became one of the most popular Nikons of all time and remains so today, in the improved version, the F8008s/F-801s.

The response to the F4, the new AF flagship in the professional range, was somewhat less than immediate. The interchangeable viewfinder system, the fast motor drive and the robust mechanics certainly met with approval. But the fact that mechanical operating controls had been retained despite the highly complex internal electronics and wide range of automatic functions, was received more critically. By trying to preserve the use of buttons and switches and not use the digital display "video game" approach, there was a necessary increase in the number and complexity of these "mechanical" operating elements. This made some of the operations less than simple or convenient. In addition, any camera which is jammed with digital electronics, from whatever manufacturer, is more susceptible to breakdown than the best mechanical models. This may come as a disappointment to some professionals who liked to think they could use an F4 to "hammer nails," as was said of older "F" models. To make matters worse, early F4 cameras were reported to have high breakdown rates which, was never true but unfortunately was a critical negative for any pro camera, especially in light of the record the other F models had established.

There was one other reservation concerning the wholehearted acceptance of the F4, which Nikon could do nothing about: the antipathy towards AF shown by many photographers. The fact that Nikon continues to offer the F3 and FM-2n attests, in part, to the preference among many professionals and serious non-professionals alike, for a manual focus camera.

On the other hand, Nikon is now producing a full line of AF lenses and is obviously completely committed to that technology. Apart from special areas for which autofocus is not suitable for technical reasons, the non-AF Nikkor range will probably be phased out in the long term. Although all non-AF Nikkors can be mounted on AF cameras, there are considerable restrictions on the automatic exposure modes available when they are used, which reduces the effectiveness of the camera's potential. Conversely, AF Nikkors can be used without any problem on the classic Nikon cameras, although the "feeling" of the mechanical focusing on most AF lenses is not nearly as refined as on conventional non-AF lenses.

Nikon's Philosophy: Compatibility with a Concentration on Essentials

Nikon stands alone today in the field of 35mm photography with its commitment to maintaining almost total compatibility between cameras and lenses produced over several generations. Though this may have been a disadvantage in the fast-changing mass market where the latest electronic marvel of a camera may have seemed to be redefining photography, it did enable Nikon to maintain its overall established position with professionals and win over newcomers who were looking for a system that provided a mix of manual-mechanical as well as automatic-electronic functions with complete compatibility among lenses. This meant, for example, having access to many more lenses and accessories available on the huge used market.

But also as regards automation, Nikon has always concentrated on what was essential and practical rather than what was possible. This is also apparent in their autofocus philosophy; whereas their competitors suggested the possibility of total automation of focusing with multi-field autofocus, Nikon has so far deliberately allowed the photographer to make a conscious decision on which part of the subject should be in focus, and Nikon has remained aloof from such complexities as chip card programming, although the N90 with its separate computer programming system, may mark the departure from this view point. As desirable as "intelligent" cameras might be in some cases (e.g. display of depth of field and picture contrast), Nikon's design philosophy is apparently that the camera should not become a computer game and the photographer lose control over key functions. In short, there seems to be a consistent strategy in their AF/all-electronic philosophy that the camera should not take the picture, but rather the photographer must, in the end, decide when to take it and under what conditions.

Nikon Cameras

Nikon F3 - The Classic Professional Camera

F3, F3HP, F3/T, Technical Data and Characteristics

Camera type: electronically-controlled 35mm SLR with interchangeable viewfinder system; with conventional mechanical operating controls and, therefore, particularly fast and direct access to the different functions; manual exposure setting and aperture priority automatic exposure; all versions with robust metal body; F3/T made of titanium for hard professional use.

Film format: 35mm film; 24 x 36mm picture format.

Lens mount: Nikon F bayonet fitting with AI aperture value transmission.

Suitable lenses: all AI/AIS Nikkors and all AF Nikkors (can only be manually focused); all older Nikkors converted to AI; older Nikkors without AI coupling after folding up the AI aperture cam on the camera body, with stopped-down metering.

Shutter: electronically-controlled horizontal-action titanium foil slit shutter.

Shutter speeds: quartz-controlled fixed speeds from 8 seconds to 1/2000 second and X-flash sync speed 1/80 second plus "B" and "T," all shutter speeds plus aperture-priority A selected directly by means of shutter speed dial; without batteries, 1/60 second and T can also be triggered mechanically using an auxiliary shutter release on the front of the camera; in aperture priority mode, stepless shutter speeds of between 8 seconds and 1/2000 second are formed according to the pre-selected aperture setting.

Shutter release: electromechanical, 2-stage function; partial depression activates exposure metering for approximately 16 seconds, full depression releases shutter; integrated main power switch; thread connection for cable release.

Remote shutter release: via cable release or electrically in combination with MD-4 winder via MC-12/12A remote shutter release cable.

Viewfinder: interchangeable DE-2 prism viewfinder standard on F3; DE-3 high-eyepoint viewfinder ideal for people wearing glasses (standard on F3HP); DE-4 high-eyepoint viewfinder with titanium body on F3/T; these viewfinders have an eyepiece shutter to keep out stray light; 3 other viewfinders can be fitted; 100% of the picture field can be seen, at 0.8 x magnification on the F3, and 0.75x magnification on the F3HP (with a 50mm lens set to infinity).

Focusing screen: type K with split-screen indicator and microprism ring as standard; can be interchanged with 20 other focusing screens.

Viewfinder information: LC display of shutter speed; in manual mode an M appears with either + or -; + and - appear together when exposure is correctly adjusted; in automatic mode, +2000 appears to indicate overexposure and -8 to indicate underexposure; direct readout of selected aperture setting in the viewfinder; an LED indicates flash readiness when compatible flash units are used; viewfinder illumination can be switched on if required.

Exposure metering: internal metering system with center-weighted open-aperture metering (80/20 weighting); metering beam is passed through a pinhole mirror and via a connected auxiliary mirror to a silicon photo diode in the base of the camera.

Exposure compensation: from +2 to -2 in 1/3 EV steps (1 EV = 1 exposure step = 1 "f stop").

Reflex mirror: quiet, air-dampened, quick-return mirror with pneumatic shock-absorber and brake. Mirror can be locked up for absolutely sharp tripod shots at slow shutter speeds.

Checking depth of field: visual assessment of the depth of field is possible using the preview button.

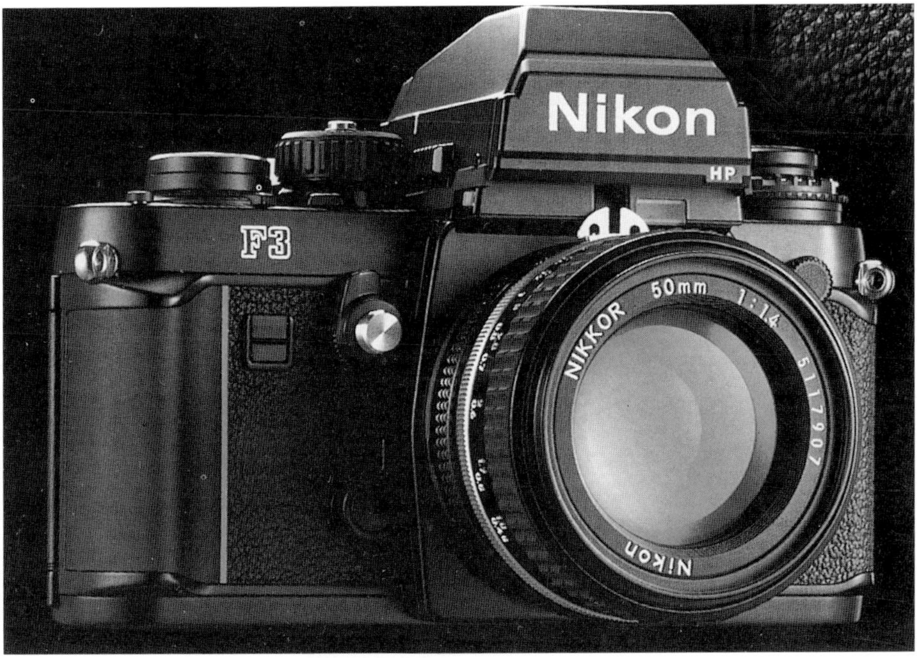

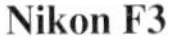

Nikon F3

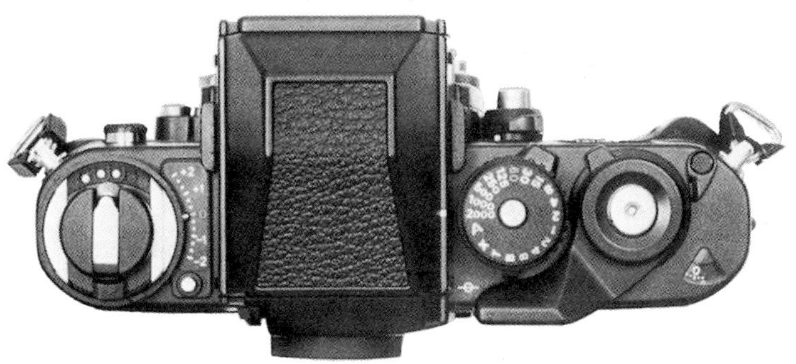

Film speed: manual setting from ISO 12 to ISO 6400.

Film loading: conventional manual method, without automatic facility; take-up spool with 6 slits for quick threading.

Film transport: conventional manual method, with quick-wind lever; folded out by 30° when in readiness; film is wound on and shutter cocked by advancing lever by 140°. The lever can also be advanced in several shorter stages, totaling 140°.

External motor drive: MD-4 with connection via motor coupling and rewind coupling plus 7 electrical control contacts; depending on the type and condition of the batteries (8 batteries or MN-2 NiCd) and the selected shutter speed, up to around 5 shots per second are possible and up to 60 rolls can be transported per set of batteries; when a motor is fitted, the motor batteries also provide the power supply for the camera; single frame and continuous advance settings are possible.

Frame counter: counts forward; is reset when camera back is opened.
Rewinding: manual with rewind crank; motorized rewind also possible when MD-4 motor is fitted (approximately 5-8 seconds).
Self-timer: electronic with 10 seconds delay and countdown display by flashing LED on front of camera.
Multiple exposures: multiple exposure lever prevents film transport; only shutter is cocked; any number of exposures on one frame possible.
Camera back: can be exchanged for MF-4 250 exposure back, which works in conjunction with MD-4 motor; also MF-17 databack (in combination with MF-4 and MD-4); and MF-18 and MF-14 databack (in combination with MD-4).
Flash connection: SB-16A and SB-17 flash units or SC-12 cable for connection to SB-11, also SC-14 TTL cord for use with SB-12, -16A, -17 and -21A; all can then be used with TTL control (flash metering is effected by silicon photo diode in the base of the camera); there is also an adapter (AS-4) for the use of flash units with a central ISO contact and one (AS-5) for older flash units designed for use with the F2. The TTL macro flash (version SB-21A) can also be used.
Flash ready display: when Nikon flash units SB-11, SB-12, SB-14, SB-140, SB-16A, SB-17 or SB-21A are connected, an LED in the viewfinder lights up when the flash is ready for use. With an AS4 or AS7 adapter the flash ready light displays with SB24, 23, 22, 20, 18 and 15 flash units.
Power supply: 2 silver oxide 1.55V button cells (type SR-44), or if necessary 2 LR44 alkaline-manganese button cells or 1.3V lithium button cell (type CR1/3N); during motorized operation with the MD-4, the camera's power is provided by the motor batteries (batteries can be removed from the body).
Battery test: if the viewfinder display goes off immediately when the shutter release is no longer depressed exposures will be incorrect!
Body: metal body, painted black.
Dimensions: width 5.8in. (48.5mm), height 3.8in. (96.5mm) [F3HP 4in. (101.5mm)], depth 2.6in. (65.5mm) [F3HP 2.7in. (69mm)].
Weight: approximately 25oz.(700g) (F3HP approximately 750g 26.5oz.).

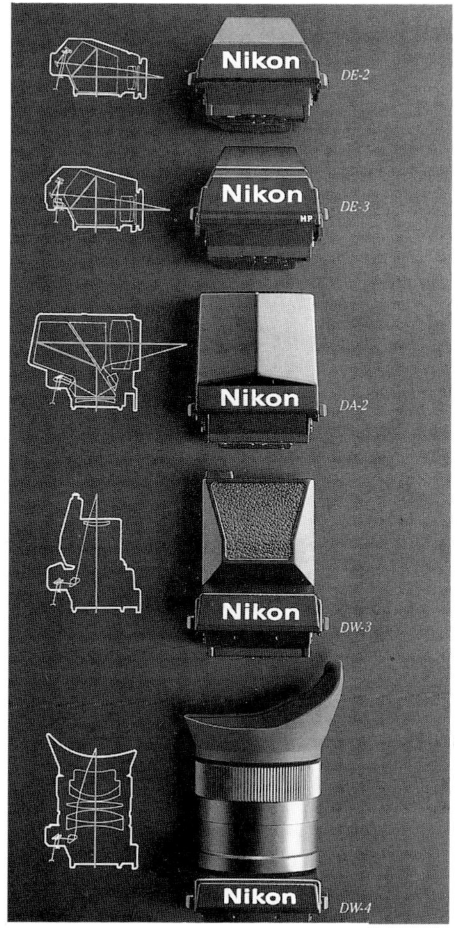

Nikon Viewfinders

Special accessories for the F3

DE-3 high-eyepoint viewfinder: eyepoint (maximum distance from which eyepiece can be viewed) 25mm 1in. from eyepiece, ideal for people wearing glasses. The DE-3 is supplied as standard with the F3HP.
DA-2 sports viewfinder: eyepoint (maximum distance from which eyepiece can be viewed)

MD-4

Nikon 1453468
ASA/ISO
L M H
COLOR 25—64 80—160 200—400
B & W 100—400
Nikon MF-14 JAPAN

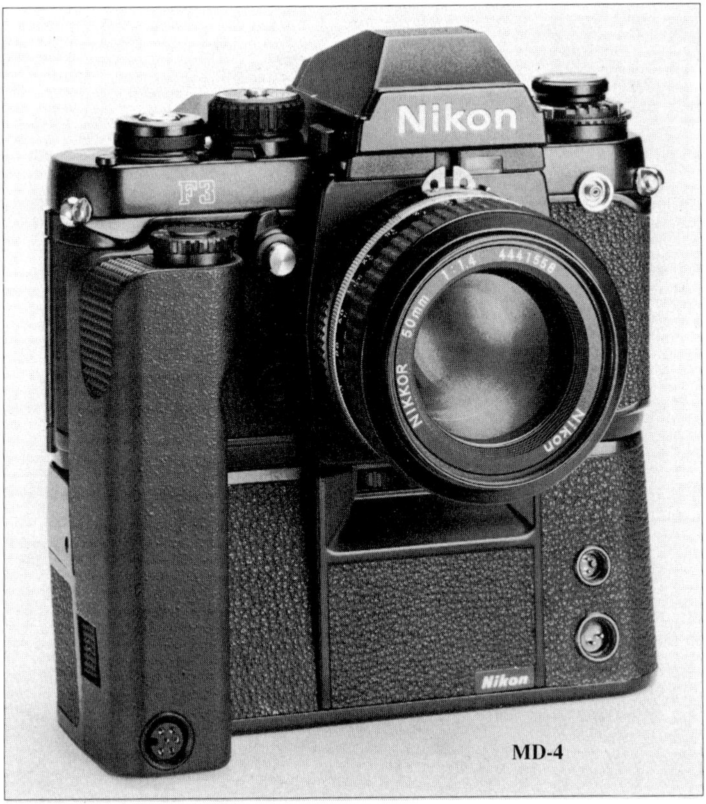

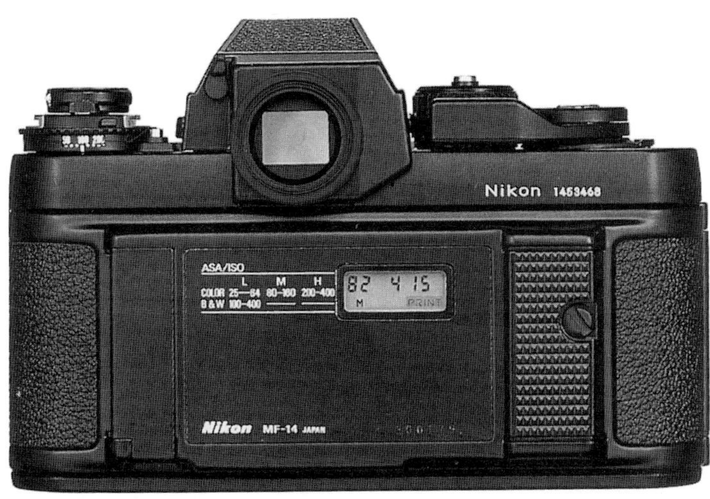

MF-14

DB-2

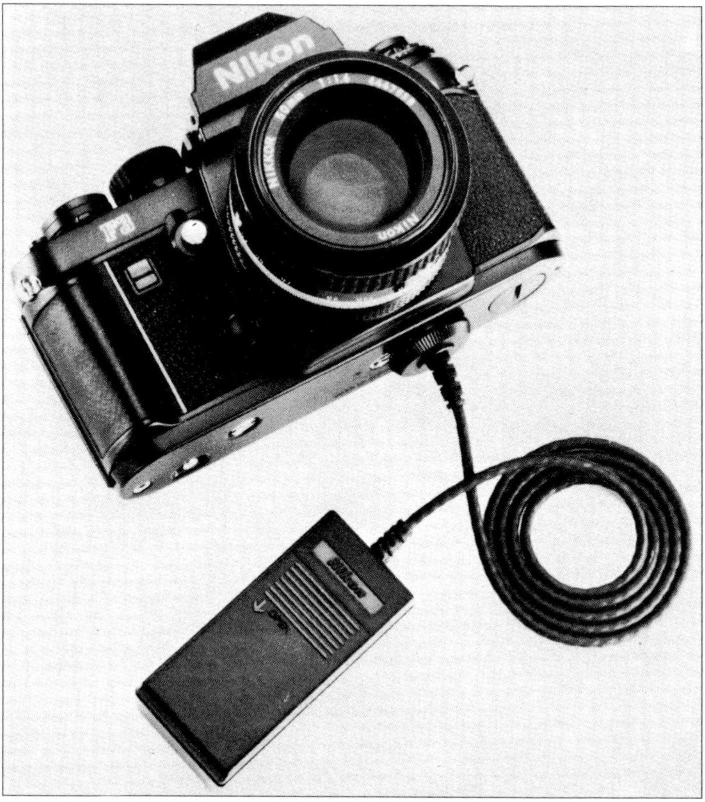

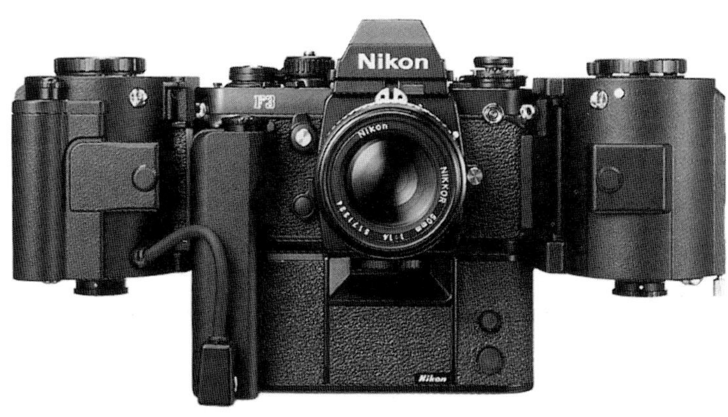

MF-4

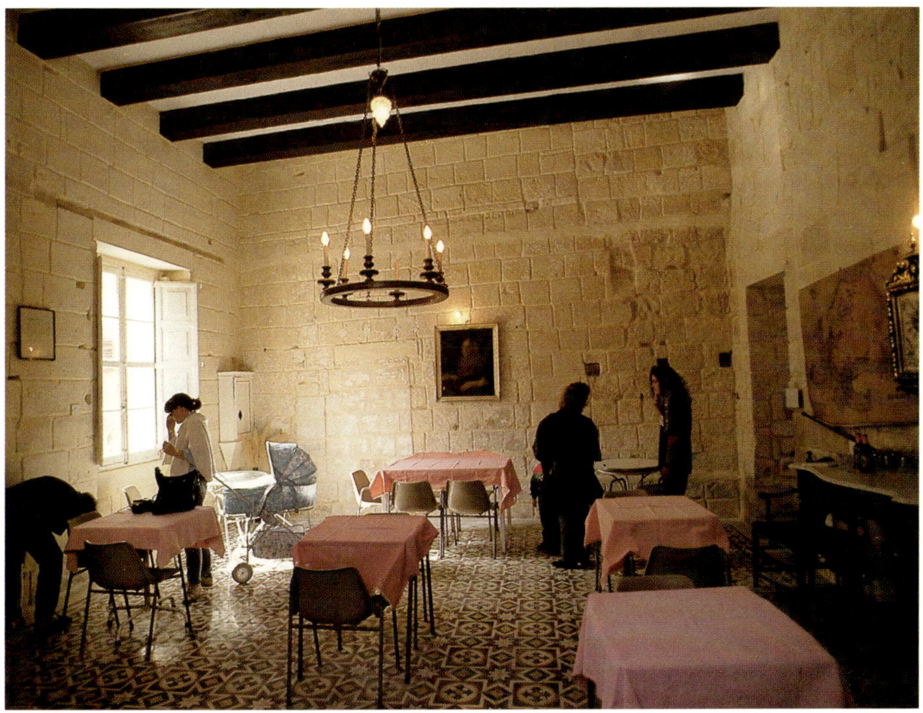

This available light image, was shot on the spur of the moment and optimally exposed thanks to Nikon's matrix metering. The challenging illumination, ranging from the bright window (left) to the deep shadows of the far corner (right) demonstrates the technological sophistication of matrix metering (1/30 sec. at f/2.8).

2.4in.(60mm) from eyepiece, ideal for keeping an eye on the general scene at the same time as the viewfinder image, but also suitable for use with underwater casings.

DW-3 waist level viewfinder: for viewing the viewfinder image from above. Folding hood with 5x auxillary magnification for focusing. Image appears reversed. Good for extreme camera positions, e.g. in copy or macro photography.

DW-4 magnifying viewfinder: for viewing the viewfinder image from above. With 1.5x magnification and eyesight diopter from +3 to -3 diopters. Image appears reversed.

MD-4 motor drive: single frame (S) or continuous (C) settings. 3.8 to 5.5 frames per second, depending on; shutter speed, power supply, and whether or not the mirror is locked up. Automatically takes over the camera's power supply functions (useful at low temperatures). Connection for MC-12/12A electrical remote shutter release. Power supply 8 x 1.5 Volt alkaline-manganese batteries (type AA) or appropriate NiCds. Used with auxillary MF-4 250 exposure back, MF-18 databack, or with MF-6/6B.

DB-2 low temperature battery protection: in case the small button cells give up at low temperatures.

MF-4 250 exposure back: used in combination with MD-4 motor drive. Can be used in combination with MF-17 databack.

MF-6/6B: used to leave film leader sticking out after rewinding (preferred by photojournalists).

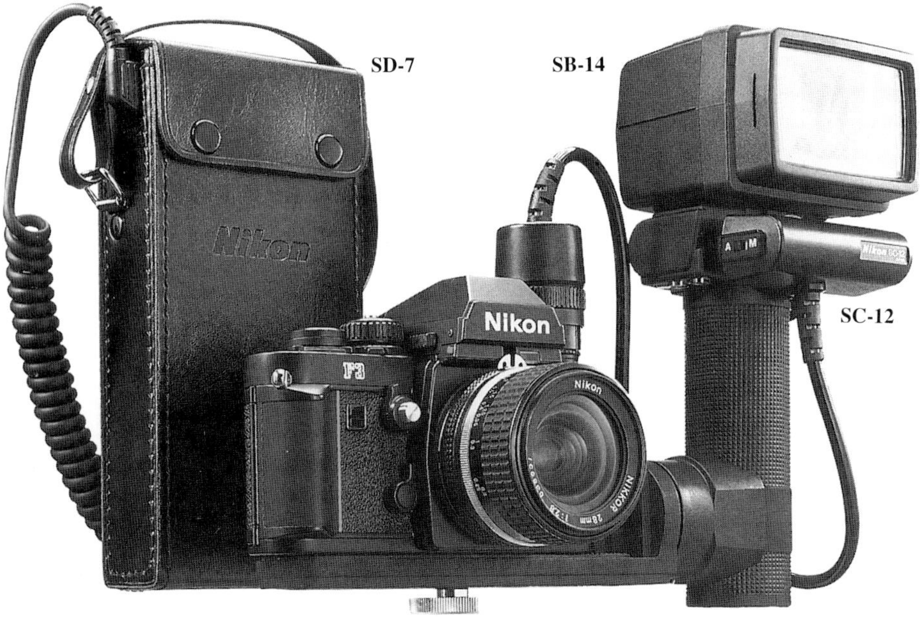

SD-7 SB-14

SC-12

MF-14 databack: allows year/month/date, date/hour/minute or serial number from 1-2000 to be exposed onto the frame.

MF-18 databack: in combination with MD-4 motor drive, allows year/month/date, date/hour/minute or serial number from 1-2000 to be exposed onto the strip of film between frames, leaves leader out after rewinding.

MF-17 databack: in combination with MF-4 bulk film back and MD-4 motor drive, allows year/month/date/hour/minute/second or space for handwritten notes to be exposed onto the frame.

Flash units: only the SB-12, SB-16A and SB-17 flash units and the SB-21A macro flash can be used with TTL control; the SB-11, SB-14 and SB-140 can be used via the SC-12 TTL cable. All modern Nikon flash units can be used via the AS-4 or AS-7 adapters, but without TTL control.

Focusing screens: 21 interchangeable focusing screens, for further details see the chapter on Nikon system accessories.

Eyecup: DE-2, DK-4, DE 3 & 4, DK-2.

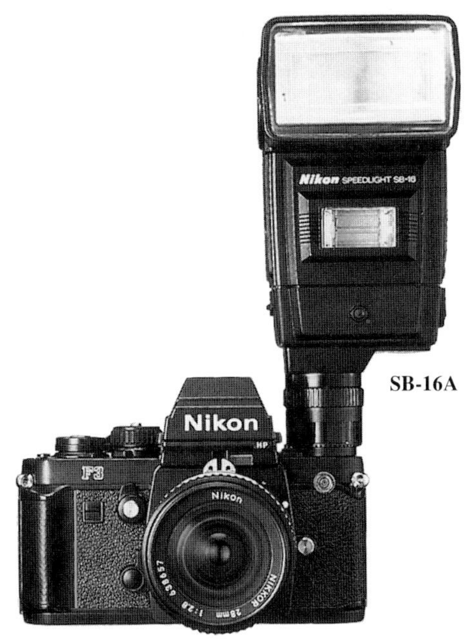

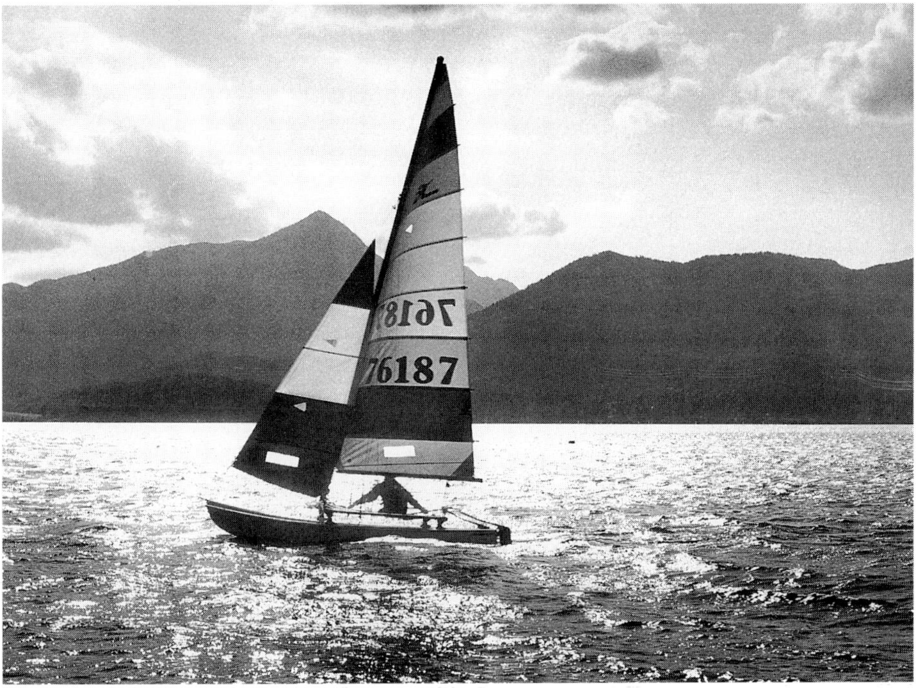

Photography is first, last and always about capturing light in all its variations. As these well-exposed pictures demonstrate, this requires excellent equipment and the knowledge of how to use it. Photos: Rudolf Dietrich

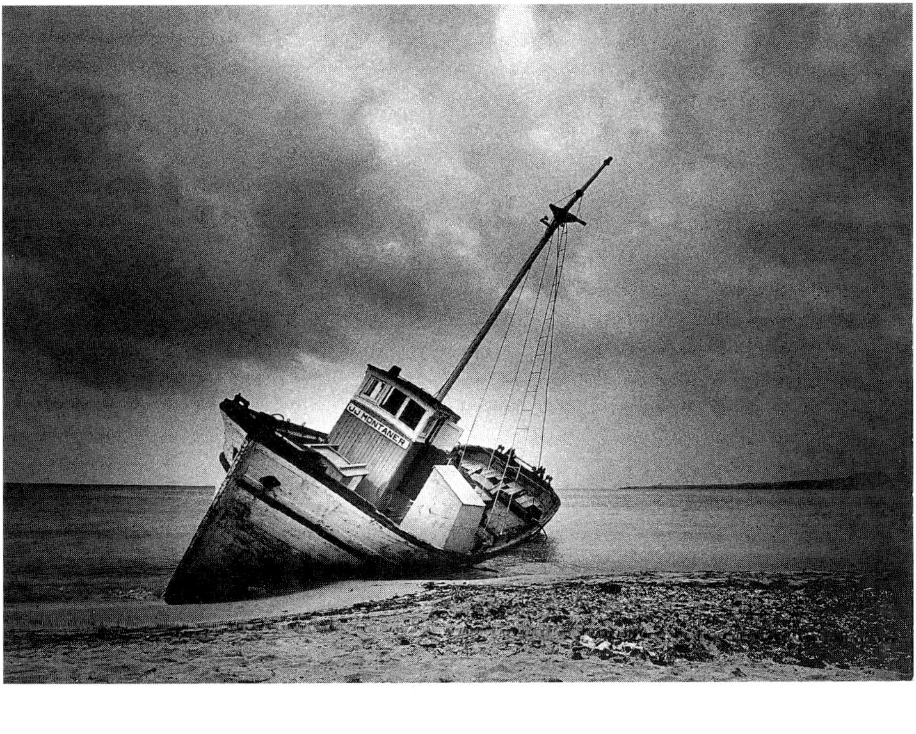

Nikon FM2n - The Fully-Mechanical Alternative

FM2n, Technical Data and Characteristics

Camera type: fully-mechanical 35mm SLR for manual exposure control, with conventional, well-proven operating controls, allowing fast and direct access to all settings. Even without batteries, all shutter speeds are available, since only the exposure metering system requires battery power.

Film format: 35mm film; 24mm x 36mm picture format.

Lens mount: Nikon-F bayonet mount

Suitable lenses: all non-AF Nikkors (type AI and AI-S); AF Nikkors, but only with manual focus; older Nikkors converted to AI; reflex Nikkors 1000mm f/11, 2000mm f/11 and 200-600mm, 180-600mm and 360-1200mm telezooms only above a certain serial number (see operating instructions).

Shutter: mechanical, vertical-action slit shutter with aluminum blinds.

Shutter speeds: fixed shutter speeds from 1 second to 1/4000 second and B, selected directly using shutter speed dial.

Shutter release: mechanical; with cable release connection; can be locked by engaging film advance lever in closed position.

Viewfinder: permanently-installed prism viewfinder; 93% of the picture area is seen at 0.86x magnification (with a 50mm lens set to infinity).

Focusing screen: K2 screen with split-image indicator and microprism ring fitted as standard. Can be exchanged for B2 full matte screen and E2 full matte screen with grid lines.

Viewfinder information: display of shutter speed, direct readout of aperture setting and LED light scale (+,0,-) for exposure adjustment; 5-stage compensation display; flash ready indication by LED when certain Nikon flash units are attached.

Exposure metering: TTL with center-weighted open-aperture metering (60/40 center-weighted) with 2 silicon photo diodes; metering range from EV 1 to EV 18 at ISO 100 and a lens speed of f/1.4 (equivalent to 1 second at f/1.4 and 1/4000 second at f/8); activated for approximately 30 seconds by partially depressing the shutter release button; the exposure metering is switched off when the shutter speed dial is set to B.

Reflex mirror: extremely fast, low-vibration and silent due to special gears and brake; cannot be locked in up position.

Depth of field check: using preview button.

Film speed: can be set from ISO 12 to ISO 6400.

Film loading: conventional manual method, non-automatic.

Film transport: conventional manual method using rapid film advance lever; the camera can only be used when the lever is extended by 30°; film is wound on and shutter cocked by advancing lever by 135°.

External motor drive: MD-12 with connection via motor coupling and 4 electrical control contacts.

Frame counter: effective, but only counts forward; is reset when camera back is opened.

Rewinding: manual, using rewind crank.

Self-timer: mechanical, with 10 scconds delay.

Multiple exposures: multiple exposure lever prevents film transport; only shutter is cocked; any number of exposures on one frame possible.

Camera back: can be exchanged for MF-16 databack

Flash connection: via flash shoe with ISO contact and additional contact for flash ready indicator in viewfinder, plus PC socket contact for connection of trigger cable for off-camera flash.

Flash synchronization: sync. speeds 1/250 second and slower.

Flash ready display: an LED in the viewfinder lights up when the flash is ready for use (only when Nikon flash units from SB-15 and later models are connected).

Power supply: 2 silver oxide 1.55V button cells (type SR-44), or if necessary 2 LR44 alkaline-manganese cells or 1.3V lithium button cell (type CR1/3N).

Battery test: the LED display in the viewfinder lights up when the shutter release button is

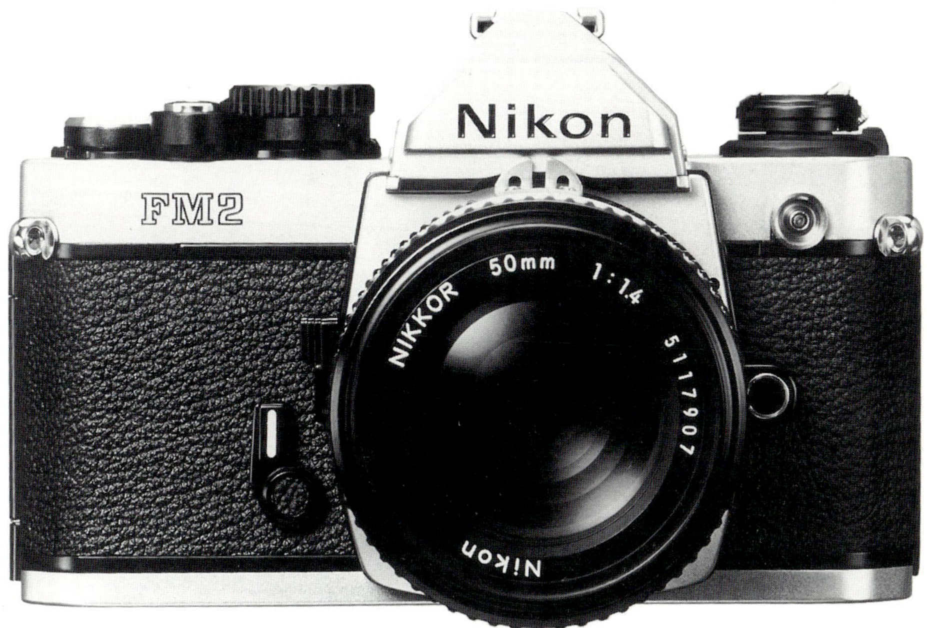

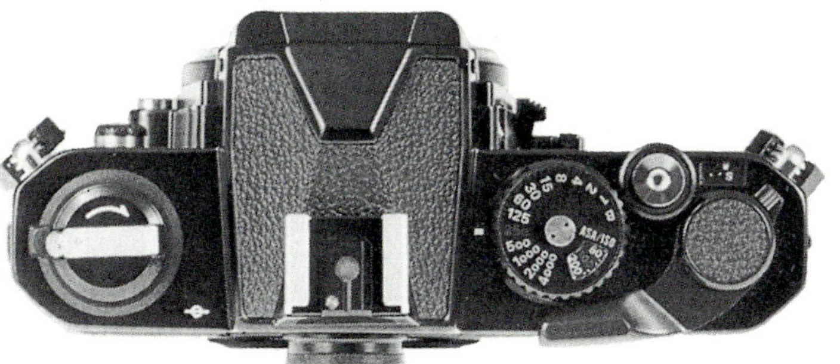

Nikon FM-2n

partially depressed, unless the shutter speed is set to B.

Body: metal body in chrome or black.

Dimensions: width 5.6in. (142.5mm), height 3.5in. (90mm), depth 2.4in. (60mm)

Weight: approx. 19.1oz. (540g)

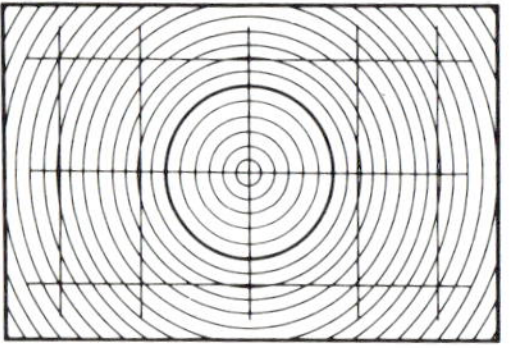

E2

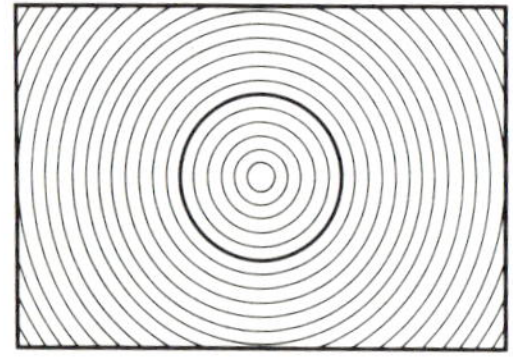

B2

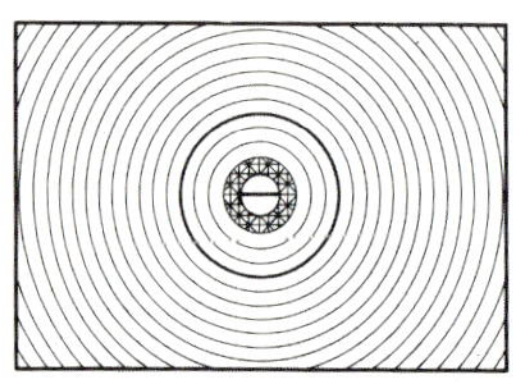

K2

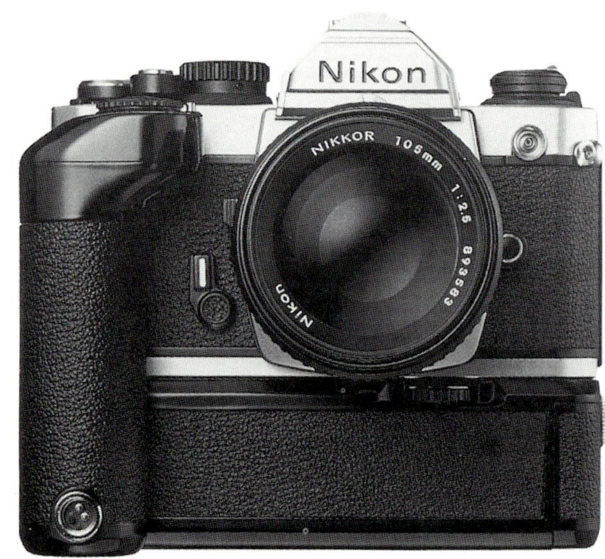

MD-12

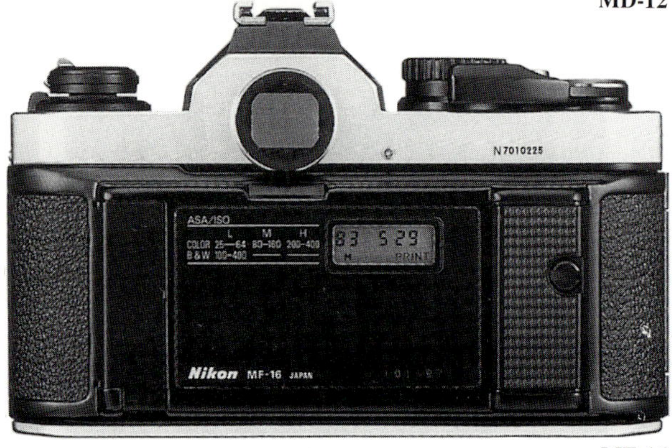

MF-16

Special Accessories for the FM2n

Focusing screens: B2 with 12mm metering circle and otherwise matte surface, for macro and telephoto work. E2 with 12mm metering circle and grid lines, otherwise matte surface, for architectural photography and extreme wide-angle shots.

Motor drive: MD-12 for up to 3.5 frames per second at shutter speeds faster than 1/125 second; up to 100 rolls are transported per set of batteries (8 AA type batteries); single frame or continuous advance settings.

Databack: MF-16 allows year/month/date, date/hour/minute or serial number from 1-2000 to be exposed onto the frame.

Eyecup: DK-3.

Matrix and spot metering: Light can produce a variety of effects setting up conditions for exposure best handled by different meter patterns. For example, using matrix metering (below) rendered the foreground too dark. Spot metering on the hedge resulted in reading that more accurately exposed the foreground (top).

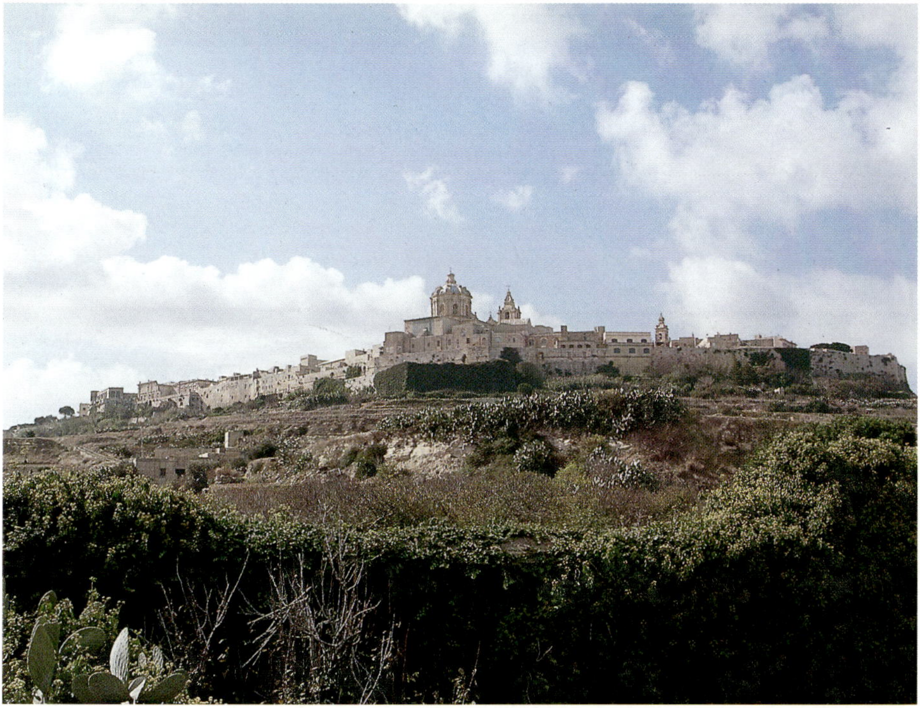

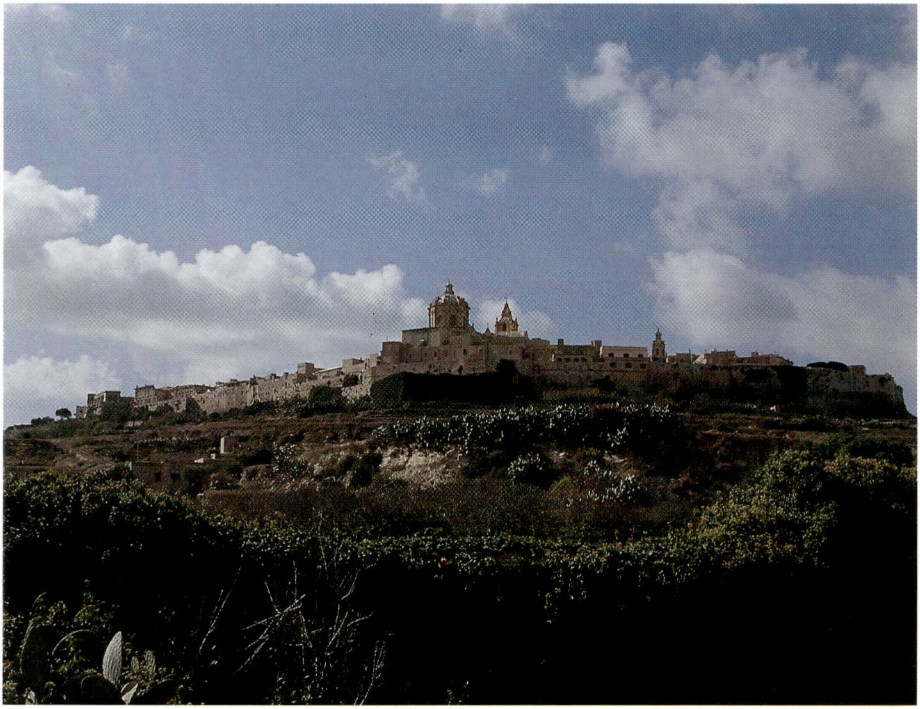

Nikon N2000/F-301 - Nikon's First Camera with Built-in Motor

N2000/F-301, Technical Data and Characteristics

Camera type: electronically-controlled 35m SLR with motorized film transport. Conventional, well-proven operating controls allowing particularly fast, direct access to all settings; manual exposure control, aperture priority mode, normal program mode and fast shutter speed program mode.

Film format: 35mm film; 24mm x 36mm picture format.

Lens mount: Nikon-F bayonet mount.

Suitable lenses: all AI-S Nikkors and all AF Nikkors (can only be used with manual focusing); all older AI Nikkors and Nikkors converted to AI (only in aperture priority mode and manual mode), plus E series Nikkors.

Shutter: electronically-controlled, vertical-action slit shutter with laminated aluminum-plastic blinds.

Shutter speeds: extremely accurate fixed shutter speeds from 1 second to 1/2000 second controlled by lithium niobate oscillator; all shutter speeds are selected directly using shutter speed dial. In aperture-priority mode and program modes, stepless shutter speeds in the range between 1/2000 second and approximately 30 seconds are formed (i.e. continuous range, not discrete values), depending on the speed of the film.

Shutter release: electromechanical, with 2-stage function; exposure metering is activated for approximately 16 seconds when partially depressed, shutter is released when fully depressed. Integrated main power switch for camera locks the shutter release. No cable release connection.

Remote shutter release: electric, e.g. using the MC-12A remote release cable.

Self-timer: electronic, with 10 seconds delay and countdown display by LED on the front of the camera, plus acoustic signal. Viewfinder: permanently-installed prism viewfinder; 92% of the picture area is seen at 0.85x magnification (with a 50mm lens set to infinity).

Focusing screen: permanently-installed extremely bright type K2 "Brite-View" screen with a central split-image indicator which hardly darkens, microprism ring and matte screen with fresnel finish; central circle of 12mm marks the center-weighting area for metering.

Viewfinder information: LED display of shutter speed, over- and underexposure, flash ready indicator (LED lights up when flash is ready); simple manual exposure balancing (-selected shutter speed is illuminated, shutter speed calculated by exposure metering system blinks).

Exposure metering: TTL with heavily center-weighted integral (60/40 weighting) open aperture metering; silicon photo diode; additional diode for TTL flash metering.

Saving of metered values: metered values in all automatic modes can be locked until the shutter is released using the exposure lock button.

Exposure compensation: from +2 to -2 in 1/3 EV steps (1 EV = 1 exposure step = 1 "f stop"); set on exposure compensation ring, with unlocking button.

Reflex mirror: cannot be locked in up position.

Depth of field check: not possible.

Film speed: manual setting from ISO 12 to ISO 3200, alternatively by DX coding, i.e. when this function is selected the camera identifies DX-coded films from ISO 25 to ISO 4000 while uncoded films are set to ISO 100.

Film loading: automatic with transport to frame 1; film transport window indicates whether film threading and transport are functioning.

Film transport: motorized. In S setting, one frame at a time is exposed and wound on. In C setting, up to 2.5 frames per second are exposed and wound on for as long as the shutter release button is held down; shuts off automatically when the film runs out.

Frame counter: forwards-counting; is reset when camera back is opened.

Rewinding: manual with rewind crank.

Multiple exposures: not possible.

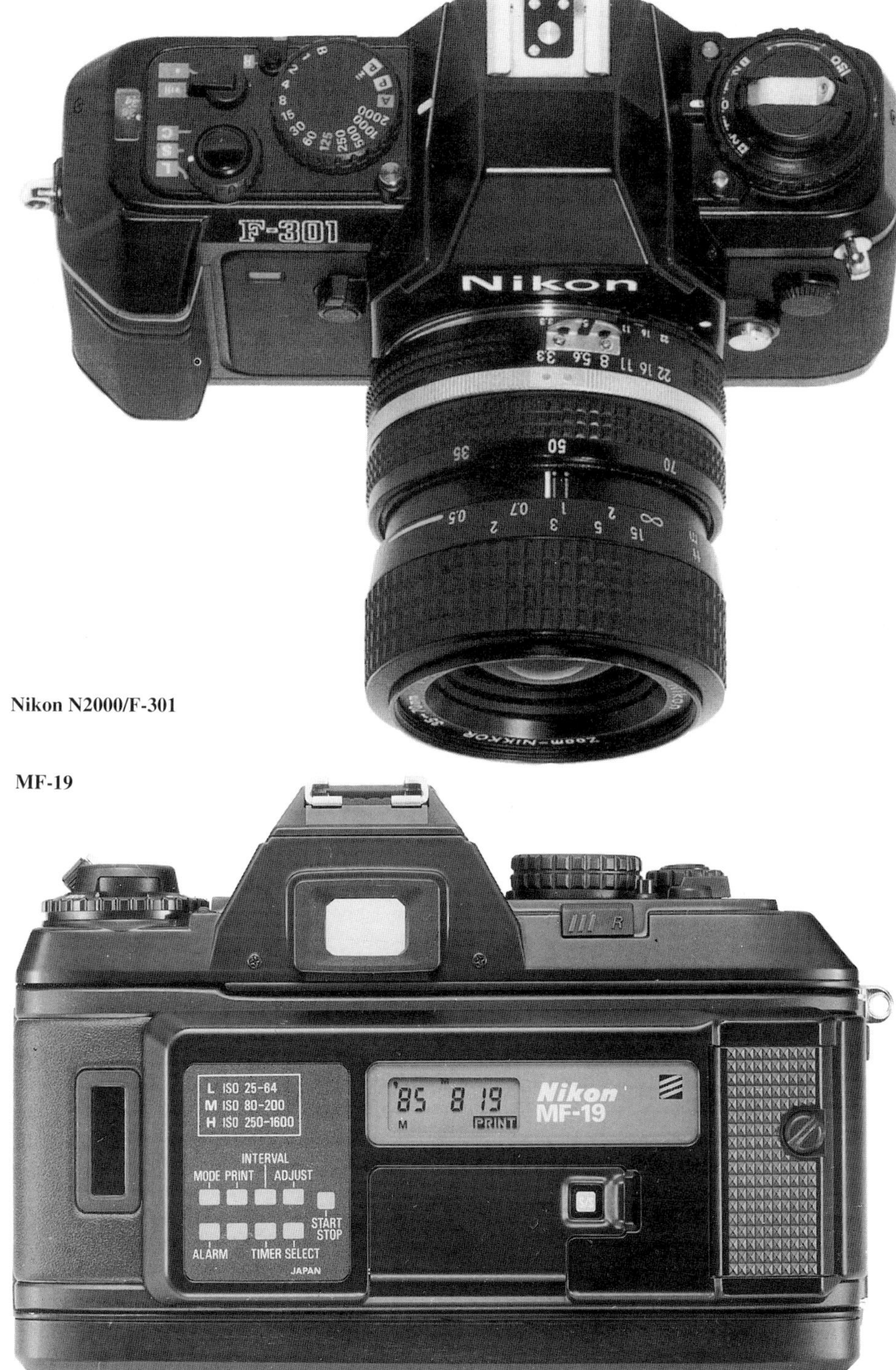

Nikon N2000/F-301

MF-19

Camera back: can be exchanged for MF-19 multi-control databack.

Flash connection: via flash shoe with ISO contact and Nikon system contacts for flash ready indicator, TTL control and monitor; the SB-15 and later Nikon flash units allow use with TTL flash program mode; the same applies to the SB-11 and SB-14 when used in combination with the SC-23 connection cable.

Flash synchronization: 1/125 second and slower speeds are possible; when using Nikon flash units in the automatic modes, a sync speed of 1/125 second is automatically set; the same applies if a shutter speed of 1/250 second or faster is selected; if a shutter speed of 1/60 second or slower is selected then this shutter speed is used.

TTL flash control range: ISO range for TTL flash is ISO 25 to ISO 1000.

Power supply: 4 alkaline-manganese micro batteries (type AAA) for up to 60 36-exposure films. Or preferably, using the MB-3 battery pack, four 1.5 V alkaline-manganese batteries (type AA) for up to 180 36-exposure rolls. It is also possible to use appropriately sizcd AA Ni-Cds.

Battery test: if the viewfinder display cuts out after 10 seconds following depression of the shutter release button, one should replace the batteries. It cuts out after 1 second at absolute minimum voltage.

Body: main body is made of metal, with some casing sections in plastic. The whole camera is painted or colored black.

Dimensions: width 5.8in. (148.5mm), height 3.8in. (97.5mm), depth 2.1in. (54.5mm).

Weight: approx. 20.1oz. (570g) without batteries.

Special Accessories for the N2000/F-301

Battery pack: MB-3 for 4 AA batteries.

Databack with interval timer: MF-19 which allows you to expose either the year/month/day, day/hour/minute or a serial number from 1-999999. Time-lapse photography: 1-99 intervals of between 1 second and 99 hours, 59 minutes and 59 seconds can be programmed, with 1-99 shots being taken per interval. Mainly used for documentation purposes in the fields of science and research.

Tripod adapter: AH-3 shifts the tripod mount ing socket to the center of the camera.

Eyecup: DK-5.

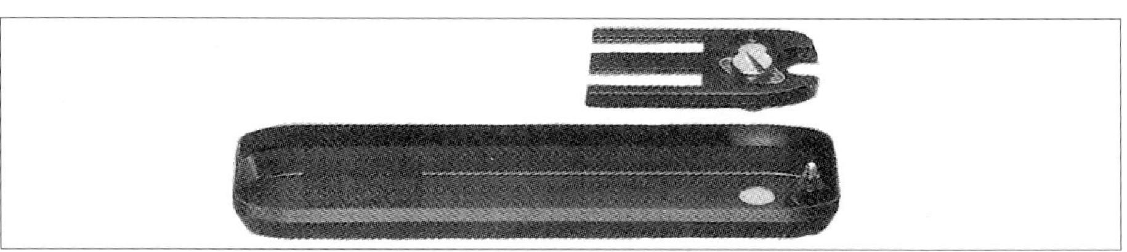

MB-3

(Top) Spot Metering: In this situation, the entire image is contrasty because of the range of brightness while the dog in the foreground is in both the brightest and darkest areas of illumination. Spot metering on the boat's hull as the key middle tone area versus the rest of the scene resulted in the optimal compromise that even captured the dog within the latitude of the film.

(Bottom) Graduated filters: The evening mood was reinforced in this shot by using a red graduated filter in the sky area. Without the filter, the image was focused manually and the exposure was selected in order not to confuse the automatic systems. Then the filter was installed thus preserving the balance of light in the foreground.

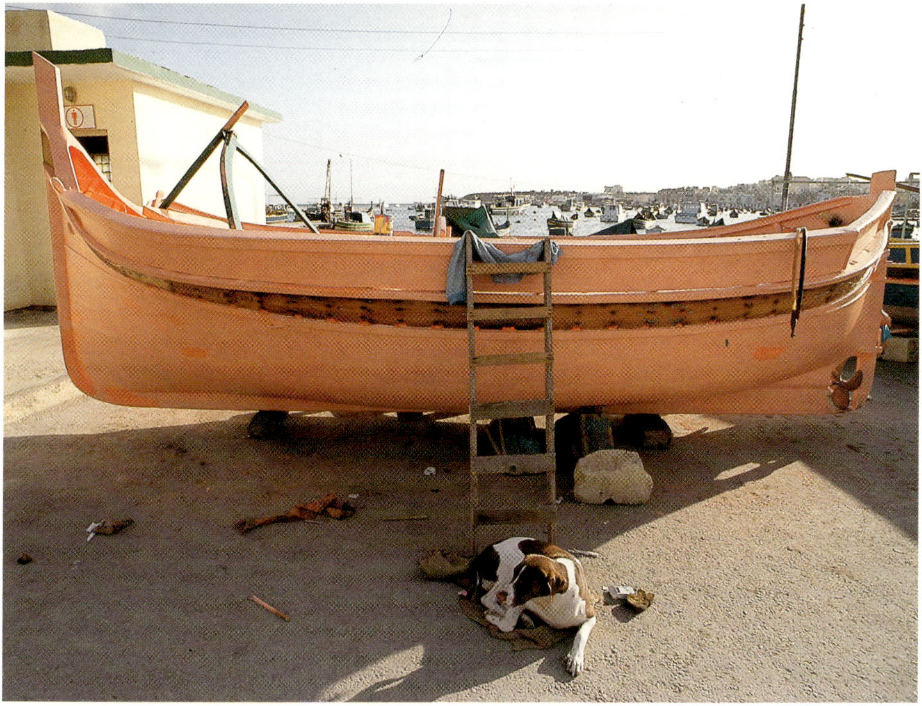

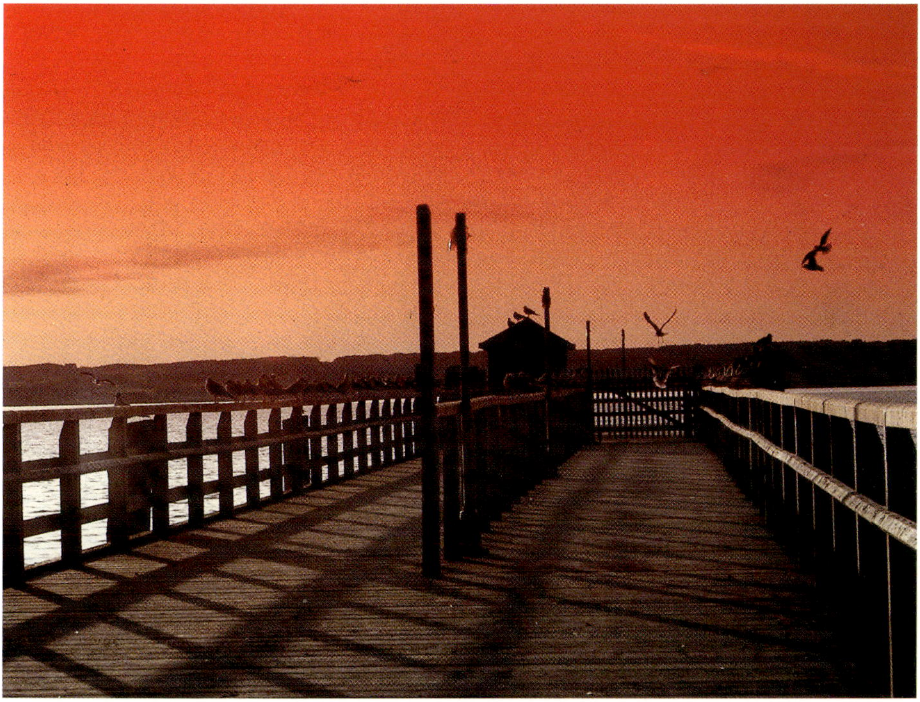

Nikon N4004s/F-401s and N5005/F-401x - An introduction to AF SLR Photography

N4004/F-401, N4004s/F-401s, N5005/F-401x, F-401x Quartz Date, Technical Data and Characteristics

Camera type: autofocus 35mm SLR with motorized film transport. Designed for fully-automatic photography.

Film format: 35mm film; 24 x 36mm picture area.

Lens mount: Nikon F-bayonet fitting with additional electronic control and data transmission contacts for AF lenses, and with integrated AF motor coupling. No mechanical aperture value transmission possible.

Suitable lenses: all AF Nikkors; neither the automatic exposure modes nor the exposure metering will function if AI and AI-S Nikkors are used. Manual setting of aperture and shutter speed on the basis of external metering is, however, possible. The AF teleconverter TC 16A should not be used.

Focusing modes: either autofocus of manual focusing using the focusing screen or with the aid of the electronic focusing aid (LED focus indicator in viewfinder) with all lenses with an aperture not slower than f/5.6.

Autofocus system: passive; TTL phase-detection with AM-200 module; working range of the N5005/F-401x and N4004s/F-401s EV -1 to EV 19 using ISO 100 film. N4004s/F-401s less fast than N5005/F-401x, N4004/F-401 less fast than N4004s/F-401s and N5005/F-401x.

Autofocus modes: only focus priority; the shutter can only be released when the subject is in focus; when the shutter button is depressed halfway, the focus setting is locked. Coupled with "tracking autofocus" in the case of the N5005/F-401x, i.e. readings are repeated in rapid succession and, for moving subjects, the camera calculates the predicted focusing distance in advance according to the speed at which the subject is moving.

Exposure metering: with silicon photo diodes; integral center-weighted metering in manual mode and if exposure locking is engaged. In the automatic exposure modes, the N5005/F-401x uses five-field metering with matrix evaluation (like the N6006/F-601, N8008/F-801 and F4); the exposure metering is activated for approximately 8 seconds by depressing the shutter release button. The N4004/F-401 and N4004s/F-401s only feature three-zone multi-field metering with simpler evaluation.

Exposure compensation: no manual compensation possible.

Exposure modes: 1. Aperture-priority mode; shutter speed dial set to A, aperture is pre-selected using aperture dial. 2. Shutter speed priority mode; Aperture dial is set to S, the shutter speed is pre-selected using the shutter speed dial. 3. Program mode; Shutter speed dial is set to A and aperture dial is set to S; the camera automatically switches between high-speed and normal program modes, depending on the focal length of the lens.

Exposure lock: activated by pressing the AE-L button while the exposure meter is switched on, whereby the camera switches to center-weighted metering; the last metered exposure value is locked in any exposure mode.

Shutter: electronically-controlled, vertical-action aluminum-plastic slit shutter; electro-magnetic shutter release.

Shutter speeds: in aperture priority and program modes, stepless speeds between 1/2000 second and 1 second (or 30 seconds on the N5005/F-401x). Fixed shutter speeds of from 1 second to 1/2000 second in shutter speed priority mode and manual mode, "B" and "T" also possible with the latter (N5005/F-401x only); Lithium niobate oscillator provides extremely precise shutter speeds.

Shutter: electromechanical with three-stage function (lightly touching the button activates the exposure metering for approximately 16 seconds, partial depression activates the autofocus, focus setting is locked by holding the shutter button in its half-depressed position; the shutter is released by pressing the shutter release button completely down). The main camera switch integrated into the shutter speed dial locks the shutter release. No cable release connection.

Nikon N5005

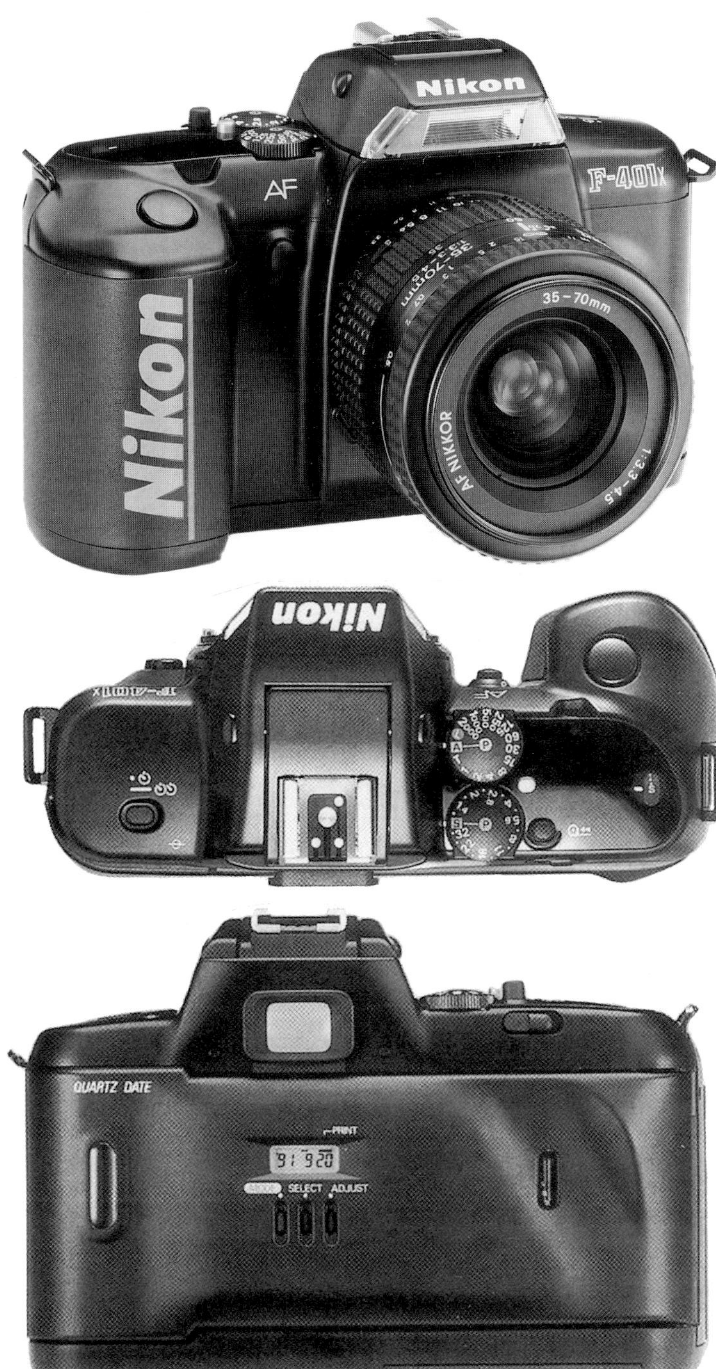

Nikon F-401x
Quartz Date

Remote control: not possible.
Self-timer: electronically-controlled delay of approximately 10 seconds; countdown is indicated by a flashing LED on the front of the camera.
Viewfinder: permanently-installed pentaprism viewfinder; 93% of the picture area is seen at 0.80x magnification (with a 50mm lens set to infinity); DK-5 eyepiece shield prevents stray light from entering the viewfinder (risk of exposure errors) during automatic operation when the eyepiece is not covered by the photographers eye.
Focusing screen: non-exchangeable "Brite-View" matte screen with marked AF focusing brackets and reference circle for center-weighted metering.
Viewfinder information: green LED as focus indicator; red LEDs warn of over- and under-exposure and indicate correct exposure; also red LED flash ready indicator.
Film speed: only automatic setting possible using DX coding from ISO 25 to ISO 5000; non-DX-coded films are set to ISO 100.
Film loading: automatic, film wound on to frame 1; effective film transport can be checked by film transport indicator on back of camera.
Film transport: motorized only; each time the shutter is released, the film is wound on within 0.4 seconds; stops automatically at the end of the film.
Frame counter: forwards-counting; resets when camera back is opened.
Rewind: motorized only, rewinds film completely into cassette.
Built-in TTL flash: guide number 40 (ft./ISO 100, 68°F). Angle of illumination corresponds to the angle of view of a 35mm lens (or that of a 28mm lens with the N5005/F-401x); TTL flash program mode with program and shutter speed priority modes; automatic TTL flash in aperture priority and manual modes.
Flash connection: only via flash shoe with ISO central contact, additional Nikon system contacts for flash ready display and TTL control with Nikon system flash units such as SB-16B or later models. Flash units by other manufacturers may only be connected if it is ensured that there is no danger of short-circuit or excess voltage.
Flash synchronization: 1/125 second automatically set in program and aperture priority modes; this also applies to shutter speed priority and manual modes if shutter speeds faster than 1/125 second are selected. If shutter speeds of 1/60 second or slower are selected in shutter speed priority and manual modes, these shutter speeds will be used for the exposure; ISO range for TTL control 25 to 400 (or ISO 25 to 800 for the N5005/F-401x).
Flash check indicator: red LED in viewfinder; lights up when Nikon system flash is ready for use; flashes if the use of flash is recommended (subject darker than EV 10 with a central area darker by more than 1 EV).
Autofocus illuminator: available if appropriate flash units such as the Nikon SB-20, SB-22, SB-23, SB-24 and SB-25 are used.
Power supply: four 1.5V alkaline-manganese batteries (type AA) for up to 50 36-exposure films at 20°C, four rechargeable NiCd batteries of the same size for up to 16 36-exposure rolls at 20°C; if 50% of shots are taken using flash the batteries will last slightly less than half as long.
Battery check: with fresh batteries the aperture and shutter speed settings are displayed for around 8 seconds; if they appear for less than 4 seconds, the batteries should be replaced.
Dimensions: width 6.1in. (154mm); height 4in. (102mm); depth 2.6in. (65.5mm)
Weight: 23oz.(650g) without batteries.
F-401x Quartz Date only: permanently-installed databack allowing year/month/date or day/hour/minute (24 hour clock notation can be selected) to be exposed onto the frame. Data exposure can be switched off.

Special Accessories for the N4004/N5005
Eyecup: #2939

Colorization: Hand coloring this black and white shot emphasized its mood and created a much stronger statement. This image became the cover of a mystery novel thanks to this effect. Photo by Wolf Huber.

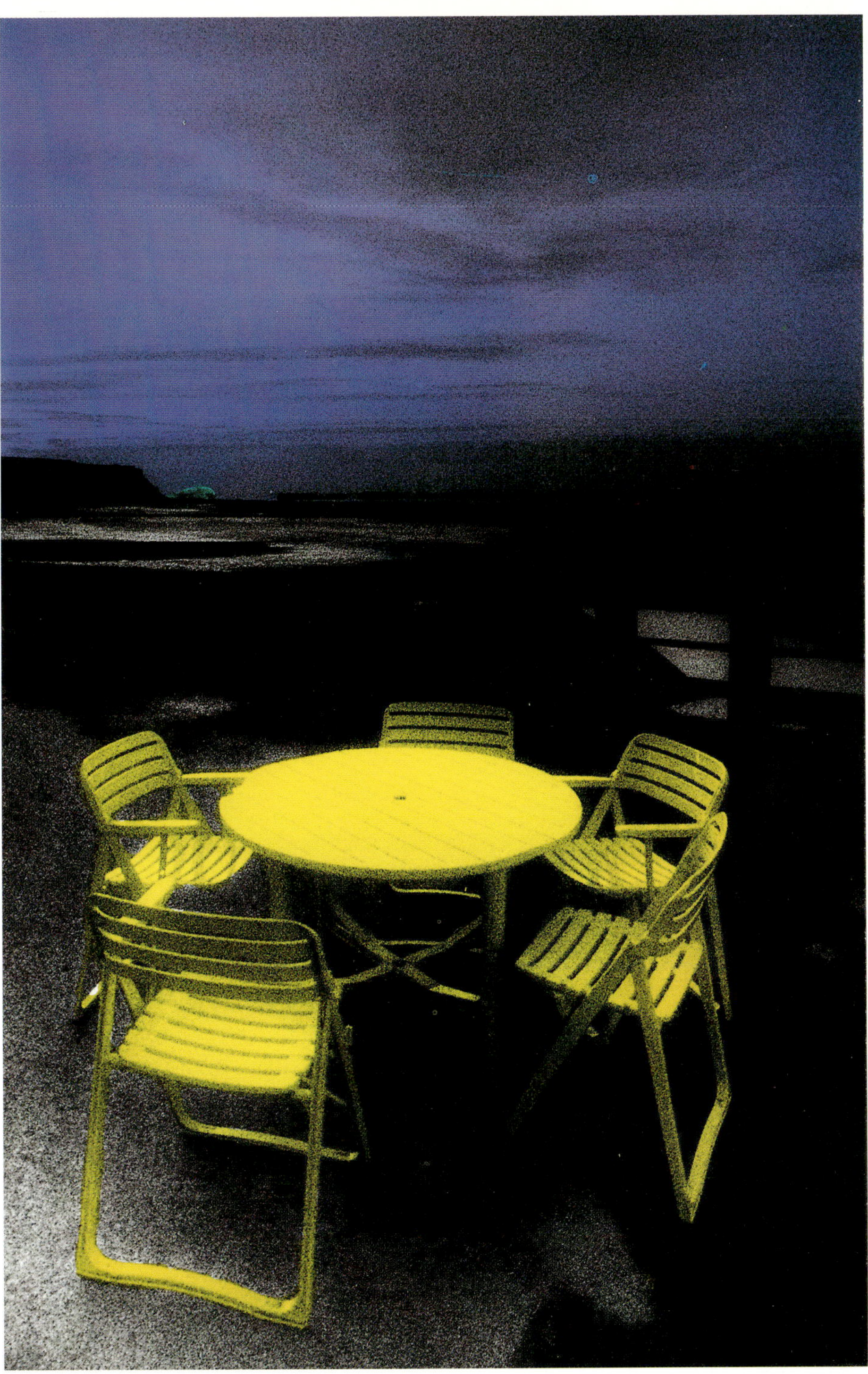

Nikon N6006/F-601 and N6000/F-601m - Extensively Equipped AF and MF Cameras

These two models are largely identical in construction, the N6006/F-601 (referred to as the N6006/F-601 AF wherever a clearer distinction appears necessary) features an autofocus facility and a built-in flash. The N6000/F-601m, for manual focusing, is designed to allow the use of the AF Nikkors in all automatic exposure modes, but has no built-in flash and no spot metering.

N6006/F-601, N6006 Quartz Date/F-601 Quartz Date, N6000/F-601m, Technical Data and Characteristics

Camera type: 35mm SLR with motorized film transport. On the one hand, the camera allows fully-automatic photography, and on the other hand, it features the widest range of options in terms of automatic flash and exposure functions currently available.

Film format: 35mm film; 24 x 36mm picture format.

Lens mount: Nikon F bayonet fitting with additional electronic control and data transmission contacts for AF lenses, and with integrated AF motor coupling.

Lenses: all AF Nikkor lenses can be used in all operating modes, without any restriction. AI/AIS Nikkors and Nikkors converted to AI can be used with the N6006/F-601 in "M" (manual) and "A" (aperture priority) modes. Matrix metering is not possible, only center-weighted and spot metering (the latter only with the N6006/F-601 AF). It is not advisable to use the TC-16A AF teleconverter or the 80mm f/2.8 and 200mm f/3.5 IF AF Nikkors since correct exposure cannot be guaranteed. The use of certain special lenses, e.g. some fisheyes, tele-Nikkors with AU-1-adjustment mount, PC- Nikkors, a number of super telezooms etc. can result in damage to the camera or lens (check with current operating instructions for camera).

Focusing system (N6006/F-601 AF only): passive, TTL phase detection with AM 200 AF module; light sensitivity and metering range from EV -1 to EV 19, with reference to ISO 100. With moving subjects the autofocus works with focusing distance calculated in advance ("prediction autofocus" or "tracking autofocus").

Autofocus modes (N6006/F-601 AF only): "S" and "CF". In both modes focusing proceeds continuously in the case of moving subjects ("AF servo" and "tracking autofocus"), and the shutter can only be released when the subject is in focus ("focus priority"). In "S" mode, when the subject is stationary, once the correct focus setting has been achieved with the shutter button depressed halfway, this focus setting is locked until the shutter is released (automatic autofocus locking).

Manual AF-locking (N6006/F-601 AF only): using AE-L slider after activation of AF-L function, only functions together with simultaneous exposure locking.

AF aid for manual focusing (N6006/F-601 AF only): this electronic rangefinding functions with all AF Nikkors and all AI and AIS Nikkors with a speed of f/5.6 or greater.

Exposure metering: choice of center-weighted metering (75/25 weighting) or five-segment metering with matrix evaluation; metering range from EV 0 to EV 19 at ISO 100 and a lens speed of f/1.4. Activated for approximately 8 seconds by lightly touching the shutter release button. N6006/F601 AF only: option of spot metering of around 1% (depending on the lens in use) of the picture area with a metering range from EV 4 to EV 19 at ISO 100 and a lens speed of f/1.4.

Automatic exposure modes: aperture priority; shutter speed priority ; program modes (normal program, multi-program, manual program shift).

Exposure locking: activated by pushing the exposure lock slider "AE-L" to the left; saves the last metered exposure value in all automatic exposure modes.

Manual exposure setting: aperture on lens, shutter speed on data input dial; selected shutter speed and aperture setting are displayed in

Nikon N6006

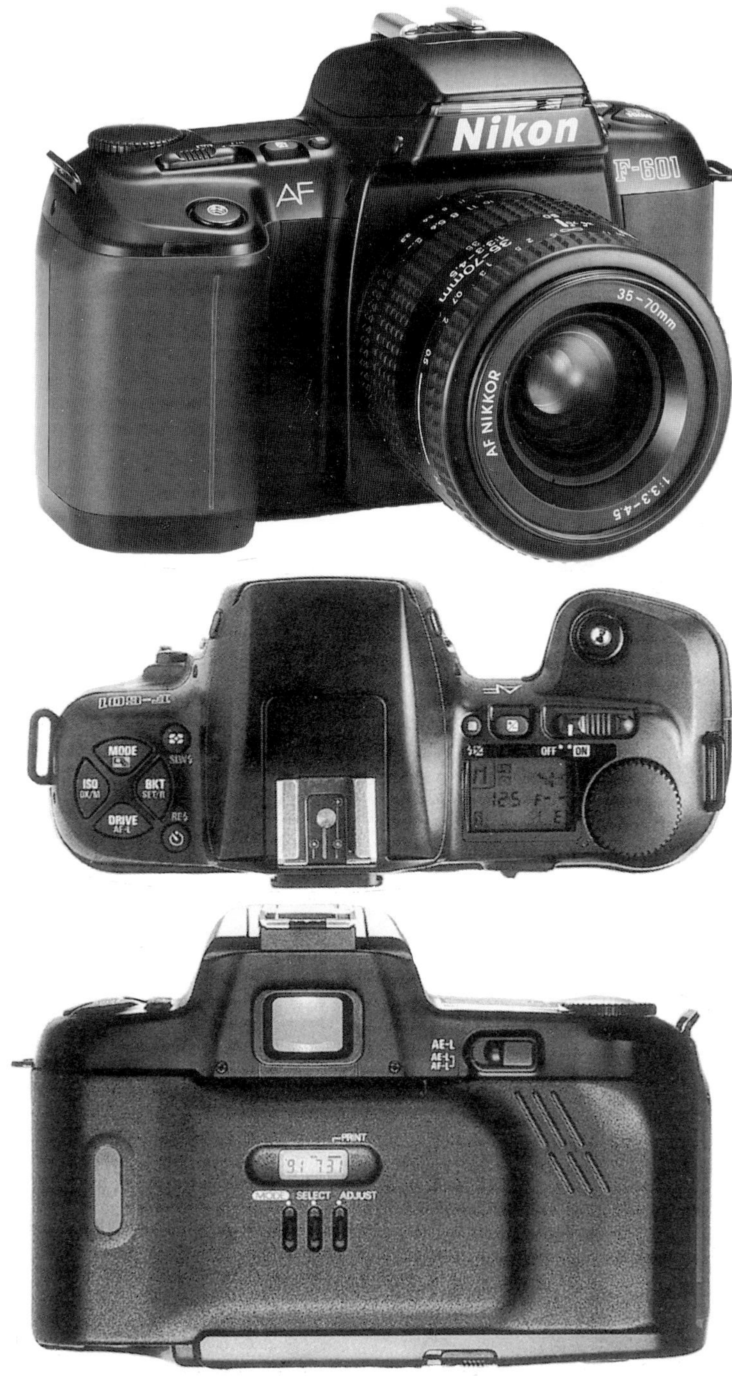

**Nikon N6006
Quartz Date**

viewfinder and on central LCD panel; display of exposure balance on light scale (electronic analog display) in 1/3 stops.

Exposure compensation: can be set manually from +5 EV to -5 EV in 1/3 steps (1 EV = exposure step = 1 "f stop"); automatic compensation with matrix metering (with the margin of error associated with an automatic mode of this sort).

Automatic exposure bracketing: automatic exposure brackets (3 or 5 frames) with exposure differences of 0.3, 0.7 or 1 EV. The middle exposure is always based on the metered exposure value. The camera is automatically reset to normal operation after the bracket has been exposed.

Shutter: electromagnetically-controlled, vertical-action slit shutter with aluminum blinds; electromagnetic shutter release.

Shutter speeds: in aperture priority and program modes, stepless speeds between 1/2000 second and 30 seconds, depending on the film speed. Fixed shutter speeds of from 30 seconds to 1/2000 second in shutter speed priority mode and manual mode. "B" is also possible with the latter; lithium niobate oscillator allows extremely precise shutter speeds.

Shutter release: electromechanical with three-stage function. The exposure metering is activated for approximately 8 seconds by lightly touching the shutter release button, partial depression activates the autofocus, focus setting is locked by holding the shutter button in its half-depressed position (N6006/F-601 AF in AF mode "S" only), the shutter is only released when the shutter release button is fully depressed. Separate main camera switch blocks the shutter release. Cable release connection.

Remote control: only possible using mechanical cable release (AR-3).

Self-timer: electronic; delay times from 2 seconds to 30 seconds. Double self-timed shots possible. Can be cancelled without taking a picture.

Viewfinder: high-eyepoint viewfinder allowing viewing from a distance of around 0.7in. (18mm), good for people wearing glasses; 92% of the picture area is seen at 0.75x magnification (with a 50mm lens set to infinity); the eyepiece can be covered using the DK-5 eyepiece cover supplied.

Focusing screen: non-interchangeable type B "Brite-View" screen with AF focusing brackets and spot metering reference circle marked (N6006/F-601 AF only). The N6000/F-601m has a non-interchangeable type K focusing screen with central split-image indicator, microprism ring and matte fresnel field. On both focusing screens, the reference area for center-weighted metering is indicated by a 12mm circle.

Viewfinder information: permanently displayed or appearing when the shutter release button is touched: exposure mode; metering method; shutter speed; aperture; risk of camera shake (flashing shutter speed LED); flash ready indicator (flash LED). The following displays can also be selected: film speed; light scale (electronic analog display); manual exposure compensation; manual flash output compensation; AF-L status (not on N6000/F-601m); automatic exposure bracketing; self-timer delay time.

Central LCD panel: permanently displayed or appearing when the shutter release button is touched: exposure mode; metering method; shutter speed; aperture; automatic DX-reading; film transport mode; film transport check; frame counter. The following displays can also be selected: film speed; light scale (electronic analog display); manual exposure compensation; automatic fill-in flash; manual flash output compensation; Slow flash mode with slow sync speeds; rear blind synchronization "REAR," AF-L status (not on N6000/F-601m); automatic exposure bracketing; frame counter or remaining number of frames in automatic exposure bracket; self-timer delay time.

Film speed: can be set automatically using DX coding from ISO 25 to ISO 5000 or manually from ISO 6 to ISO 6400.

Film loading: automatic, film wound on to frame 1; effective film transport is indicated.

Film transport: motorized only, following each exposure; single shot setting "S," continuous

Nikon N6000

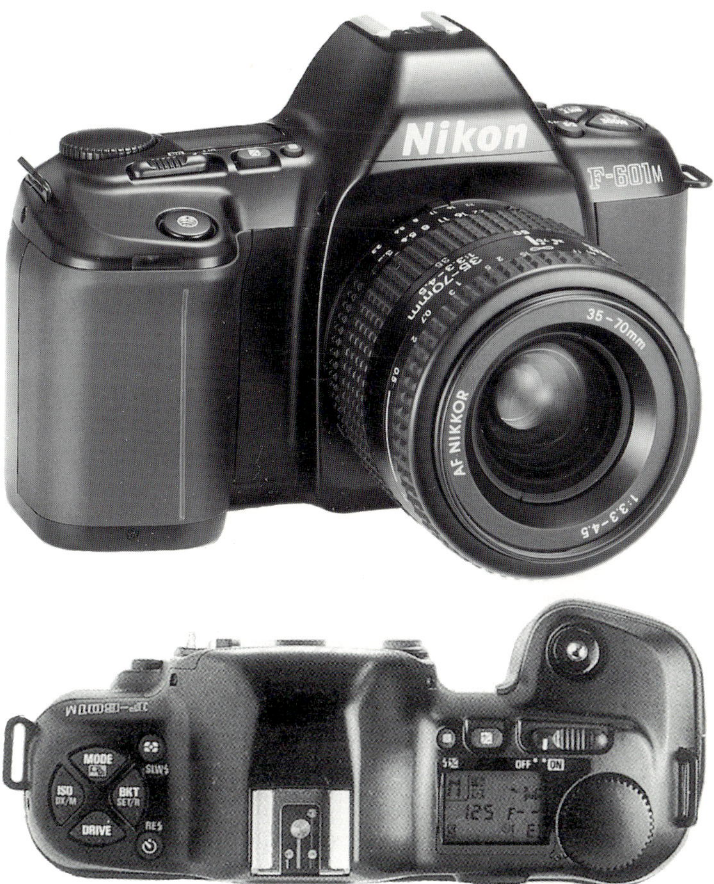

setting "CL" with up to 1.2 frames per second; continuous setting "CH" with up to 2 frames per second; effective transport is indicated; stops automatically at the end of the film.

Frame counter: forward-counting, counts backwards when the film is rewound.

Rewind: motorized only, approximately 26 seconds; rewinds film leader completely into cassette.

Built-in flash (N6006/F-601 AF only): guide number 43 (ft./ISO 100, 68°F). Fixed reflector illuminates the angle of view of a 28mm lens; works together with all the camera's automatic flash modes.

Automatic flash modes: normal TTL-controlled flash; automatically-balanced fill-in flash; manual compensation only affecting the amount of light emitted by the flash, in 1/3 steps from +1 EV to -3 EV. All automatic modes function with all Nikon system flash units from SB-16B onwards.

Flash connection: only via flash shoe, ISO contacts and additional Nikon system contacts. More recent Nikon flash units (from SB-15 onwards) allow all the flash functions which are controlled by the camera (even with the N6000/F-601m). Flash units made by other manufacturers may only be connected if it is ensured that there is no danger of short-circuit or excess voltage.

Flash synchronization: 1/125 second to 30 seconds in manual or shutter speed priority

Comparison of 6000 Series Camera Features

	N6006 F-601 AF	N6006 Quartz Date F-601 Quartz Date	N6000 F-601m
Autofocus:	yes	yes	no
Spot metering:	yes	yes	no
Built-in flash:	yes	yes	no
Databack:	no	yes	no
Other functions:	identical	identical	identical

modes; 1/125 second (or possibly 1/60 second with automatic fill flash) in aperture priority and program modes. In aperture priority and program modes, automatic flash with slow sync. speeds, "SLOW" is also possible (the camera automatically selects a sync speed between 1/125 second and 30 seconds, depending on subject brightness and film speed). In all modes and at any sync speed, synchronization can be timed to the action of either the first, "NORMAL" or the second, "REAR" shutter curtain.

Flash check indicator: red LED in viewfinder lights up when flash is ready for use; flashes after the exposure if the flash was too weak for correct exposure; if the flash is switched off or no flash is fitted, the flash LED flashes if the use of flash is recommended.

Autofocus illuminator: available if appropriate flash units with AF illuminator are used and camera is set to proper modes.

Power supply: 6V lithium block battery (Duracell DL-223 A, Panasonic CR-P2P or equivalent). At 68°F (20°C), a battery will last for around 75 rolls, N6006/F-601 AF without flash, or 140 rolls, N6000/F-601m; at -10°C it will last for around 22 rolls, N6006/F-601 AF without flash, or 80 rolls with the N6000/F601m. If 50% of shots are taken using flash, the battery will last for 16 films at 68°F (20°C),or only around 3 rolls at 15°F (-10°C) with the N6006 using built-in flash. This sort of power supply is ideal for sporadic photography, since the lithium battery loses virtually none of its capacity during storage. However, when used for frequent photography, it can be seen that the capacity is clearly less than that of four fresh alkaline-manganese batteries.

Battery check: with fresh batteries, the aperture and shutter speed settings are displayed for around 8 seconds after the shutter release button is touched; shorter display times, flashing of the display or blocking of the shutter release indicate that the batteries are run down.

Dimensions: N6006/F-601 AF: width 6.1in. (154.5mm); height 4in. (100mm), depth 2.6in. (65.5mm), N6000/F601m: width 6.1in. (154.5mm); height 3.8in. (96mm); depth 2.6in. (65mm)

Weight (without batteries): N6006/F-601 AF: 23oz. (650g), N6000/F-601m 20oz.(565g)

N6006 Quartz Date/F-601 Quartz Date only: as N6006/F-601 AF but with permanently-installed databack allowing either year/month/date or day/hour/minute (24 hour clock notation can be selected) to be exposed onto the frame. Data exposure can be switched off. This model is also referred to as the "N6006 Data/F-601 Data".

Special Accessories for the N6006/F-601

Eyecup: #2939.

This gate in Spanish Granada was taken with the F3. It lacks the absolutely correct rendering of perspective of a pure architecture shot since it was taken without a tripod or shift lens (note the slight converging line of the building to the right). In this situation a PC lens would have eliminated the converging lines but in doing so, would have taken away some of the dynamic quality of the shot. Photo Rudolf Dietrich

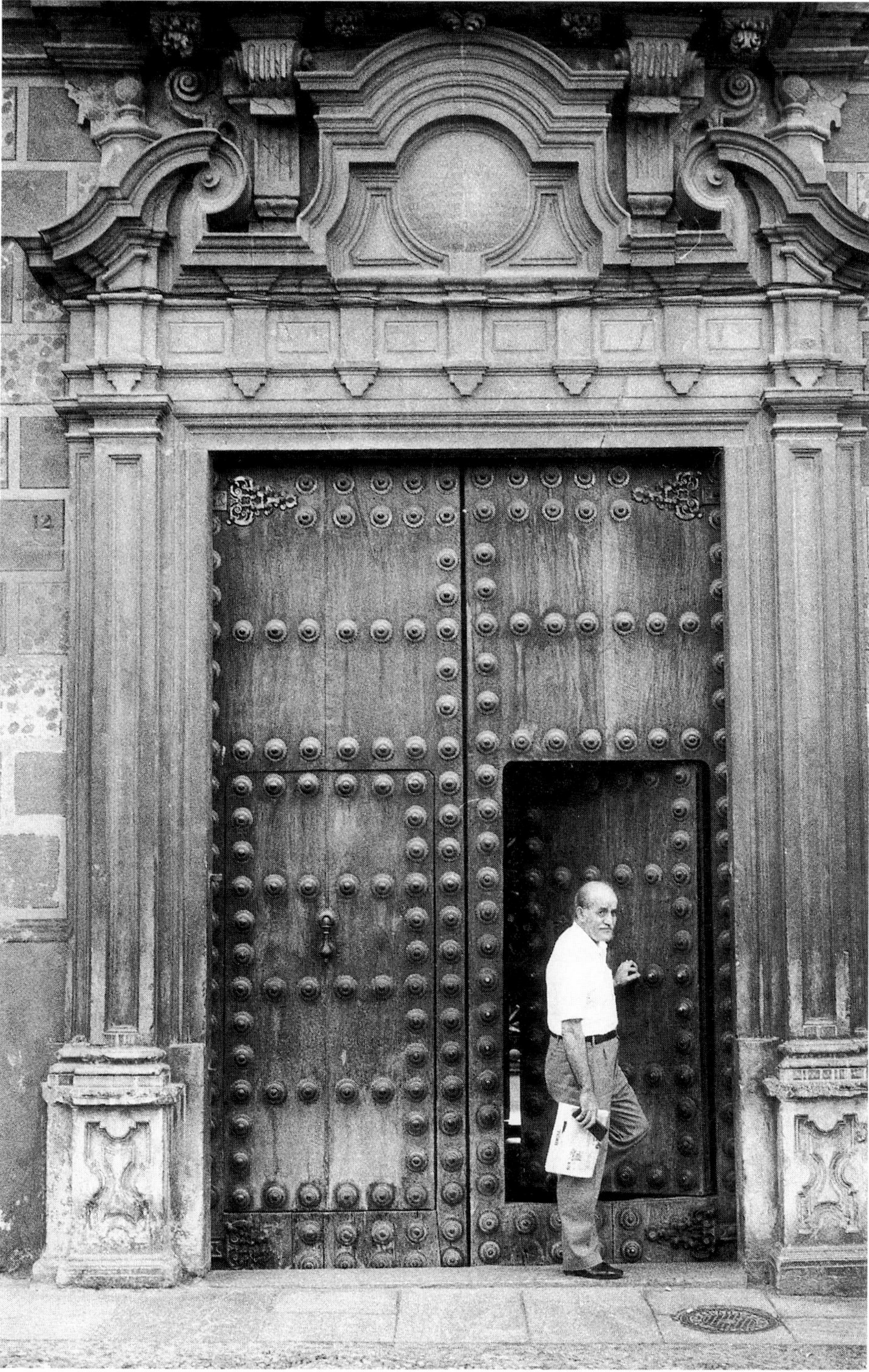
12

Nikon N8008/F-801 - The Semi-Professional AF SLR

N8008/F-801, N8008s/F-801s, Technical Data and Characteristics

Camera type: 35mm autofocus SLR with motorized film transport and operating controls and features designed to meet professional requirements.

Film format: 35mm film; 24 x 36mm picture format.

Lens mount: Nikon F-bayonet fitting with additional electronic control and data transmission contacts for AF lenses, and with integrated AF motor coupling. Mechanical transmission of aperture values with AI and AI-S Nikkors.

Suitable lenses: all AF Nikkors; all non-AF Nikkors (type AI-S and older AI Nikkors) with manual focusing and center-weighted metering (plus spot metering with N8008s/F-801s only) in manual and aperture priority modes. The non-AF Nikkors with a speed of f/5.6 and above can also be focused using the AF focusing aid. AF operation is possible using most non-AF fixed focal lengths in combination with the TC-16 A autofocus teleconverter, as long as the lens has a speed of f/3.5 or above.

Focusing system: 1. "S" Single servo: the shutter can only be released when the subject is in focus ("focus priority"); the focus setting is locked when the shutter release button is held in half-depressed position. 2. "C" Continuous servo: the focus is continuously adjusted as long as the shutter release button is held in half-depressed position, and the shutter can be released at any time, even if the autofocus facility has not yet got the subject in focus ("-release priority"). 3. "Tracking autofocus" (only on N8008s/F-801s): if film transport mode "CL" and AF mode "C" are selected together, the autofocus always takes two readings and uses these to calculate the focusing distance from a moving subject in advance "prediction autofocus." Focus priority is used initially, but the camera automatically switches to release priority after a certain delay if the subject is not suitable for automatic focusing.

Manual AF-locking: using the AF-L button.

AF focusing aid for manual focusing: the electronic rangefinding (LCD display in viewfinder) functions with all AF Nikkors and most AI and AI-S Nikkors with a speed of f/5.6 or greater.

Exposure metering: using silicon multi-field sensor. 1. Center-weighted metering (75/25 weighting); 2. Five-segment metering with matrix evaluation; metering range from EV 0 to EV 21 (at ISO 100 and a lens speed of f/1.4). 3. (N8008s/F-801s only) Spot metering [in center of matte screen, approximately 1% (depending on the lens) of the picture area], metering range from EV 4 to EV 21 (at ISO 100 and a lens with a speed of f/1.4). Metering is activated for approximately 8 seconds by lightly touching the shutter release button.

Exposure locking: activated by pressing the AE-L button. Saves the last metered exposure value in all automatic exposure modes.

Manual exposure setting: aperture on lens, shutter speed on central data input dial; both settings are displayed in the viewfinder and on the central LCD panel, but in both places the aperture is only displayed when using AF or P lenses; display of exposure balance on light scale in 1/3 steps. If these values are being set on the basis of external metering - e.g. metering of flash lighting in the studio - the aperture values can only be set by "sight and feeling" on the aperture ring of the lens, since the displays in the viewfinder and LCD panel only show full 'f stops'.

Exposure compensation: can be set manually from +5 EV to -5 EV in 1/3 steps (1 EV = exposure step = 1 "f stop").

Automatic exposure bracketing: only possible with MF-21 databack; up to 19 exposures with exposure differences ranging from 1/3 to 2 EV.

Shutter: electronically-controlled, vertical-action slit shutter with aluminum blinds; electromagnetic shutter release.

Shutter speeds: stepless speeds between 1/8000 second and 30 seconds in aperture priority and program modes; fixed shutter speeds from 30 seconds to 1/8000 second in shutter speed priority mode and manual mode, also B

Nikon N8008s

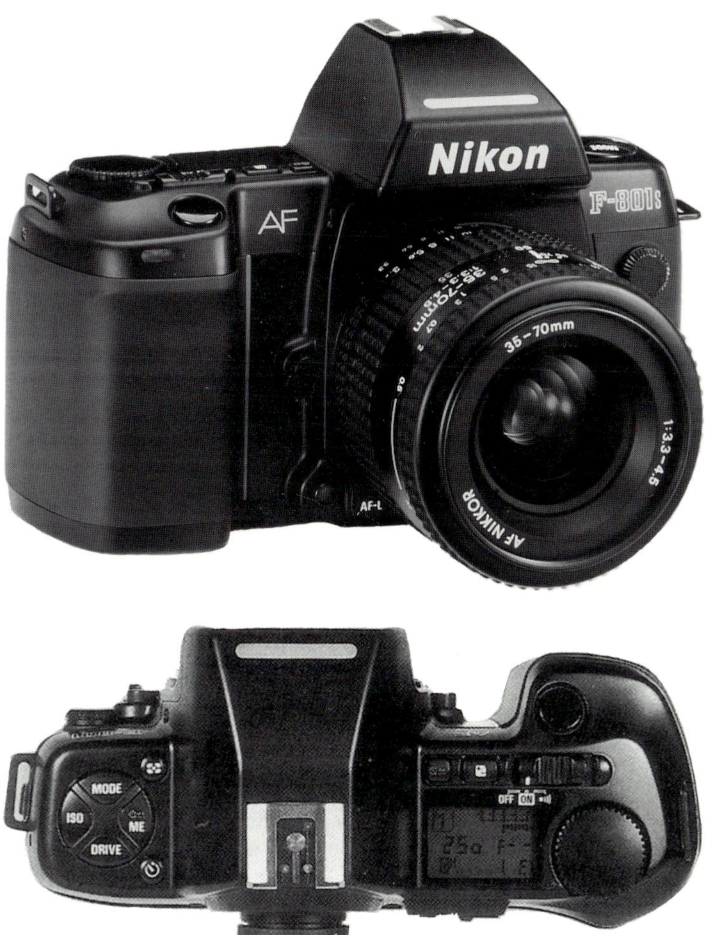

with the latter; lithium niobate oscillator allows extremely precise shutter speeds.

Shutter release: electromechanical with three-stage function. The exposure metering is activated for approximately 8 seconds by lightly touching the shutter release button, partial depression activates the autofocus, and the focus setting is locked by holding the shutter button in its half-depressed position (in AF mode "S"). The shutter is only released when the shutter release button is fully depressed. Separate main camera switch blocks the shutter release. Cable release connection.

Remote control: electronic, using MC-12A remote cord. Self-timer: electronic; delay times from 2 seconds to 30 seconds Countdown is indicated by a flashing LED on the front of the camera. Double self-timed shots are possible. Function can be cancelled without taking a shot.

Multiple exposures: up to 9 exposures on one frame are possible.

Viewfinder: permanently-installed high-eye-point viewfinder allowing viewing from a distance up to around 3/4in.(19mm) (good for people wearing glasses); 92% of the picture area is seen at 0.75x magnification (with a 50mm lens set to infinity); the DK-8 eyepiece cover prevents stray light from entering the viewfinder (causing risk of incorrect exposure) during timed exposures in automatic operation, when the eyepiece is not covered by the eye.
Focusing screen: type B "Brite-View" screen supplied as standard; can be exchanged for type E.
Viewfinder information: permanently displayed or appearing when the shutter release button is touched: focus indicator, exposure mode, shutter speed, aperture, flash ready indicator where suitable system flash units are used, exposure compensation indicator. The following displays can also be selected: film speed, light scale, exposure compensation value.
Central LCD panel: permanently displayed or appearing when the shutter release button is touched: exposure mode; metering method; shutter speed; aperture; symbol for exposure compensation; automatic DX-reading; film transport mode; film transport check; frame counter. The following displays can also be selected: film speed; light scale; exposure compensation value; self-timer delay time; multiple-exposure; rewind.
Warning beeper: can be switched off; signals end of film, completion of rewinding and self-timer countdown; warns of risk of over- and underexposure and camera shake (shutter speeds below 1/60 second) in aperture priority and program modes; in DX mode, warns when films without DX-coding or with defective coding are loaded; warns of film transport defects such as torn or jammed film.
Film speed: can be set automatically using DX coding from ISO 25 to ISO 5000 or manually from ISO 6 to ISO 6400.
Film loading: automatic, film wound to frame 1; effective film transport is indicated.
Film transport: motorized only, following each exposure, single frame setting "S;" continuous setting "CL" with up to 2 frames per second; continuous setting "CH" with up to 3.3 frames per second with new batteries, at normal temperature and at shutter speeds faster than 1/125 seconds; effective transport is indicated; stops automatically at the end of the film.
Frame counter: forwards-counting, counts backwards when the film is rewound.
Rewind: motorized only, approximately 15 seconds, rewinds film leader completely into cassette. (can be reprogrammed by Nikon service to leave leader exposed).
Depth of field check: visual assessment of the depth of field on the focusing screen is possible in aperture priority and manual modes using the preview button.
Camera back: can be exchanged for MF-20 databack, which allows the date and time to be exposed onto the film, and the MF-21, which also allows time exposures, automatic exposure bracketing, pre-programmed timer exposures and autofocus trap facility.
Flash connection: only via flash shoe with ISO contact and additional Nikon system contacts for the display of flash ready status, TTL control and data transmission. ISO range for TTL metering ISO 25 to ISO 1000. Flash units made by other manufacturers, particularly older models, may damage the camera's electronics through excess voltage (more than 12 volts) or short-circuiting of the system contacts.
Flash synchronization: from 1/60 second to 1/250 second in aperture priority and program modes. In manual or shutter speed priority modes, the selected shutter speed is used (1/250 second is automatically used if shutter speeds faster than 1/250 second are selected, although slower speeds can be set manually). Synchronization to the rear shutter curtain is possible with the SB-24 and SB-25 flash (in program and aperture priority modes with automatic sync speeds down to 30 seconds).
Automatic fill-in flash: in additional to conventional TTL flash, all the Nikon system flash units also allow automatic, center-weighted fill-in flash. With backlit subjects, this automatic fill-in flash takes into account the

subject contrast and background brightness, as well as remaining ambient light in twilight shots, adjusting the flash sync speed and/or aperture setting accordingly. In addition, the SB-24 and SB-25 allow fill-in flash with camera set to center-weighted metering or spot metering (N8008s only).

Manual flash output compensation: with **SB-24/25** from -1 EV to +3 EV (1 EV = 1 exposure step = 1 "f stop").

Flash check indicator: red LED in viewfinder lights up when Nikon system flash is ready for use; flashes if the flash was too weak for correct exposure or in the event of a loose contact between flash unit and shoe.

Autofocus illuminator: available if appropriate flash units such as Nikon SB-20, SB-22, SB-23 SB-24 and SB-25 are used.

Power supply: four 1.5V alkaline-manganese batteries (type AA) for up to 100 36-exposure rolls at 20(°)C or four rechargeable NiCd batteries of the same size for around 75 36-exposure rolls at 68°F (20°C).

Battery check: with fresh batteries the aperture and shutter speed settings are displayed for around 8 seconds after the shutter release button is touched; significantly shorter display times indicate that the batteries are running down.

Dimensions: width 6.1in (153.6mm); height 4in. (102.5mm); depth 2.7in. (67.5mm)

Weight: 24.5oz. (695g) without batteries.

Special Accessories for the N8008/F-801

Eyepiece adapter DK-7: for the connection of the DR-3 right-angle viewing attachment or the DG-2 eyepiece magnifier.

Eyecup: DK-6.

Focusing screens: type E matte screen with 12mm center circle, AF metering brackets and fresnel finish plus additional grid marking of vertical and horizontal lines. For reproduction work, architectural photography, extreme wide-angle shots.

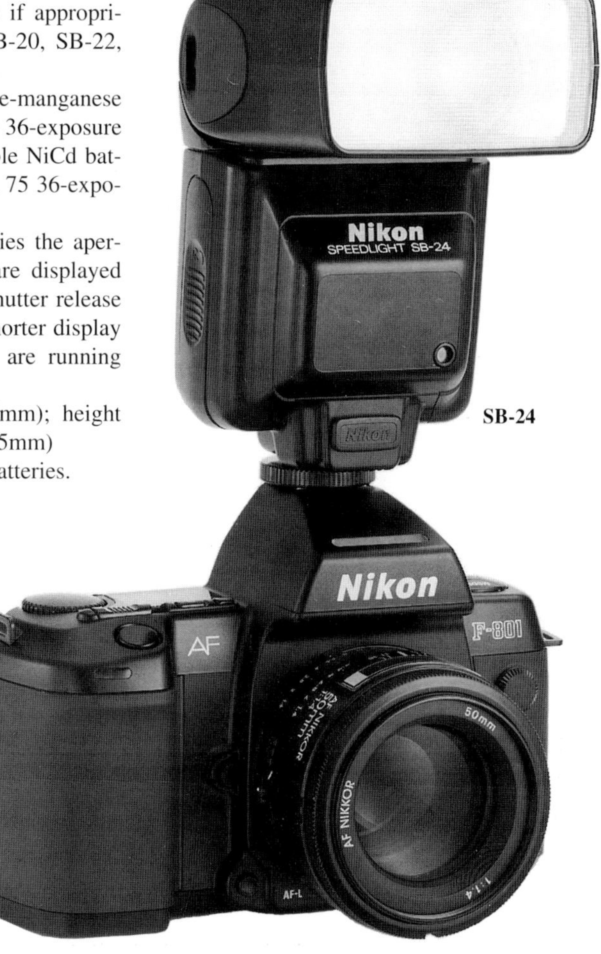

SB-24

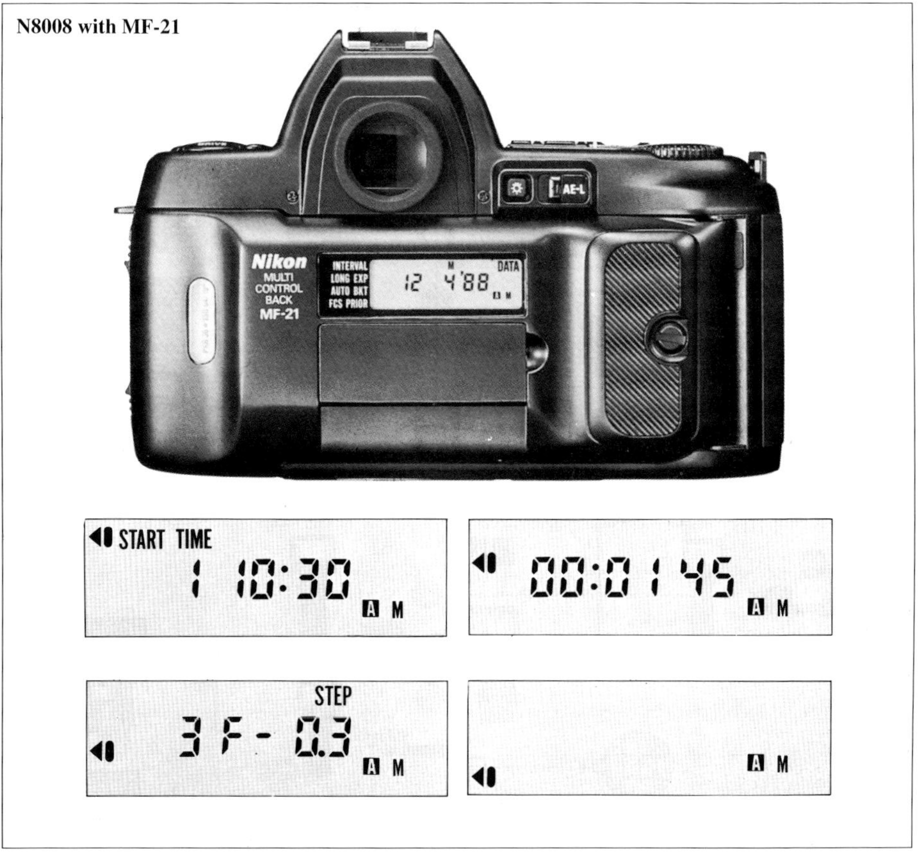

N8008 with MF-21

MS-7 reserve battery pack: pre-loaded battery pack allows you to change batteries quickly and continue taking pictures without a lengthy interruption.

DB-5 low-temperature protection for batteries: external battery holder can be carried close to the body, allowing reliable photography even at extremely low temperatures.

MC-12A remote shutter release cord: for electrical remote shutter release, also automatic AF focus trap in combination with MF-21.

MF-20 databack: allows year/month/date or day/hour/minute to be exposed onto film.

MF-21 Multi Control Back: *data exposure:* year/month/date or day/hour/minute; two-digit frame number; serial numbers from 1 to 999999; shutter speed and aperture setting. Interval *timer:* intervals and number of exposures per interval can be programmed. *Timer:* up to 99 exposures per day on 99 different days or monthly on a set day. Automatic exposure bracketing: up to 19 exposures with exposure differences of between 1/3 and 2 EV. *Time exposures:* from 1 second to 99 hours 59 minutes and 59 seconds. Autofocus trap: the shutter release button is held down after the camera has been focused manually on a particular spot. When an object enters this field of focus, the shutter of the N8008/F-801 is automatically released (the MC-12A release cord can be used to lock the shutter release button down allowing you to set up a truly automatic photo trap). In the field of photographic technology, the MF-21 has proven to be perfect for

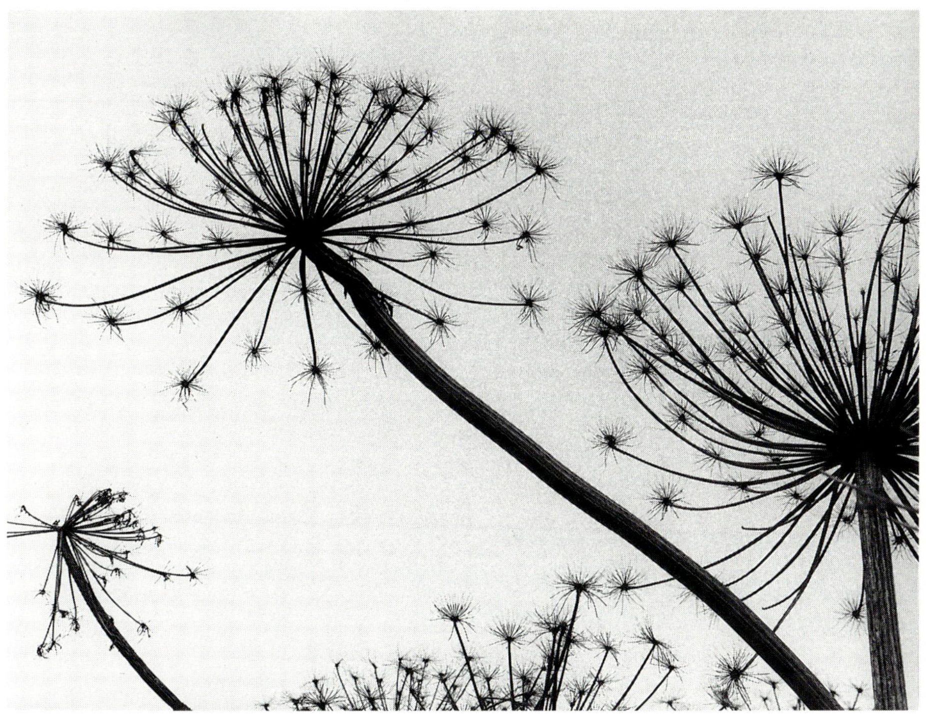

**This low angle shot of withered hemlock demonstrates that camera angle and perspective are often crucial for making a dramatic presentation of a rather simple, mundane subject.
Photo Rudolf Dietrich**

the testing of films and lenses. In the fields of research and development in industry and at universities, it offers a wide range of options for documentation.

Flash units: practically all Nikon system flash units (see above, and in the chapter "Nikon Flash" page 153).

Nikon F4 - The AF Camera for Professionals

F4, F4S, F4E, Technical Data and Characteristics

Camera type: 35mm autofocus SLR designed to meet the requirements of professional use with motorized film transport, interchangeable viewfinders, and other professional accessories. Conventional mechanical design of operating controls is intended to allow extremely fast and direct access. Both manual exposure metering and a variety of automatic exposure, focusing and flash modes are available. Currently, it is the Nikon AF SLR with the widest degree of compatibility with conventional non-AF lenses. It has an extremely durable body for demanding professional use.

Film format: type 35mm film; picture format 24 x 36mm.

Lens mount: Nikon F-bayonet fitting with additional electronic control and data transmission contacts for AF lenses, and with integrated AF motor coupling. Also features all mechanical transmission elements for AIS-type non-AF lenses.

Suitable lenses: all AF Nikkors; all non-AF Nikkors (type AI-S and AI Nikkors) but only with manual exposure control or aperture priority mode. Center-weighted, matrix and spot metering are all possible with all the above-mentioned lenses (in contrast to the N6006/F-601 and N8008/F-801). AF operation is possible in combination with the TC-16A autofocus teleconverter, as long as the lens has a speed of f/3.5 or faster.

Autofocus system: passive; TTL phase detection; Nikon AM 200 autofocus module; working range EV -1 to EV 18 at ISO 100.

Autofocus modes: 1. "S" Single servo: the shutter can only be released when the subject is in focus ("focus priority"); the focus setting is locked when the shutter release button is held in half-depressed position. 2. "C" Continuous servo: the shutter can be released at any time, "release priority." The camera continuously focuses on the subject as long as the shutter release button is held in the half-depressed position, and the shutter can be released at any time, even if the autofocus facility has not yet got the subject in focus. 3. "Tracking autofocus" If film transport mode "CL" and AF mode "C" are selected together, the autofocus always takes two readings and uses these to calculate the focusing distance from a moving subject in advance, "prediction autofocus." Focus priority is used initially, but the camera automatically switches to release priority after a certain delay if the subject is not suitable for autofocus.

Manual AF-lock: using the AF-L button.

AF focusing aid for manual focusing: the electronic rangefinder (LCD display in viewfinder) functions with all AF Nikkors and most AI and AI-S Nikkors, as well as with non-AI Nikkors and AI-modified Nikkors with a speed of f/5.6 or greater.

Exposure metering: using silicon multi-field sensor. 1. Center-weighted metering (60/40 weighting). 2. Five-field metering with matrix evaluation and automatic exposure compensation. Automatic adjustment of weighting for horizontal and vertical format shots. 3. Spot metering (in center of matte screen, approximately 2.5% of the picture area). All metering methods can be used with the DP-20 multimeter viewfinder, matrix metering is not possible with the other interchangeable viewfinders. Metering range from EV 0 to EV 21 with center-weighted metering and matrix metering, EV 2 to EV 21 with spot metering at ISO 100 and using a lens with a speed of f/1.4. Metering is activated for approximately 16 seconds by lightly touching the shutter release button.

Automatic exposure modes: shutter speed priority, normal program mode and slow-speed program mode, all three are only possible with AF Nikkors (with built-in CPU) or with the 500mm f/4, P Nikkor. Aperture priority also functions with all non-AF Nikkors of type AI and AI-S; the automatically-selected shutter speeds and/or apertures are displayed in the viewfinder LC display in 1/2 EV steps.

Exposure lock: activated by pressing the AE-L or AF-L button; saves the last metered exposure value in all automatic exposure modes.

Nikon F4

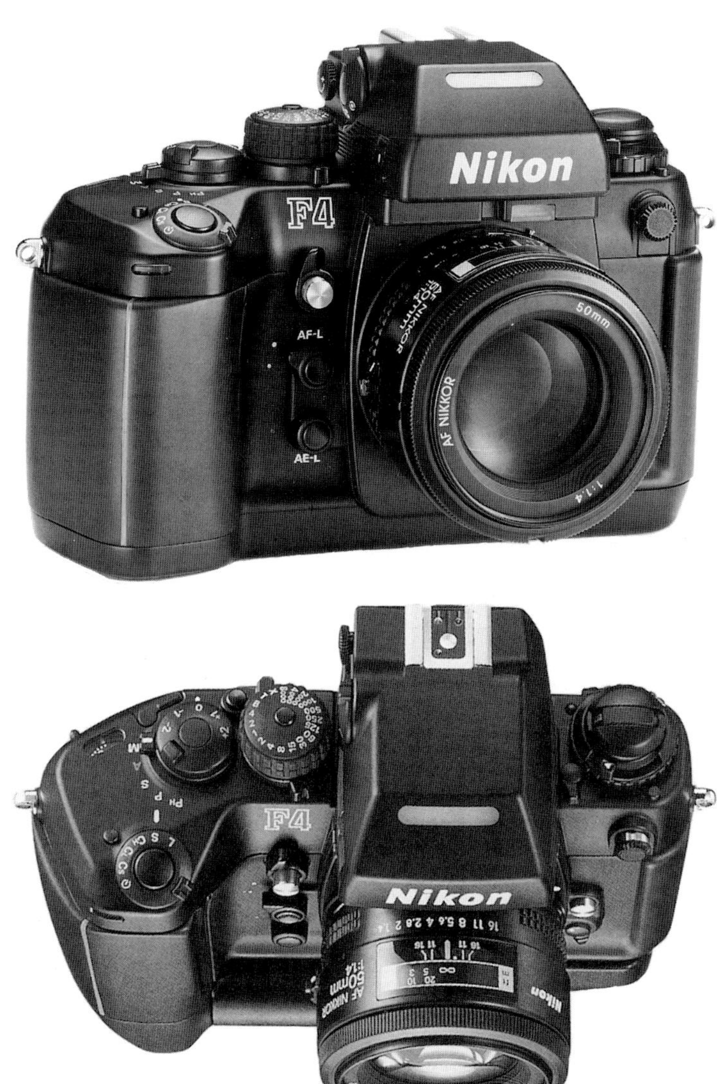

Manual exposure setting: aperture on lens, shutter speed on shutter speed dial; the selected shutter speed and deviation from metered value are displayed in 1/2 stops on the light scale in the viewfinder LCD; direct read-out of the aperture setting in the viewfinder. *Note:* if set on the basis of external metering - e.g. metering of flash lighting in the studio - the aperture values can only be set by "sight and feel" on the aperture ring of the lens, since the LC displays in the viewfinder only show the aperture values in 1/2 "f stops" in aperture priority and program modes.

Exposure compensation: can be set manually from +2 EV to -2 EV in 1/3 stops on exposure compensation dial (1 EV = exposure step = 1 "f-stop"). The selected compensation value can not only be seen clearly on the exposure compensation dial, it also appears in the viewfinder display as a real numerical value (in contrast to all other AF Nikons).

Automatic exposure bracketing: only possible with MF-23 databack; up to 19 exposures with varying exposure value.

Shutter: electronically-controlled, vertical-action double slit shutter with aluminum and epoxy-carbon blinds; a wolfram counterweight and shutter brake eliminate practically all vibration due to shutter action; electromagnetic shutter release.

Shutter speeds: any speed between 30 seconds and 1/8000 second in aperture priority and program modes; fixed shutter speeds from 4 seconds to 1/8000 second in shutter speed priority mode and manual mode, also B, T and X (1/250 second) with the latter. Lithium niobate oscillator allows extremely precise shutter speeds.

Shutter release: electromechanical with three-stage function. The exposure metering is activated for approximately 16 seconds by lightly touching the shutter release button, partial depression activates the autofocus, and the focus setting is locked, in AF mode "S," by holding the shutter button in its half-depressed position. The shutter is only released when the shutter release button is fully depressed. Integrated main camera switch blocks the shutter release. Cable-release connection on camera body.

Remote control: via cable release or electronic, via MB-21 or MB-23 battery sections, e.g. with MC-12A remote cord.

Self-timer: electronic; delay time 10 seconds. Function can be cancelled.

Viewfinder: interchangeable high-eyepoint viewfinder (DP-20 supplied as standard, with selector switch for 3 exposure metering methods) allowing viewing from a distance up to around 22mm (good for people wearing glasses); 100% of the picture area is seen at 0.70x magnification (with a 50mm lens set to infinity); the built-in eyepiece shutter prevents stray light from entering the viewfinder (risk of incorrect exposure) during time exposures or automatic operation, when the eyepiece is not covered by the eye; eyepiece features diopter adjustment to compensate for eyesight defects; exposure compensation when focusing screens are changed; and flash shoe. The standard viewfinder can be exchanged for the DA-20 sports viewfinder, the DW-20 waist-level viewfinder, or the DW-21 6x magnification viewfinder.

Focusing screen: type B "Brite-View" screen supplied as standard; can be exchanged for other focusing screens (see below).

Viewfinder information: the LC display shows the exposure compensation value, frame counter, metering system, shutter speed, aperture in 1/2 "f-stops" (only in shutter speed and program modes), exposure mode, light scale (in manual mode), AE-L indicator; LEDs for AF system focus indicators, exposure compensation indicator, flash ready indicator where suitable system flash units are used; direct readout of aperture setting; viewfinder illumination is also available.

Film speed: can be set automatically using DX coding from ISO 25 to ISO 5000 or manually from ISO 6 to ISO 6400.

Film loading: automatic, film wound to frame 1; effective film transport is indicated.

Film transport: motorized only, following each exposure, single frame setting "S>;" continuous setting "CL" with up to 3.3 frames per second (Nikon F4S and F4E up to 3.4 frames per second); fast continuous setting "CH" with up to 4 frames per second, Nikon F4S and F4E up to 5.5 frames per second) depending on the condition of the batteries, the temperature and pre selected or automatically set shutter speeds, as well as AF mode; also silent continuous setting "CS" (approx. 14 dB) with 1 frame per second. Effective transport is indicated; transport stops automatically at the end of the film. The transport speed also depends on the battery pack used (F4, slow; F4S, medium; F4E, fast). Thus, for example, an F4 can be converted into an F4S or F4E by the attachment of either MB-21 or MB-23.

Frame counter: forwards-counting, mechanical display on top of camera and electronic display in viewfinder LCD.

Rewind: either motorized or manual, using rewind crank.
Multiple exposures: any number of exposures on one frame are possible using multiple exposure lever.
Depth of field check: visual assessment of the depth of field on the focusing screen is possible in aperture priority and manual modes using the preview button.
Camera back: can be exchanged for MF-22 databack, which allows the date and time to be exposed onto the film, and the MF-23, which also offers a number of other functions such as timed exposures, automatic exposure bracketing, pre-programmed timer exposures and autofocus trap facility, as well as a feature known as film stop which allows the film advance to stop at a predetermined frame number; the MF-24 databack 250 exposure back holding around 250 exposures and has the same functions as the MF-23.
Flash connection: via flash PC socket or flash shoe with ISO center contacts (with DA-20 and DP-20 viewfinders) and additional Nikon system contacts for the display of flash ready status, TTL control and monitor function. ISO range for TTL metering ISO 25 to ISO 1000. *Warning:* flash units made by other manufacturers, particularly older models, may damage the camera's electronics through excess voltage (more than 12 volts) or short-circuiting of the system contacts.
Flash synchronization: from 1/60 second to 1/250 second in aperture priority and program modes; in manual or shutter speed priority modes, the selected shutter speed is used (1/250 second is automatically used if shutter speeds faster than 1/250 second are selected). Synchronization to the rear shutter curtain is possible with the SB-24 and SB-25 flash (in program and aperture priority modes with stepless sync. speeds down to 30 seconds).
Flash check indicator: red LED in viewfinder; lights up when Nikon system flash is ready for use; flashes if the flash was too weak for correct exposure or in the event of a loose contact between flash unit and shoe.
Automatic fill-in flash: in addition to conventional TTL flash, all the Nikon system flash units also allow automatic, matrix-controlled fill-in flash. With backlit subjects, this automatic fill-in flash takes into account the subject contrast and background brightness, as well as remaining ambient light in twilight shots, adjusting the flash sync speed and/or aperture setting accordingly. In addition, the SB-24 also allows fill-in flash with camera set to center-weighted metering or spot metering.
Manual flash output compensation: with SB-24 from -1 EV to +3 EV (1 EV = 1 exposure step = 1 "f stop"). **SB-25**
Autofocus illuminator: available when appropriate flash units such as Nikon SB-20, SB-22, SB-23 SB-24 and SB-25 are used.
Power supply: MB-20 battery pack takes four 1.5V alkaline- manganese batteries (type AA) for around 30 36-exposure films (the use of "generic" rechargeable NiCds is not recommended with this camera). MB-21 uses 6 AA; MB-23 uses 6 AA or MN-20 NiCd.
Battery check: with fresh batteries, the aperture and shutter speed settings are displayed for around 16 seconds after the shutter release button is touched; significantly shorter display times indicate that the batteries are running down.
Dimensions: F4: width 6.63in. (168.5mm); height 4.6in. (117mm); depth 3in. (76.6mm) F4S: width 6.63in. (168.5mm); height 5.4in. (138mm); depth 3in. (76.6mm) F4E: width 6.63in. (168.5mm); height 6.1in. (156mm); depth 3in. (76.6mm)
Weight (without batteries): F4 approx. 38.5oz. (1090g), F4S approximately 45.2oz. (1280g), F4E approximately 48.3oz. (1370g)

Special Accessories for the F4
Eyepiece adapter: DK-7: for the connection of the DR-3 right-angle viewing attachment or the DG-2 eyepiece magnifier.
DA-20 action viewfinder: can be viewed from a distance of up to 23.7in. (60cm) from the eyepiece, ideal for viewing the viewfinder image and the general scene at the same time, also useful with special housings for underwater photography. This viewfinder allows cen-

ter-weighted integral metering and spot metering, but not matrix metering.

DW-20 waist-level viewfinder: allows the viewfinder image to be viewed from above. Folding hood with 5x auxillary magnifier. Connection for SC-24 TTL flash cable. This viewfinder only allows spot metering, no center-weighted integral metering or matrix metering. The DW-20 is good for extreme camera positions, e.g. in copy or macrophotography.

DW-21 high-magnification viewfinder: allows the viewfinder image to be viewed from above. With 6x magnifier and diopter adjustment from +3 to -3 diopters. Built-in eyepiece cover. Connection for SC-24 TTL flash cable. This viewfinder only allows spot metering, no center-weighted integral metering or matrix metering. The DW-21 is good for macro- or microphotography when used in combination with appropriate focusing screens.

SC-24 TTL flash cable: for the connection of Nikon flash units when DW-20 or DW-21 viewfinders are fitted.

MB-20 reserve battery pack: pre-loaded battery pack allows you to change batteries quickly and continue using the F4 without a lengthy interruption

MB-21 battery pack: converts the F4 into an F4S (F4 with MB-21 supplied as standard). The MB-21 battery pack holds six 1.5V alkaline-manganese batteries (type AA) for approximately up to 90 36-exposure films or equivalent NiCd batteries for approximately up to 70 rolls; the number of rolls is based on a temperature of 68°F(20°C). The MB-21 battery pack incorporates a handgrip which features an additional shutter release button for vertical-format shots.

MB-23 battery pack: converts the F4 into an F4E (F4 with MB-23 supplied as standard). The MB-23 battery pack holds six 1.5V alkaline-manganese batteries (type AA) or equivalent NiCd batteries. Alternatively, the quickly rechargeable MN-20 battery can be used, providing enough power for up to 190 36-exposure rolls. The number of rolls is based on a

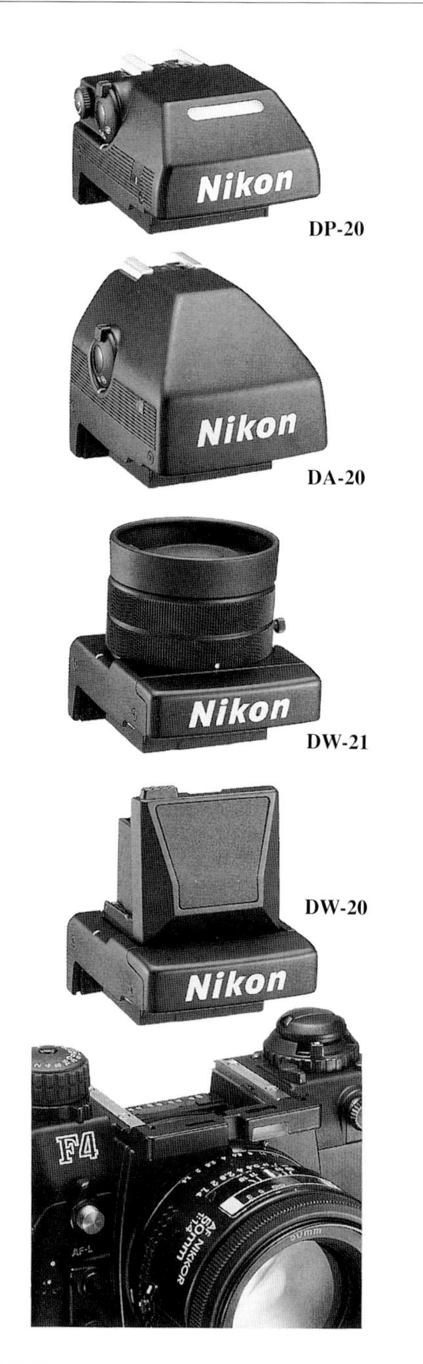

DP-20

DA-20

DW-21

DW-20

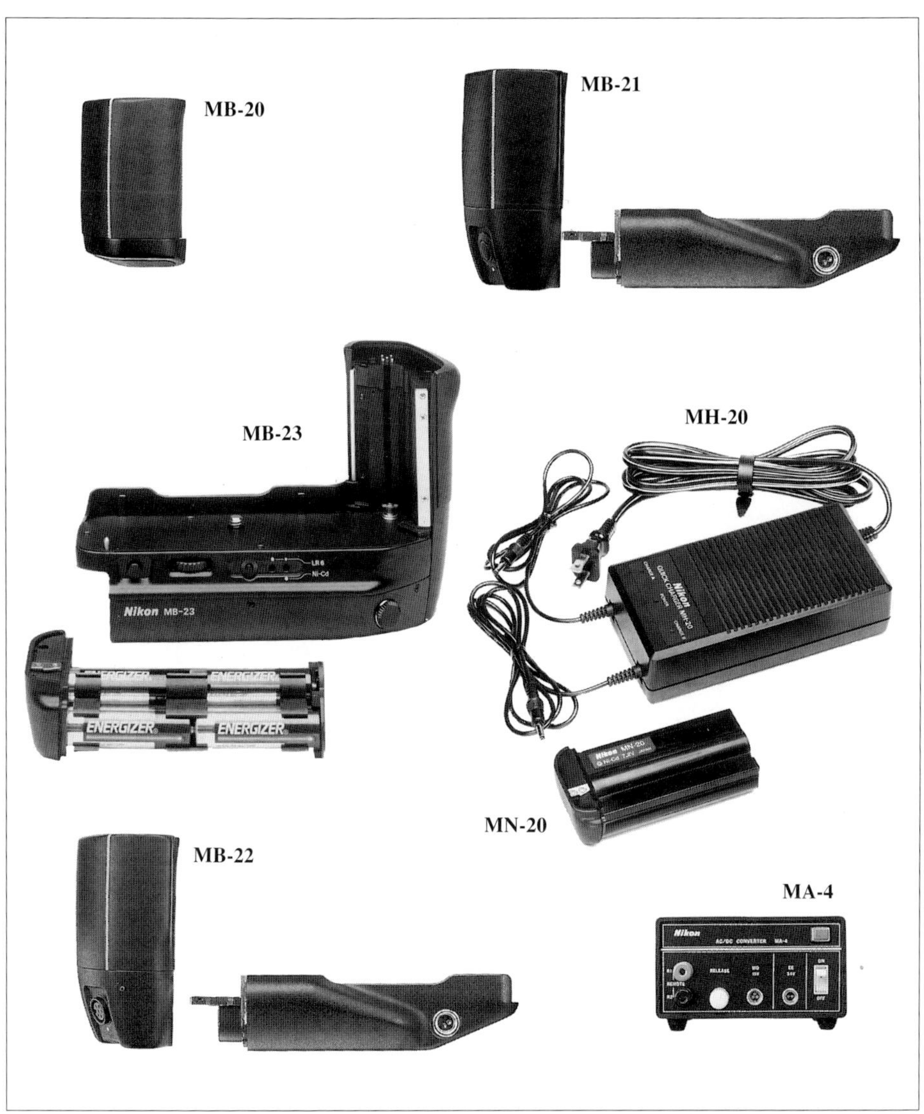

temperature of 20(°)C. This battery can be recharged using the MH-20 rapid-charging unit. The MB-23 battery pack incorporates a handgrip which features an additional shutter release button for vertical-format shots.

MH-20 rapid-charging unit for the MN-20 battery pack (for MB-23): charges the battery pack within 90 minutes using a voltage of 110 V to 240 V (making it international in use).

MB-22 external power regulator and MA-4 power adapter: allow the F4 and F4S to be operated on AC power, e.g. in the studio.

MC-12A remote shutter release cord: for electrical remote shutter release with MB-21 and MB-23, and for automatic AF focus trap in combination with MF-23.

MF-22 databack: allows year/month/date or day/hour/minute to be exposed onto film.

MF-23 multi-control back: data exposure: year/month/date or day/hour/minute; two-digit

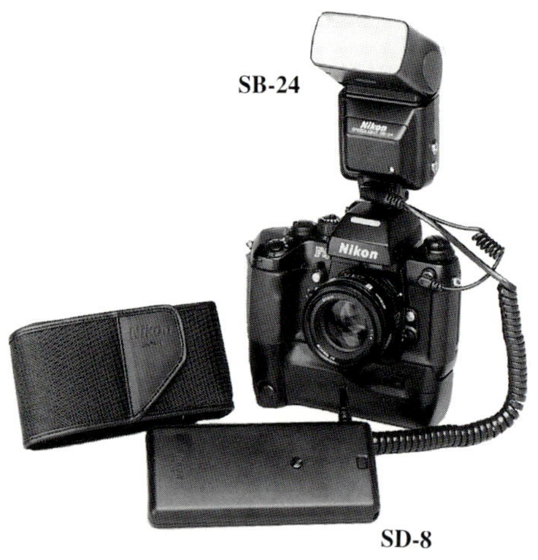

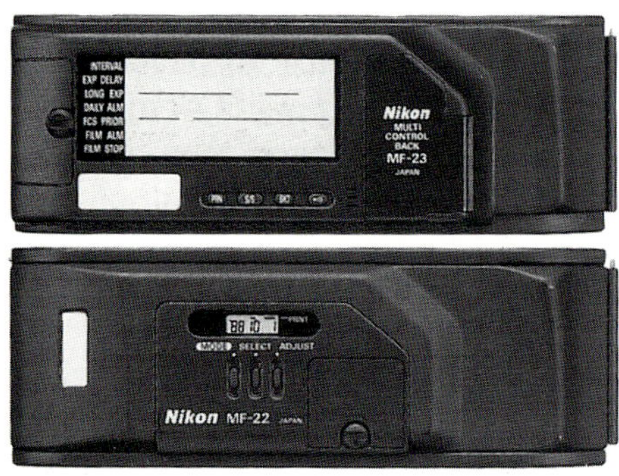

Above: MF-23; Below: MF-22

frame number; any number in series from 1 to 999999; shutter speed and aperture setting. Interval timer: intervals and number of exposures per interval can be programmed. Delayed release timer: delay before first exposure and number of exposures can be programmed. Automatic exposure bracketing: up to 19 exposures with exposure differences of between 1/3 and 2 EV. Time exposures: from 1 seconds to 1000 hours. Autofocus trap; the shutter release button is held down after the F4 has been focused manually on a particular spot. When an object enters this field of focus, the shutter is automatically released (with the MB-21 or MB-23, the MC-12A release cord can be used to lock the shutter release button down, allowing you to set up a truly automatic photo trap). Acoustic signal: at a preset time or with various film functions. Film stop: blocks the shutter release when a pre-selected frame number is reached. In the field of photographic technology, the MF-23 has proven to be ideal for the testing of films and lenses. In the fields of research and development in industry and at universities it offers a wide range of options for automatic documentation.

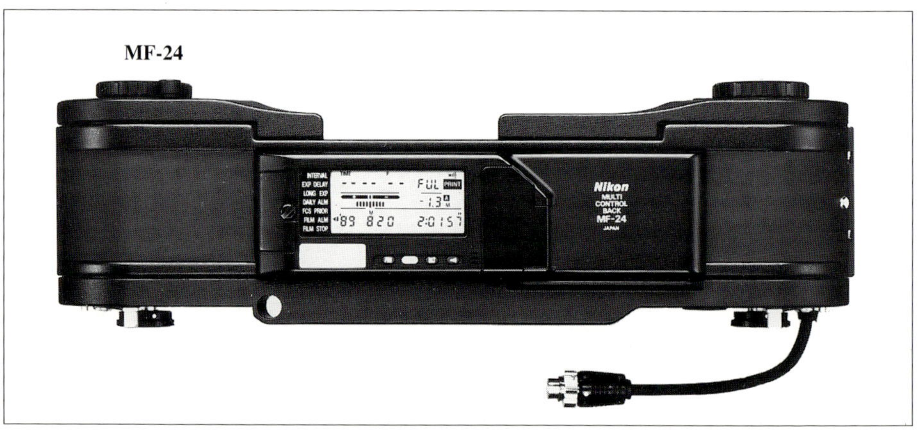

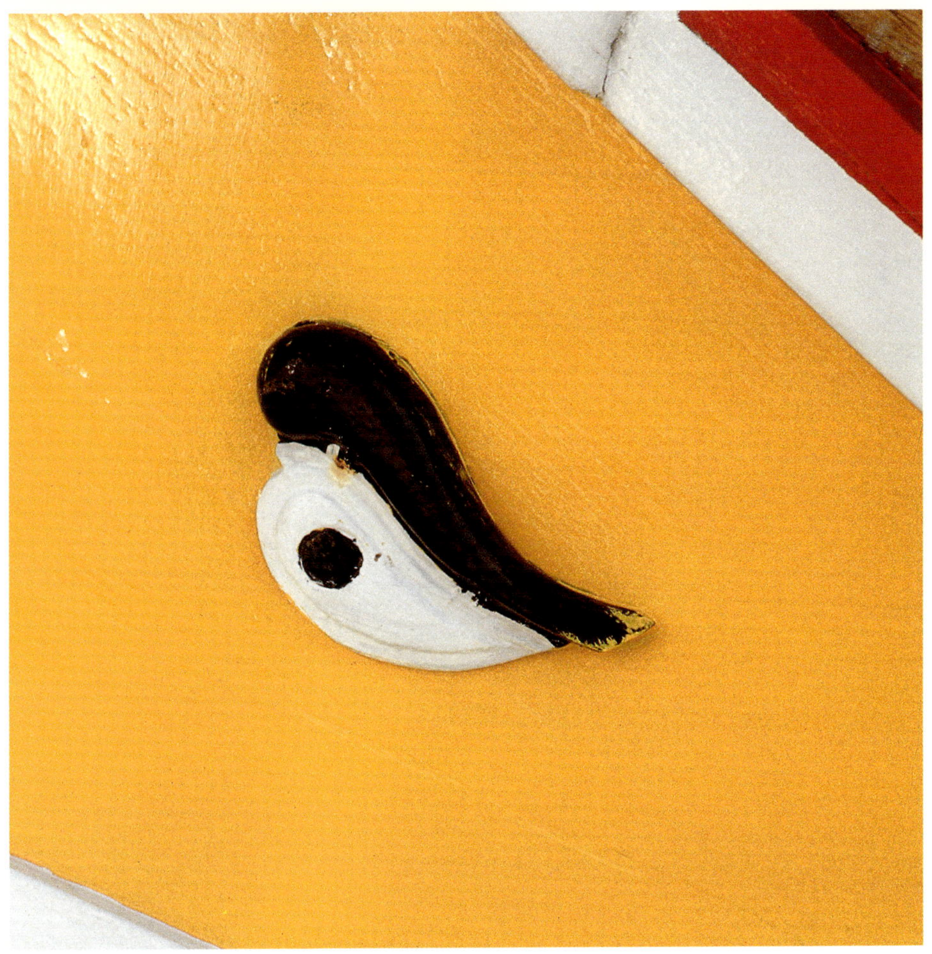

Color and shape: This close-up of a fishing boat's bow is not only aesthetically pleasing but it has a documentary quality due to the precise way the details were recorded. The stylized eye on the bow is a centuries old Phoenician tradition that is still alive in the Mediterranean area.

MF-24 250 exposure back: can only be used in combination with MB-21, MB-23 or MB-22. Remote control output for connection to MB-21, MB-23 and MB-22, remote control input for connection of MC-12A etc. The MF-24 incorporates an integrated data and multi-control back which offers exactly the same features as the MF-23.

Flash units: practically all Nikon system flash units (see above, and in the special chapter on flash units).

Focusing screens: 21 additional interchangeable focusing screens, see also viewfinder accessories in chapter on Nikon System Accessories.

Eyecup: DK-6.

Nikon N90/F90 - Exposure Genius with Computer Connection

Nikon N90/F90 - Technical Data and Characteristics

Camera Type: Autofocus, small format, mirror reflex camera with motorized film transport and electronic functions and features optimized for the professional user. Data-Link connection for remote display and control, programming, data storage, etc.

Film Format: 36mm; 24x36mm picture format.

Lens mount: Nikon F Bayonet with additional electronic control and data transmission contacts for AF lenses and with integrated AF motor drive. Additional electronic contacts for transmission of actual focus distance with Type D AF Nikkors and for use of the built-in AF motors on AF-I Nikkors. Mechanical transmission of aperture values with AI and AI-S Nikkors.

Compatible lenses: all AF Nikkors; all Type D AF Nikkors, all non-AF Nikkors (Type AI-S as well as older AI Nikkors) manual focusing allowing center-weighted or spot metering in manual exposure and aperture preferred modes. Non-AF Nikkors of f/5.6 and faster can also be focused with AF Focus-assist. Most non-AF fixed focal length lenses can be used in autofocus mode in conjunction with the AF Teleconverter TC-16A, provided the lens is f/3.5 or faster.

Autofocus system: passive; TTL phase detection; Nikon CAM 246 autofocus sensor module in cross configuration; selectable, two size AF Field. Working range from -1 EV to 19 EV with respect to ISO 100. Dynamic autofocus (tracking) in all AF modes. Particularly fast AF focusing algorithms.

Autofocus modes: 1. "S" Single AF with sharpness priority: the shutter can only be released when the subject is in focus; when the trigger is depressed half-way, the focus setting is stored. 2. "C" Continuous Autofocus: When the trigger is depressed half-way, the system is continually focusing (tracking). An exposure can be made at any time even if the autofocus has not focused yet. 3. Sharpness prediction: This function (dynamic autofocus) is active in "S" and "C" modes. It recognizes moving objects by taking two measurements and calculates the subject's speed and hence the focus setting at the time of the exposure.

Manual AF locking: With the AF-L key, can be combined with exposure storage using the MF-26 back.

AF Focus-Assist for manual focusing: Besides working with AF Nikkors, the electronic distance meter (LCD panel in the viewfinder) also works with most AI and AI-S Nikkors which are f/5.6 or faster.

Exposure metering: Selenium multi-field sensor. 1. Center-weighted metering (75/25 weighting); 2. Spot metering (center of the viewfinder, approximately 1% of the image area), sensitivity EV 3 to EV 21 (at ISO 100 with an f/1.4 lens); 3. Eight-field metering with matrix evaluation and automatic exposure correction; sensitivity EV -1 to EV 21 (at ISO 100 with an f/1.4 lens) with both; 4. 3D Matrix metering with automatic exposure correction with particular emphasis on the focused subject. Exposure metering is activated for approximately 8 seconds by touching the trigger (programmable to 4, 16, 30 or 60 seconds via Data Link).

Exposure modes: aperture priority; shutter priority; multi-program mode (automatic shift program that accommodates itself to the focal length), manual program shift. In addition, 7 subject-optimized Vari-programs: portrait, portrait with flash and pre-flash, silhouette, high depth of field, landscape, sport, macro.

Exposure lock: Activated by pressing the AE-L key; the last metered exposure value is stored in all exposure modes. Can be combined with sharpness storage with the MF-26 back or Data Link.

Manual exposure selection: Aperture on the lens' aperture ring, shutter speed on the central command dial; selected values shown on the LCD displays in the viewfinder and central panel; matching exposures shown on an analog display in 1/3 stops. *Note:* The N90 display is not suited to selecting exposure according to external metering - i.e: with flash metering in a

studio - since the displays only show full stops (set using "feel" on the lens's aperture ring).
Exposure compensation: Manually from +5 EV to -3 EV in steps of 1/3 (1 EV = 1 exposure level = 1 exposure "step"); automatic corrections with matrix metering or 3D matrix (with the inherent error factor of such automations).
Automatic bracketing: Only with MF-26 data back or Data Link; 3 to 19 images with exposure differences of 1/3 to 2 EV.
Shutter: Electronically controlled, vertical metal focal plane shutter made of a special light-metal alloy; electromagnetic release.
Shutter speeds: Stepless from 30 seconds to 1/8000 second in aperture priority and program modes; discrete shutter speeds from 30 seconds to 1/8000 second in shutter preferred and manual modes, also "B" in the latter; very accurate times through a lithium-niobate oscillator. Long time exposures up to 99 hours, 59 minutes and 59 seconds possible with the Multi-function Back MF-26. The N90 works with "T"-shutter with the MC-20 remote control, that is that the first release opens the shutter while the second closes it again.
Shutter release: Elector-mechanical in three steps. Light touch activates the exposure metering for about 8 seconds, half depression activates the autofocus and stores the focus distance (in "S" mode) when the trigger is held in the half depressed position; exposure results only when the trigger is completely depressed. Separate main camera switch blocks the trigger. No cable release connection.
Remote triggering: Electrically via the MC-20 remote release cable. When using the MC-12A

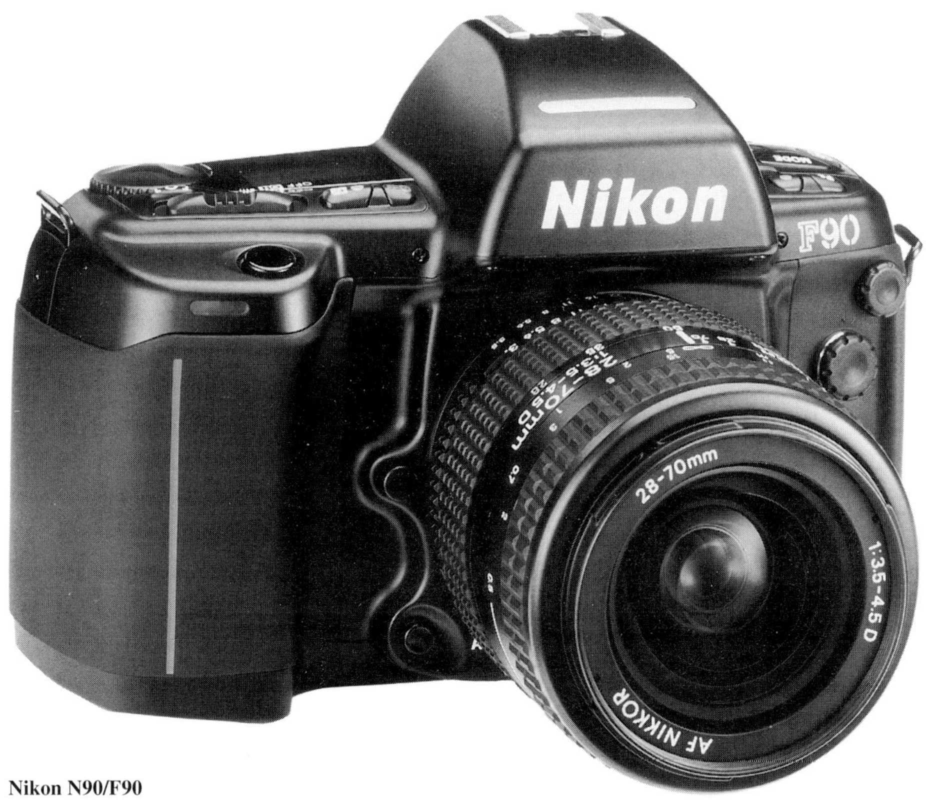

Nikon N90/F90

remote release cable, the MC-25 adapter cable in required. Interval release possible with the MF-26 multi-function back.

Self-timer: double self-timer: electronic; duration's from 2 to 30 seconds; progress shown via a blinking LED on the front of the camera; double self-timer in intervals of 10 seconds possible; reset without exposure possible.

Multiple exposures: only with MF-26 Data back or Data Link; it is possible to expose 2-19 images on one frame.

Viewfinder: Built-in high-eyepoint viewfinder for viewing distances up to 19mm 0.7in. (good for people with glasses); 92% of the image is shown at a ratio of .78 (with a 50mm lens at infinity); built-in eye-piece cover prevents stray light from entering the viewfinder during long-time exposures when the eye is not at the eye-piece.

Focusing screen: Brite-View Type B; can be interchanged with Type E with grid lines.

Viewfinder information: always shown or when the trigger is depressed: AF Field size, sharpness indicator, exposure mode, shutter speed, aperture, frame number, flash indicator, flash ready indicator (only when using appropriate system flash units). Alternatively or in addition depending on mode or condition: incorrect exposure warning, light scale or exposure correction indicator, end of film. Optional when touching the function key: exposure correction value.

Central LCD Panel: constantly shown: exposure mode, exposure metering system, six of the AF field, frame counter, film transport method. If these indicators blink, the film is stuck or torn. After touching the trigger, the following are shown for approximately 8 seconds: exposure time including B, over- or under exposure warning, aperture; AF mode, manual focus, auto-flash mode (other than normal TTL), loaded film, film transport control, battery load indicator; via the Electronic Organizer connected by Data Link, functions programmed via Data Link. Shown according to the function key touched: film speed, exposure correction values, self-timer delay, selected Vari-program.

Beeper: can be turned off and is intended as a warning, information and OK beeper. Warnings: Aperture ring not set to maximum aperture number in "P;" flash unit not set to TTL in program mode; over and under exposure; use of non-AF lenses with incompatible programs; selection of "bulb" in inappropriate modes; danger of camera shake (exposure times over 1/focal length seconds) in time and program modes; warning when films without or with faulty DX codes are loaded in DX mode; warns if there are film transport problems such as torn or stuck film. Information: end of film; rewind complete and self-timer progress. OK: Focus completed in AF mode "S."

Film speed: Automatic selection from ISO 25 to ISO 5000 via DX coding or manually from ISO 6 to ISO 6400.

Film load: automatic advance to frame 1; monitor of effective film transport.

Film transport: only motorized after every exposure; single picture mode "S;" continuous shooting mode "L" with 2 exposures per second and continuous shooting mode "H" with up to 3.6 exposures per second (with new batteries, normal temperatures and exposure times less than 1/250 second); monitor of effective transport; automatic stop at the end of the film.

Counter: increasing and decreasing during rewind.

Rewind: only motorized, pulls the film leader in. (Can be programmed to leave leader out by Nikon service).

Depth of field control: the depth of field can be visually checked on the viewfinder by depressing the preview button in aperture preferred and manual exposure modes.

Camera back: interchangeable with MF-25 Global time data back for superimposition of date and time and MF-26 multi-function back (see N90 Accessories as well as the "data and Multi-Function Backs" chapter).

Flash connection: via hot shoe with central ISO contact and additional Nikon System contacts for display of flash readiness, TTL control and data transmission; ISO range ISO 25 to ISO 1000 in TTL metering mode. Additional flash PC port on the camera body. Older non-

Nikon units could possibly damage the camera's electronics through overload (more than 12V) or by shorting the system contacts. ***Flash sync:*** Normal: from 1/60 to 1/250 second in aperture preferred and program modes. In manual and shutter preferred modes, the selected time is used (times faster than 1/250 second will automatically be changed to 1/250 second). Slow: longer exposure times up to 30 seconds will be automatically set in aperture preferred and program modes. Rear: after selecting flash operation on the camera, flash output will be synchronized with the rear shutter curtain with any flash unit (set on the flash unit with the SB-24 and SB-25 flashes). FP high speed sync: sync speeds from 1/250 to 1/4000 second possible with the SB-25.

Conventional TTL flash: only possible with the N90 and all Nikkors when using the SB-24 and SB-25. The units have to be switched over with the "M" switch for this purpose.

Conventional TTL fill-flash: in this flash mode, ambient light is automatically considered with combinations of all modern Nikon System flashes and non-AF Nikkors. The fill-flash mode sets the appropriate flash sync speed and/or aperture based on an ambient light metering and performs an automatic flash intensity correction. TTL flash duration control occurs during the exposure based on a lightly center-weighted metering.

TTL Fill-flash with multi-sensor: in this flash mode, ambient light is automatically considered with combinations of all modern Nikon System flashes and AF Nikkors. The fill-flash mode sets the appropriate flash sync speed and/or aperture and performs an automatic flash intensity correction. TTL flash duration control occurs during the exposure based on a five-field multi-sensor metering.

Multi-Sensor fill-flash with test flash: only when using AF Nikkors and the SB-25 does the flash send out a series of invisible test flashes that are evaluated by the multi-sensor after the trigger has been depressed. The flash automation hence obtains information regarding the reflective properties and spatial distribution of the subject and background.

3D Multi-sensor fill-flash with test flash: only when using Type D AF Nikkors and the SB-25 are the focus distance and the position of the main subject also taken into consideration.

Manual flash exposure corrections: can be set on the flash units from +1 EV to -3 EV with SB-24. With MF-26 multi-function back with all other modern Nikon System flashes (see below "Special accessories for the N90).

Flash exposure bracketing: with multi-function back MF-26 with all modern Nikon System flashes (see below, "Special Accessories for the N90).

Flash control indicator: red LED illuminates in the viewfinder when the Nikon System flash is ready to fire; flashes or goes out if the flash was too weak for appropriate exposure, or if there was a loose contact between the flash and the shoe. Only with SB-25: Under exposure warning accurate to 1/3 stop.

Autofocus test flash: possible when using appropriate flash units such as SB-22, SB-23, SB-24 and SB-25.

Power supply: four 1.5V alkaline batteries (AA) suffice for about 75 films (36 exposure) at 20 ° C or four rechargeable batteries of the same size for about 55 films (36 exposure) at 20 ° C.

Battery check: when the batteries are fresh, aperture and shutter speed are shown for about 8 seconds after touching the trigger; noticeably shorter display times indicate low battery power. Additional battery power indicator via Battery Symbol.

Data Link Connection: 10-pin port for both remote control (MC-20) or Data Cable (MC-27) for connection to the Electronic Organizer.

Data Link System: See "Special Accessories for the N90," next page.

Size: width 6.1in. (154mm), height 4.2in. (106mm); depth 2.7in. (69mm), 2.8in. (71mm) with the Data Back.

Weight: 27.3oz. (775g) without batteries.

Note: the F90D and F90S models (available in some markets) are nothing other than the N90/F90 with the MF-25 Databack and the MF-26 Multi-function Back respectively. More detailed information regarding the functions of these backs can be found the following section.

Special Accessories for the N90

Eyepiece adapter DK-7: for mounting angle-finder DR-3 or loupe DG-2.

Eyecup: DK-6

Focusing screens: type E screen with 12mm central circle, 2 AF fields and fresnel ground with additional grid lines of horizontal and vertical lines. For reproduction, architecture, extreme wide-angle.

External battery pack DB-6: with six cells, it has the capacity for 10 times as many exposures. Also ideal for stationary constant use such as scientific documentation, etc.

Remote triggering cord MC-20: for electrical remote triggering, long time exposures ("T" connector). See also "Mechanical and electrical cable releases, remote triggering" in the "Other Accessories" section of the main chapter.

Remote triggering adapter MC-25: alternatively, use MC-12A plus the adapter cable MC-25 (this combination is also required for automatic AF sharpness instances in conjunction with the MF-26). See also "Mechanical and electrical cable releases, remote triggering" in the "Other Accessories" section of the main chapter.

Sync Triggering cord MC-23: two N90's can be simultaneously fired with the MC-23 cable. See also "Mechanical and electrical cable releases, remote triggering" in the "Other Accessories" section of the main chapter.

Data back MF-25: the following can be added to the frame: Year, month, day; day, hour, minute; day, month year. World time function, alarm.

Multi-Function Back MF-26: the following is only a brief listing of the most important facts. Information regarding practical use can be found in the special section, "Data and Multi-Function Backs." Data superimposition: Year, month, day or day, hour, minute (based on a 24 hour world clock); 2 digit frame number; index number continuously increasing from 1-999999 or constant; shutter speed and aperture. Auto series exposure: up to 19 frames with one shutter release. Interval timer: Time intervals can be selected from 1 second to 99 hours, 59 minutes, 59 seconds, can be combined with auto series. Long time exposure: from 1 second to 99 hours, 59 minutes, 59 seconds. Multiple Exposure: 2 to 19 exposures on one frame. Automatic bracketing: 3 to 19 exposures with exposure differences from 1/3 to 2 EV. Flash exposure correction: Can be selected from +1 to -3 in steps of 0.3 EV. Flash exposure bracketing: 3 to 19 exposures with exposure differences from 1/3 to 2 EV that effect flash output like manual single corrections. AE/AF storage: simultaneous storage of exposure and distance settings. AF Sharpness Priority: AF sharpness priority in conjunction with manual sharpness pre-selection and AF mode "C". Autofocus pre-sets: the trigger is depressed on an N90 that is focused on a specific location. If something moves into this spot, the camera automatically fires. Reset to individual camera defaults: the standard selection for metering method, exposure mode, flash mode, AF field size and film transport can be freely programmed.

DB-6

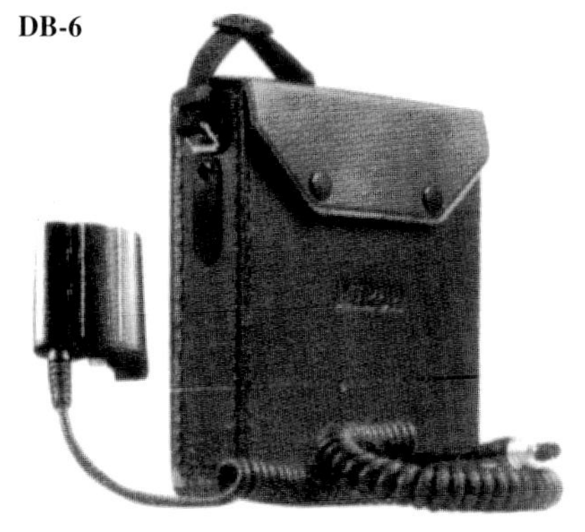

Data Link Systems components: the Data Link System enables the N90 to be connected to Sharp's Electronic Organizer models 8000, 8100M, 82000, 8300M, 84000 and 8500M pocket computers. Nikon supplies an N90

cable MC-27 that connects to the Electronic Organizer as well as an IC chip AC-IE. card that can be inserted into the Organizer.

Data Link Off-line mode: the Electronic Organizer offers the following photographic possibilities without being connected to the N90/F90. Instruction manual for the N90, photographic handbook with glossary and formula sheets, utility program to manage stored data.

Data Link On-Line mode: when connected to the N90/F90 with the chip card, the Electronic Organizer offers the following photographic possibilities, (among others). Remote control

Databack MF-25

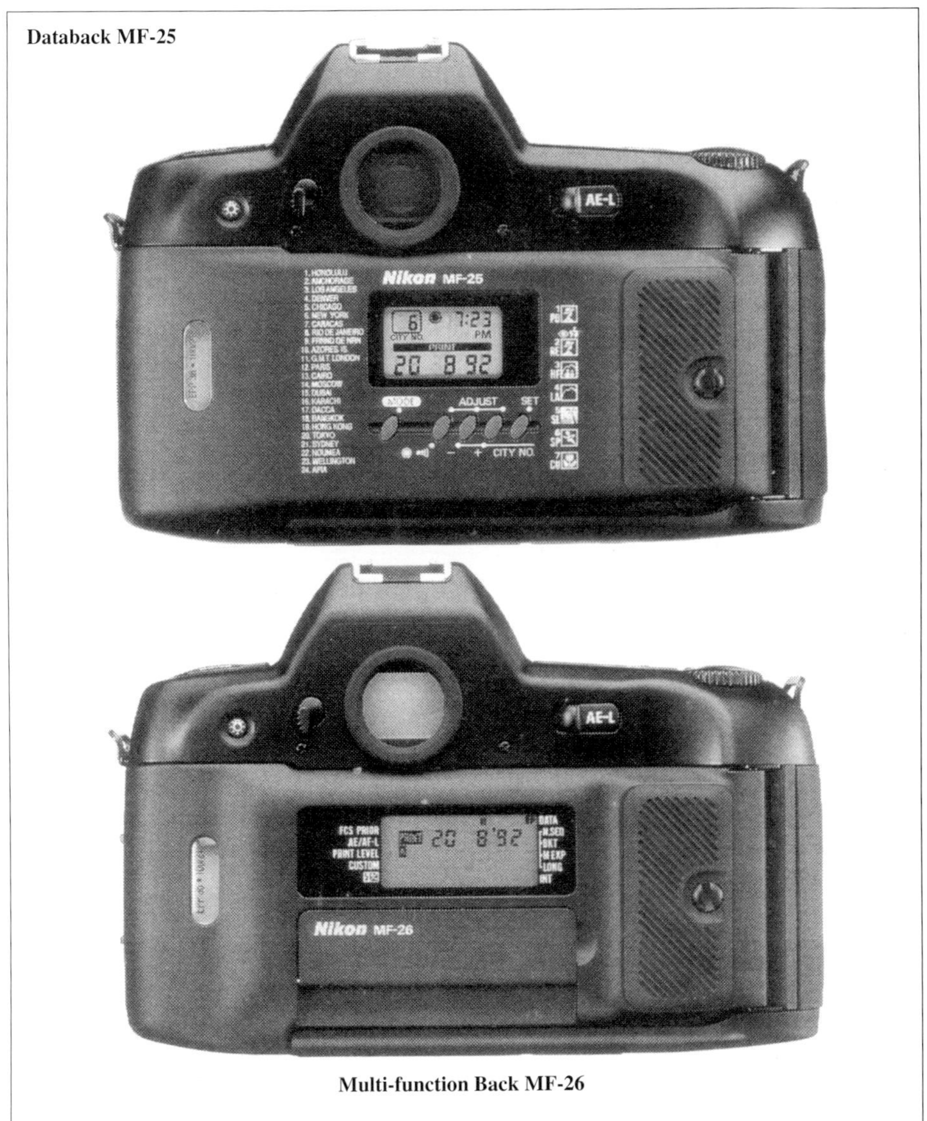

Multi-function Back MF-26

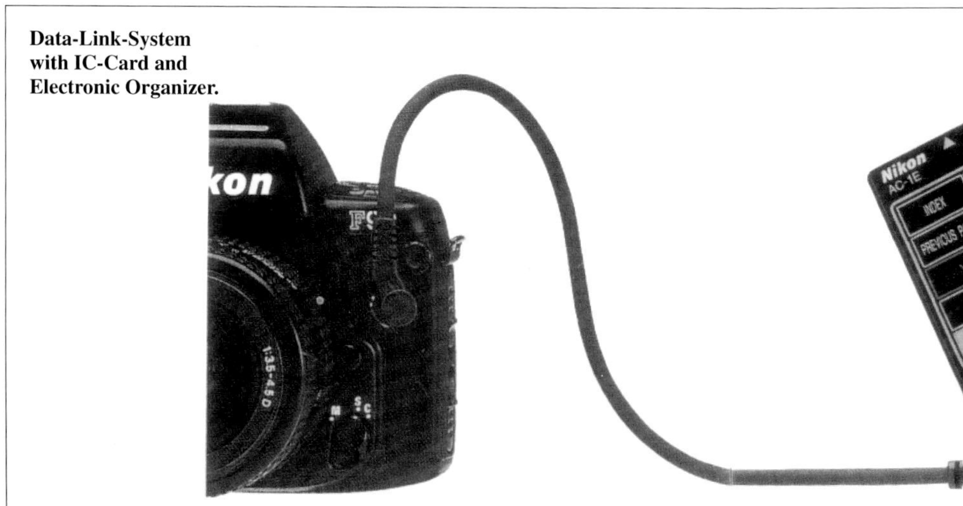

Data-Link-System with IC-Card and Electronic Organizer.

and remote display of camera functions, individual programming of basic camera functions (during reset), programming an individual program curve, extending the N90's functions to include those only available through the MF-26, reprogramming some of the MF-26's functions, automatic storage of all image data.
Flash Units: the full range of the N90/F90's flash options can only be taken advantage of with the SB-25. Otherwise, practically all modern Nikon System flashes can be used (see the special flash unit chapter).

SHARP IQ-8300M MULTILINGUAL
Electronic Organizer 128KB
INDEX
HELP
PREVIOUS PAGE
NEXT PAGE
Y
N
ESC
EDIT
COMMUNICATE
ENTER EXECUTE
CARD

Nikon
SPEEDLIGHT SB-25
Nikon
F90
28-70mm
1:3.5-4.5 D
AF NIKKOR

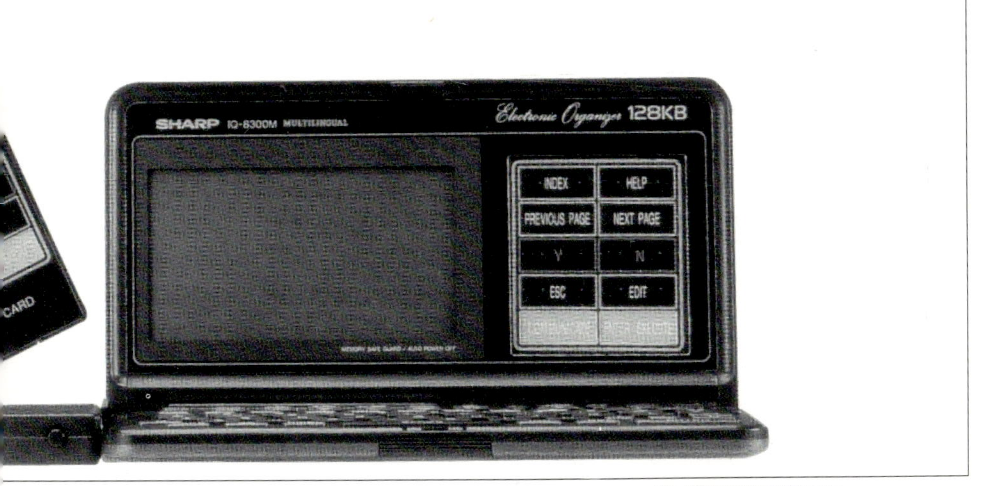

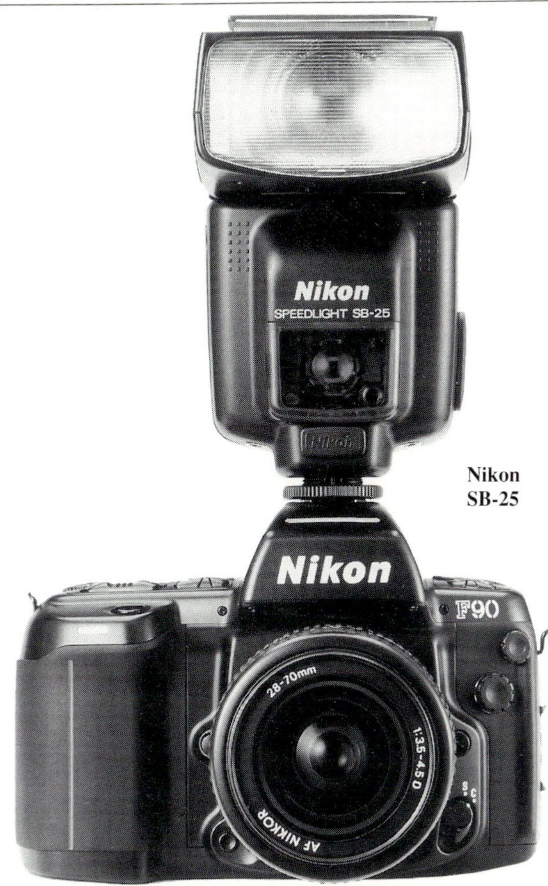

Nikon SB-25

Overview of Nikon SLRs

The following table contains, in abbreviated form, the most important technical features of Nikon SLR Cameras. For more details the reader is referred to the appropriate preceding sections. The comparison table is useful in that it allows a direct comparison between different Nikon cameras and it simplifies a comparison with equivalent cameras by other manufacturers. However, it should be remembered that the practical value of a camera is not determined simply by the number and sophistication of the functions listed in its specifications since this does not take into consideration such key points as the quality of construction and practical operating logic of the camera.

Comments and Suggestions
The following comments and assessments are intended to be of assistance to anyone planning to buy a new camera outfit or update their old equipment. It is possible that some owners of a certain Nikon model may not agree with the comments contained herein. But bear in mind that an objective assessment must always be based on the characteristics of a camera as currently available, and that standards and criteria inevitably change along with technical advances for a range of cameras. So someone who, in 1986, chose the best model available at the time in terms of their individual requirements would usually come to a different decision in 1992, if they applied objective criteria to their choice in both cases.

Nikon F3: If it were not for the fact that the range of modern non-AF lenses is decreasing, it would be tempting to call the Nikon F3 "timeless." While AF lenses certainly work with this body, many are often a poor substitute in terms of smoothness and handling when used in manual focus. The F3 is also dependent on its electronics thus, nothing will function without batteries apart from a single emergency shutter speed. In this respect it is, therefore, not a true alternative to the all-electronic modern AF models. Nonetheless, compared with all-electronic cameras, the F3 is far less prone to breakdowns and it is considered by many photographers the most durable camera currently on the market.

In the professional field, the F3 can be recommended to anyone who cannot, or does not want to accustom themselves to modern autofocus photography. It can also serve as a second or third camera body to an AF camera, providing any professional photographer with a reliable emergency reserve for normal working conditions, or the camera of choice in particularly difficult climatic conditions, or any circumstances where only the most durable of cameras will do. For a serious non-professional photographer, the expense of an F3 has to be weighted against their individual needs. The primary reason for buying this camera is to take advantage of its ability to work under adverse conditions, to be able to shoot hundreds and hundreds of rolls of film without fear of failure and to use the interchangeable prism feature for special needs such as a magnifying hood or mirror lock up for close-up work. If the work load and special needs warrant any of these considerations, then the F3 is the camera of choice, otherwise, real thought should be given to the FM-2n.

Nikon FM-2n: As with the F3, the restricted availability of non-AF lenses in the future is likely to prove a problem with this all-manual camera. As has been pointed out for the F3, AF lenses can be used, though not as efficiently as with conventional lenses. On the other hand, many special lenses are not, in any case, suitable for AF, and virtually the entire range of conventional Nikkor lenses will continue to be available on the second-hand market for many years to come. In addition, the FM-2n is one of the last fully-mechanical cameras without automatic exposure functions left on the world market. That is, the entire range of shutter speeds is always available, even without batteries, since the battery controls only the meter's function. Relatively compact in construction, it offers everything you really need in order to take photographs.

	F3 FE HP, F3 T	FM-2n	N2000/ F-301	N4004/s N5005 F-401/s/x	N6006/ F-601	N6000/ F-601m	N8008/s/ F-801/s	F4 F4S, F4E	N90/ F90
Lens Mount *	AI, (AI--S, AF)	AI, (AI--S, AF)	AI, (AI--S, AF)	AF, ((AI, AI--S))	AF, (AI-S, AI)	AF, (AI-S, AI)	AF, (AI-S, AI)	AF, (AI-S, AI)	AF, (AI-S, AI)
Shutter									
Action	Horizontal	Vertical	Vertical	Vertical	Vertical	Vertical	Vertical	Vertical	Vertical
Type	Roll	Blade	Blade	Blade	Blade	Blade	Blade	Blade	Blade
Material	Titanium	Titanium	AL & Plastic	AL & Plastic	Aluminum	Aluminum	Aluminum	AL & Plastic	AL & Plastic
Control	Electronic	Mechanical	Electronic	Electronic	Electronic	Electronic	Electronic	Electronic	Electronic
Shutter Speeds **									
Automatic	1/2000s - 8s;	-	1/2000s - 30s	1/2000s -1s/1s/30s	1/2000s - 30s	1/2000s - 30s	1/8000s - 30s	1/8000s - 30s	1/8000s - 30s
Manual	1/2000s - 8s, B. T. X	1/4000s - 1s; B	1/2000s - 1s; B	1/2000s - 1s; B // T	1/2000s - 30s; B	1/2000s - 30s; B	1/8000s - 30s; B	1/8000s - 4s; B: T: X	1/8000s - 4s; B: (T): X
Mechanical	1/60s	1/4000s - 1s	-	-	-	-	-	-	-
Shutter Release									
Self-timer	Electronic	Mechanical	Electronic	Electronic	Electronic	Electronic	Electronic	Electronic	Electronic
Cable Release	+	AR-3	-	AR-3	AR-3	AR-3	-	AR-3	-
Electronic Remote with	MD-4 + MC-12A	MD-12 + MC-12A	Cable MC-12A	-	-	-	Cable MC-12A	Cable MC-12A	Cable MC-20
Exposure Modes									
Manual	+	+	+	+	+	+	+	+	+
Automatic ***	A	-	A - P - PH	A - S - P	A - S - P - PM	A - S - P - PM	A - S - P - PH - PD	A - S - P - PH	A - S - PM - PV
Program	-	-	-	-	-	-	-	-	via Data-Link
Auto Bracketing	-	-	-	-	+	+	with MF-21	with MF-23, MF-24	with MF-26
Exposure Compensation EV	+/-2	-	+/-2	-	+/-5	+/-5	+/-5	+/-2	+/-5
Exposure Metering									
Metering Range EV)	1 -18	1 -18	1 - 19	1 - 19	0 - 19 (4 - 19 Spot)	0 - 19	0 - 21 (4 - 21 Spot)	0 - 21 (2 - 21 Spot)	-1 - 21 (3 - 21 Spot)
Matrix Metering	-	-	-	3 // 5 Field	5 Field	5 Field	5 Field	5 Field	8 Field
Center-weighted Integral	80:20	60:40	60:40	75 : 25	75:25	75:25	75:25	60:40	75:25
Spot Metering	-	-	-	-	+	-	- / +	+	+
AE-Lock	+	-	+	+	+	+	+	+	+
Film Speed									
Manual (ISO)	12 - 6400	12 - 6400	12 - 3200	100	6 - 6400	6 - 6400	6 - 6400	6 - 6400	6 - 6400
DX-Automatic (ISO)	-	-	25 - 4000	25 - 5000	25 - 5000	25 - 5000	25 - 5000	25 - 5000	25 - 5000
Viewfinder		-							
Interchangeable Viewfinders	4	-	-	-	-	-	-	3	-
Viewfinder Information ****	B - Z - M - V	M - Z - V	M - Z - V	M - V - S	B - Z - V - M - S	B - Z - V - M	B - Z - M - V - S	B - Z - M - V - A - S - N	B - Z - M - V - A - S - N
Type of Readout	LCD	LED	LED	LED	LCD	LCD	LCD	LED + LCD	LCD
Interchangealbe Screens	21	3	-	-	-	-	2	21	1
Frame Coverage	100%	93%	92%	93%	92%	92%	92%	100%	92%
Illumination	+	-	-	-	+	+	+	+	+
Eyecup	F3 - DK4; F3HP - DK2	DK-3	#2939	#2939	#2939	#2939	DK-6	DK-2	DK-6

	F3 FE HP, F3 T	FM-2n	N2000/ F-301	N4004/s N5005 F-401/s/x	N6006/ F-601	N6000/ F-601 M	N8008/s/ F-801/s	F4 F4S, F4E	N90/ F90
Flash									
TTL Flash	+	-	+	+	+	+	+	+	+
Auto Fill Flash	-	-	-	+	+	+	+	+	+
Multisensor Fill Flash	-	-	-	-	-	-	-	-	+
3D-Fill Flash	-	-	-	-	-	-	-	-	+
Built-in Flash	-	-	-	+	+	-	-	-	-
Sync Speeds	1/80s	1/250s- 1s	1/125s - 1s	1/125s - 30s	1/125s-30s	1/125s - 30s	1/250s - 30s	1/250s - 30s	1/250s - 30s
REAR Synchronization	-	-	-	-	+	+	with SB-24, SB-25	with SB-24, SB-25	with SB-24, SB-25
FP - Slow Synchronization	-	-	-	-	-	-	-	-	up to 1/4000s
ISO PC Connection	+	+	(AS-15)	(AS-15)	(AS-15)	(AS-15)	(AS-15)	+	+
Flash Shoe Type	F3-Type	ISO Hot Shoe	ISO Hot Shoe	ISO Hot Shoe	ISO Hot Shoe	ISO Hot Shoe	ISO Hot Shoe	ISO Hot Shoe	ISO Hot Shoe
Flash Ready Indicator	+	+	+	+	+	+	+	+	+
Film ISO Range for TTL	25 - 400	-	25 - 1000	25 - 400	25 - 1000	25 - 1000	25 - 1000	25 - 1000	25 - 1000
Film Advance									
Manual	+	+	-	-	-	-	-	-	-
Motorized	with MD-4	with MD-12	built-in	built-in	built-in	built-in	built-in	built-in	built-in
Maximum FPS	5.5	3.5	2.5	2.5	2	2	3.3	4 / 5.5 / 6	3.6
Multiple Exposure	+	+	-	-	-	-	+	+	with MF-26
Rewind	Manual	Manual	Manual	motorized	motorized	motorized	motorized	manual or motorized	motorized
Autofocus									
AF Operating range	-	-	-	-1 - 17 / -1 - 19	-1 - 19	-	-1 - 19	-1 - 18	-1 - 19
Focus Priority	-	-	-	+	+	-	+	+	+
Release Priority	-	-	-	-	+	-	+	+	+
Tracking -AF	-	-	-	- / - / +	+	-	- / +	+	+
AF Self-timer	-	-	-	-	-	-	with MF-21	with MF-23, MF-24	with MF-26
Accepts Teleconverter TC-16A	-	-	-	-	+	-	+	+	+
Data Link	-	-	-	-	-	-	-	-	+ (*****)
Other Features									
Central LCD Display	-	-	-	-	+	+	+	-	+ (lighted)
Mirror Lock-up	+	-	-	-	-	-	-	+	-
D-O-F Preview	+	+	-	-	-	-	+	+	+
Changeable Back	+	+	+	-	-	-	+	+	+
Type of Polarizer	linear	linear	linear	circular	circular	circular	circular	circular	circular
Weight oz. (w/o batt.)	24.5, 26.1	19.3	20	22.9	22.8	19.8	20.9	38.2/44.8/48	27.1
Dimensions (in.)	3.8x4x2.7	3.5x5.6x2.4	3.8x5.8x2	4x6. x2.6	3.9x6.1x2.6	3.7x6.1x2.6	4x6x2.6	(4.6,5.4,6)x6.6x3	4.2x6.1x2.7

/ When more than one variation of a camera model is listed data following the first slash refers to the 2nd variant, after the 2nd slash, the 3rd variant, etc.

* Lenses in brackets can only be used with some restrictions; in double brackets with extreme restrictions.

** Shutter speed ranges in automatic modes depend on the selected mode and the ISO film speed. Thus, stated values are maximum values.

*** A=Aperture priority mode, S=Shutter priority mode, P=Program mode, PM,PD multi-program mode with auto adaptation to focal length, PH=High speed program mode.

**** B=aperture, Z=shutter speed, M=exposure meter display, V=flash ready indicator, A=exposure mode, δ=AF focus indicator.

***** Via Data-Link system. Enables almost all MF-26 functions in addition to remote control, remote display, exposure-data storage, optional program modifications, etc.

In this sense, it will certainly continue to represent the non-AF alternative market for quite a while. The FM-2n is without a doubt the number one choice for non-professional photographers who do not want to get involved with "automatic photography". It is an ideal camera with which to learn the craft of photography since it allows the user to become familiar with the basic principles of photography without any "automatic short-cuts". In the professional field, its rugged construction and all-mechanical configuration make it the ideal reserve camera behind an F3 or, for that matter, an F4. It has only one serious drawback as a substitute for the F3, and that is its lack of a mirror lock up to prevent "mirror slap" vibration in long telephoto and close-up work.

Nikon N2000/F-301: In terms of sheer numbers sold, this motorized camera is one of Nikon's most successful models. Apart from its good practical features, as in ease of operation, the reason for its success is probably that it offered what was, at that time, a good range of automatic exposure modes combined with the option of complete manual control. With respect to lenses, what was said about the F3 and FM-2n also applies here. Although production was discontinued in 1991, there is such general high regard for this camera that it has been included here. For non-professionals who are not interested in autofocus, it is the ideal camera for testing the extent of one's photographic ambitions without investing too much money. This economical camera is another good camera to learn on, especially where photography is a secondary area of study, such as graphic design and advertising. In the professional field it was, for a brief period, in use as a second or third camera, but in this regard the choices already cited are better.

Nikon N4004/F-401 & N5005/F-401x: With their technical features and operation designed for fully-automatic use, these cameras are ideal for the beginner. Their fully-automatic configuration limits use to the AF Nikkor range, but without any restrictions. Whereas the FM-2n or N2000/F-301 principally appeal to the user who is not afraid of making decisions, or who wishes to learn the basic principles of photography, with the N4004/F-401 or the N5005/F-401x you can get by with just pressing the shutter release button. They will produce better pictures in fully-automatic mode than an inexperienced photographer would in manual mode. What distinguishes them from similar models by other manufacturers is the deliberate omission of any "computer games" in the display, limiting functions to self-evident representations. These cameras, however, cannot be recommended to the serious photographer. Anyone with an FM-2n, N2000/F-301, F3 or other non-AF Nikon who is considering changing over to AF photography would be better off opting for the N8008/F-801.

Nikon N6006/F-601 AF: This camera allows limited use of conventional Nikkor lenses and unrestricted use of the complete AF Nikkor lens range. The N6006/F-601 AF is distinguished from the N5005/F-401x principally by the high-eyepoint viewfinder and the much wider range of exposure metering and automatic exposure options. In terms of the wealth of features offered, such as built-in flash and the wide range of exposure and flash functions, the N6006/F-601 AF is in some respects actually ahead of the N8008/F-801 and F4. This will appeal to many photographers who routinely use a fraction of these possibilities, but who like to have the option of using them if they wish. The drawback of such a multi-function camera shows up in the operating logic where, for many users, there are too many buttons serving double functions which increases the chances of confusion. The lack of a preview button is also a serious drawback in many general picture taking situations. The N6006/F-601 AF is the ideal camera for the non-professional photographer who only occasionally takes pictures, but who does so "intensively" on these occasions. The built-in pop-up flash is certainly a real plus, but for the serious non-professional photographer, the N8008s/F-801s is a better over-all choice.

Nikon N6000/F-601m: According to the marketing experts at Nikon, this was supposed to be the non-AF successor to the N2000/F-301 by virtue of its more highly-developed automatic exposure functions. The actual concept behind this camera was probably that, as the conventional Nikkors are gradually taken out of production, a manual focus camera must be offered which makes use of at least the automatic exposure functions of the AF Nikkors. That sounds reasonable, but it does not take into consideration the corollary that anyone put off by the idea of AF photography will probably also be deterred by the N6000/F-601m with all its buttons and functions. Furthermore, despite all of the electronics in this camera, it lacks some vital functions expected by the serious non-professional, such as a preview button. Conclusion: this camera is ideal for the amateur photographer who is not interested in autofocus photography, but who otherwise likes "technology."

Nikon N8008s/F-801s: Like the N6006/F-601 AF and the F4, the N8008/F-801 allows use of conventional Nikkor lenses in some of its automatic meter modes and unrestricted use of the complete AF Nikkor range. In comparison with the N6006/F-601 AF, the N8008/F-801, along with its 's' upgrade, offers significantly more professional features: namely the power supply is based on the omni-present AA batteries which are now available in the even longer lasting Lithium form, the fast top shutter speed of 1/8000 seconds, flash synchronization to 1/250 seconds, film transport at 3.3 frames per second, electrical remote shutter release, multiple exposures, interchangeable focusing screens, preview button for depth of field control, and a very versatile programmable databack (including auto bracketing). The straight forward design of the operating controls is a particularly useful feature. When using AF lenses, all important functions can be operated without having to take the eye from the viewfinder (with the exception of the film counter), and even the more specialized functions, which require some attention at first such as multiple exposure, can soon be operated "blind". Many Nikon photographers regard the N8008/F-801 as one of the easiest to operate, fully-electronic camera on the market. The only drawbacks are the lack of a mirror lock up, no option to boost the motor drive to a true motor drive level of 5 frames per second or more, and the reality that electronic cameras are, by nature, not as resistant to abuse as fully-mechanical models. For example, extreme humidity, salt water spray etc. can sometimes cause problems with electronic cameras, making it useful in critical circumstances to carry a fully-mechanical camera in reserve.

These reservations aside, the N8008/F-801 has an extremely broad scope of use. It can be recommended to any serious photographer as their primary camera, or to a professional as an ideal second camera behind the F4. It is also excellent for documentation purposes in the fields of research, development, and science and technology, where the F4 is simply too expensive or too big. The N8008/F-801 is also ideal for photography students who want to get straight into AF photography, but who can still operate the camera in a manual mode and learn the effects of depth of field control and shutter speed selection. For professional photography it is used as a second or third body by many press and sports photographers who have already changed over to autofocus, and as a first choice camera when size and weight are critical as in any backpacking situation. Many professionals who still swear by the F3 seem to prefer the N8008/F-801 for a tentative involvement with AF photography.

Nikon F4: all AF Nikkor lenses can be used with the F4 without any restriction, whereas there are a number of limitations on the use of non-AF Nikkors, though these are less than with all other Nikon AF cameras. In operation, the F4 leans towards classical mechanics with its "pseudo mechanical" controls. Presumably Nikon wanted to make the transition to AF photography more palatable to professionals accustomed to working with the F2 and F3. In view of the F4's wide range of electronic functions, this may have been more wishful thinking on their part than reality. But in fairness to Nikon, no other manufacturer has even attempted to deal with this question of mechanical to electronic transition in a top-of-the-line, professional AF camera.

In addition to the interchangeable viewfinder system and mirror lock up, both of which can be useful in many typical professional circumstances, such as the use of extreme telephotos and close-up equipment, the F4 is also the camera of choice when there is a need for high speed exposures. This is primarily because it has the fastest motor drive of the Nikon line. Whatever the need, from sports to nature or in action situations in photojournalism, the generous power supply, fast built-in motor drive, and if necessary, an accessory bulk film magazine, put the F4 in a class by itself at the top of the Nikon line.

Again, however, as with any fully-electronic camera, one cannot necessarily expect the F4 to be as reliable in operation as a good fully-mechanical camera. On the other hand, the F4, with its strong construction, is probably the most robust camera currently available for all areas of professional AF photography. It has certainly outlived the bad reports concerning breakdowns with very early units and is now considered a real "electronic workhorse."

Even though this camera is directed specifically at the working professional, it does not preclude its purchase by a serious non-professional. The real question is why should they do so? As always, the answer must depend on the individual photographer's needs and, to be perfectly honest, how strongly the photographer feels about having Nikon's top-of-the-line camera in their camera bag. As far as photography students in training, the full range of manual to all-automatic features of the F4 certainly will permit one to learn all the basics, but that can just as well be done with the less expensive FM-2 and 8008/F-801. If money is not a major consideration, then there is much to be said for someone who is aspiring to be a working professional to start off from the beginning with the most commonly used tool of their profession. So, for the professional, the F4 is the camera of choice and in some areas such as where high speed photography with AF capability is required, it is the only real choice.

Nikon N90/F90

The N90/F90 not only offers complete compatibility with AF Nikkor lenses but also, like the F4 and N8008, with conventional non-AF Nikkors in aperture priority and manual modes. Like the F4, the N90/F90 utilizes all of the features of AF-I Nikkor lenses and it is the only camera so far that can make full use of D-type Nikkors. Although it has more functions than the N8008, the N90 is easier to handle since all important functions can be controlled without having to put the camera down. This is due to ingenious design work on Nikon's part: the more refined camera functions have been transferred to the Multi-function Back thus, eliminating cumbersome function and double-function keys. When combined with the MF-26 Multi-function Back, the N90/F90 offers the widest range of sophisticated features available. I find the ability to store and retrieve a wide range of auto functions such as exposure bracketing, flash corrections and data super-imposition extremely useful. Also outstanding are the many flash functions which when combined with the SB-25, leave virtually no photographic situation uncovered.

The N90/F90 is a perfect choice for the advanced amateur, semi-pro and professional photographer. It is also an ideal complement to the F4 since it makes full use to the new D-type lenses. With the Data Link for remote display, control and storage of image data the N90/F90 is an ideal choice for commercial uses such as in catalog and documentation photography. As computers become more integrated as tools of the photographic trade, the N90/F90 with Data Link will become even more useful in photographic training and record keeping.

Nikkor Lenses

This chapter provides a review of the important characteristics of the currently available Nikkor lenses and their applications, beginning first with fixed focal length designs and then zoom lenses. Special lenses are covered in the same way in the next section. In the case of non-AF lenses, only lenses for which there is as yet no modern AF version will be discussed. Anyone interested in more detail on Nikon lenses should refer to the *Magic Lantern Guide to Nikon Lenses* by B. "Moose" Peterson.

Fixed Focal Length Lenses

Ultra Wide-Angle

Nikkor 13mm f/5.6: *Applications:* essential in situations where as much of the scene as possible has to be included in the picture, i.e. where the maximum possible angle of view is required, as commonly happens in landscape or architectural photography. Also, for interior shots where the greatest possible effect of spatial depth is to be achieved, or in confined spaces where the photographer's back is literally up against the wall as, for example, for photographing large instrument panels in limited settings.

This extreme wide-angle lens, with an angle of view of 118° and rectilinear design, is practically without competition on the market. But with its very high price it is only manufactured to order. It is also a bulky lens with a diameter of 4.5in. (115mm). a length of 4in. (101mm) and a weight of 42.3oz.(1200g). This lens requires 16 elements for optical correction and the use of floating elements for close-up correction ("CRC") down to 11.9in. (0.3m). It is supplied with 4 filters, which fit behind the rear element.

Nikkor 15mm f/3.5: *Applications:* similar to the 13mm lens, with a slightly reduced wide-angle effect, but same rectilinear design.

With a weight half that of the 13mm lens, slightly smaller dimensions, faster speed and about a quarter of the price, this lens still provides an impressive angle of view of 110°. 14 elements are used to provide maximum optical quality, including CRC close-up correction down to 11.9in. (0.3m). Slight vignetting can occur in the corners of the frame. This lens is

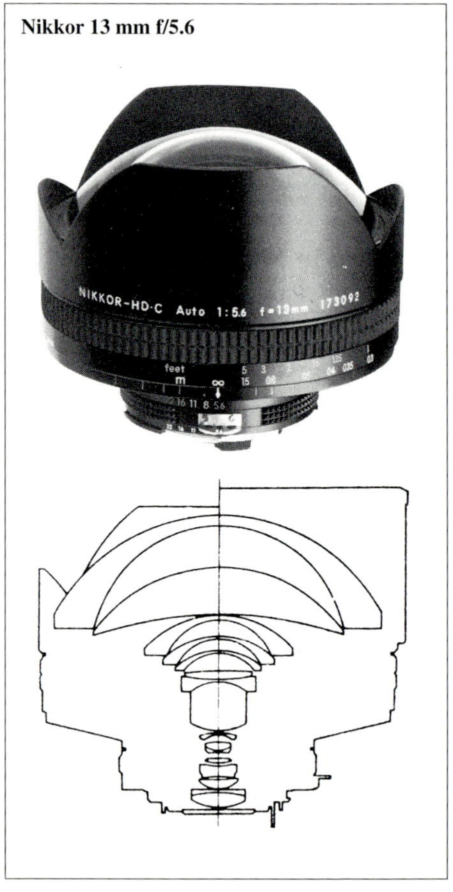

Nikkor 13 mm f/5.6

Nikkor 15mm f/3.5

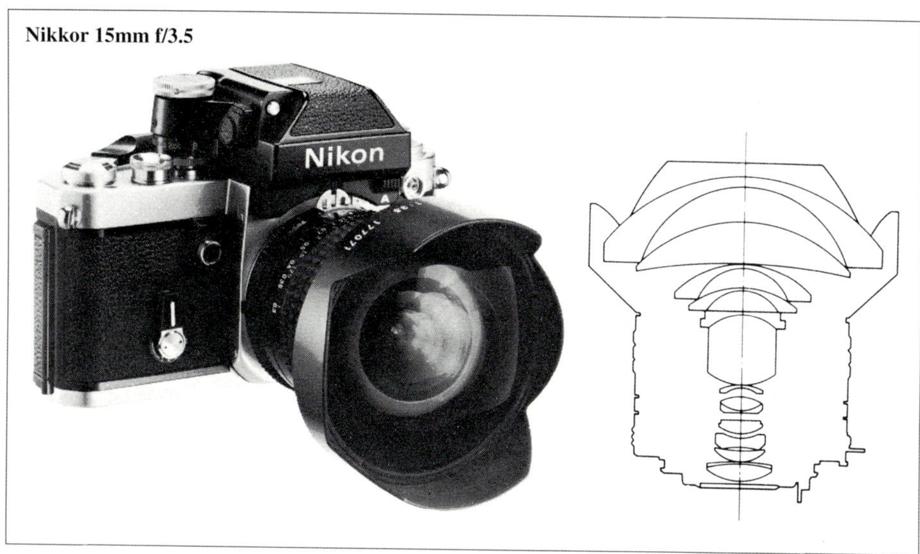

also supplied with 4 filters which bayonet behind the rear element.

Nikkor 18mm f/3.5: ***Applications:*** This lens has a more moderate ultra wide angle effect than the 13mm and 15mm lenses. Many photojournalists carry this lens as their shortest focal length and it is also used frequently in landscape and travel photography. This lens is half the weight and price of the 15mm lens, with significantly smaller overall dimensions that permits the use of 72mm screw-in filters while delivering an angle of view of 100°. This is a significant point since in rough working conditions it is a definite advantage for photographers to be able to protect their expensive lens with a UV filter. The cost of replacing a front element far outweighs the very slight loss in picture quality that might be caused by the addition of a another glass surface. Besides, the filter can always be removed if necessary. There is also the advantage of being able to use a complete range of filters with this lens, and not being limited to the custom size selection of rear mounted filters as with the other super wide-angle optics covered so far. This

Nikkor 18 mm f/3.5

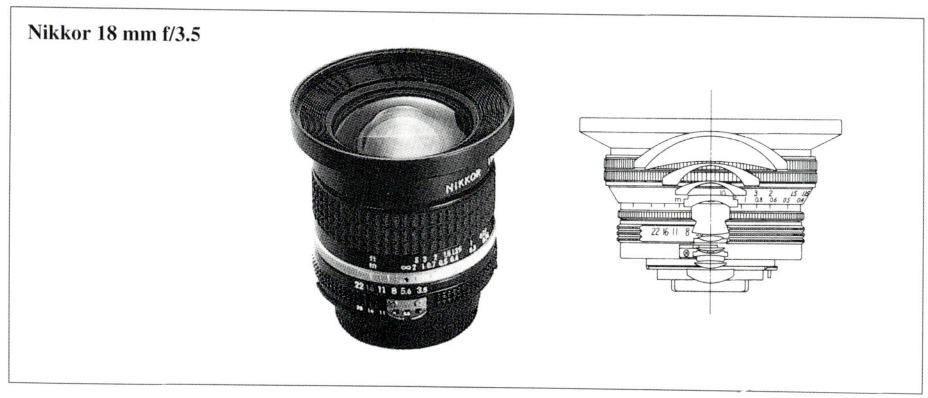

lens has "only" 11 elements and allows CRC close-up correction down to 9.8in. (0.25m). Lens may vignette with filters. It is not recommended to stack filters.

AF Nikkor 20mm f/2.8: *Applications:* For a long time the 20mm focal length was at the end of the wide-angle selection list as widest focal length available at an affordable price, but in recent years, this focal length has become established as a popular lens among photojournalists and travel photographers. It is recommended for those photographers who require the so-called super wide-angle effect. In addition, because this lens can also deliver relatively normal looking wide-angle effects when held level, parallel and at a reasonable distance to the subject, it is far more useful than any of the other extremely wide optics mentioned as yet.

This lens is the shortest focal length currently available in an AF version. It is faster by 1/2 a stop than the 18mm lens, has an angle of view of 94° and CRC close-up correction down to 9.8in. (0.25m). It contains 12 elements and takes 62mm filters. A reasonable price, compact dimensions and a weight of only 9.2oz. (260g) also add to its popularity. Here again, as with the above lenses, slight vignetting may occur in the corners of the frame at full aperture, but this disappears as the lens is stopped down.

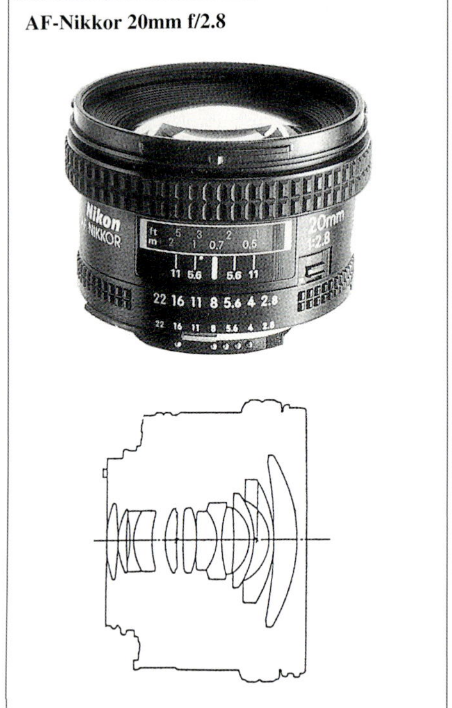

AF-Nikkor 20mm f/2.8

Wide-Angle

AF Nikkor 24mm f/2.8 N: *Applications:* The 24mm it is a very popular focal length in photojournalism, particularly where the photographer is dealing with people indoors and wishes to convey a sense of space without too much of an exaggerated wide-angle effect. The improper use of focal lengths shorter than 24mm typically leads to unnatural distortion of heads and limbs. This effect becomes more pronounced the closer the camera is to the person, and the nearer the subject is to the edge of the frame. When taking pictures of people with wide-angle lenses in this category, one should avoid getting any closer than about 3 feet (1m) and compose the shot so that the subject is more or less in or near the center of the frame. Most photojournalist today own either a 20mm or 24mm and there are many who have both.

This lens is almost identical in size and weight to the 20mm lens. It has an angle of view of 84 degrees with 9 elements and CRC close-up correction down to 11.9in. (0.3m). It is essentially based on a construction design dating from 1967 which has been repeatedly updated and thoroughly proven in practice. It has a 52mm filter thread, like many of Nikon's medium speed lenses in the range 24mm to 200mm.

AF Nikkor 28mm f/2.8 N: *Applications:* a travel and photojournalist lens much like the 24mm lens, except that the wide-angle effect (and consequently the risk of distortion) is diminished. Today the 28mm is regarded as the "standard wide-angle" as opposed to the 35mm which was the mainstay wide-angle focal length several decades ago. In the hands of more conservative photographers, it produces quite conventional-looking pictures that cover a wide field, yet it allows adventurous users to create more unusual images. If candid pictures of people in their natural surroundings were the goal and only one lens could be used, a 28mm or 24mm would be the best choices since they have enough of a wide-angle of view to take in the necessary subject matter, but can also be used to provide undistorted views. The choice between the two is more a matter of personal taste in terms of the slightly different looks they give rather than any major technical difference. With a little practice these lenses are also particularly good for "shooting from the hip" as in situations where it would not be appropriate to hold the camera up to the eye.

The 28mm f/2.8 is a first generation AF lens with an angle of view of 74° with only 5 elements and a minimum focusing distance of 11.9in. (0.3m), without CRC. Based on an E series lens, it is of relatively straightforward optical construction and is therefore particularly inexpensive. An alternative which will deliver approximately the same optical quality would be a 28-85mm zoom. Anyone looking for a 28mm lens of particularly high quality can always opt for a non-AF fixed focal length model, e.g. the Nikkor 28mm f/2.8 with 8 elements and CRC close-up correction down to 7.9in. (0.2m) or the Nikkor 28mm f/2 with 9 elements and CRC close-up correction down to 9.8in. (0.25m).

AF Nikkor 28mm f/1.4 D: An AF lens in the new D generation series with automated transmission of subject distance to the AF camera (to date only the N90/F90). With an angle of view of 74° and a close-focus distance of 13.8in. (0.35m), this lens is almost the same as the 28mm f/2.8. In order to offer f/1.4 speed in

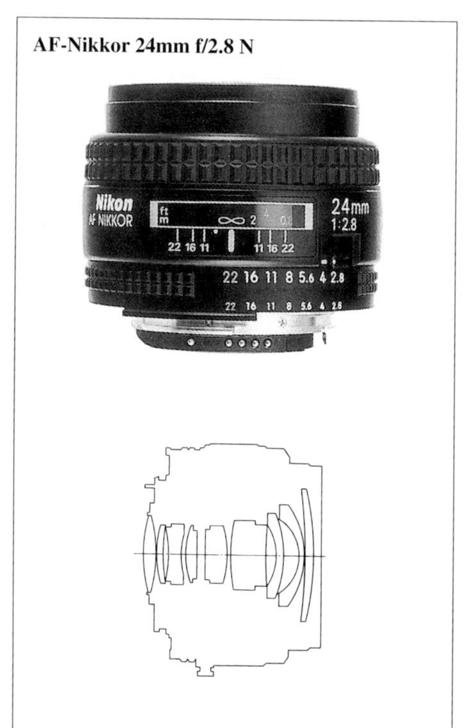

AF-Nikkor 24mm f/2.8 N

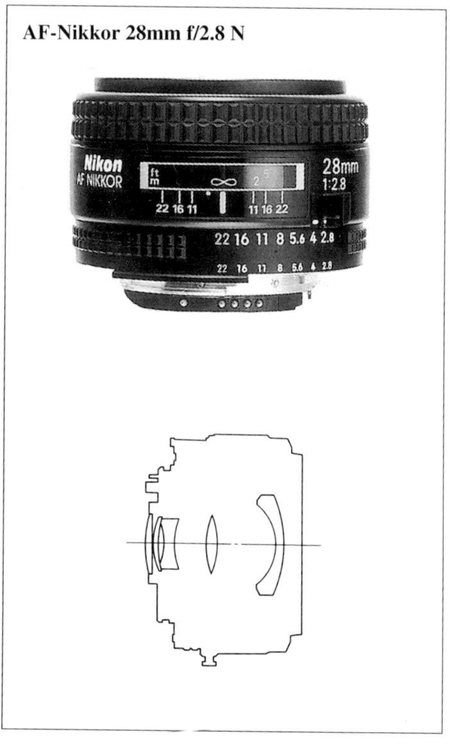

AF-Nikkor 28mm f/2.8 N

this focal length, it has a complex construction consisting of 11 elements. Thanks to outstanding corrections, including an aspherical element, the lens, however, offers excellent sharpness throughout the focusing range.

Applications: Like the previously reviewed 28mm f/2.8, but in addition, the range of available light in which pictures can be taken and the reduced depth of field effect are increased thanks to the larger minimum aperture which makes this lens more applicable to professional needs.

AF Nikkor 35mm f/2: ***Applications:*** similar to those for the 28mm, only the wide-angle effect is even "tamer." This is the classic wide-angle focal length which was, up until the early 50s, the widest view lens available to photographers using Canon, Contax, Leica and Nikon (viewfinder) cameras. In many cases, the 35mm makes a perfectly good substitute for the normal focal length lens, since it is possible to move in fairly close to the subject (certainly much closer then with a 28mm or 24mm) when the maximum distance is limited by circumstances as in the size of a room. Thus, the 35mm is a good choice in a typical three lens outfit for shooting in tight spaces (along with a 20mm and 85mm) because it will still give you a "normal" look when you cannot back up far enough with a 50mm. The 35mm also works particularly well for landscape, architectural photography, and environmental portraits where the point is to bring in a significant amount of the setting while rendering the subject with normal proportions.

This fast and compact lens with an angle of view of 62° is a successful new design with 6 elements and a minimum focusing distance of 9.8in. (0.25m), without CRC.

AF-Nikkor 28mm f/1.4 D

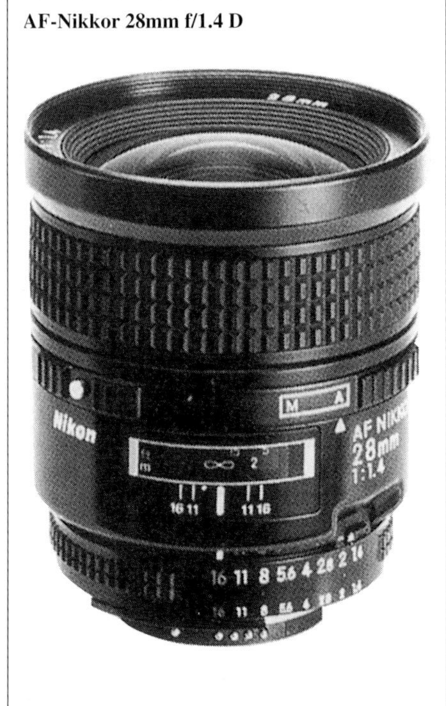

AF-Nikkor 35mm f/2.0

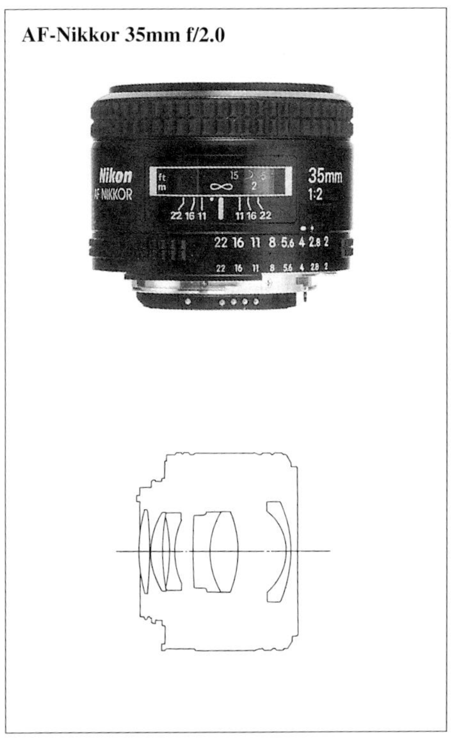

Normal Focal Lengths

AF Nikkor 50mm f/1.8 N: *Applications:* See 50mm f/1.4. A light 5.5oz. (55g) compact, fast, and inexpensive lens with 6 elements, an angle of view of 46° and a minimum focusing distance of17.7in. (0.45m), without CRC.

AF Nikkor 50mm f/1.4 N: *Applications:* the f/1.8 is often supplied with the camera as part of the basic outfit and, because of the high volume of production, it is very inexpensive. An increasing number of camera buyers today, however, opt for a 28-70mm, 28-85mm or 35-70mm zoom as their first lens. When compared to the 50mm f/1.4 , however, these zooms are slower by about 2-3 stops and, because of the increased number of elements, they may not be able to match the excellent image quality that is typical of the normal lens. So, for certain situations, especially when speed with the highest image quality at the widest apertures is paramount, it is well worth considering the additional purchase, for a modest price, of a normal lens. Someone for whom faster speed and even greater influence on depth of field are of prime

Page 84: Wide-angle lens in architectural photography: There was hardly any space in which to move back when shooting this passageway in a megalithic temple. Though a 20mm wide-angle was used, strongly converging lines were prevented by keeping the lens level. Since this temple area was probably used for astronomical sun observations among other things, the sunburst was consciously included in the image.

Page 85: Wide-angle lens in landscape photography: The extremely wide 20mm lens emphasizes the depth of the scene. Normally, the human eye would have had to sweep the coast from left to right to take in the entire scene; the photograph allows the viewer to see it at a glance.

AF-Nikkor 50mm f/1.8 N

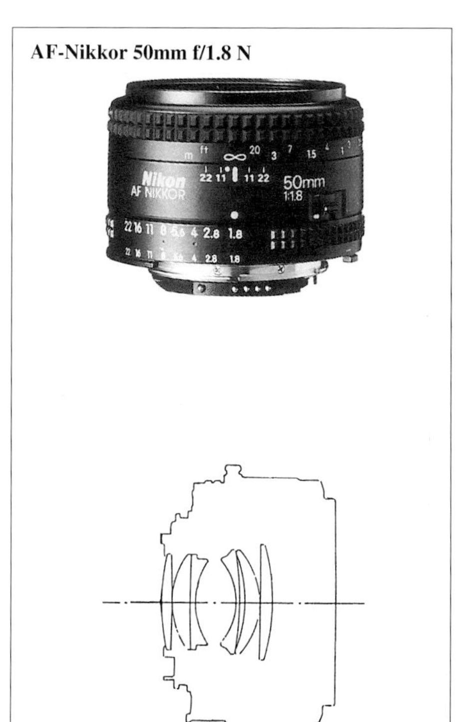

AF-Nikkor 50mm f/1.4 N

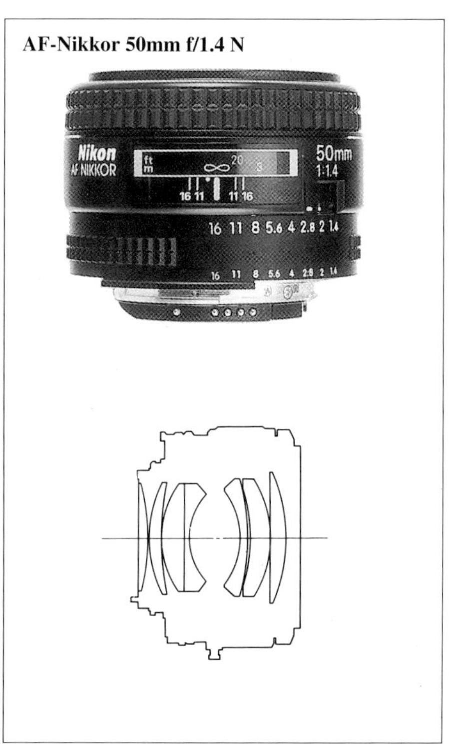

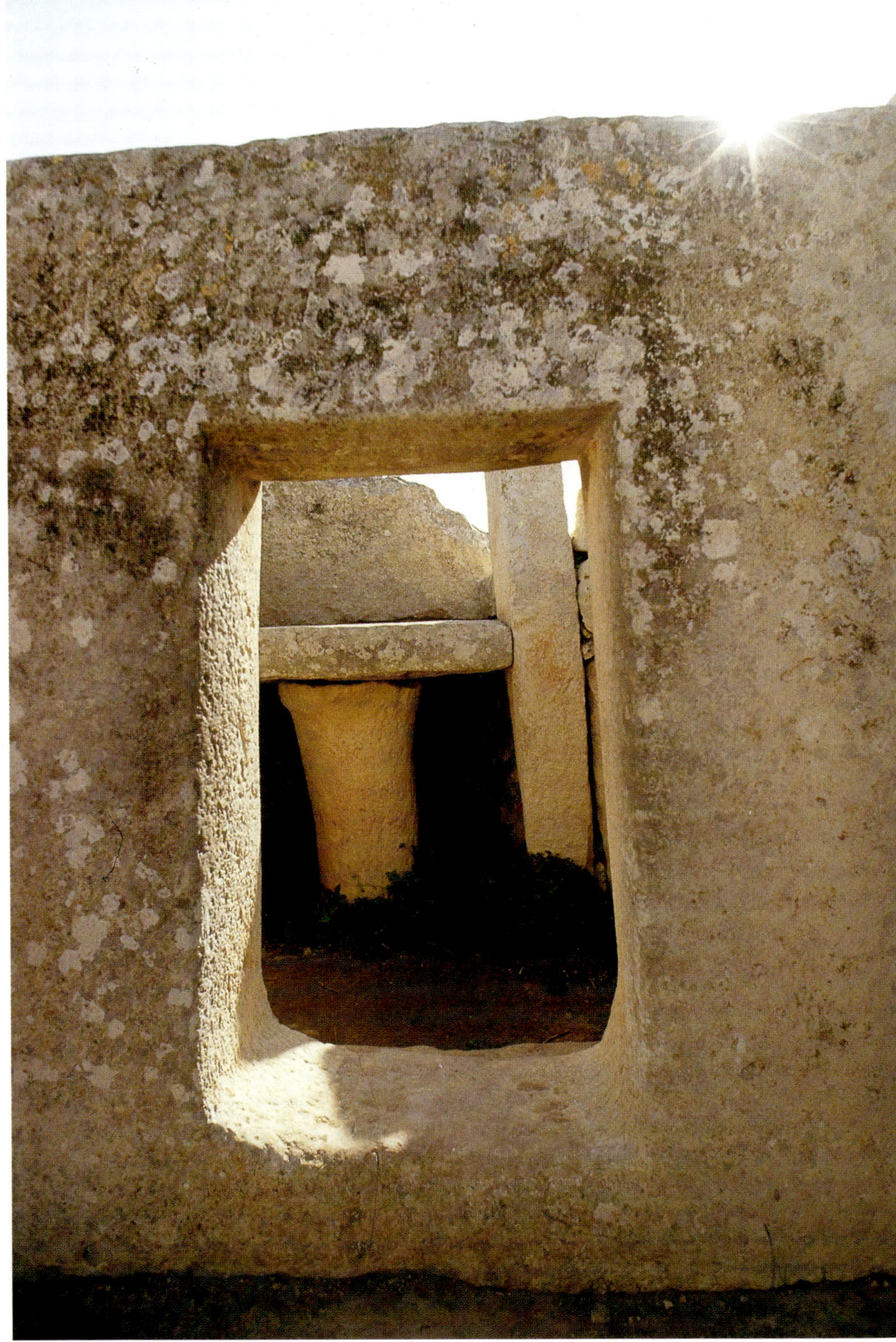

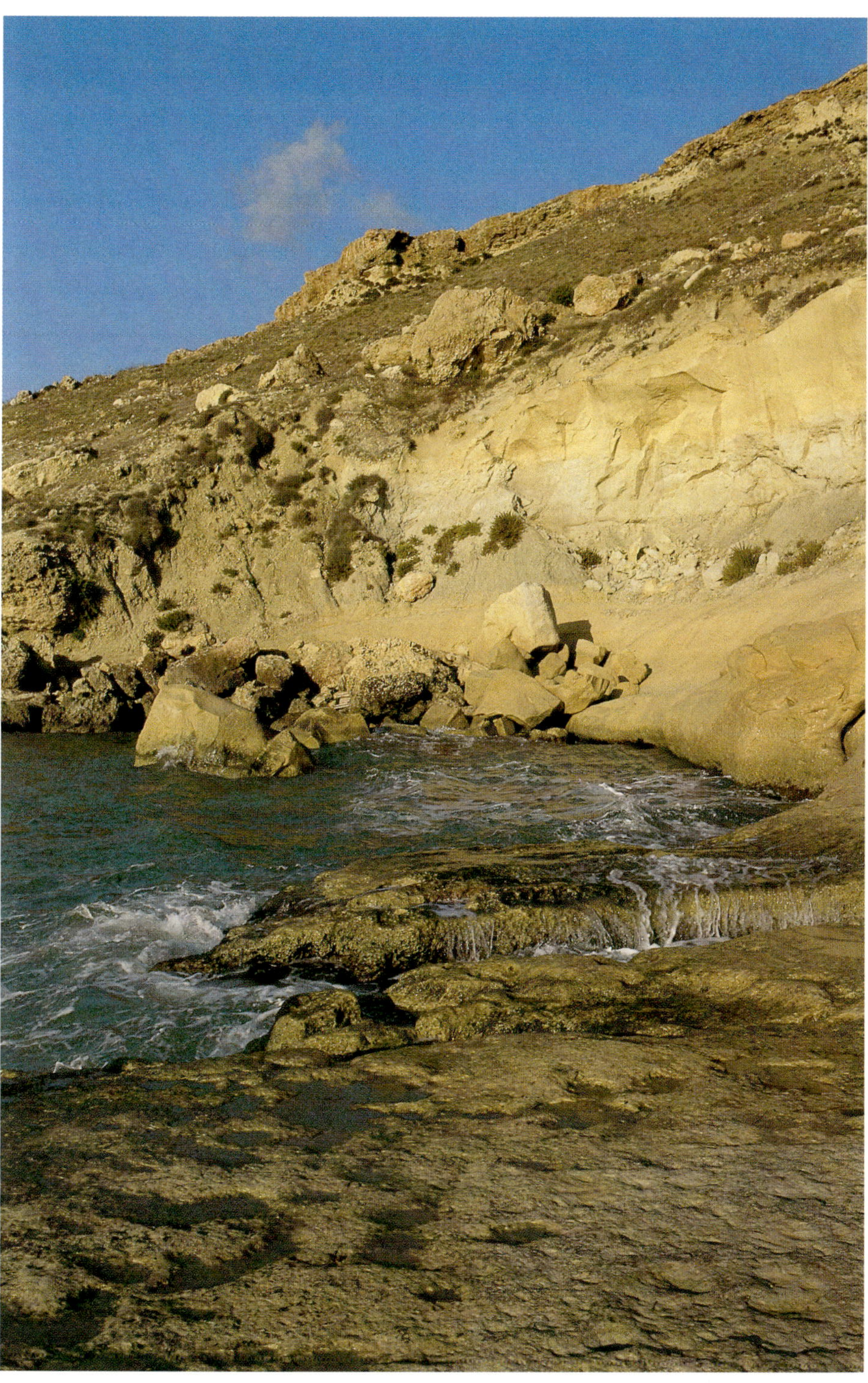

importance would probably be better served by the f/1.4.

It has often been written that normal lenses are called by that name because their angle of view corresponds to our angle of vision. The angle of view which the human eye can effectively take in is significantly greater though not with the same level of acuity. In fact, the angle of view within which we can see in sharp focus is much narrower and very close to that of a 50mm lens. These technicalities aside, the fact is, the so-called normal focal length of 50mm does, in fact, produce pictures that correspond roughly to the "average" human angle of vision and thus, for years, the "normal" focal length for 35mm cameras has been the 50mm lens. Furthermore, the fact that they became the focal length that came with new cameras, no doubt, led to their further designation as the "standard lens in 35mm photography." Perhaps the greatest case for touting the 50mm as the most useful single focal length in 35mm photography is to study the work of one of the greatest of all candid photographers, Henri Cartier-Bresson, who achieved worldwide fame with pictures taken with lenses of this focal length.

In comparison with the f/1.8 lens, the f/1.4 is about half a stop faster, heavier 3.5oz. (100g), slightly longer, has 7 elements and the same minimum focusing distance, also without CRC.

AF Micro-Nikkor 60mm f/2.8: ***Applications:*** close up photography including nature photography, work on a copy stand, and other situations where you need to get close to a subject in order to magnify its size on film. The macro lens, (or as Nikon calls their version, the micro), has the distinct advantage of being able to focus down to a magnification that will produce 1:1, life size images on film. By comparison, zooms with so-called macro ranges or lens

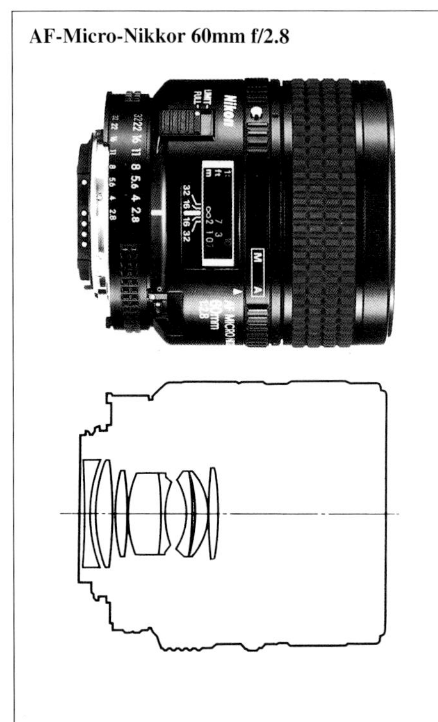

AF-Micro-Nikkor 60mm f/2.8

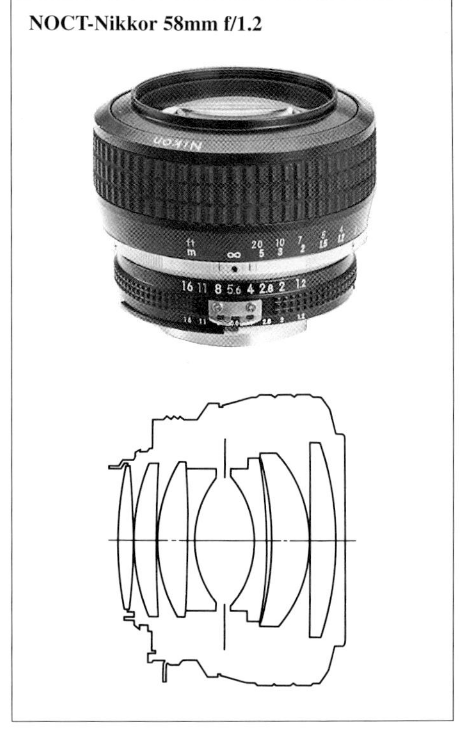

NOCT-Nikkor 58mm f/1.2

attachments such as extension rings used in combination with fixed (or zoom) focal lengths generally limit the focusing range to a specific close-up distance. While these close-up adaptations will give reasonably good results, they cannot match the superb quality of lens specifically corrected for close-up work as in the case of the Micro-Nikkors.

The 60mm Micro-Nikkor is a true macro optic in the sense that it meets the definition of a macro close-up in being able to produce 1:1 magnification ratios. (Its predecessor, the 55mm micro, went to a 1:2 ratio requiring an extension tube to reach 1:1.) It has 8 elements and CRC close-up correction down to 0.22m 8.7in. with an outstanding level of correction over the entire focusing range. In contrast to most AF Nikkors, with which manual focusing lacks the feel of a manual lens, the focusing mechanism of this optic can actually be switched from AF to manual, allowing the lens to be focused manually using the wide focusing ring, without any loss of comfort or accuracy.

NOCT-Nikkor 58mm f/1.2: ***Applications:*** available low-light photography.

A non-AF special lens of maximum speed. The aspherical front element practically eliminates any coma effect so that, when used at night with wide-open aperture, light sources are sharply reproduced, even around the edges of the frame. It is about one stop faster than the f/1.8, has 7 elements and a minimum focusing distance of 19.7in. (0.5m) without CRC.

Telephoto Lenses

(For teleconverters, AF teleconverters: see page 114.)

AF Nikkor 85mm f/1.8: ***Applications:*** This moderate focal length is a favorite for reporters, fashion, portrait and studio photographers. Its speed makes it ideal for available light

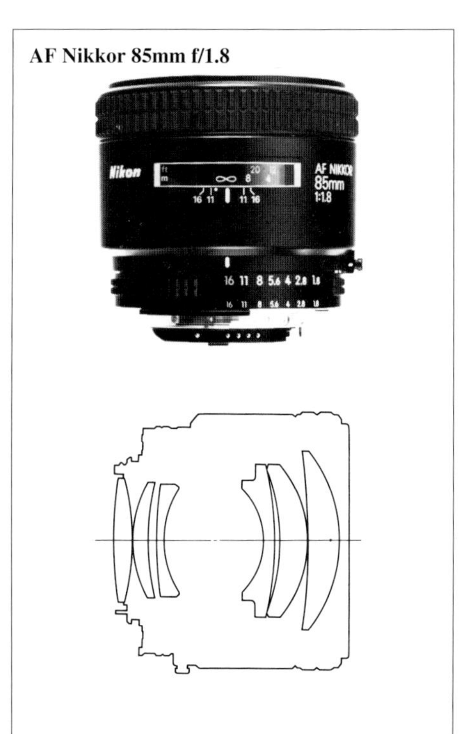

AF Nikkor 85mm f/1.8

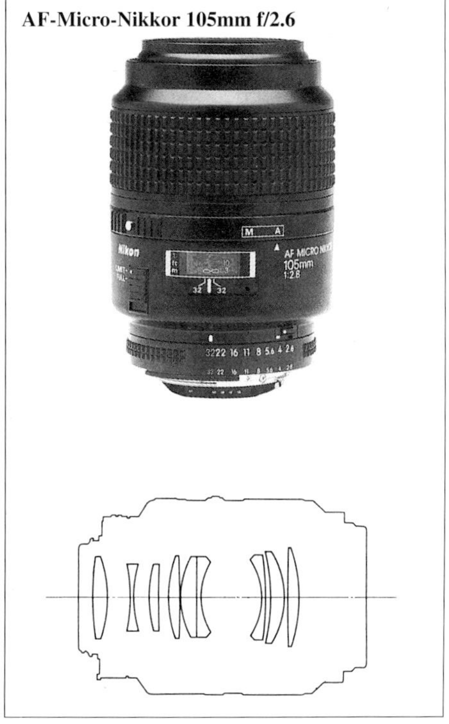

AF-Micro-Nikkor 105mm f/2.6

photography, and in the case of portrait photography it allows the background or surroundings to be either included in the picture in sharp focus or put out of focus by opening up the aperture. The focal length of 85mm produces a natural, undistorted perspective for people photography such as in fashion, portrait or nude photography. When using this lens at a range of around 3.3ft. (1 m), the ideal distance for undistorted portraits, the subject's head will more or less fill the frame. Faces, bodies and solid objects retain their three-dimensional appearance in the image without being flattened by the telephoto effect typical of longer focal lengths, making it very useful for portrait.

A moderate telephoto lens of compact design, weighing 14.6oz. (415g), with 6 elements, an angle of view of 28 degrees and a minimum focusing distance of 2.8ft. (0.85m).

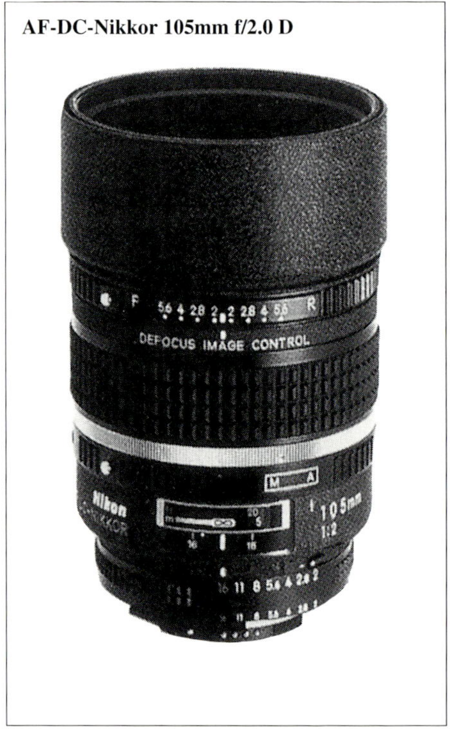

AF-DC-Nikkor 105mm f/2.0 D

AF Micro-Nikkor 105mm f/2.8: ***Applications:*** the 105mm Micro-Nikkor allows you to achieve the same maximum 1:1 magnification ratio as the 60mm Micro-Nikkor, but with the front of the lens further from the subject. This increase in "working distance" is an important, indeed critical, advantage when it comes to photographing easily-startled, small animals at extremely close range, or for reducing the danger of casting a shadow with any subject. On the other hand, this focal length is unsatisfactory for work on a copy stand whose limited column height does not allow the raising of the lens enough to compensate for the larger working distance. Thus, for macro users working in the field, the 100mm is preferable to the 60mm lens. Furthermore, the 100mm (like the 60mm) can also be used as a lens for general photography where the results are no less than those of comparable normal distance focusing lenses.

A special lens for the close-up range up to 1:1 (without extension ring) with 9 elements, it focuses down to 1ft. (0.31m). Like its 60mm relative, the level of optical correction across the entire focusing range is outstanding. It can also be switched from AF to manual, allowing the lens to be focused manually using its wide focusing ring with the "feel" of a manual focus lens as noted for the 60mm Micro-Nikkor.

AF DC-Nikkor 105mm f/2.8 D: An AF lens in the new generation of D lenses with automatic transmission of subject distance to the AF camera (to date the N90/F90). This fast lens has 6 elements and a close-focus distance of 3ft. (0.9m). Its feature of steplessly adjustable "out of focus" is similar to the DC 135mm f/2.0 (see below).

Applications: Although a superb portrait lens with the N90/F90 its expense makes it a strong choice only for serious professionals.

Using a short telephoto lens, such as contained within the range of many zooms (perhaps with the aid of an extension tube or close-up filter), enables one to take a detail shot quite easily while walking through a town. 

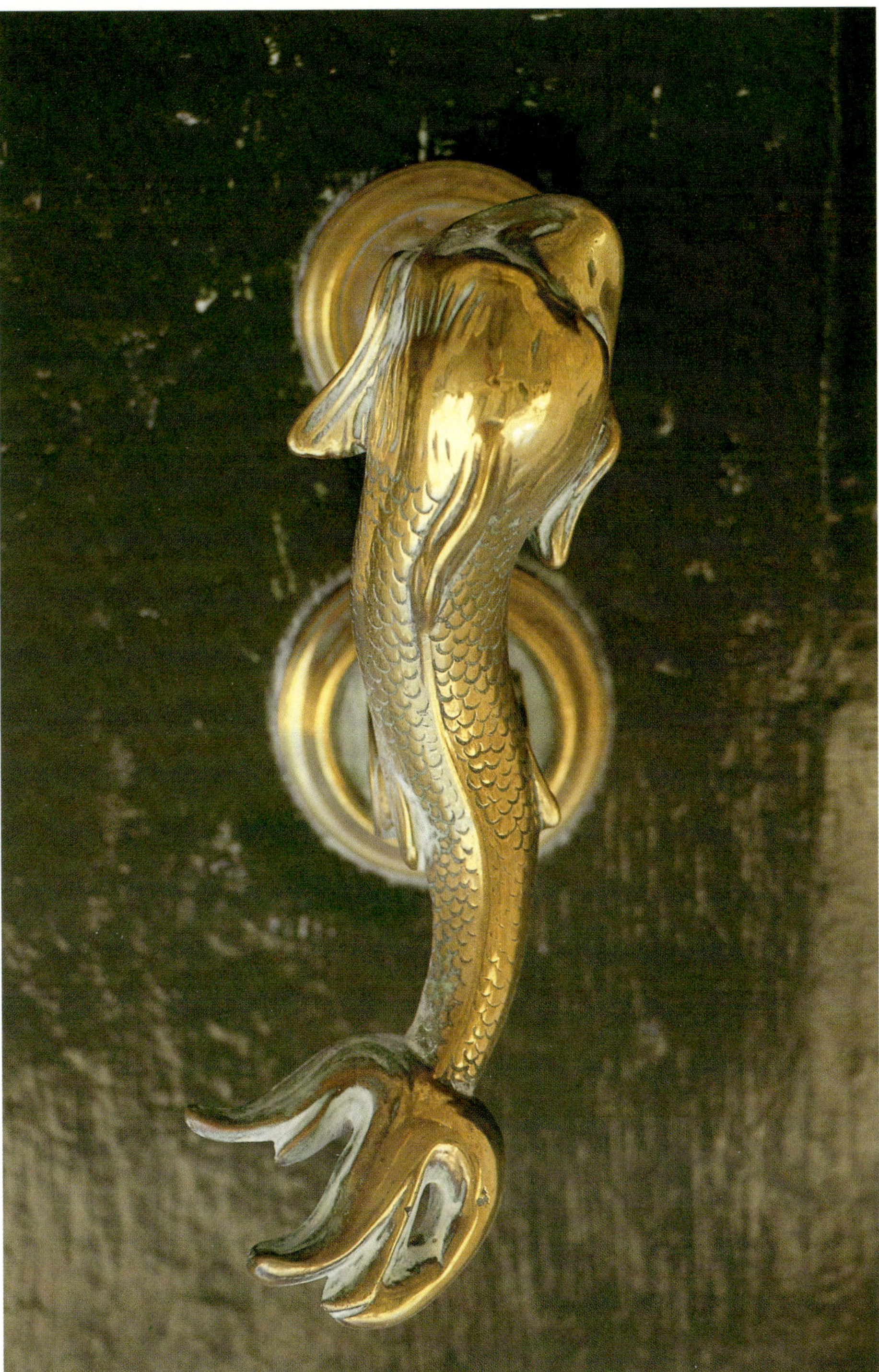

AF DC-Nikkor 135mm f/2: ***Applications:*** portraits with special "defocus effect".

This extremely fast lens has 7 elements and a minimum focusing distance of 3.6ft. (1.1m). Its special feature is a built-in and separate "defocus control" ring which, when turned, will result in various degrees of out of focus background, independent and beyond that of the aperture setting. This makes this lens especially useful to anyone who has to shoot portrait in a situation where there is no direct control over backgrounds that might distract from the subject. The length of only 5.1in. (13cm), and weight of 30.7oz. (870g) along with a reasonable price are further positive characteristics.

Before the advent of zooms, the medium telephoto focal length of 135mm was quite popular, particularly for amateurs (the range of lenses offered by independent manufacturers actually included a huge gap between 28mm and 135mm at that time). Among professionals, this focal length has had a somewhat ambiguous reputation. In day-to-day use it tends to be either too short or too long with the 80 to 100mm or a 100 to 200mm range finding more uses.

AF Nikkor 180mm f/2.8 IF-ED N: Applications: in action photography such as wildlife, sports and photojournalism or any candid situation which requires you to stay a distance from the subject. In the field of fashion photography or other areas of creative photography with people, the fast aperture can be used effectively to separate the figure from the background. Faces and other three-dimensional objects, however, do appear noticeably flatter and an arm stretched out towards the camera will appear very foreshortened. These effects are more pronounced with even longer focal lengths, and the result is pleasing for some photographers and rejected by others. For example, a traditional portrait shooter is

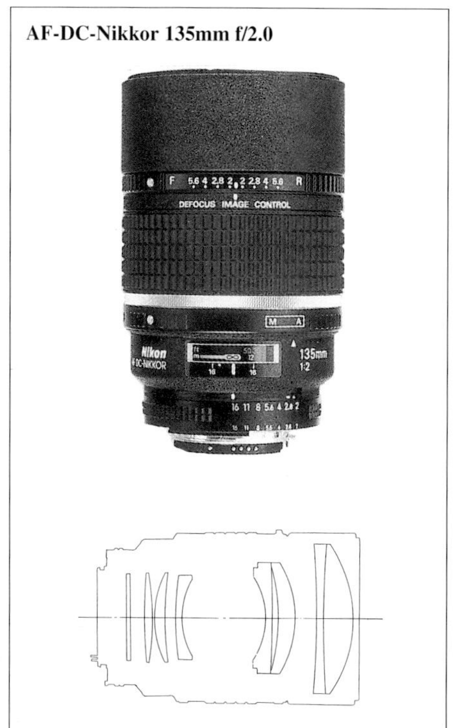

AF-DC-Nikkor 135mm f/2.0

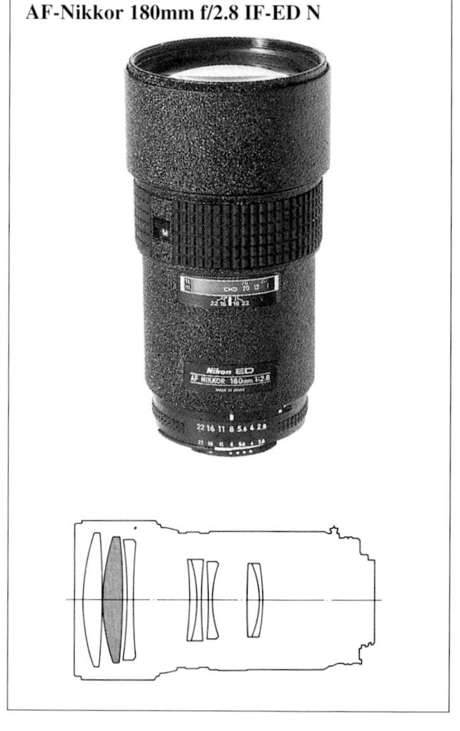

AF-Nikkor 180mm f/2.8 IF-ED N

more likely to be put off by this and opt for a 105mm or 85mm lens, but fashion shooters are using this and even longer lengths such as 300mm for the control of backgrounds and the way the model's geometry is subdued in favor of the garment itself.

This lens has a minimum focusing distance of 4.9ft. (1.50m) and can be focused very quickly using autofocus, thanks to its internal focusing mechanism. Its front lens element of ED glass largely eliminates chromatic aberration, and its construction using only 8 elements avoids unnecessary reflections. These factors ensure very sharp, brilliant pictures even with the aperture wide open. Weighing only 26.4oz. (750g) and around 6.3in. (16cm) in length, it fits easily into any camera bag and has been, like the 105mm and 85mm a very popular lens.

Nikkor 200mm f/2 IF-ED: *Applications:* basically the same as for the 180mm. How-

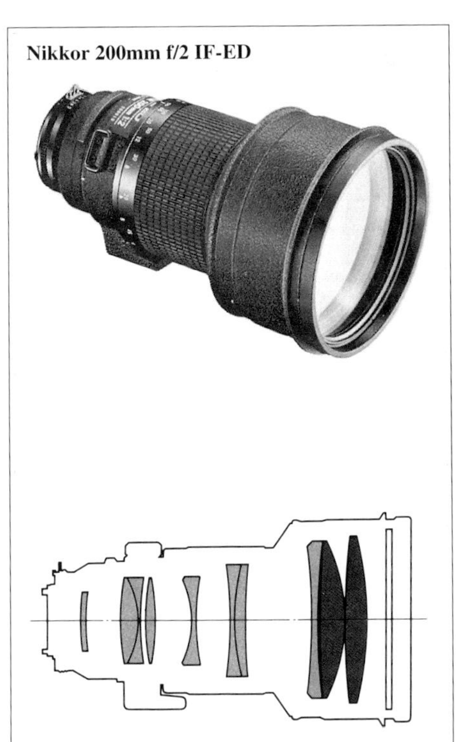

Nikkor 200mm f/2 IF-ED

AF-Nikkor 300mm f74.0 IF-ED

ever, this 200mm lens is preferable for manual focusing. Its greater weight and size is actually an advantage for stationary photography using a monopod. Whereas the 180mm AF telephoto is particularly good for hand-held photography from different camera positions, the 200mm non-AF telephoto is ideal for taking pictures from a fixed position in the stands of an event or at the edge of playing field, etc.

Anyone looking for a lens which is faster by 1 stop, and who can afford its high price, might be interested in this non-AF lens with internal focusing which, because of its wide maximum aperture, provides a very bright viewfinder image and brilliant focus. The high speed of the lens also enables it to be focused very quickly and accurately, even by hand. But weighing 5.6lbs. (2550g) with a front element diameter of 3.9in. (10cm) and corresponding bulk, it is really more at home on a tripod (or monopod). In addition to a pair of front elements of ED glass, the lens further uses 8 elements for perfect correction so that high-quality results can be obtained even using a wide-open aperture. The minimum focusing distance is 8.2ft. (2.5m) and the lens features a filter drawer for gelatin filters.

AF-Nikkor 300mm f/2.8 IF-ED N

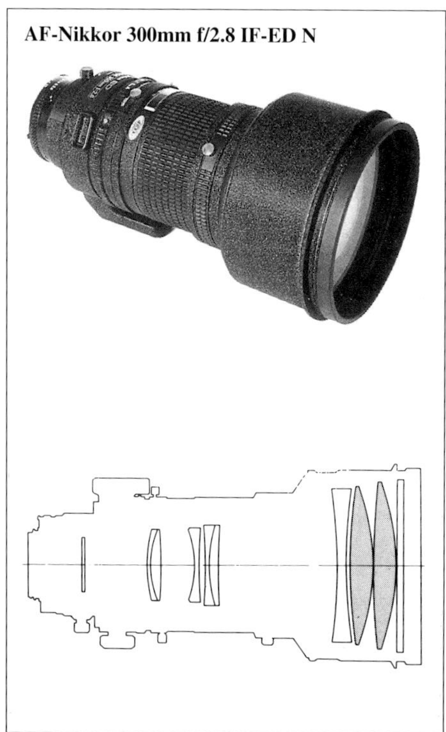

AF Nikkor 300mm f/4 IF-ED: ***Applications:*** in contrast to the 180 or 200mm lenses, the use of the 300mm lens is reserved for situations when the subject is at an extensive distance from the camera position as in sports, nature and action photography. For many wildlife and sports photographers, this is, in fact, considered the "medium" telephoto lens. The 300mm f/4 is preferred to the f/2.8 lens for photojournalism, travel and landscape work because of its comparatively lighter weight, but in the case of many nature and sport shooters, that extra stop and the higher shutter speed it permits is worth the weight.

While the 300mm focal length may be the "-medium" size for nature and sports photographers, it represents the beginning of the longer telephoto class for most and brings up the question of which focal length in this class is best? A 300mm lens, a 400mm or even a 500mm? Apart from the cost factor, the major considerations in this choice are whether or not you need the wide aperture for low light shooting, or the reduced depth of field for isolating the subject and the need, as mentioned already, to shoot at higher shutter speeds. As far as the specific focal length, that will depend primarily on how close you can get to your subject. In other words, the subject-to-camera distance versus how big you want the subject to appear on film. Two other factors related to the focal length choice, which are for some equally important questions; will the lens have to be hand-held? (The 300mm is the last of the hand-held focal lengths for most of us). And, is the "telephoto compression" of the scene important? (As in landscape work where the object is to draw together widely separated, but related subjects to improve the composition).

There is also the influence on these options brought about by the now common use of high quality Nikon teleconverters, in particular, the 1.4X which add significantly more focal length (as for example; 300mm x 1.4X = 420mm) without any loss of quality and at a fraction of the cost of a lens of the next larger focal length.

The AF 300mm f/4 IF-ED is a compact 300mm telephoto with internal focusing, weighing 2.9lbs. (1330g) measuring 8.6 x 3.5in. (219 x 89mm). As with all Nikon lenses using ED glass elements, the sharpness of focus is practically the same whether the aperture is wide open or stopped down. The lens has 8 elements and a minimum focusing distance of 8.2ft. (2.5m) and uses either 82mm front element filters or 39mm glass and gelatin filters.

AF Nikkor 300mm f/2.8 IF-ED N: ***Applications:*** when an important meeting is covered on the television news, and we see the familiar shot panning across the crowd of waiting news photographers with their rows of tripods set up, you will find that a good many of them will be using a 300mm f/2.8 lens as well as a lens of even longer focal length. In fashion photography, the f/2.8 lens is used with open aperture to separate the main subject from the background. (But only from relatively long range, so that the flattened perspective is not too apparent). In other words, the f/2.8 lens is used in much the same way as the f/4 lens, with the restriction that it is best used from a "stationary" position on a tripod or monopod. Weighing 5.9lbs. (2700g), this lens is about three times as expensive and twice as heavy as its 1-stop slower equivalent. Its optical performance is more or less the same. It also has 8 elements and a minimum focusing distance of 9.8ft. (3m). Like the f/4 lens, it has a built-in, dust-proof filter holder for 39mm filters and gelatin filters. The lens has a length of 10.3in. (263mm) and a diameter of 5.2in. (133mm).

AF-I Nikkor 300mm f/2.8D IF-ED N

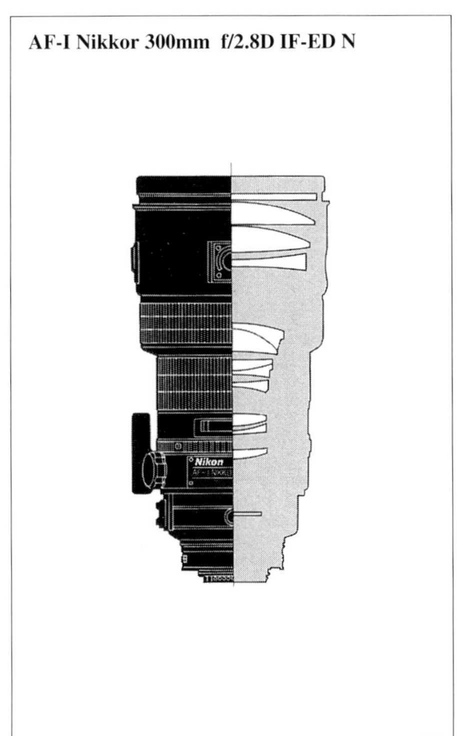

AF-I Nikkor 300mm f/2.8 D IF-ED: ***Applications:*** same as for the AF 300mm f/2.8. In terms of handling and additional features, it is probably the ultimate lens for sports, action or fashion photographers.

This is an internally-focusing apochromatic lens with 11 elements in 9 groups and has an additional plane-parallel glass plate to protect the front element. It features a filter holder for 39mm filters and gelatin filters and with a weight of 6.4lbs. (2900g), it is slightly heavier than the non-D version, but it is around 0.8in. (2cm) shorter and 0.8in. (2cm) narrower. The special feature of the AF-I Nikkor is an extremely fast, coreless DC motor built into the lens. The focusing range can be limited in order to allow very fast AF focusing over a specific near/far range. In addition, up to four focusing distances can be indexed and recalled at any time using a focus lock button. Alternatively, the present model can be focused just as well by hand, with the familiar feel of a manual focus lens. The interesting feature here is that the lens does not need to be switched from autofocus to manual; it automatically switches to manual focusing when the focusing ring on the lens is turned.

Note: Since the AF functions of this lens require a special interaction with the camera, it can only be used with the F4 and N90/F90 in the AF functions to date. Transmitting the subject distance to the camera (it is a generation D lens) can only be used with the N90/F90 so far. With the other Nikon AF cameras it only allows manual focusing, but all automatic exposure functions can be used.

Extreme Telephoto Lenses

Nikkor 400mm f/5.6 IF-ED: *Applications:* lenses with focal lengths of between 400 and 800mm are used to overcome otherwise insuperable distances in situations where the photographer either cannot or is not allowed to get any closer to the subject or wants to photograph something secretly or unobtrusively. For example, those paparazzi who are prepared to spend days up a tree in order to get a shot of royalty, prominent prisoners in the exercise yard, or film stars sunbathing in the nude around their swimming pools. Nature and sports photographers, and photojournalists specializing in taking pictures of politicians, also find these long lenses indispensable.

With these longer focal lengths, it takes a very steady hand and a fair amount of practice to achieve any sort of sharp hand-held pictures, with the lighter lenses. The faster but heavier versions of this class of super telephotos can only be used from a tripod effectively for long periods of time as at a sporting event or in wildlife shooting. It is possible to handhold them using very fast shutter speeds but for many photographers to do this, it is more for winning an argument then for setting up those conditions which will allow you to make the most of what these lenses can give.

Nikkor 400mm f/5.6 IF-ED

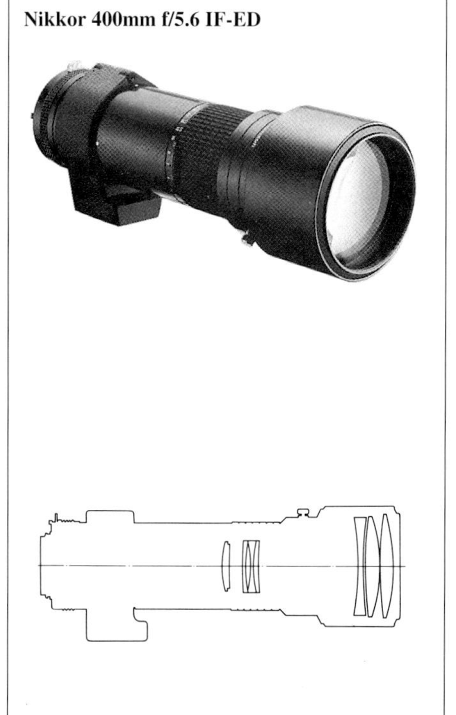

Nikkor 400mm f/3.5 IF-ED

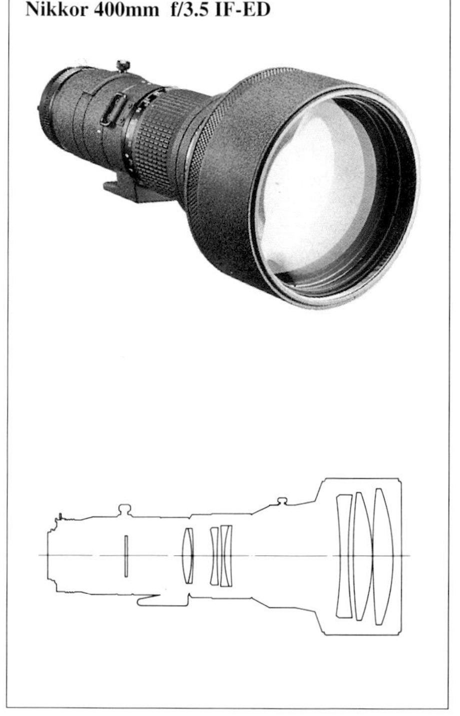

So the upshot of "super telephoto reality" is that all of the faster larger lenses have to be tripod or monopod mounted and if the smaller, lighter versions are hand held, at least moderate speed film has to be used to allow for higher shutter speeds. Even with a steady hand, shake-free shots can generally only be achieved at shutter speeds which at least correspond to the reciprocal value of the lens' focal length, i.e. at least 1/500 second (and that's minimal) for a 400mm lens or 500mm lens. Alternatively, the use of a monopod or chest-support allows the use of slightly slower shutter speeds. The 400mm f/5.6 is the least cumbersome of the big lenses and is the most suitable for mobile use.

A 7 element non-AF lens with a minimum focusing distance of 4m 13.1ft., a "reasonable" filter thread of 72mm and a relatively handy weight of 1200g 2.6lbs., dimensions 262 x 85mm 10.3in.x3.3in.

Note: Internal focusing and ED front elements are standard features of all of Nikon's conventional super telephotos, so no further mention of them will be made in the following descriptions.

Nikkor 400mm f/3.5 IF-ED: ***Applications:*** in comparison with the f/5.6, this is a typical tripod lens.

This 8 element non-AF lens is 1.5 stops faster, weighs in at 6.2lbs. (2800g) with dimensions of12 x 5.3in. (304 x134mm). The minimum focusing distance is 14.8ft. (4.5m). Either 122mm screw-in front element filters can be used or 39mm glass filters or gelatin filters in a special mount inserted into the optical path of the lens.

Nikkor 400mm f/2.8 IF-ED: ***Applications:*** The f/2.8 aperture makes this lens an excellent choice (in spite of its price) for sports and wildlife photography due to its excellent ability to isolate the subject.

AF-I Nikkor 400mm f/2.8 D IF-ED

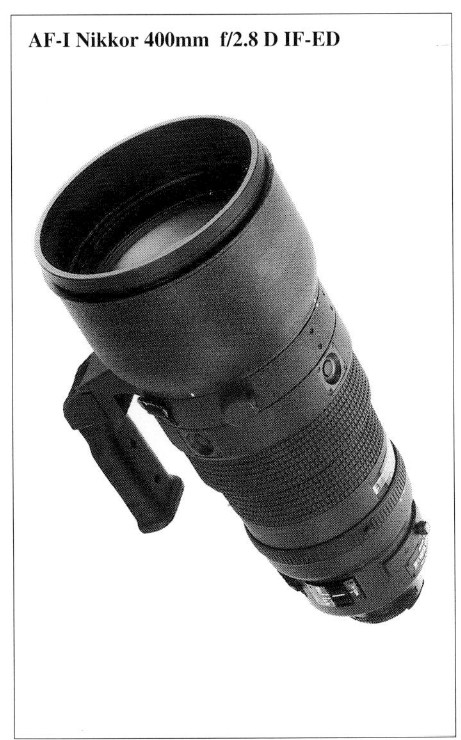

Nikkor 500mm f/4 P IF-ED

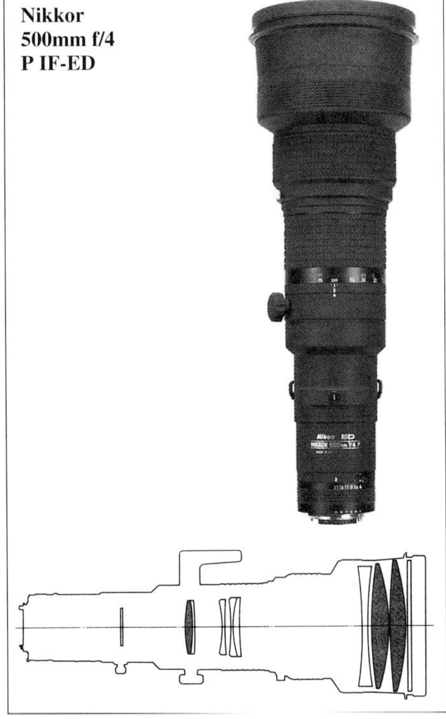

Only 1/2 a stop faster, with a minimum focusing distance of 13.1ft. (4m), this 8 element lens weighs all of 11.3lbs. (5150g) and measures 17 x 6.8in. (432 x 172mm). It has a permanently built-in UV filter to protect the front element and also uses the special mountings for 39mm filters and gelatin filters. With these faster versions and with the even longer focal lengths, Nikon has obviously made no compromises in terms of weight, size or price. Their only concern is to provide the photographer with the best possible lens.

Nikkor 500mm f/4 P IF-ED: ***Special applications:*** as with the above lenses, but with slightly greater magnification. This can be considered the "long" telephoto lens for use with the N8008/F-801 or F4.

This 500mm lens has 8 elements and can be focused down to a range of 16.4ft. (5m). It weighs 6.6lbs. (3000g) and measures 15.3 x 5.4in. (387 x 138mm). However, this is the only non-AF lens with a built-in CPU, which allows it to be used with Nikon AF cameras (though without the AF function) in any exposure mode, e.g. shutter speed priority mode. This mode is useful in sports photography or when taking pictures of moving subjects, since one can deliberately avoid loss of sharpness through camera shake or select an appropriate shutter speed to match the anticipated movement of the subject.

Note. This lens also has a permanently built-in UV filter in front of the front element and special 39mm filter holder. All the other super telephoto lenses also have these two technical features, so no further mention will be made of these features in the following.

AF-I Nikkor 600mm f/4 D IF-ED: ***Applications:*** generally the same as for the other 500mm and 600mm lenses above and below. In

AF-I Nikkor 600mm f/4.0 D IF-ED

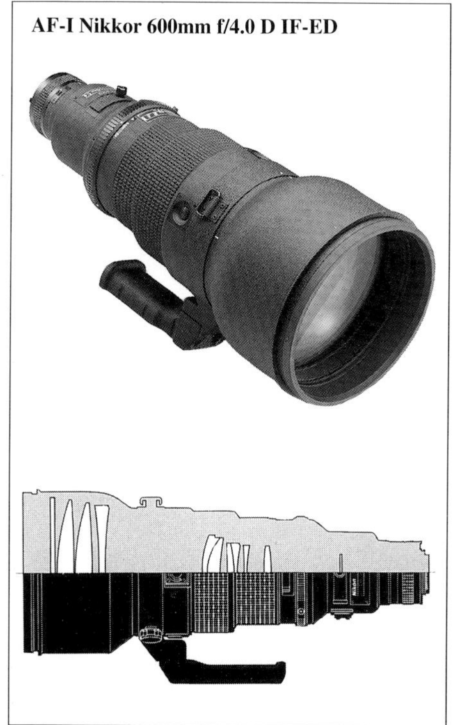

Nikkor 600mm f/5.6 IF-ED

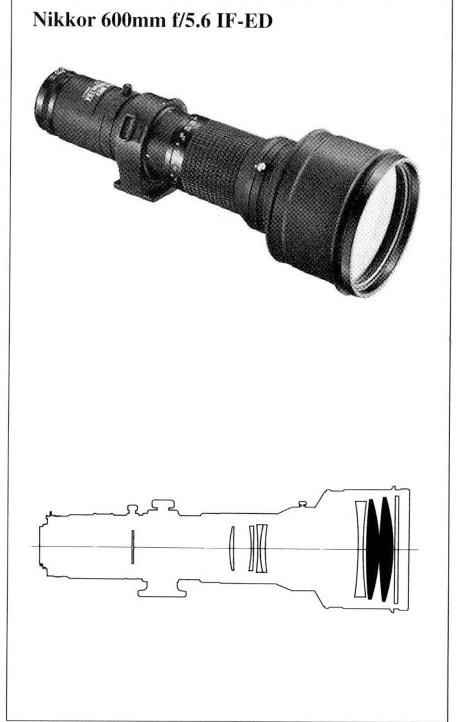

terms of handling and additional features, it is probably the ultimate lens for AF photography with long focal lengths.

This is an internally-focusing apochromatic lens with 9 elements in 7 groups with an additional plane-parallel glass plate to protect the front element. It features a filter holder for 39mm filters and gelatin filters. The weight of 13.3lbs. (6050g) is considerable, and with a length of 16.5in. (42cm) and a diameter of around 6.7in. (17cm), it is quite cumbersome. The special feature of this AF-I Nikkor is an extremely fast, coreless DC motor built into the lens. The focusing range can be limited in order to allow very fast AF focusing. In addition, up to four focusing distances can be indexed and recalled at any time using a focus lock button. Alternatively, the lens can be focused just as well by hand, with the familiar feel of manual focusing. The lens automatically switches to manual focusing when the focusing ring on the lens is turned as described above for the 300mm f/2.8 D IF-ED lens.

Since the AF functions of this lens require a special interaction with the camera, it can only be used with the F4 and N90/F90 in the AF functions to date. Transmitting the subject distance to the camera (it is a generation D lens) can only be used with the N90/F90 so far. It only works in manual focus mode and in any auto exposure mode with all other AF Nikon cameras.

Nikkor 600mm f/5.6 IF-ED N: *Applications:* similar to preceding lens. In comparison with the 600mm f/4 and AF-I 600mm f/4 D IF-ED, and intended use versus differences in weight and bulk (as described in the section under the AF Nikkor 300mm f/4 IF-ED) will be the deciding factors in the selection of which of these larger telephotos to use.

7 elements, 16.4ft. (5m) minimum focusing

Nikkor 600mm f/4.0 IF-ED

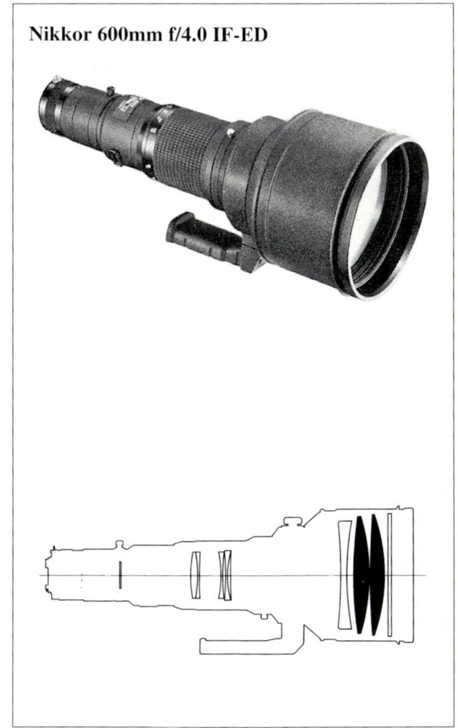

Nikkor 800mm f/8 IF-ED

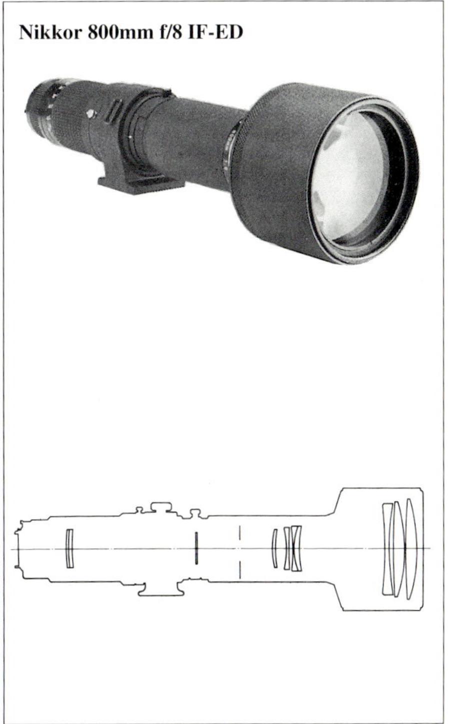

distance and a weight of 6.2lbs. (2800g), with dimensions of 15.5 x 5.2in. (395 x 132mm).

Nikkor 600mm f/4 IF-ED: ***Applications:*** similar to preceding lenses.

8 elements, 21.3ft. (6.5m) minimum focusing distance and a weight of 12.4lbs. (5650g), with dimensions of 18.6in. x 6.8in. (473 x 173mm).

Nikkor 800mm f/5.6 IF-ED: ***Applications:*** similar to preceding lenses. In comparison with the 600mm lenses, the subject is brought closer by a factor of around 1.3X.

8 elements, 26.2ft. (8m) minimum focusing distance and a weight of 12lbs. (5450g), with dimensions of 21.8in. x 6.4in. (554 x 163mm).

Reflex Telephoto Lenses

Reflex Nikkor 500mm f/8 N: ***About reflex lenses:*** Reflex or mirror telephotos, as they are also known, represent a different optic design from the conventional telephoto we have been discussing. Reflex lenses work on the principle of the magnifying effect of reflections off curved surfaces. The light rays pass through the large, circular front element onto a circular concave mirror at the rear end of the lens and are reflected from there onto a round mirror located on the internal slide of the front element. The light rays are then reflected back to the film and focused to a focal point on the film plane. Folding the path of the light rays twice in this way allows a very short construction. The 500 f/8 N has no significant chromatic aberrations, due to its design incorporating expensive ED glass. On the other hand, this same reflex design is usually limited to just one fixed f/stop, resulting in the loss of the option to increase depth of field by stopping down. Furthermore, when using very fast films with a camera which has a maximum shutter speed of only 1/1000 or 1/2000 second, you have to screw grey neutral density filters

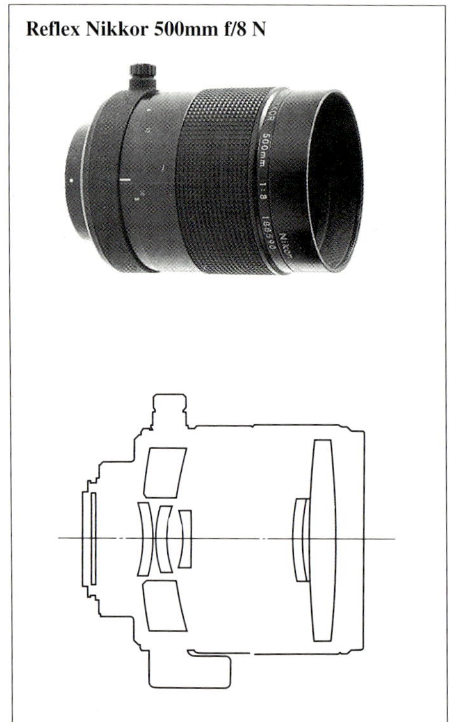

Reflex Nikkor 500mm f/8 N

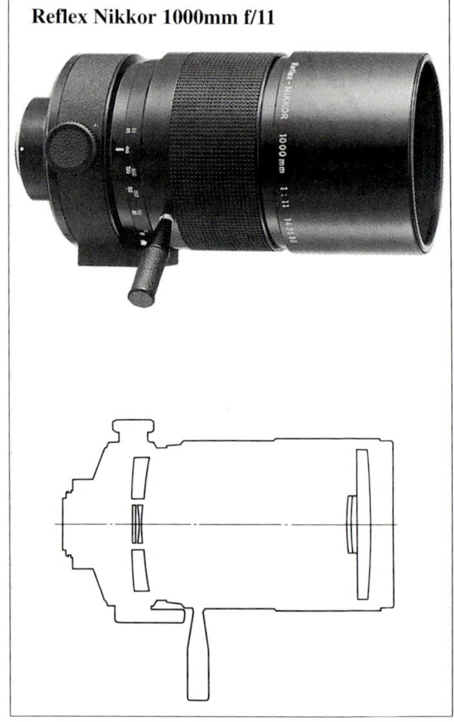

Reflex Nikkor 1000mm f/11

onto the rear of the lens in order to avoid overexposure in bright conditions. Since a filter always has to be fitted for optical reasons (normally a UV filter), this can become an irritating business under changeable lighting conditions. Characteristically, photographs taken with reflex lenses can be recognized by blurred, donut or ring-shaped highlights in the unfocused areas of the picture which appear, for example, from reflections on water surfaces in sunlight.

Applications: with their very small maximum apertures, these lenses produce a relatively dark image in the viewfinder without the brilliant sharpness of faster lenses of comparable focal lengths, so that even the 500mm, which is really designed for hand-held use, can be difficult to focus in anything less than bright, natural light. While the reflex Nikkors are probably not so suitable for sports photography under dimmer lighting conditions as at the end of the day or under outside lighting in anything other than an major league stadium, they are well suited to all types of long distance photography which allow enough time for accurate focusing. Thus, both the 500mm and the 1000mm are used by landscape and travel photographers. The 500mm in particular is a lens which can still be carried in the camera bag ready for use in case unexpected opportunities arise, whereas you would probably think twice before taking a 500mm lens of conventional construction with you.

The 500mm Reflex Nikkor has a length of 116mm and a diameter of 89mm and weighs only 840g. This is an incredibly compact lens for this focal length. It also has a minimum focusing distance of.4.9ft. (1.5m), which is unusual for such a focal length. 5 different filters are supplied with the lens, including an ND.

Reflex Nikkor 1000mm f/11: ***Applications:*** as for the 500mm, but for even more distant subjects. It should, however, be noted that in bringing extremely distant subjects closer, all atmospheric "interference" such as smog, haze and dust are also magnified. This is a problem in all telephoto photography but when you get to a focal length of, it can really be detrimental to picture contrast, although the effects of haze and sometimes dust can be diminished by the use of a UV filter and accepts 39mm screw filters (also orange filters for black-and-white photography).

This lens, with a weight of.4.2lbs. (1900g), a length of. 9.5in. (241mm) and a diameter of 4.7in. (119mm) is remarkably handy for a lens of this extreme focal length. It can also be used for hand-held shots, with the limitation that one only has an aperture of f/11 to work with and a shutter speed of 1/1000 second or more is required. That means both good lighting conditions and the use of a fast film. The minimum range of this lens is 26.3ft. (8m). 5 different 39mm filters are also supplied with this lens.

AF-Nikkor 20-35mm f/2.8 D

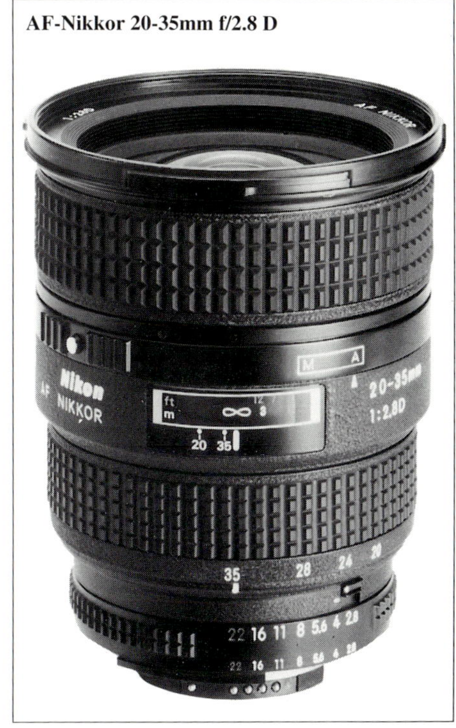

Zoom Lenses

Understandably, zoom lenses enjoy massive popularity since they seem to offer a whole range of focal lengths in a single lens. But the use of zoom lenses does involve certain specific limitations and therefore the reader is referred to the section "Zoom or Fixed Focal Length?"

AF Nikkor 20-35mm f/2.8 D: An AF lens of the new D generation with automatic transmission of subject distance to the AF camera (to date only the N90/F90). It covers the traditional wide-angle range with angles of view from 94° to 64°. Even though it is very fast, it offers excellent sharpness throughout the entire zoom range thanks to a complex construction consisting of 14 elements, one of which is aspherical. The close-focus distance of 1.6ft. (0.5m) is a bit far for some applications (9.8in. would be required for product shots with perceptively increased foregrounds). Sensitivity to flare caused by reflective surfaces are higher in zooms as compared to high-quality fixed focal length lenses.
Note: Transmission of subject distance to the camera (it is also a new type D lens) can only be used with the N90/F90 to date.
Applications: Although excellent for product shots, architecture and landscape photography, the high price and fact that filtration is very difficult due to vignetting make this lens not highly recommended. However, for the reporter on the move who does not have time to change lenses, or travel and nature photographers who have to travel light, a zoom such as this one may be an option.

AF Nikkor 24-50mm f/3.3-4.5: ***Applications:*** same as for the corresponding fixed focal lengths in its range.

A two-ring zoom lens (also known as a

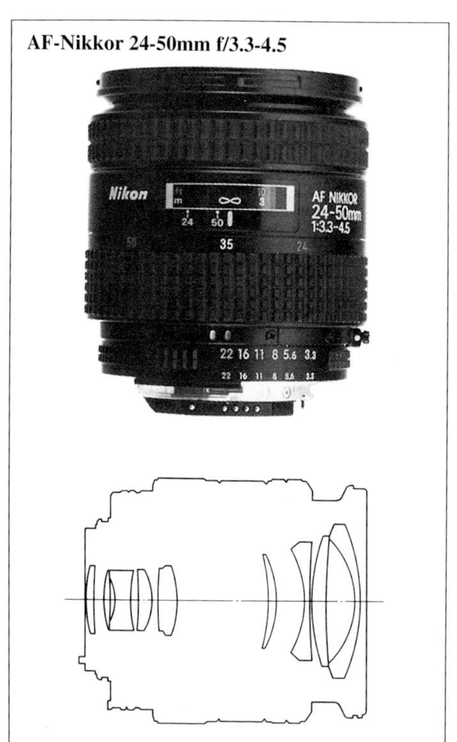

AF-Nikkor 24-50mm f/3.3-4.5

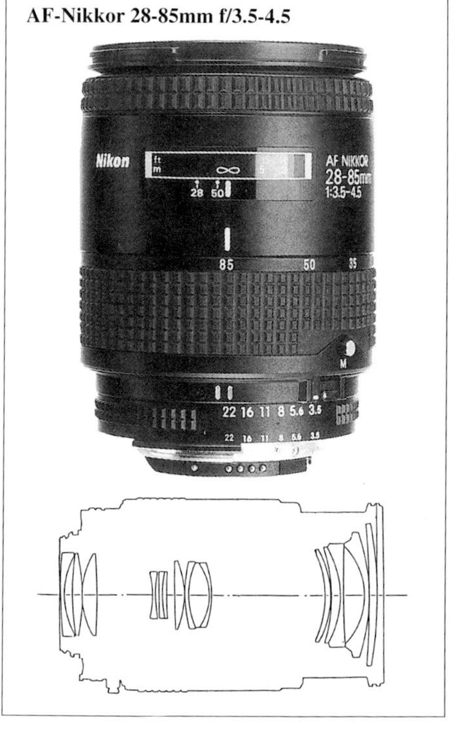

AF-Nikkor 28-85mm f/3.5-4.5

"variable-zoom") which only has a 2x zoom range, but which, for a zoom lens, has a very wide-angle minimum focal length of 24mm. Unfortunately, the range only extends to 50mm. This is probably because the manufacturers wanted to construct a compact and really first-class lens without any compromises, and in this they have been successful. The lens has 9 elements, weighs 13.2oz. (375g) and has a normal minimum focusing distance of 2ft. (0.6m) plus a slightly closer macro range of 1.6ft. (0.5m). It is worth considering whether one would be better off opting instead for an AF Nikkor 24mm f/2.8 N and an AF Nikkor 50mm f/1.8 N as a fixed focal length, two-lens combination. In terms of speed, there is a gain of 1/2 a stop with the first lens and 3 whole stops with the latter, at a total additional weight of only 1.4oz. (40g) and at a virtually negligible extra cost. Anyone who favors the two extreme focal lengths of this zoom lens and is prepared to change lenses from time to time would almost certainly be better served by this two-lens combination. Otherwise, the convenience of the zoom lens wins out when making a choice.

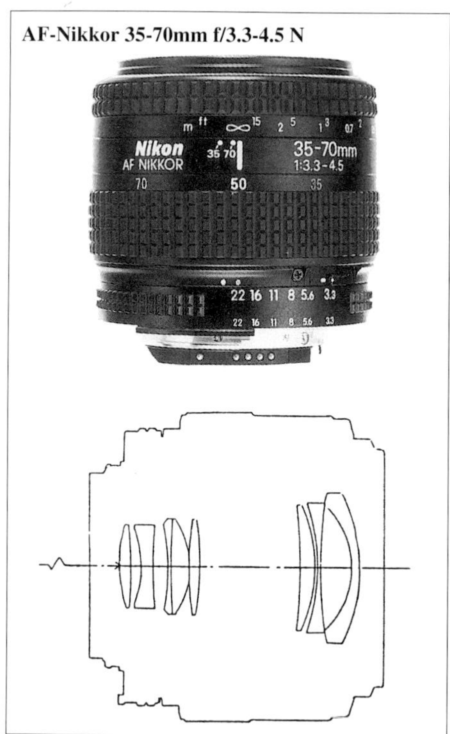

AF-Nikkor 35-70mm f/3.3-4.5 N

AF Nikkor 28-85mm f/3.5-4.5 N: ***Applications:*** same as for the corresponding fixed focal lengths within its range. This is the ideal zoom for anyone starting out in SLR photography, e.g. as a first lens for the N8008/F801. At 28mm it contains a wide-angle lens which already displays the typical wide-angle characteristics and can also convey an idea of the effect of lenses with shorter focal lengths. At 85mm it acts as a moderate telephoto lens, which is ideal for portraits and the experience gained with this longer focal length is useful when it comes to choosing a lens of longer focal length at a later stage. After a certain time, one will probably develop a preference for certain subjects or a particular focal length and feel the need to expand the range of available focal lengths. That, in turn, might lead very logically to the purchase of an additional lens of the appropriate fixed focal length with greater speed (up to 3 stops), or a macro lens which provides much better quality in the extended macro range than a zoom lens on macro setting.

With a 3x zoom range, this two-ring zoom has a 15mm advantage over the 28-70mm standard zoom which has been showing up of late as a possible replacement offered by some manufacturers with their middle range cameras. With 15 elements, it is so well corrected in terms of sharpness that it can bear comparison with equivalent fixed focal lengths. The large number of elements does tend to make it more susceptible to stray light, so it should not be used without a lens hood. The lens weighs 19oz. (540g) and has a minimum focusing distance of 2.6ft. (0.8m) plus a macro range down to 9in. (0.23m).

AF Nikkor 35-70mm f/3.3-4.5 N: ***Applications:*** same as for the corresponding fixed focal lengths in its range. A typical first lens for amateur photographers, made even more attractive by its reasonable price.

A "tame" standard two-ring zoom with only a 2x range of focal lengths. Compact and weighing only 8.5oz. (240g), this 8 element lens has a minimum focusing distance of 1.6ft. (0.5m) and a macro range down to 13.8in. (0.35m). In terms of focal length, it covers approximately the range which photographers had to be content with during the early decades of 35mm photography, i.e. 35mm, 50mm and, with 70mm, not quite the classic 90mm. And yet, even with such a limited range of focal lengths to choose from, many photographers in the 1920s and 1930s developed a visual style which still seems modern today. The lesson taught by this lens is that masterpieces can be created even with limited means.

AF Nikkor 35-70mm f/2.8: Except for transmission of subject distance information which is featured in the D series lenses, it is identical to the AF Nikkor 35-70mm f/2.8 D as described below.

AF Nikkor 35-70mm f/2.8 D: With a constant aperture of f/2.8 throughout the zoom range, it is a push-zoom (also known as "true zoom") weighing 1.5 lbs. (675g). Its close-focus distance is 11in. (0.28m) with a maximum magnification ratio of one quarter life-size. The image quality is comparable to the fixed focal lengths right down into the close-up range which is limited, however, to only the 35mm setting. 15 elements are required to provide this performance, which provides lower control of flare as compared to fixed focal length designs when stray light is not controlled, or in backlight situations. *Note:* The automatic transmission of subject distance to the AF camera can only be used with the N90/F90 to date.
Applications: Like the corresponding fixed

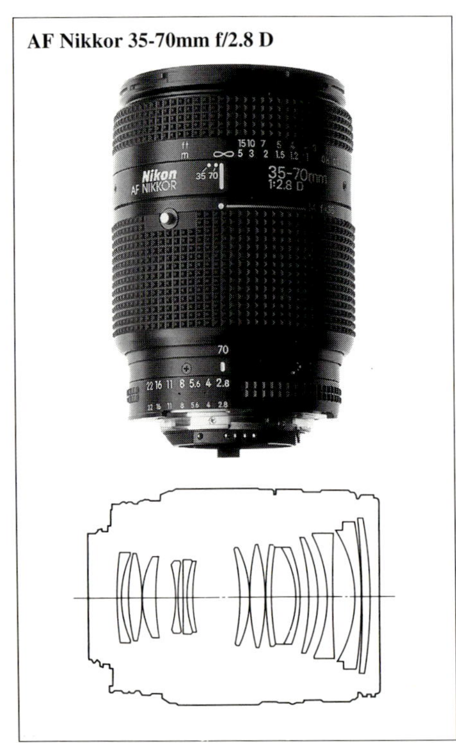

AF Nikkor 35-70mm f/2.8 D

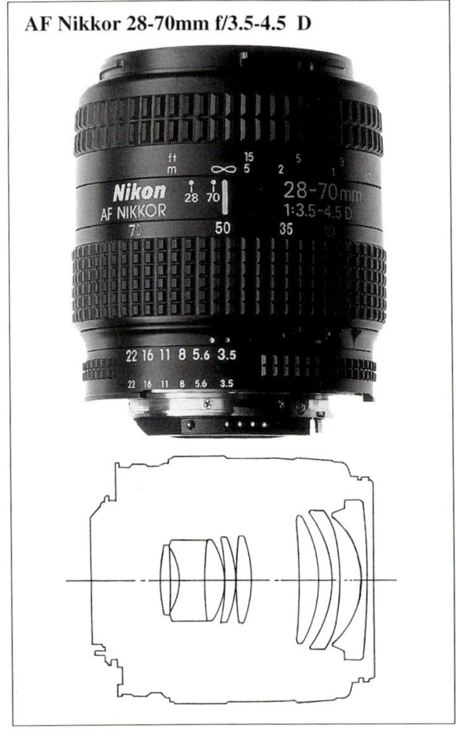

AF Nikkor 28-70mm f/3.5-4.5 D

focal length in its range. It is intended as a fast, zoom alternative for these fixed lenses for the pro and serious non-pro markets.

AF Nikkor 28-70mm f/3.5-4.5: Except for transmission of subject distance characteristic of the D series, identical to the AF Nikkor 28-70mm f/3.5-4.5 D below.

AF Nikkor 28-70mm f/3.5-4.5 D: A conventional two ring-zoom with a 2.5X zoom range. The largest magnification ratio is 1:4.6 at 1.3ft. (0.39m) distance. It weighs 12.3oz. (350g) and has 8 elements without sacrificing sharpness. It can get by with so few elements because an aspherical element reduces spherical aberration and the fairly symmetrical optical construction minimizes distortion. Its mechanical construction is noticeably better than lenses of comparable quality made by other manufacturers. *Note:* Transmission of the subject distance to the AF camera (it is a new D generation lens) can only be used with the N90/F90 to date.
Applications: Same as the corresponding fixed focal length lenses in its range. This 28-70mm zoom lens appears to be the best compromise of quality, speed, handling and price for the serious non-professional and professional.

AF Nikkor 35-80mm f/4.0-5.6 D: A zoom of the new D generation that only weighs 7.9oz. (225g). The image quality is excellent thanks to an aspheric element. The almost fixed focal number of elements (six) promises good contrast levels under all light conditions. The close-focus distance is 1.6ft. (0.5m), in manual mode with the "macro ring" at 13.8in. (0.35m). *Note:* Transmission of the subject distance to the AF camera (it is a new D generation lens) can only be used with the N90/F90 to date.
Applications: Like the corresponding fixed focal lengths in its range. A particularly light and

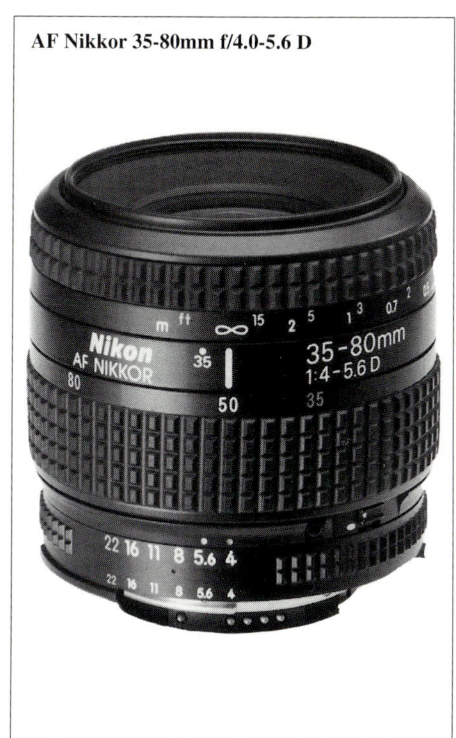

AF Nikkor 35-80mm f/4.0-5.6 D

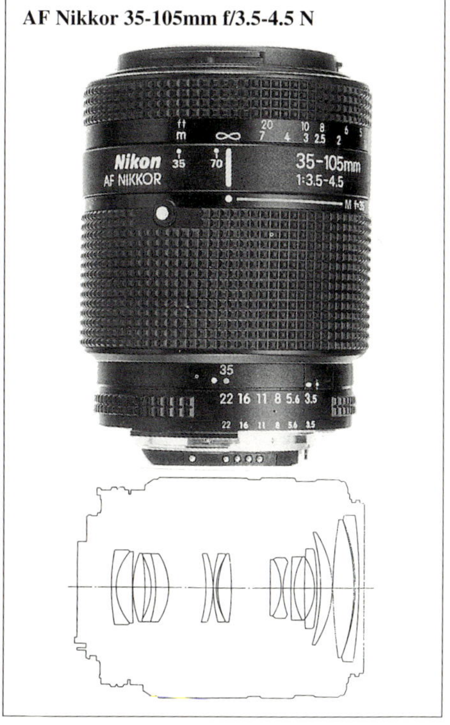

AF Nikkor 35-105mm f/3.5-4.5 N

high-quality "all-purpose" zoom for demanding non-professionals and professionals alike.

AF Nikkor 35-105mm f/3.5-4.5 N: ***Applications:*** same as for the corresponding fixed focal lengths in its range with the above-mentioned limitations.

Though it only starts at 35mm, this lens goes up to 105mm, providing a 3x zoom range. With 16 elements, it is a well-corrected lens weighing 1lb. (460g). As mentioned, the high number of elements can reduce image quality under poor lighting conditions. The 105mm would be a very good focal length for portrait photography, but unfortunately the lens will only focus down to a distance of 4.6ft. (1.4m). This rules out frame-filling head shots, and the macro range of 1.2ft. (0.38m) is no help in this situation since the gap between the shortest normal focusing distance and the macro range is, generally speaking, too great for portrait work.

AF Nikkor 35-135mm f/3.5-4.5 N: ***Applications:*** same as for the corresponding fixed focal lengths in its range with the above-mentioned limitations.

Again, this lens starts at 35mm and allows a 4x zoom up to 135mm. But also, again, the minimum focusing distance of 4.9ft. (1.5m) which is rather unsatisfactory, particularly in the shorter focal length range, even though a macro range of 11.9in. (0.3m) is available. If it is bought by a beginner as their first lens, the unsatisfactory minimum focusing distance will impose a severe restriction on tight compositions. The only possible compromise would be the use of an appropriate close-up lens or extension ring. This rather expensive lens with 15 elements and weighing 1.5lbs. (685g) is optically sound, but, as already mentioned, the high number of elements may reduce image quality under poor lighting conditions.

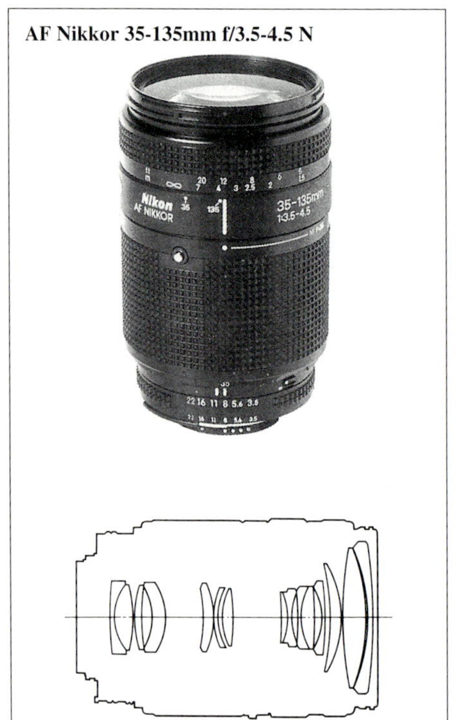

AF Nikkor 35-135mm f/3.5-4.5 N

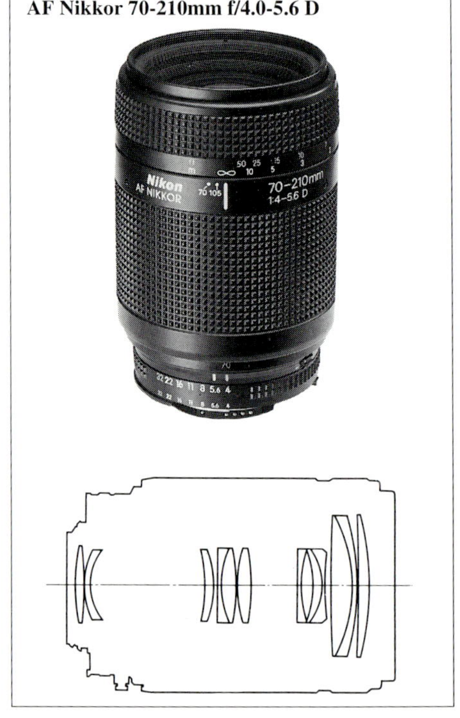

AF Nikkor 70-210mm f/4.0-5.6 D

AF Nikkor 70-210mm f/4.0-5.6 D: This lens should be considered the D equivalent of the standard telephoto zoom range that has been popular in 35mm photography since the days of Nikon's legendary 80-200 f/4.5 manual zoom of twenty years ago. This slightly longer and wider version offers a full 3x zoom range, with the same speed and focal length characteristics now available from every independent lens manufacturer. The lens has a macro range down to 3.9ft. (1.2m), is optically well corrected with 12 elements and is also compact and weighs 1.3lbs. (590g). Here again, the minimum focusing distance of 4.9ft. (1.5m) is not quite satisfactory, particularly in the shorter focal length range.

Applications: same as for the corresponding fixed focal lengths in its range, with limitations mentioned above. For professional requirements, this very good lens has to be measured against improved sharpness and brilliance that can be achieved using the appropriate fixed focal length lenses (85mm, 180 or 200mm) and against the superior performance, but much larger 80-200mm f/2.8 D ED Nikkor. There are differences in image quality, but they are slight and not necessarily critical for most photographers. The real advantage of the single focal length lenses and the ED zoom over the 70mm-210mm is speed.

Note: Transmission of the subject distance to the AF camera (it is a new D generation lens) can only be used with the N90/F90 to date.

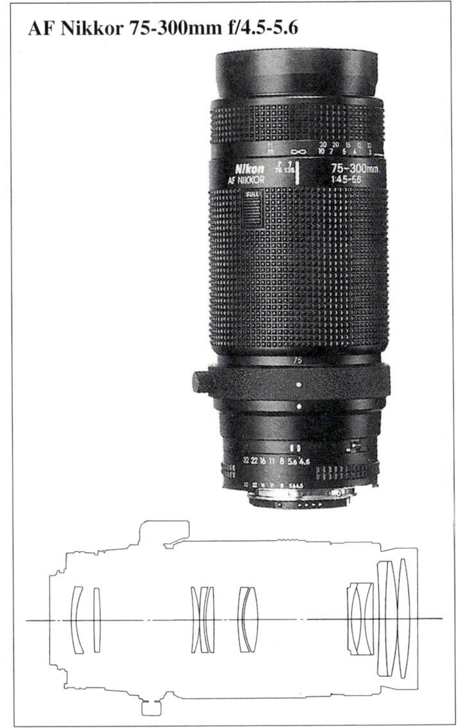

AF Nikkor 75-300mm f/4.5-5.6

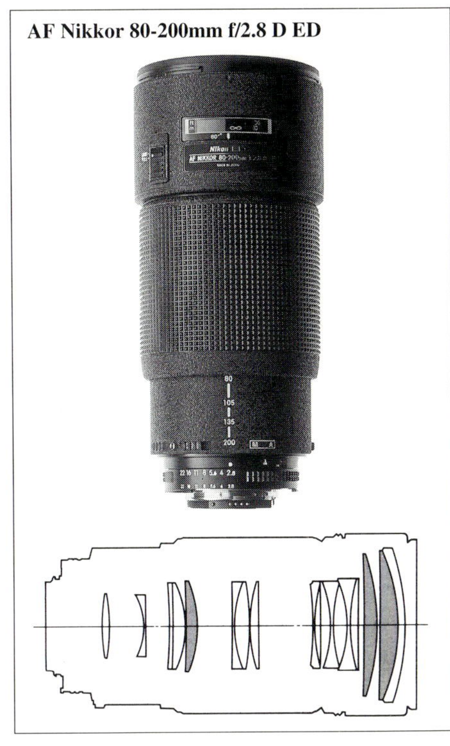

AF Nikkor 80-200mm f/2.8 D ED

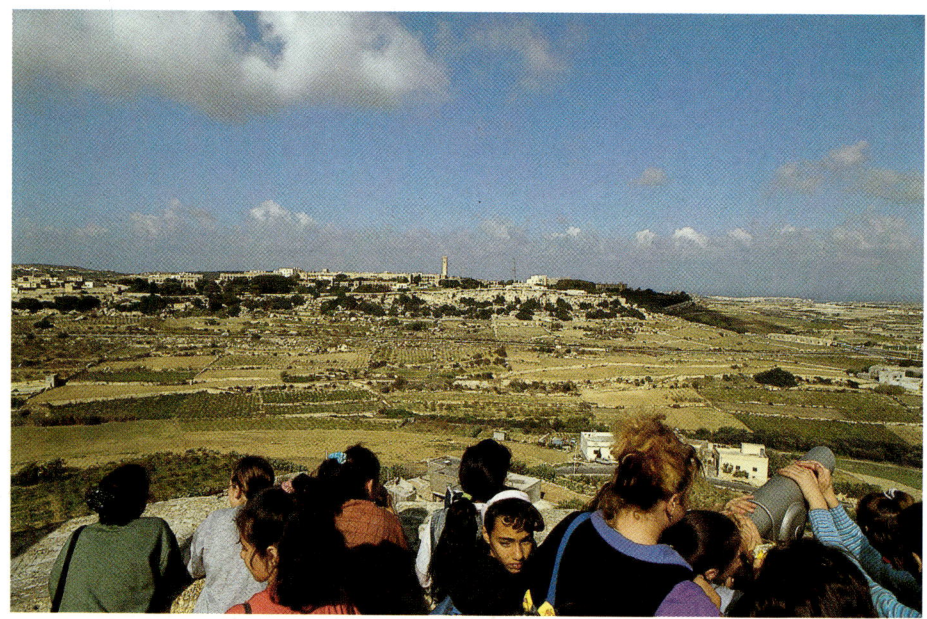

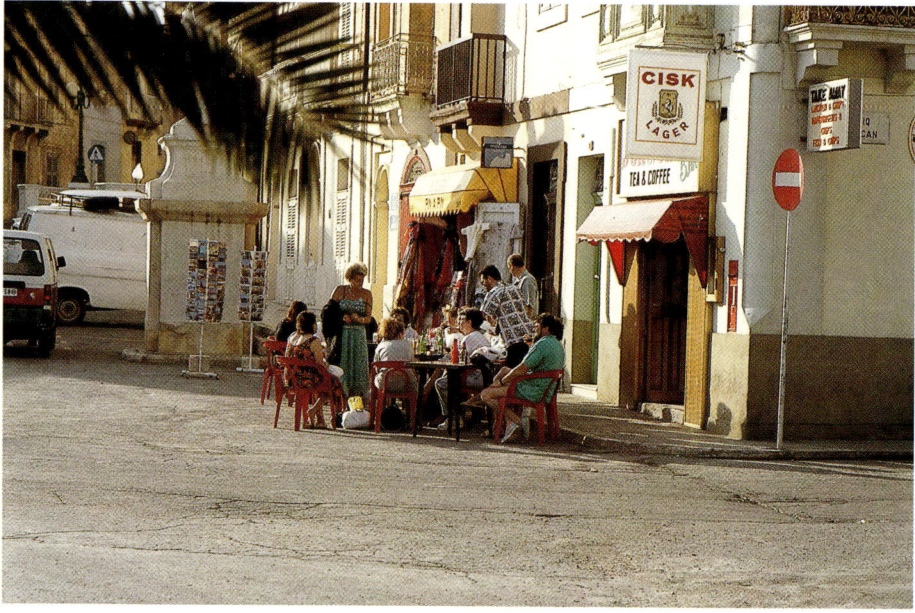

Even the most routine tourist snapshots can be troublesome in terms of exposure because of bright areas that can fool less sophisticated metering systems. In the landscape it is the large bright area of the sky that can cause over-exposure (20mm lens) while in the street scene the same effect can be caused by the white face of the building in the sun (180mm lens). Dual or multi-program modes of modern AF Nikons handle such lighting situations very well.

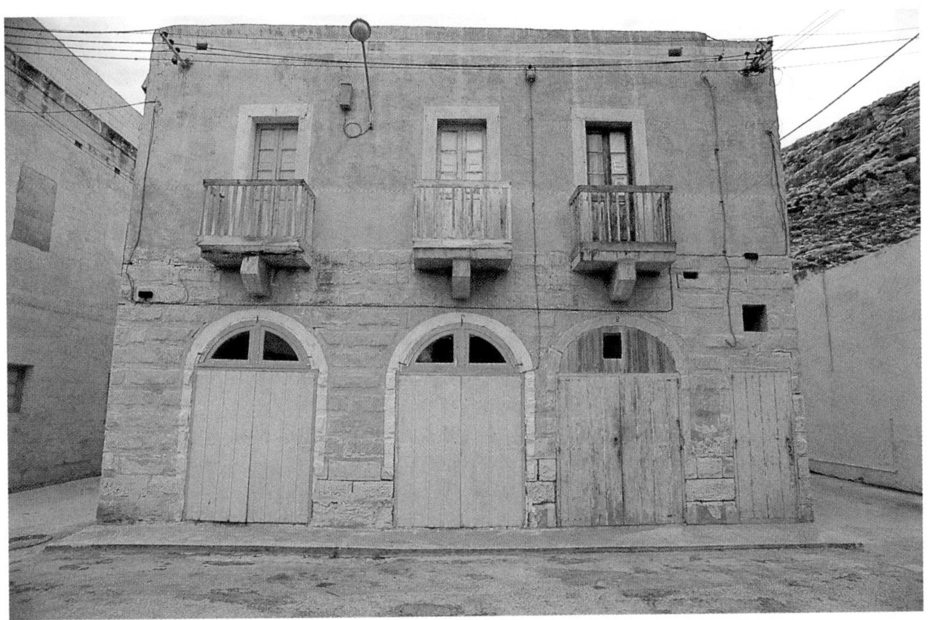

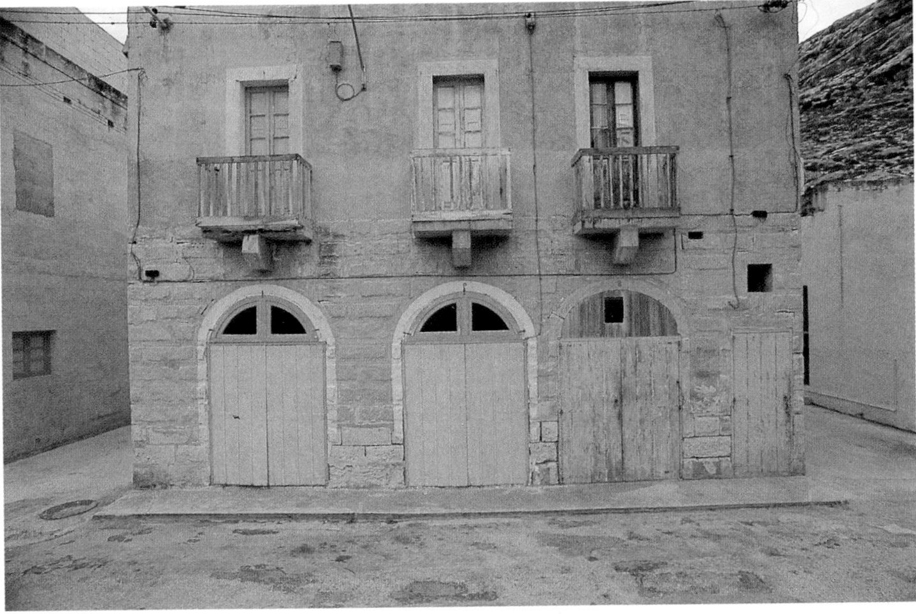

Converging lines: The top picture taken from street level shows typical convergence distortion because of the low point of view. The second image, taken from atop a wall is more or less distortion free thanks to the higher vantage point. An optimal image from the original low vantage point could only have been achieved with a PC shift lens.

AF Nikkor 75-300mm f/4.5-5.6: ***Applications:*** same as for the corresponding fixed focal lengths within its range. This is an exceptional good zoom that covers its wide range with near ED quality, though Nikon says it does not have any of this special glass in its construction. With a 4x telephoto range, it has a normal minimum focusing distance of 9.8ft. (3m), is very useful for the focal length range approaching 300mm, but in the shorter focal length range it is significantly greater. There is a macro range of 4.9ft. (1.5m) The lens has 13 elements and weighs 1.9lbs. (850g).

AF Nikkor 80-200mm f/2.8 ED: Identical to the AF Nikkor 80-200mm f/2.8 D ED with the exception of the automatic transmission of subject distance as described below.

AF Nikkor 80-200mm f/2.8 D ED: A fast telephoto zoom with constant f-stop throughout the zoom range. It is extremely well corrected using ED glass and a total of 16 elements. As already mentioned, however, the high number of elements may reduce brilliance under poor lighting conditions, though the correction of this lens holds down these detrimental effects as well. The normal minimum focusing distance is 5.9ft. (1.8m), the macro range is 4.9ft.(1.5m). The lens weighs 2.9lbs. (1300g), is suited to hand-held use, and can also be focused very accurately by hand (a wide ring with a gear system helps the manual feel). This lens focuses particularly fast in both manual and auto focus modes. In short, it is the ideal zoom if one prefers to focus manually with an AF camera on certain occasions, or if one wants to use this modern AF zoom on non-AF Nikons. There has been much written about the "need" for a tripod collar on this already large lens by those who like to operate it from a tripod or monopod.
Note: transmission of the subject distance to the AF camera (it is a new D generation lens) can only be used with the N90/F90 to date.
Applications: same as for the corresponding fixed focal lengths in its range, with the above-mentioned limitations. Because of its fast speed and suitability for manual focusing it is a favorite with reporters, sports photographers, wildlife photographers and other professionals who work in changing light conditions and action situations.

Special Purpose Lenses

Fisheye Lenses

The unique effect of fisheye lenses is derived from their curvilinear optical design which produces the characteristic spherical perspective. Some of the non-fisheye, wide-angle lenses

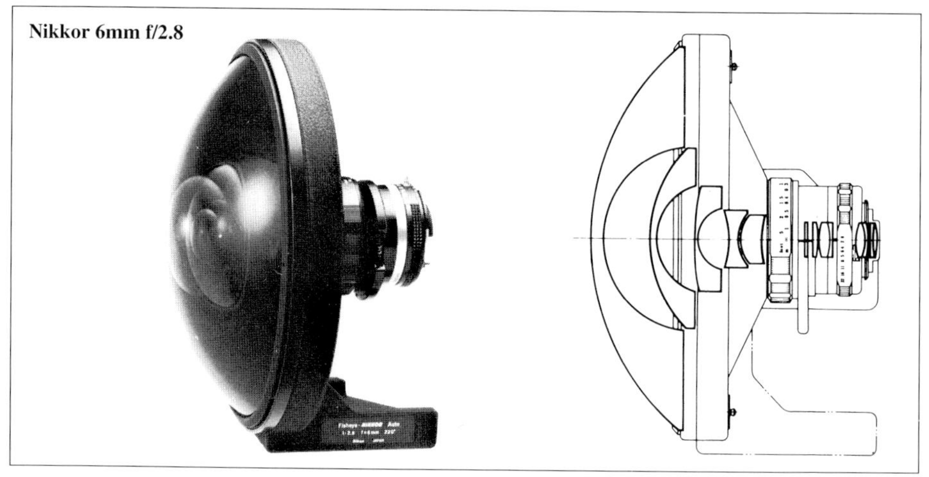
Nikkor 6mm f/2.8

Nikkor 8mm f/2.8

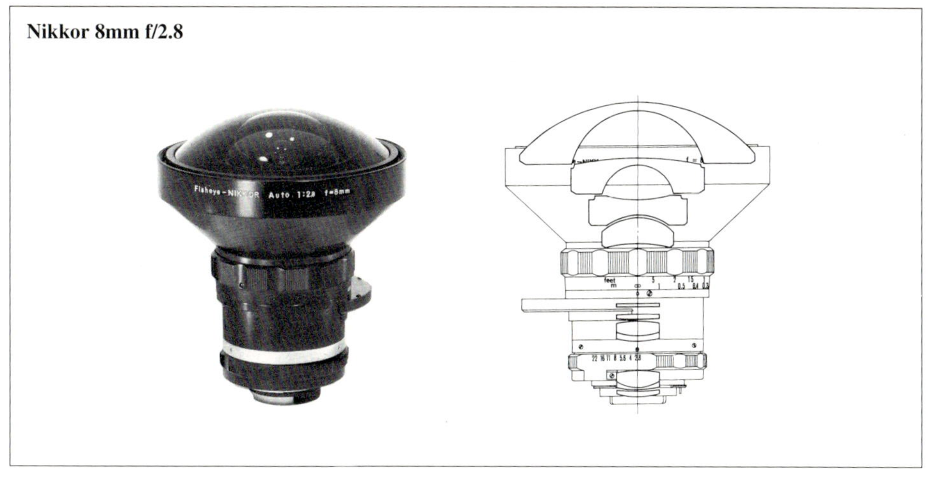

Nikkor 16mm f/2.8

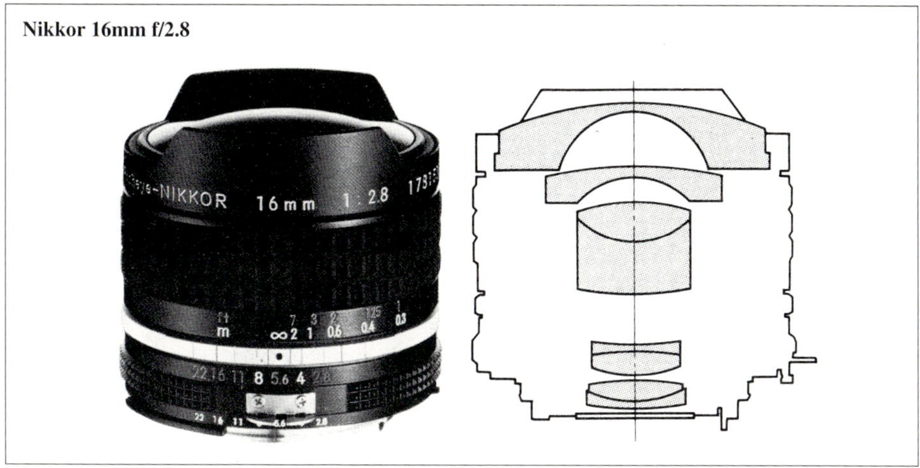

described earlier, are based on a rectilinear design in which straight lines appear straight, provided the camera is held parallel, level and at a distance to the subject. Fisheye optics will show straight lines as curved around the center of the field, regardless of the camera's placement. Only lines passing through the dead center of the field will appear straight. Thus, the further a line is away from the center, the more curved it appears in the image. What one sees in the image then is similar to looking at a mirrored ball, or through the "spy hole" in a door.

There are really two distinct varieties of this type of lens; the circular fisheye, in which the final image is a circle on film, and the semi-fisheye or "full-frame fisheye," in which the entire film frame is filled with this curvilinear perspective. Coupled with the spheric perspective of these lenses is a huge angle of coverage of up to 220°. The name hails from fishes' eyes that have a similarly large angle of view. They were originally used for aerial photography, meteorological and astronomical research as well as for technical monitoring applications. (In aerial photography, central perspective can be calculated from the spheric shape by computers if necessary.) Using fisheye lenses takes some getting used to as in being careful that one's own feet do not end up in the shot. These are special purpose lenses, especially in the case of the circular variety, and many professionals tend to rent them as needed. The semi-fisheye versions are, however, far more useful and, when used skillfully, produce some of the most dramatic images.

Fisheye Nikkor 6mm f/2.8: A heavy, 12 element beast weighing 11.4lbs. (5200g) with a length of 6.7in. (17cm) and a diameter of 9.4in. (24cm) that even an F4 can hide behind. It has an astonishing angle of view of 220° and close focus distance of 9.8in. (0.25m), with five built-in filters. *For applications:* see above.

Fisheye Nikkor 8mm f/2.8: In contrast to the preceding lens, this one weighs a mere 2.4lbs. (1100g) even though it "only" has an angle of 180° and uses only 10 elements. Close focus is 11.9in. (0.3m) and it has 5 built-in filters. *For applications:* see above.

AF Fisheye Nikkor 16mm f/2.8 D: This full-frame fisheye has a 180° angle of view over the diagonal section of the frame. Essentially, this full frame is achieved by increasing the size of the circular image until it covers the entire image area, so much of the curvilinear optical effect remains and becomes more obvious the closer the lens is held to a straight line subject. It has 8 elements and weighs 11.5oz. (325g) with a close focus distance of 9.8in. (0.25m). At a length of 2.2in. (55mm) and a 2.5in. (63mm) diameter, it is barely larger than a normal lens, which makes it easy to carry around for those occasional situations when this sort of extreme view is appropriate.

Although this lens is naturally unsuitable for conventional portraiture or architectural photography, some once-in-a-lifetime landscape or travel shots result with feel and experience. Quite frankly, when used appropriately, a semi-fisheye can produce some of the most dramatic if not unusual pictures, to say nothing of those times when its extreme wide angle is the only way to get the shot because of close shooting quarters. Note: Transmission of the focus distance to the camera (it is at the same time a lens of the new D generation) can only be used with the N90/F90 at the moment. For applications: See above.

Shift Lenses

What are Shift Lenses and how do they work? Shift or PC (perspective control) lenses, as they

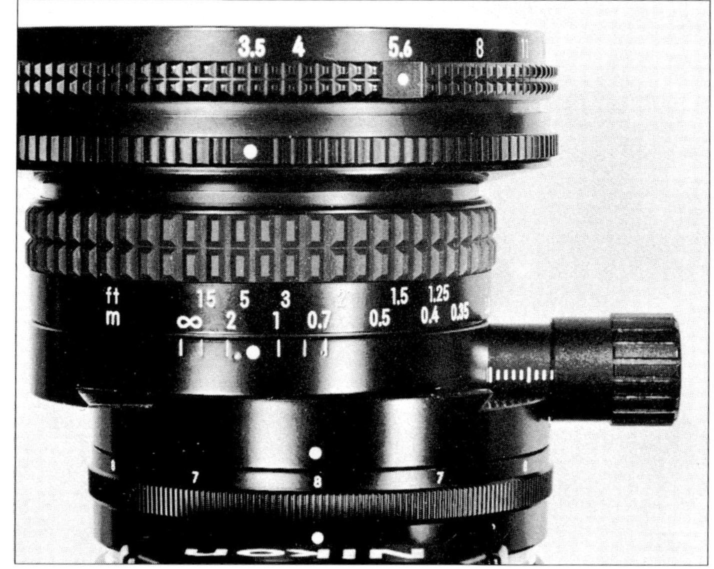

The amount of shift with a PC lens can be read off the shift knob on the side (8mm shown here). The white dot on the ring closest to the camera body is the maximum shift possible at the current settings without vignetting (also 8mm).

are also known, permit the front of the lens to move (that is, shift) a short distance while remaining parallel to the film plane, similar to what a large format camera is capable of. Also, like a typical large format lens, shift lenses for 35mm film must have a larger image circle to cover the image area as it is shifted off center. The main reason for using a shift lens is to compensate for converging lines that are caused when a camera, particularly in the case of a wide-angle lens, is tilted up or down. The result is the pyramid shaped convergence of the sides of a building, for example, toward the direction of the tilt. Typically, the camera is pointed up to take in more of the building and the result is those characteristic pyramid shaped walls. By returning the camera to a parallel position and just raising the lens in a shift, more of the building is placed on film, this time without convergence because the film and subject planes remain parallel.

Their main area of use with small format cameras is, understandably, in photographing architecture and in this regard the 28mm (versus the 35mm) version is far more useful. Nikkor shift lenses are also equipped with a circular plate that allows the user to revolve the shift mechanism so that the shift off center can be in any north-south-east-west direction. This means being able to correct for convergence when the camera is tilted down or up as well as shifting the lens left or right to "get around" an object, such as a telephone pole, when you cannot move the camera position. These shift lenses have preset aperture arrangements in which you focus and compose wide open and then set the f/stop for TTL-stopdown metering in the unshifted position. This is a bother, but that is the price of being able to make perspective controlled pictures. To precisely align the camera and lens, a tripod and a viewing screen with grid lines are recommended. The total shift distance of both lenses allow a shift of up to 11mm (with restrictions) from the normal optical center of the image.

PC Nikkor 28mm f/3.5: This 380g 13.4oz. lens has 9 elements with a close focus distance of 11.9in. (0.3m). It has an angle of view of 74° which is the same as a normal 28mm lens. Through the shift option of 11mm in all directions, a usable angle of 92° results, comparable, by the way, to a 21mm lens. Shifting the lens along each diagonal, taking 3 shots and mounting them together would result in an image that a 21mm lens would deliver horizontally with one shot.

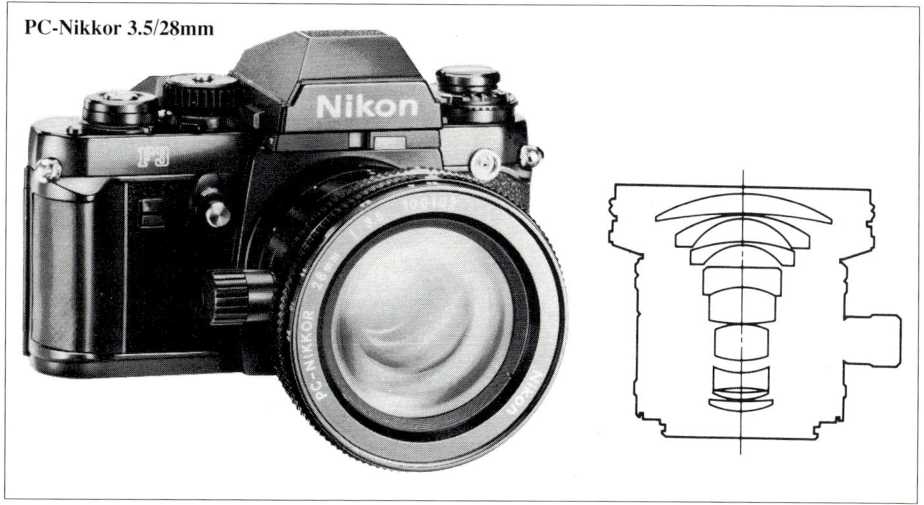

PC-Nikkor 3.5/28mm

PC-Nikkor 35mm f/2.8

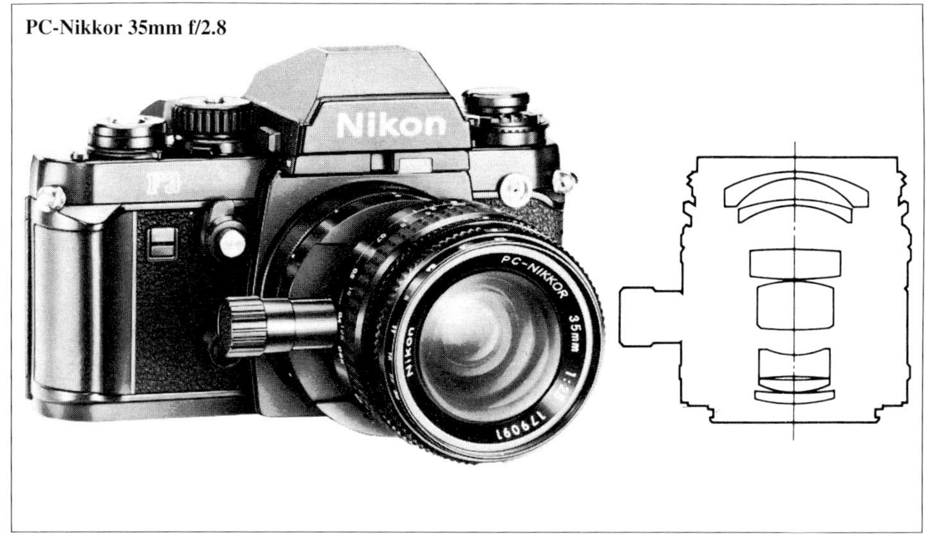

For applications: see above description of shift lenses.

PC Nikkor 35mm f/2.8: 7 elements; 11.3oz. (320g); close focus 11.9in. (0.3m); angle of view 62°; usable angle of view 78°. For applications: see above. Compared to the 28mm f/3.5, significantly less correction than the 28mm because of the narrower angle of view.

Macro Lenses

The specialized macro lenses from Nikon that carry the names "medical" or "micro" can achieve magnification ratios of 1:2 or 1:1 without extension tubes or close-up filters and are optimized optically for macro work as well. The AF-Micro Nikkor 60mm f/2.8 and the AF-Micro Nikkor 105mm f/2.8 have been covered above since they are a real alternative to the corresponding "normal" fixed focal length lenses for general picture taking as well as for close-up work.

Note: Important information regarding macro lenses can also be found in the Macro Accessories chapter.

AF-Micro Nikkor 60mm f/2.8: See above under fixed focal length lenses.

AF-Micro Nikkor 105mm f/2.8: See above under fixed focal length lenses.

Medical Nikkor 120mm f/4 IF: A specialized lens for close-up work in the range of 5.2ft. (1.6m) at 1:11 to 11.9in. (0.35m) at 1:1 only, and with a special close-up filter up to 2:1. The lens has 9 elements and weighs 2lbs. (890g). It has a built-in ring flash with modeling light that is designed specially for medical or dental applications. The reproduction scale can be super-imposed onto the image. If the focal length is not long enough, the TC-14A/B teleconverter can extend the focal length through a factor of 1.4 to 170mm. The flash requires a separate battery pack that takes eight 1.5V alkaline batteries. Since this lens was designed before TTL was widely available, the medical Nikkor has a completely different "flash automation" system. The flash output is calibrated according to the focus distance (set manually). Apparently, this is a macro flash control method that could not be improved to date. ***Applications:*** Dentists, pathologists, surgeons, collectors, product photographers. Ease of handling is the strong point for taking strictly macro range documentation-type photographs as opposed to offering features for creative control.

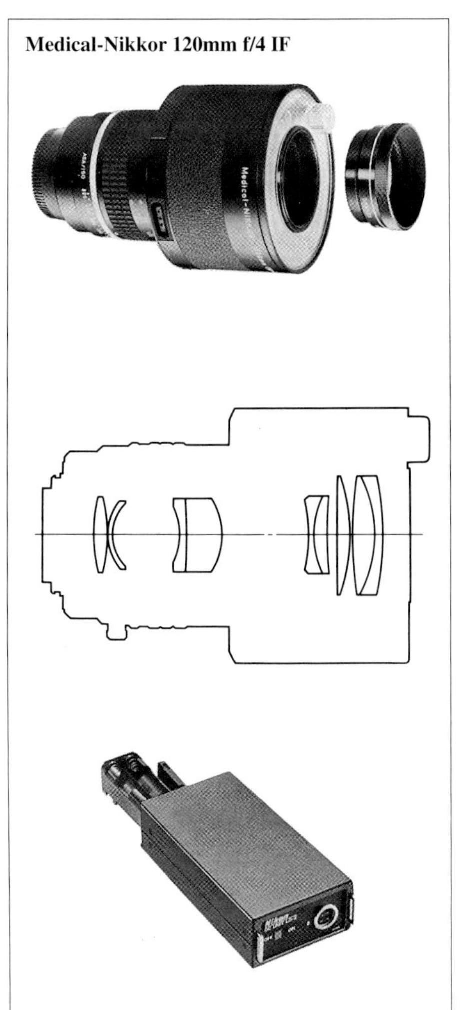

Medical-Nikkor 120mm f/4 IF

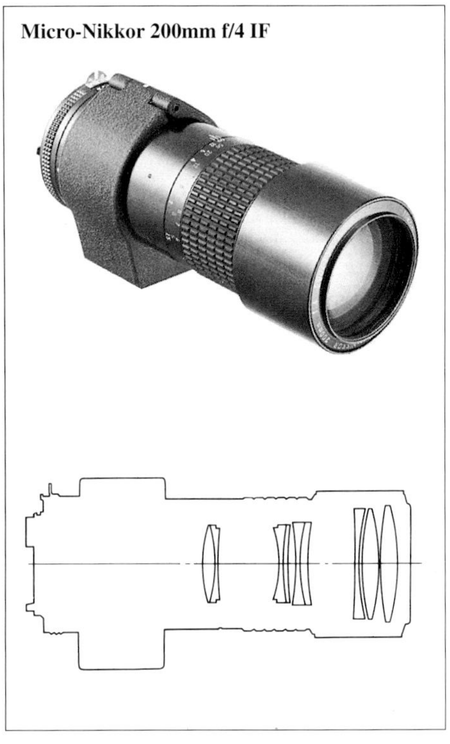

Micro-Nikkor 200mm f/4 IF

Micro-Nikkor 200mm f/4 IF: 9 Elements, 1.8lbs. (800g) and a close focus distance of 2.3ft. (0.71m) with a magnification ratio of 2:1. It has internal focusing, a rotatable tripod mount and is corrected for distance photography as well. In order to obtain 1:1 macro, one can use either two PN-11 extension tubes (now discontinued) or a TC300/301 or TC-200/201 teleconverter.

Applications: Macro photographs that have to be taken from a greater distance.

Teleconverters

These devices are intended to fit between the lens and the body of the camera. A teleconverter contains its own lens elements which functions to multiply the focal length of the prime lens. Thus, a 2X converter will change a 200mm lens to a 400mm lens and a 1.4X will produce a 280mm lens. There is a loss of light in this process such that one more stop exposure is needed for the 1.4X and two stops for the 2X version. Early teleconverters significantly reduced the image quality of the prime lens and, in fact, Nikon did not even make them. But in 1978, Nikon took the leap and has been producing converters ever since. Today, the quality of those converters that increase focal length by about half are so good that pros in sport and nature photography use them routinely. With the exception of the TC-20, the quality with 2X converters is not quite as good, but certainly more than acceptable in most cases.

A rough guideline for the compatibility of Nikon lenses and teleconverters is that the TC-14A (1.4x) and TC-201 (2x) are made for lenses shorter than 300mm and only give good results with these. They can be used with longer focal lengths if necessary, but one should be prepared for vignetting or lower image quality. To counteract this reduction in quality, the teleconverters TC-14B (1.4x) and TC-301 (2x) have elements that extend into the lens they are mounted on. These converters are thus intended for lenses with focal lengths of 300mm or longer whose back elements are recessed into the housing. They can, therefore, not be used with shorter focal length lenses

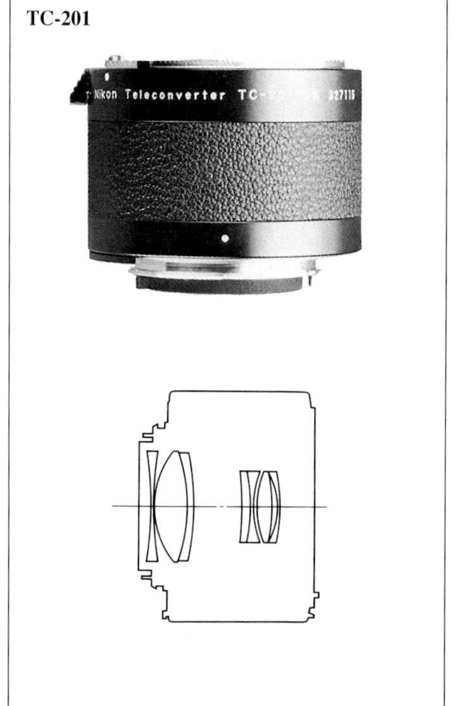

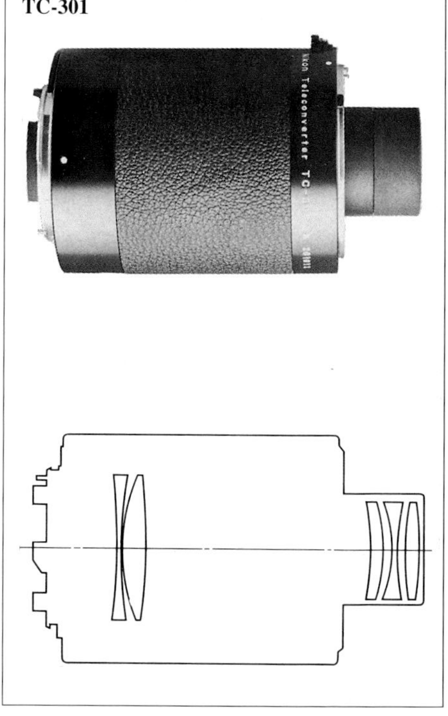

that have back elements that come up to, or even extend beyond, the bayonet mounting ring. The only exceptions are the 105mm and 200mm Micro Nikkors.

Important note regarding converter/lens compatibility: Some converters have elements that protrude beyond the bayonet mounting ring. These converters are therefore only compatible with lenses that have a sufficiently recessed rear element. If you are not sure if your lens is compatible with a given converter, you should ask Nikon or carefully read the instruction manual that comes with your converter. The compatibility of certain converters with the AF and exposure automation differs from camera to camera. So again, you are urged to carefully read the instruction manuals of camera, lens and converter.

AF TC-16A Converter: The TC-16A converter has a movable element that can be focused by a camera's AF mechanism. It is designed for use with a non-AF lens on an AF body such as the N8008/F-801, N90/F90 and F4. Since this movement is limited to about 5mm, the range of focus distances with longer focal lengths is constrained. The focus must be roughly pre-set manually on the lens. Even here, the combined maximum aperture of lens and converter cannot be more than f/5.6 if the camera's AF automatic should focus. (The TC-16A cannot be used with every Nikon AF reflex camera; check the camera manual.)

TC-14E Converter: This unit is specially designed to lengthen the focal lengths of the AF-I Nikkors 300mm f/2.8 D IF-ED, 400mm

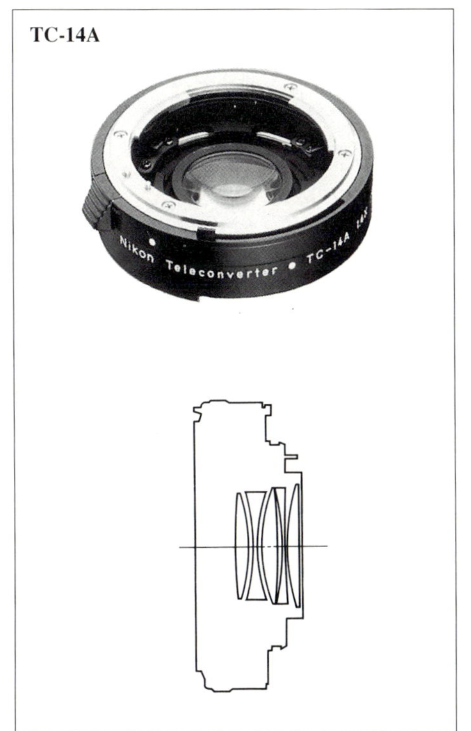

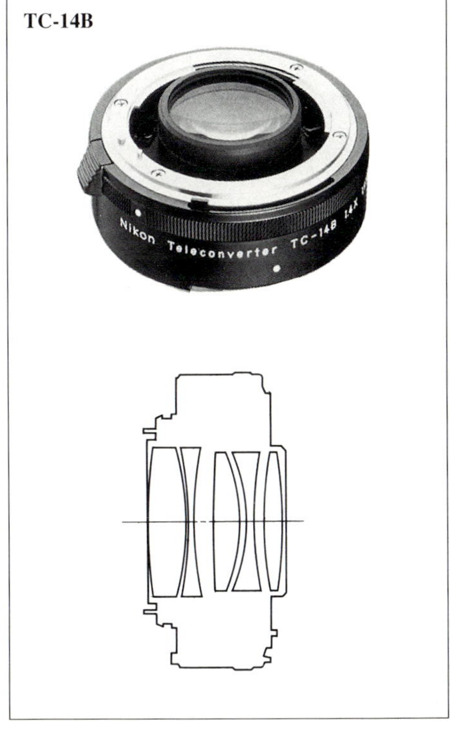

f/2.8 D IF-ED and 600mm f/4 D IF-ED and increase focal length by a factor of 1.4. The design principle was to maintain the image quality as much as possible with an optimum speed of focusing. Since the speed of the lens only drops by 1 stop, it does not reduce the maximum aperture below the f/5.6 cutoff and so these lenses remain fully AF compatible. *Note:* According to Nikon, this converter is not compatible with lenses other than the AF-I Nikkors.

TC-20E Converter: This converter is specially designed to lengthen the AF-I Nikkors 300mm f/2.8 D IF-ED and 400mm D IF-ED by a factor of 2. The basic design principle was to maintain the image quality as much as possible with an optimum focusing speed. Since the speed of the lenses drops by 2 stops, the 300mm and 400mm remain fully AF compatible, while the 600mm falls above the f/5.6 cutoff and has to be manually focused. *Note:* According to Nikon, this teleconverter is not compatible with lenses other than the AF-I Nikkors.

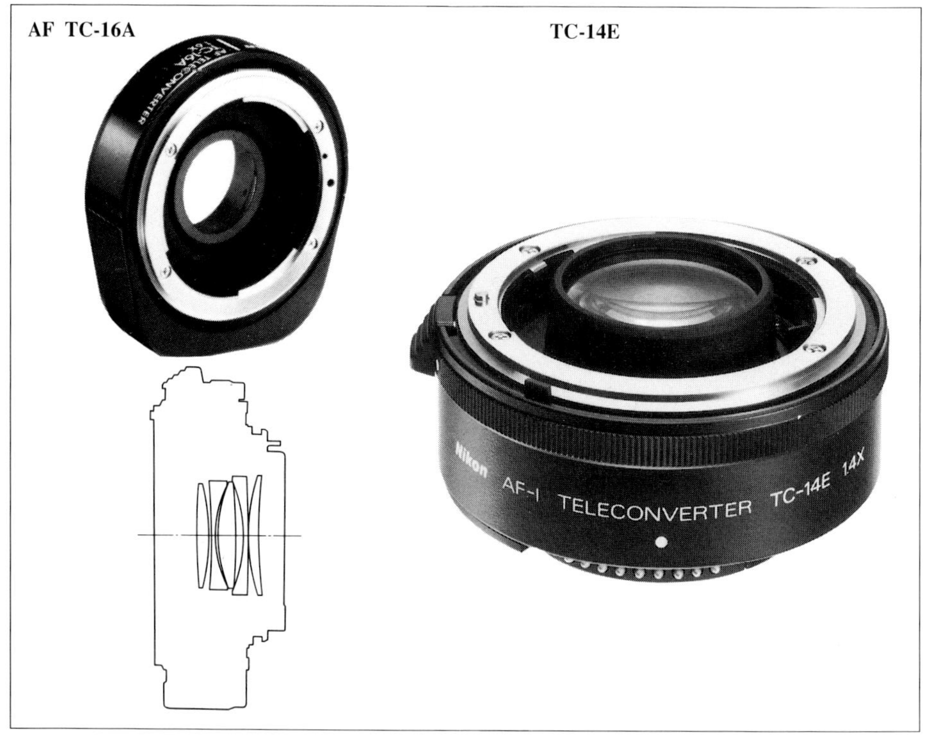

	Effect on Focal Length	Light Loss in EV	Number of Elements/Groups	Weight oz./g	Size in inches	Lens Type	Focal Length Compatibility *	Camera-Compatibility **
Teleconverter								
TC-201	x2	2	7 / 5	8.1/230	2x2.5	AI-S	A	F
TC-301	x2	2	5 / 5	9.8/280	4.5x2.5	AI-S	B	F
TC-14A	x1.4	1	5 / 5	5.1/145	1x2.5	AI-S	A	F
TC-14B	x1.4	1	5 / 5	5.8/165	1.3x2.5	AI-S	B	F
TC-16A AF	x1.6	11/3	5 / 5	5.3/150	1.2x2.7	AF (AI-S)	C	G
TC-14E AF-I	x1.4	1	5 / 5	7.0/200	0.9x2.6	AF-I	D	H
TC-20E AF-I	x2	2	7 / 6	11.9/340	2.2x2.5	AF-I	E	H

* See the actual lens instruction manual.

** See the camera instruction manual.

A Recommended for focal lengths up to 200mm.

B Recommended for focal lengths over 300mm. These converters have elements that protrude past the bayonet mount and hence into the lens itself. They can therefore only be used with shorter focal lengths if there is sufficient distance between bayonet and rear element.

C AF mode only with lenses of f/3.5 or faster. Otherwise compatible with all focal lengths of mechanical lenses.

D Only AF-I lenses of f/4 and faster. Slower AF-I lenses only with manual focus.

E Only with AF-I lenses of f/2.8 and faster. Slower AF-I lense only with manual focusing.

F With all non-AF and AF cameras (no AF functions though!)

G Only for certain AF cameras (N8008, F4, N90). Only some meter and exposure modes function.

H Autofocus possible only with F4 or N90/F90 (see also D or E).

TC-20E

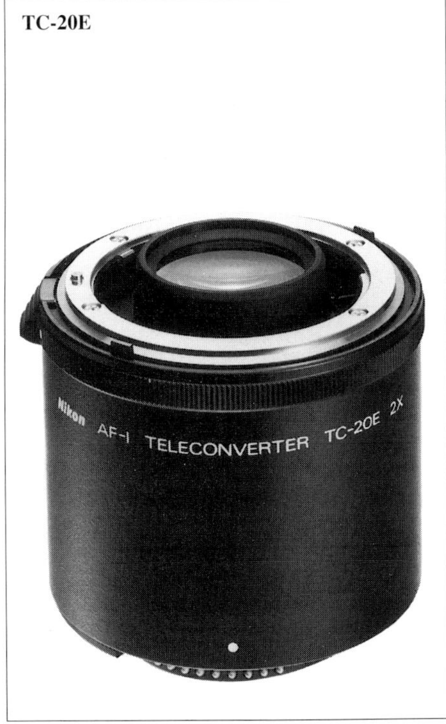

Focal length and perspective: The perspective differences between lenses are particularly apparent when the size of the subject is kept constant and the background is very deep. While the normal focal length of a 50mm lens (left side) is roughly equivalent to the perspective of the human eye, the 16mm fisheye (right side, top left) makes the background seem very deep and distorts the lines in the foreground. The main subject and background are less distorted since their straight lines pass approximately through the center of the image. With the 20mm wide angle (right side, top right), the foreground is no longer so completely overpowering and the spheric distortions are minimal when compared to the fisheye. The 180mm telephoto lens (right side, bottom left) reduces the depth of the image and brings the background closer to the subject (compression). This effect is even more noticeable with the 300mm (right side, bottom right).

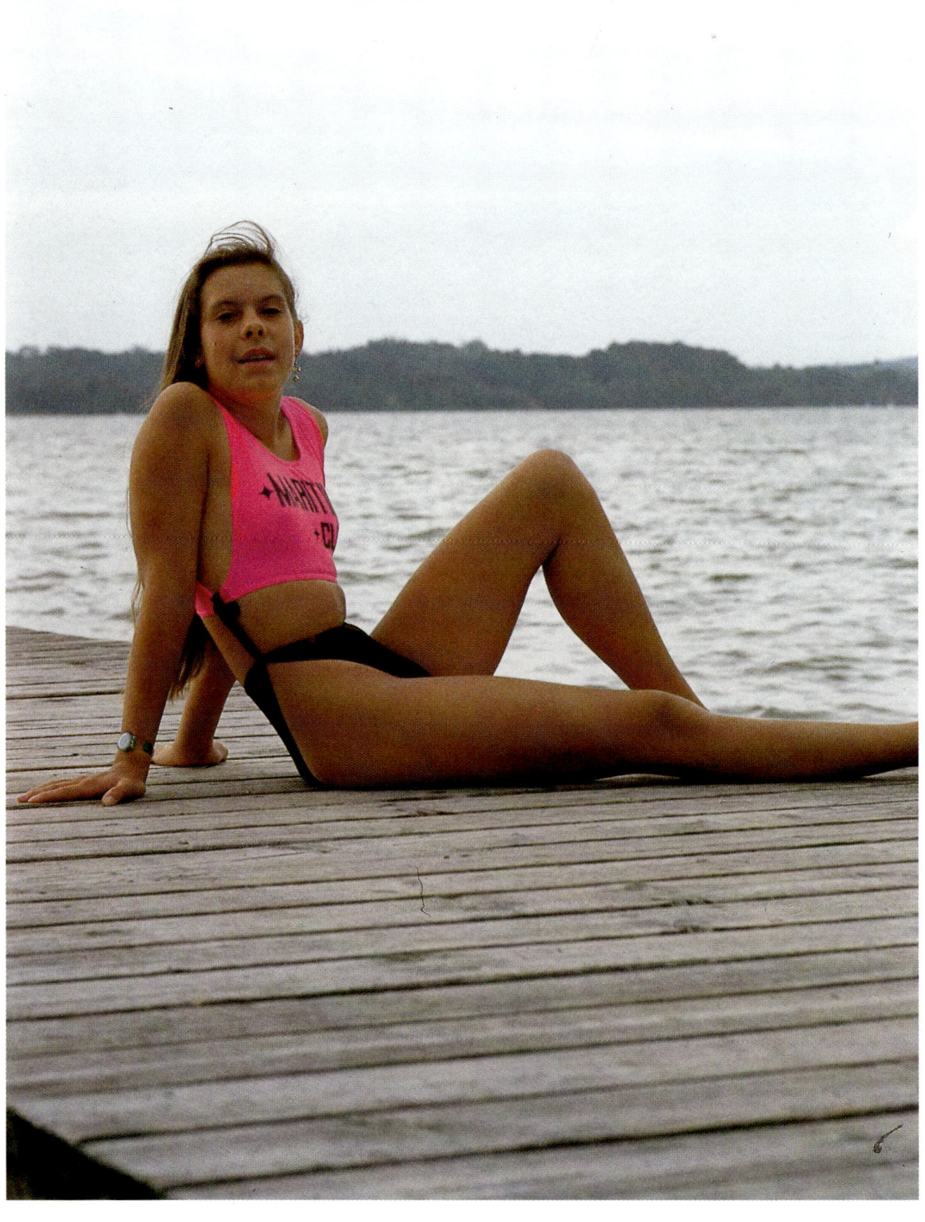

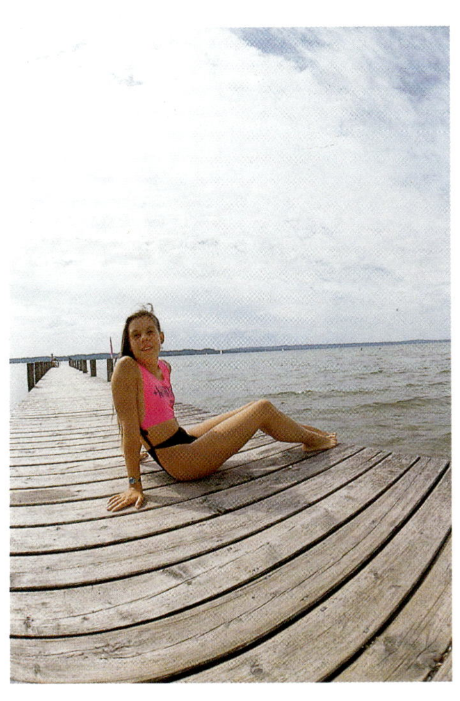

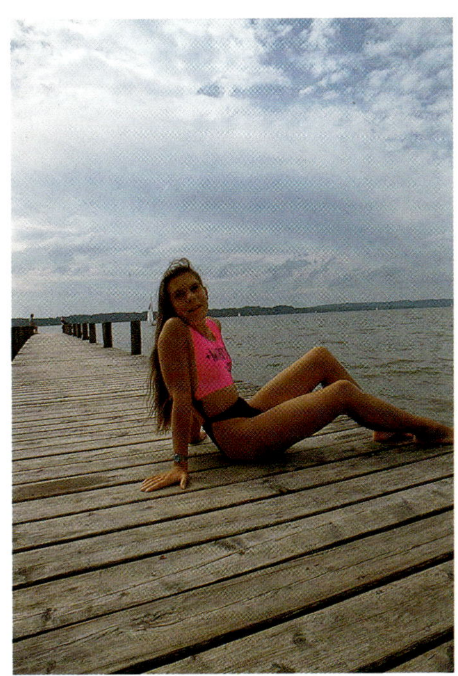

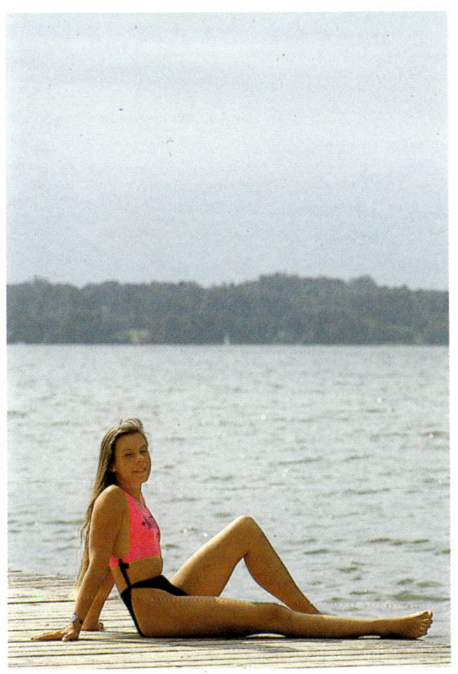

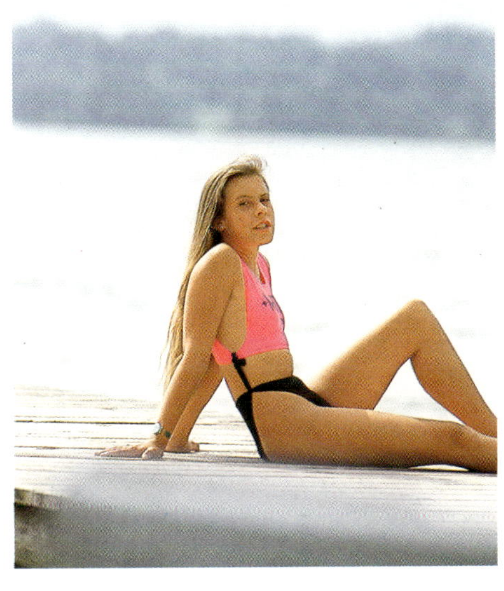

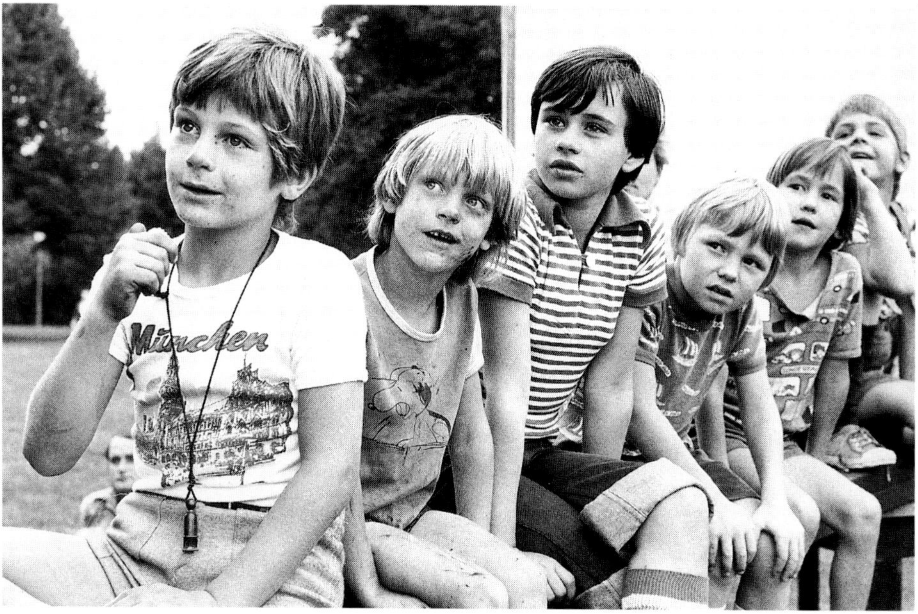

The expressions of children captured during a theater presentation. The photo demonstrates the need to make decisions about depth of field. A focus point has to be chosen along with an appropriate camera position so that everyone is in focus. Photo: Rudolf Dietrich.

UV-Micro-Nikkor 105mm f/4.5

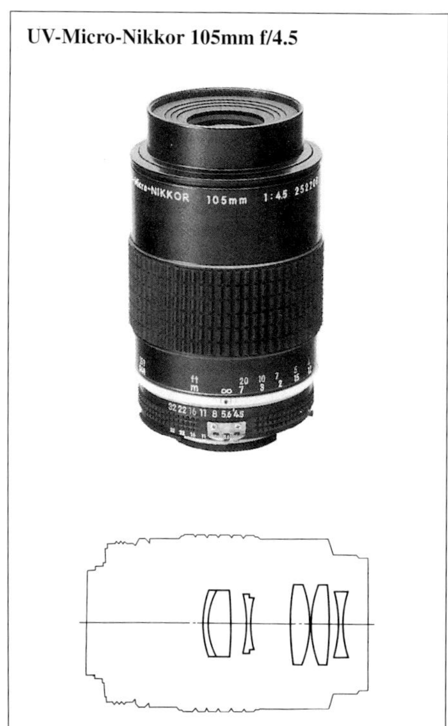

Other Special Purpose Lenses

UV-Nikkor 105mm f/4.5: A specialized lens for photography with UV light, constructed with 6 elements made of fluoride and quartz glass so that UV radiation can pass easily through the lens system. Most lenses allow wavelengths from 220nm in the UV region through the visible spectrum from 400-750nm into the infra-red region of 1100nm to pass through. In order to do pure UV photography, a specialized filter transmits only the invisible UV rays from 200-400nm out is necessary. It can be combined with a specialized SB-140 flash unit that produces UV and infra-red thanks to a filter. Special applications: This lens, which can be focused to 1:2, is used primarily for scientific, medical and forensic purposes.

NOCT-Nikkor 58mm f/1.2: See above, fixed focal length lenses.

Magnifying lenses: See section, Macro Photography with Close-Up Filters, p. 140.

Choosing the Right Lens

Zoom or Fixed Focal Length?

Not too long ago zoom lenses were consider second best in quality to single focal length lenses. That is no longer the case. Most of the top zoom lenses are now equaling the performance of their single focal length counterparts in the middle stop range, and some wide open. Certainly, the zoom lenses have advantages inherent in their design. They represent a range of focal lengths, so there is no need to change lenses when taking pictures, which makes the photographer a faster and more flexible shooter. You do not have to carry as many lenses around, and zoom lenses are usually cheaper than the combined cost of the equivalent individual focal length lenses. (Whether this is true in every case, however, depends on the range of focal lengths involved).

Price and quality: it is often said that zoom lenses represent a particularly good value. Certainly, a good zoom lens will generally cost less than two fixed focal length lenses. But whether or not this represents good value depends on the quality of the lens. Any zoom lens which matches up with a fixed focal length lens in terms of quality will cost a lot of money. It is only possible to construct zoom lenses which are as sharp as high-quality fixed focal length lenses by using special types of glass and element forms, floating elements and high-precision mechanics. If the zoom is to be as fast as the fixed focal length lens, the technical investment required to provide excellent performance in terms of preventing flare and ghost images ("brilliance") is very costly.

Zoom lenses are, as a rule, generally slower, and because their construction includes many more elements, they are also larger and heavier as a single unit. These extra elements are necessary to correct most optical defects and despite multi-coating, these extra surfaces will affect contrast and make the lens more susceptible to flare. Another disadvantage is that, even with well-corrected lenses, slight pincushion- or barrel-formed distortions can occur which are easier to rectify with fixed focal length lenses. The problem is that the necessary corrective measures for shorter focal lengths run counter to those for longer focal lengths, so that the distortions become more apparent as one approaches the two extreme focal lengths of a wide to telephoto zoom lens. Zoom lenses are therefore less suitable for such exacting situations as architectural photography and reproduction work, since straight lines near the edges of the frame might be reproduced with convex or concave curvature. In addition, zooms with a wide angle range tend, at this setting, to be affected by vignetting in the corners of the frame which only disappears when the lens is stopped down. Even the tendency towards particularly light, fast and, above all, small zoom lenses, including AF zooms, is a retrograde step in terms of optical quality, since these desirable physical characteristics, that make the lens so easy to use, work against what is needed for the best correction.

So when buying a lens, it is generally a good idea to look at the number of elements in the design as an indication (in theory at least) of how well corrected the lens is. With the disclaimers for critical copy and architectural work aside, today's best zooms are nothing short of remarkably delivering very good to excellent images for the working pro and serious photographer and snap shooter alike. The decision to buy a zoom versus a fixed focal length lens should really be made more on the grounds of how fast your lens needs to be, the weight of the equipment carried, and the shooting situation itself. For example, do you need to change focal lengths very quickly as in an action situation, or do you favor the "look" of a particular focal length rather than worry about any great differences in quality. Listed below are some of the specifics of this type of comparison.

Weight and volume: if we compare the AF lenses in the range 70mm to 210mm: the fixed focal length AF 85mm, f/1.8 has 6 elements, weighs 14.6oz. (415g) and is 2.3in. (58mm)

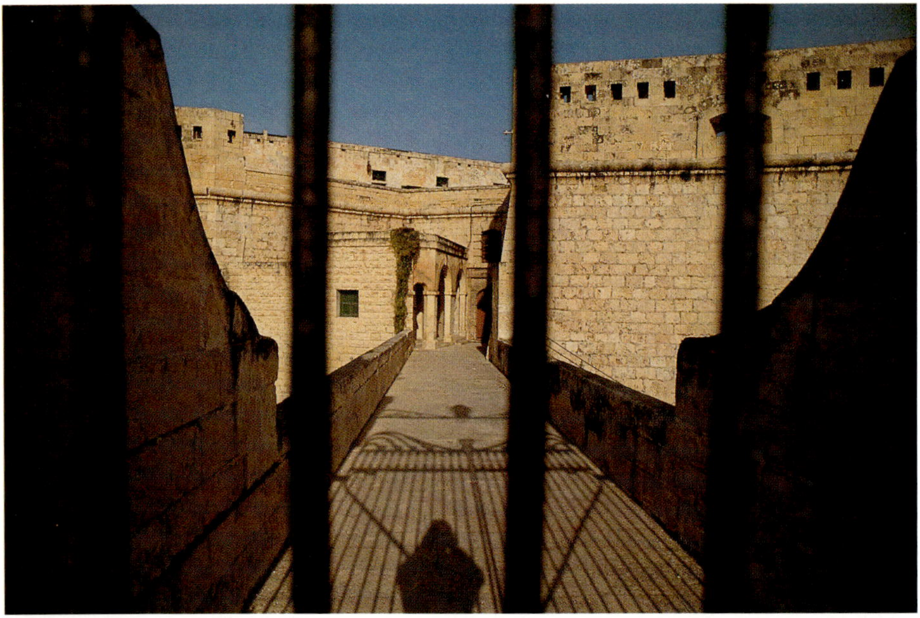

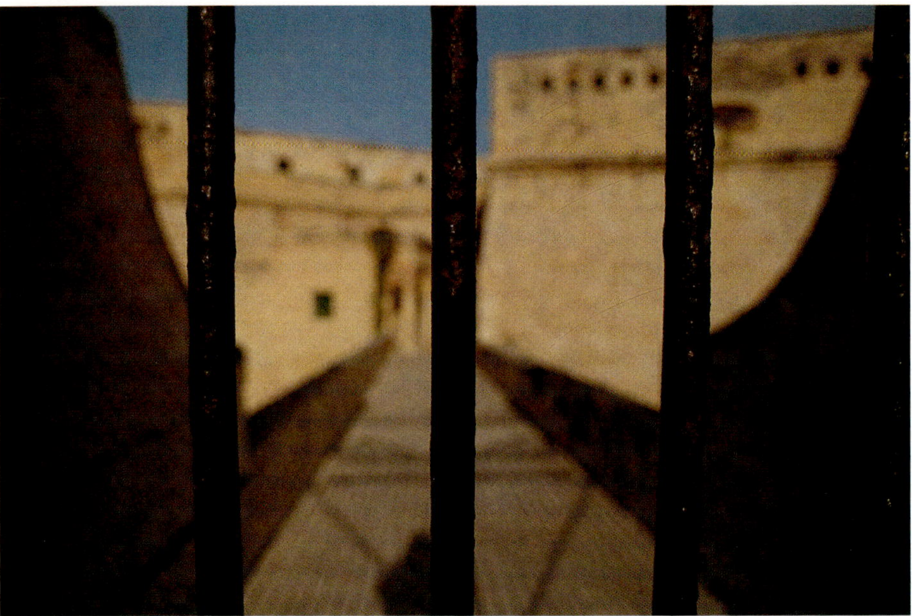

The decision as to what will be in focus with an autofocus camera is a matter of where the photographer chooses to place the focus point as shown in these two examples with very different effects. The fact that the camera has autofocus does not mean that the photographer has surrendered control over the image; on the contrary, this camera function actually gives him more control when used to its fullest potential.

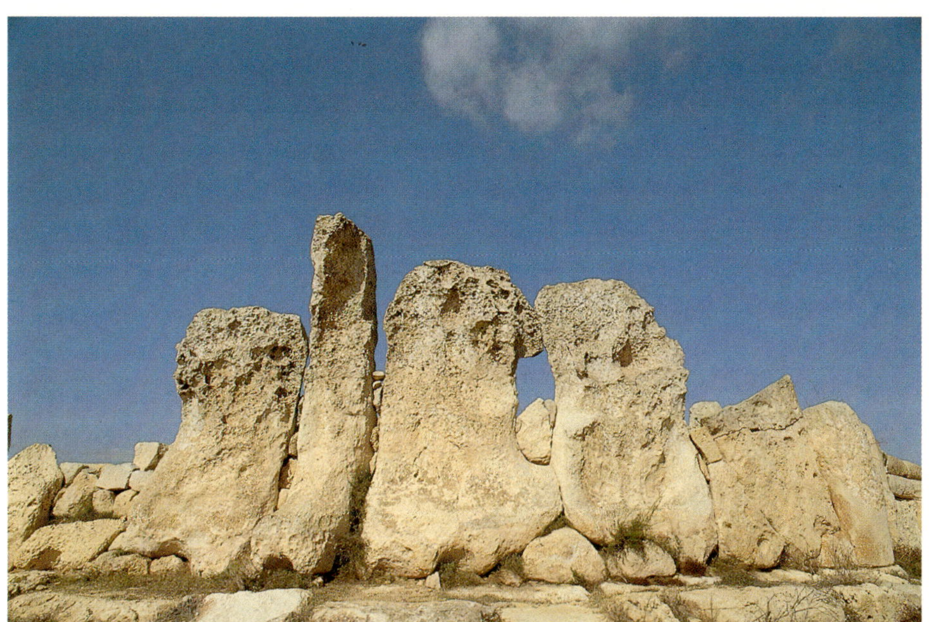

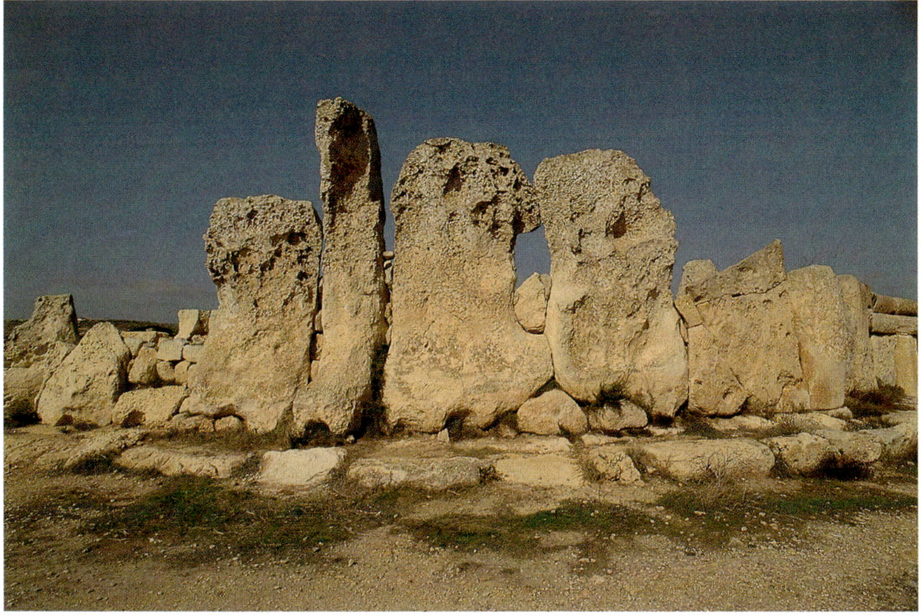

Matrix metering and image area: Matrix metering determines the correct exposure values according to the illumination of the main subject. However, the accuracy of matrix metering is dependent, among other things, on the overall subject brightness, the size of the main subject and its reflective properties. The photographer needs to be aware of this when using the camera's meter to read a scene.

long. The fixed focal length lens AF 180mm, f/2.8 IF-D has 8 elements, weighs 26.4oz. (750g) and is 5.7in. (144mm) long. The comparable AF 70-210mm, f/4-5.6 zoom is, at 20.8oz. (590g), only half as heavy and, with a length of 4.3in. (108mm), slightly more compact than the two fixed focal length lenses together. However, in terms of speed and optical quality, the zoom is clearly inferior to the two fixed focal length lenses. Nor is the AF 80-200mm, f/2.8 ED zoom entirely convincing as an alternative. Even though it is fast, and the optical quality is in most cases excellent, despite the 16 elements, its weight of 42.3oz. (1200g) already equals the total weight of the two fixed focal length lenses. And its length of 6.9in. (176mm), with a diameter of 3.3in. (85mm) makes it fairly bulky. Even though you shouldn't really weigh speed and optical quality against size and weight, the fixed focal length lenses come out quite well, even by this comparison. On the other hand, what is inescapable is the speed at which a zoom can change focal lengths.

Zooms as a compromise: even more so than with fixed focal length lenses, any zoom lens is a compromise involving range of focal lengths, quality of reproduction, speed, weight, size, and price. On the other hand, the basic amount of technology required by a fixed focal length lens is less, so, in theory at least, they should be less expensive, or they should contain more complex technology than a zoom lens of the same price. However, since modern zoom lenses are usually manufactured on a larger scale than conventional fixed focal length lenses, most manufacturers of zoom lenses have more than compensated for this price disadvantage. Whether the economic advantages of this mass production is passed on to the customer, or invested in more or improved technology, nobody can say. The retail price is a subject of its own, in any case, since the pricing policies of most manufacturers (including Nikon) are rather obscure. The important thing is that Nikon offers a whole selection of zoom lenses in the range 28mm to 105mm, with the emphasis on price, compactness or optical quality varying from model to model. This allows the user to choose the best compromise for their purposes.

Practical disadvantages: in order to keep zooms light and compact while achieving an acceptable degree of sharpness, their initial speed is often very low and usually decreases by a further stop towards maximum focal length. This is not a disadvantage if one is going to stop down the lens in any case and allow the autofocus facility to take care of focusing (it can sometimes be quite difficult to focus a lens of f/5.6 manually). The focal-length related variation in the effective aperture of a zoom lens can, however, prove to be very inconvenient when using flash in the studio, when it is only possible to set the right aperture value using a separate flash exposure meter. In order to achieve consistent exposure of negatives or, worse still, transparencies, it is often necessary to correct the setting whenever one changes the focal length. A further disadvantage is the usually unsatisfactory correction of a zoom lens in the close-up range, which is why the minimum focusing distance is often inadequate. In conclusion, it can be said that the claim that fixed focal length lenses are a thing of the past is just as mistaken as the assertion that zooms are a waste of time. However, if you are looking for maximum optical quality at a particular focal length, you will have to carefully examine the choices and assume that it is only at the wide open apertures that the fixed focal length still maintains an overall lead in quality as well as in the wider maximum aperture setting. This is probably the reason why Nikon now offers a very balanced range of zoom lenses and fixed focal length lenses.

Criteria for Lens Quality

Lens quality is revealed in a number of ways. Among the key points are sharpness, freedom from distortion, no falloff in illumination towards the edge of the frame, sharpness at close and long range, lack of chromatic and spherical aberration, mechanical robustness, and accuracy of manual setting.

Distortion, loss of light: these are particular problems with wide-angle lenses. Due to their construction, wide-angle lenses suffer from a significantly greater loss of light from the center of the frame to the edges, than occurs with standard lenses. This effect becomes increasingly evident with decreasing focal lengths. Extreme wide-angle lenses are also affected by distortion which is particularly noticeable towards the edges of the frame. This also becomes more apparent at shorter focal lengths. These typical wide-angle defects have largely been corrected in modern, high-quality lenses.

Optimization for close and long range: previously, it was not possible to optimize lenses so that they performed equally well at both close and long range. Lenses were either optimized for infinity or for the close-up range. That is to say, their defects were minimized either when set to infinity, or when set to a short distance. Today, typical close-up defects, such as barrel distortion or aperture aberration, can largely be corrected with the help of additional moving optical elements. Whereas, with most normal lenses, two main groups of elements shift their positions relative to one another, these lenses also feature a third group of elements which shifts between the other two groups. Using this close-range correction (CRC), Nikon has made some of their lenses equally suitable for both normal shots and close-up photography. This technology has also been incorporated in the construction of Nikon zoom lenses, such as today's AF zoom lenses.

Chromatic aberration and ED lenses: chromatic aberration plays an unpleasant role in lenses with long focal lengths. It is very difficult to get blue, green and red light to focus at a common focal point, and the failure to do so causes bands of colored outlines which obviously effect sharpness. Of course, all modern lenses are achromatic, which provides a certain degree of chromatic correction, so that actual rainbow effects are seldom seen nowadays. But that does not mean to say that outlines will be perfectly sharp. Only true apochromatic lenses can guarantee this. These are constructed using types of glass with extremely low dispersion characteristics, so-called LD or ED glass (Low or Extraordinary Dispersion), which facilitate the focusing of the three colors as close to the same point as physically possible. With these glasses, there is virtually no separation of the light into its spectral components and this separation is balanced in such a way, that the use of these glasses within the total combination of elements in the lens results in virtually zero chromatic aberration. Most modern Nikkors and AF-Nikkors with a focal length of 180mm or above contain elements of ED glass for apochromatic correction.

Spherical aberration and aspherical elements: in the case of optical elements with spherically-curved surfaces, the light rays which pass through the element close to the edges do not converge exactly at the focal point with those which pass through the center of the element. The resulting loss of sharpness is called spherical aberration. This defect can be limited by slower lenses and special combinations of elements. Today, the use of aspherical elements (with aspherically-curved surfaces) allows lenses to be constructed using relatively few elements, which guarantees sharpness and brilliance even with high speeds.

Internal focusing: in order to focus normal telephoto lenses, the relative positions of the main element groups are adjusted, which causes the total length of the lens to change considerably. Because of this, the longer the focal length, the more the lens is extended during focusing. This can make manual focusing very awkward and inexact, and it makes the autofocus response very slow. This problem is solved by telephoto lenses with so-called internal focusing (IF). With these lenses, the total length of the lens remains constant, and focusing is effected by shifting the position of an optical element group between the two main element groups. This element group only needs to move a very short distance. This sort of lens not only allows faster and more precise manual focusing, it also provides unbeatable speed of automatic focusing. In addition, internal focusing can be combined with automatic correction, which leads to a general improvement in the quality of reproduction. Because of these advantages, Nikon offers IF versions of all AF telephoto lenses in the longer focal lengths.

The Best Combination of Lenses
It is perfectly acceptable to cover the most important range of focal lengths with two zoom lenses, e.g. 28-70mm and 70-210mm if you do not need fast lenses, and the zoom design of quick changes in focal length is at least somewhat important. As a first investment, the zoom gives you more choices to start with. Then, as you identify a particular range (moderate wide angle, medium telephoto) it might be worth considering the single focal length lenses as faster favorites. There may also be specialized needs, as in landscape and architectural photography, where one might also buy a 24mm or even a 20mm wide-angle lens, or possibly a 300mm telephoto for sport and action photography. The choices for the professional or serious non-professional would be based on more specific needs, as in the frequency of portraits, close-up work, interiors etc. Here you are more likely to see decisions made according to individual requirements. Very likely, there will be a need for a zoom covering their range of work as a backup or general purpose lens, along with several specific focal lengths which are "just right" for specific situations.

The Nikon Bayonet Mount

Anyone who has invested thousands in high-quality lenses is not pleased when the manufacturer devalues their investment by introducing new cameras with a different lens mount. The fact, that the Nikon bayonet mount has remained largely compatible over decades of technical development, may have been one of the most important reasons that professional photographers have remained loyal to Nikon. However, since not every Nikon photographer may be aware of the continued development of the lens mount, the following brief summary is intended to answer the most important questions on this subject.

Important Note Related to Compatibility
In general, the AF, AF-D, AF-I Nikon lenses for the F3 and newer cameras are "downwards" compatible. The opposite holds for older lenses which cannot, or should not, be used with newer cameras. See also "The Nikon Bayonet" section and the Lens-Camera Compatibility table.

Erroneous Exposure Reading or Auto-Exposure: When using, for example, non-AI Nikkors on modern cameras, exposure errors will always occur.

Damage Warning: Certain AI-Nikkors and some older versions of AI-Nikkors, some extension tube models, and non-AF Special purpose lenses, such as certain fish-eyes or older PC-Nikkors, may not be mounted on modern Nikon cameras. Mechanical or electro-mechanical damage (i.e. to the AF contacts) could occur!

VERY IMPORTANT: *Always read the instruction manuals of both lens and camera before trying to combine units from different generations.*

The lens-camera compatibility chart in this book can only give a basic overview of the situation due to space constraints.

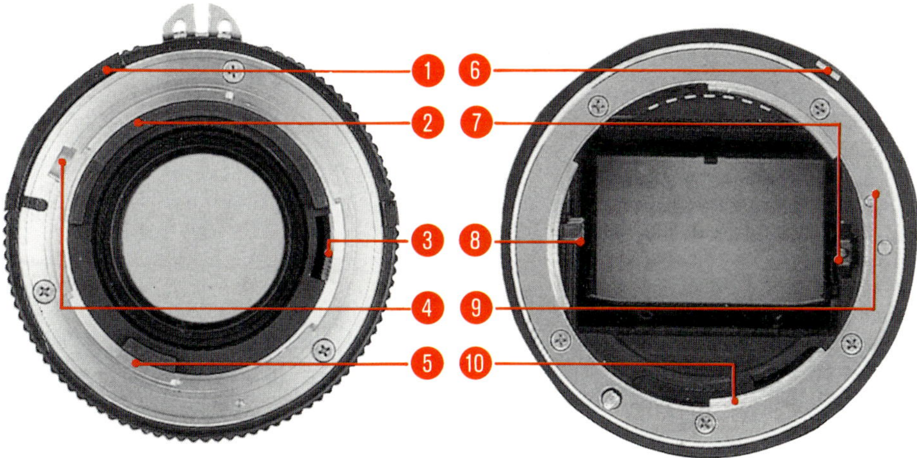

AIS Bayonet Mount

1. Meter coupling ridge
2. Protective collar
3. Auto aperture coupling lever
4. Focal length identification notch
5. Aperture indexing post
6. AIS Meter coupling
7. Focal length indicator
8. Aperture stop-down lever
9. Lens mounting flange
10. F bayonet mount flange

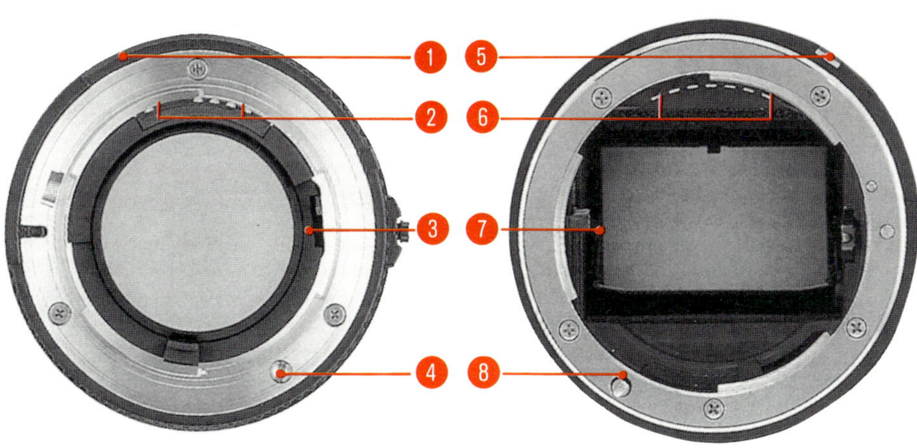

AF Bayonet Mount

1. Meter coupling ridge
2. CPU contacts
3. Auto aperture coupling lever
4. Autofocus coupler
5. AIS meter coupler
6. CPU contacts
7. Aperture stop-down lever
8. AF drive shaft

Metal Bayonet and Mounting Specification: The bayonet mount on both Nikon cameras and lenses consists of high-performance metal alloys. Its composition is carefully selected so that it works perfectly in a wide range of temperatures, from Arctic to tropical conditions. A perfectly parallel film plane and lens plane is crucial. The distance from film plane to bayonet must also be a constant 46.5mm. This so-called mounting specification must be accurate to 1/100mm. If it should change because of impact (with the mounted lens, for example), send it to Nikon service. The distance will be measured from all four corners of the film plane and the bayonet will be justified or exchanged. Generally, it is not possible to perform this kind of work on plastic bayonets, which speaks for the time-proven Nikon metal bayonet of 35 years.

Various Bayonet Generations

Non-AI Nikkors with aperture "fork": When this generation of lenses appeared, complicated automatic exposure functions had yet to be developed, it was simply a question of allowing open-aperture metering. With stopped down metering which had been used previously, the aperture had to be closed down to its working value for TTL metering. The resulting dark viewfinder image often made accurate framing impossible and the metering procedure tended to interrupt the flow of work. With open-aperture metering, on the other hand, although the aperture ring is set to the working value, the aperture remains wide open during metering. In order to allow accurate exposure metering, the working aperture setting therefore has to be transmitted to the camera's exposure metering electronics.

In the case of non-AI lenses, this was effected by means of a fork (or "rabbit ears") connected to the aperture ring. When the lens was fitted, the pin of a cam located above the camera bayonet had to be engaged with this fork. As the aperture ring was turned, the pin automatically moved with it, thus transmitting the setting of the aperture ring to the camera. Since, in order to meter the exposure, the camera had to know which absolute aperture value corresponded to the relative position of the aperture ring, the lens had to be adjusted to its "maximum aperture setting" (lens speed) after being fitted. This is why Nikon photographers of the time always turned the aperture ring after changing a lens. The aperture fork made the metering procedure itself faster and simpler, but changing lenses was still a little awkward. Note: exposure metering and automatic exposure modes will not function when non-AI lenses are used on cameras with an AI bayonet mount. For a long time, Nikon's Customer Service department offered to convert suitable non-AI lenses into AI versions.

AI lenses with automatic aperture value transmission: this generation of lenses made the special adjustment process on changing the lens a matter of just a single twist on, since the speed of the lens was now automatically transmitted. The lenses communicated defined position and length through a sort of mechanical coding, and the camera bayonet featured a mechanical cam for reading this data. In addition, the aperture fork was replaced by a cam integrated in the lens bayonet into which the reading pin of the camera's cam automatically clicked when the lens was twisted into place. *Note:* only those AI lenses which are also equipped with an aperture fork are fully compatible with non-AI cameras. AI lenses can generally be used on modern AF cameras, with manual focusing and restricted exposure metering and automatic exposure functions. Various AI-Nikkors of older production runs, certain extension tubes and some non-AF special-purpose lenses like some fish-eyes or older PC-Nikkors may not be used with modern Nikon cameras. *Mechanical or electro-mechanical failure could result!*

AI-S lenses for program and shutter speed priority modes: on non-AI and AI lenses, only a simple automatic diaphragm mechanism was required in order to allow the aperture of the lens to close down to the working aperture value set on the lens when the shutter was released. This was also perfectly adequate for aperture priority mode (working aperture value set on the lens). However, in program mode or shutter speed priority mode, the aperture has to be closed down with great precision to the working value calculated by the camera when the shutter is released. This required a completely new transmission mechanism, which was incorporated into the AI-S lenses. The AI-S lenses also featured mechanical coding for focal length (for focal length-dependent program modes). *Note:* AI-S lenses can be used in place of the corresponding AI lenses without any problem, but using earlier AI lenses on AI-S cameras (e.g. the N2000/F-301) restricts one to the use of aperture priority mode.

AI-P lenses: these lenses feature a built-in microchip and transmit typical lens data such as speed, aperture setting, and focal length to the camera by electronic means. They are, therefore, fully compatible with all modern AF cameras except for the AF function. However, like the AI-S lenses, they also feature all the mechanical transmission elements and can therefore, like these, be used on the non-AF cameras.

AF Nikkors with electronic data transmission for focusing and exposure: these lenses not only possess the mechanical coupling for the motorized focusing of the lens, they also contain a built-in microcomputer chip which determines all the lens data required for focusing and exposure. Thus, information on required focusing movements, current position of elements, lens speed, aperture setting, and focal length is transmitted to the camera by electronic means. *Note:* like the AI-S lenses, they also feature all the mechanical transmission elements and can therefore, like these, be used on the non-AF cameras.

AF-D Nikkors for 3D auto-modes: The micro-chip in previous AF-Nikkors did not give the camera a value for the subject's distance, but rather transmitted a value for the number of motor-revolutions that were necessary to achieve focus. The chip in the Type D lenses, on the other hand, gives the absolute distance in meters. The "D," therefore, stands for "distance." The 3D "intelligent" exposure and flash modes that are found in the N90/F90 are thus made possible. *Note:* The transmission of subject distance can only be used with the N90/F90 to date. Otherwise, D lenses are fully compatible with all non-3D AF functions, such as auto-exposure, and are also completely downwards compatible with non-AF SLRs.

AF-I Nikkors with AF motor built into the lens: except for the lack of the AF motor coupling, the bayonet is the same as that on normal AF Nikkors. The AF contacts are the same, but are more extensively utilized. The special feature of the AF-I Nikkors (e.g. the AF- I 300mm f/2.8 D IF-ED) is a super-fast, coreless DC motor which is built into the lens. Focusing distances can be indexed and recalled at any time using the focus lock button. The AF-I lens can also be focused just as well by hand, with the traditional "mechanical" feel. The special feature here is that the lens does not first have to be switched from autofocus to manual, it does so automatically when the focusing ring on the lens is turned. Since all these AF functions require a special interaction with the camera, the AF functions of AF-I lenses can currently only be used in combination with the F4, F4S, F4E, and N90/F90. With all other Nikon AF cameras, these lenses allow all automatic exposure functions but only manual focusing.

Review of Nikkor Lenses

In contrast to the next two chapters, the following table includes the full range of Nikon AF and non-AF lenses available at the time of writing.

Nikon Camera and Lens Compatibility *

Camera	F3	FM-2	N2000 F-301	N5005 F-401x	N6006 F-601/F-601m	N8008s F-801s	F4	N90 F90
Lens Type								
AF Nikkor	+	+	+	+	+	+	+	+
AF-D Nikkor	+	+	+	+	+	+	+	++
AF-I-Nikkor	+	+	+	X	X	X	++	++
AI-P-Nikkor	+	+	+	+	+	+	+	+
AI-S Nikkor	+	+	+	0	F	F	E	F
AI-Nikkor	+	+	C	0	F	F	E	F
AI Converted Nikkor	+	+	D	0	F	F	F	F
NON-AI Nikkor	A	-	-	-	-	-	A	-
Series E Nikkor	+	+	+	0	F	F	E	F
Medical Nikkor	A	A	B	-	B	B	A	A
Reflex and PC Nikkor	A	A	A	0	A	A	A	A
PB-6 Bellows	A	A	A	0	A	A	F	F
Extension Tubes **(PK-11A, PK-12, PK-13, PN-11)**	+	+	D	0	F	F	F	F
TC-14A/B; TC-201/301	+	+	+	0	A	F	E	F
TC-16A	-	-	-	-	-	F	E	F
TC-14E, TC-20E ***	+	+	+	X	X	X	++	++

* Possibility of damage! Certain non-AI Nikkors as well as some older AI Nikkors, extension tubes and several non-AI special purpose lenses such as Fisheyes or older PC Nikkors cannot be used with modern Nikon cameras. Mechanical or electrical damage can result! This table provides only an overview. Always refer to the camera and lens instruction manual to determine compatibility.

** On AF cameras or with AF Nikkors, only PK 11A may be used, not PK 11 (only DR-2A reversing ring may be used, not BR-2).

*** Data applies only for combinations with AF-I lenses.

+ Can be used without restrictions.

++ The unique AF or exposure modes can only be used with this camera.

- Not compatible. Not recommended or possibility of damage!

0 Can be fitted but often not practical due to severe limitations.

X Only with manual focus. Auto exposure modes can be used.

A Only with Aperture priority automatic mode and center-weighted metering. Display readouts may not correspond to actual values.

B Correct exposure only possible with flash.

C No dual program, no flash program

D No dual program, no flash program; displayed shutter speed may not correspond with actual values.

E Only manual exposure or aperture priority with all metering methods (matrix, center-weighted, spot).

F Only manual exposure or aperture priority; only center-weighted or spot metering.

Overview of AF Nikkor Lenses

Lens Description	Elements/ Groups	Angle of View	Minimum Aperture	Close-focus Distance (ft./m)	Macro (ft./m)	Max. Magnification Ratio	Filter Size	Lens Hood	Weight (oz.)	Size (mm)
AF 16mm/2.8 D Fisheye	8 - 5	180°	22	0.8	-	?	Bayonet	built-in	11.3	63 x 54.8
AF 20mm/2.8	12 - 9	94°	22	0.8	-	1 : 8.4	62 mm	HB-4	9.1	69 x 52
AF 24mm/2.8 N	9 - 9	84°	22	1.0	-	1 : 8.8	52 mm	HN-1	9.1	65 x 55,5
AF 28mm/1.4 D	11 - 8	74°	16	1.1	-	?	72 mm	HK-7	19.8	75 x 77.5
AF 28mm/2.8 N	5 - 5	74°	22	1.0	-	1 : 7.6	52 mm	HN-2	6.8	65 x 48,7
AF 35mm/2.0	6 - 5	62°	22	0.8	-	1 : 4.2	52 mm	HN-3	2.0	63 x 43,5
AF 50mm/1.4 N	7 - 6	46°	16	1.5	-	1 : 6.8	52 mm	HR-2	8.9	65 x 52,5
AF 50mm/1.8 N	6 - 5	46°	22	1.5	-	1 : 6.6	52 mm	HR-2	7.4	65 x 48
AF 60mm/2.8 Micro	8 - 7	39° 40'	32	0.7	-	1 : 1	62 mm	HN-22	15.9	70 x 74.5
AF 85mm/1.8	6 - 6	28° 30'	16	2.8	-	1 : 9.2	62 mm	HN-23	14.5	71 x 69
AF 105mm/2.0 D DC	6 - 6	23° 20´	16	2.9	-	?	72 mm	built-in	22.4	79 x 111
AF 105mm/2.8 Micro	9 - 8	23° 20'	32	1.0	-	1 : 1	52 mm	HS-7	19.4	75 x 104.5
AF 135mm/2.0 DC	7 - 6	18°	16	3.6	-	1 : 7	72 mm	built-in	30.9	79 x 128
AF 180mm/2.8 IF-ED N	8 - 6	13° 40'	22	4.9	-	1 : 6.4	72 mm	built-in	26.3	78,5 x 153
AF 300mm/2.8 IF-ED N	8 - 6	8° 10'	22	1	-	1 : 8.4	39 mm	HE-6	94.5	133 x 263
AF 300mm/4.0 IF-ED	8 - 6	8° 10'	32	0.8	-	1 : 7.0	39 mm	built-in	46.5	89 x 227
AF-I 300mm/2.8D IF-ED*	11 - 9	8° 10'	22	0.8	-	?	39 mm	HK-19	103.3	124 xs 241
AF-I 400mm/2.8D IF-ED*	10 - 7	6° 10´	22	10.8	-	?	52 mm	?	221.0	158 x 375
AF-I 600mm/4.0D IF-ED*	9 - 7	4° 10'	22	19.7	-	?	39 mm	HK-18	211.8	166 x 417
AF 20-35mm/2.8 D	14 - 11	94° - 64°	22	1.6	-	?	77 mm	HB-8	20.5	82 x 94
AF 24-50mm/3.3-4.5	9 - 9	84° - 46°	22	1.9	1.6	1 : 8	62 mm	HB-3	13.1	70,5 x 82,5
AF 28-70mm/3.5-4.5	8 - 7	74° - 34° 20'	22	1.6	1.3	1 : 4.6	52 mm	HB-6	12.3	67.5 x 71
AF 28-70mm/3.5-4.5 D	8 - 7	74° - 34° 20'	22	1.6	1.3	1 : 4.6	52 mm	HB-6	12.4	67.5 x 71
AF 28-85mm/3.3-4.5 N	15 - 11	74° - 28° 30'	22	2.6	0.75	1 : 3.4	62 mm	HB-1	18.9	71 x 97,5
AF 35-70mm/2.8	15 - 12	62° - 34° 20'	22	1.9	0.92	1 : 4.0	62 mm	HB-1	23.3	72 x 105

Lens Description	Elements/ Groups	Angle of View	Minimum Aperture	Close-focus Distance (ft.)	Macro (ft.)	Max. Magnification Ratio	Filter Size	Lens Hood	Weight (oz.)	Size (mm)
AF 35-70mm/2.8 D	15 - 12	62° - 34° 20'	22	1.9	0.92	1 : 4.0	62 mm	HB-1	23.6	71.5 x 105
AF 35-70mm/3.3-4.5 N	8 - 7	62° - 34° 20'	22	1.6	1.1	1 : 4.4	52 mm	HN-2	9.6	70,5 x 69
AF 35-80mm/4.0-5.6 D	6 - 6	62° - 30° 10'	22	1.6	1.1	?	52 mm	HN-2	8.9	66,5 x 60
AF 35-105mm/3.5-4.5 N	16 - 12	62° - 23° 20'	22	4.6	0.92	1 : 4	52 mm	HB-5	16.1	69 x 95,5
AF 35-135mm/3.5-4.5 N	15 - 12	62° - 18°	22	4.9	1.4	1 : 4	52 mm	HB-5	24.0	72,5 x 117
AF 70-210mm/4.0-5.6 D	12 - 9	34° 20 '- 11° 50'	32	4.9	3.9	1 : 4.5	62 mm	HN-24	20.7	73,5 x 116
AF 75-300mm/4.5-5.6	13 - 11	31° 10' - 8° 10'	32	9.8	4.9	1 : 3.8	62 mm	HN-24	30.1	72 x 166
AF 80-200mm/2.8 ED	16 - 11	30° 10' - 12° 20'	22	5.9	4.9	1 : 5.9	77 mm	HN-28	42.0	85,5 x 184,5
AF 80-200mm/2.8 D ED	16 - 11	30° 10' - 12° 20'	22	5.9	4.9	1 : 5.9	77 mm	HB-7	45.5	87 x 187
AF TC-16A 1.6x **	5 - 5	-	-1.3 EV	****	-	-	-	-	5.3	69 x 30
AF-I TC-14E 1,4x ***	5 - 5	-	-1 EV	****	-	-	-	-	7.0	65 x 24.5
AF-I TC-20E 2x ***	7 - 6	-	-2 EV	****	-	-	-	-	11.9	65 x 55

- Not applicable.
? Information not available as of publication.
* Autofocus possible with N90/F90 and F4 only, with all other AF cameras only manual focusing, but with all automatic exposure modes.
** Complete compatibility with N90/F90, F4 and N8008/F-801 only.
*** Only use in combination with AF-I Nikkors.
**** Same as main lens.

Overview of Non-AF Nikkor Lenses

	Elements Groups	Angle of View	Minimum Aperture	Close-Focus Distance	Macro	Max. Repro. Ratio (approx.)	Filter Size/Type	Lenshood	Weight oz.	Size in inches	TC 201	TC 301	TC 14A	TC 14B
Fisheye														
6mm/2.8	12 - 9	220°	22	9.8in.	-	1 : 21	5 - built-in	-	182	9.3x6.7	+	X	+	X
8mm/2.8	10 - 8	180°	22	11.8in.	-	1 : 20	5 - built-in	-	38.5	4.8x5.5	+	X	+	X
16mm/2.8	8 - 5	180°	22	11.8in.		1 : 13	4- supplied	built-in	11.5	2.5x2.6	+	X	+	X
Wide Angle														
13mm/5.6	16 - 12	118°	22	11.8in.	-	?	4 - supplied	built-in	42	4.5x4.0	+	X	+	X
15mm/3.5	14 - 11	110°	22	11.8in.	-	1 : 13	4 - supplied	built-in	22	3.5x3.7	+	X	+	X
18mm/3.5	11 - 10	100°	22	9.8in.	-	1 : 8.5	72 mm	HK-9	12.3	3.0x2.9	+	X	#	X
20mm/2.8	12 - 9	94°	22	9.8in.	-	1 : 8.4	62 mm	HK-14	9	2.6x2.1	+	X	+	X
24mm/2.0	11 - 10	84°	22	11.8in.	-	1 : 8.6	52 mm	HK-2	10.5	2.5x2.5	+	X	+	X
24mm/2.8	9 - 9	84°	22	11.8in.	-	1 : 8.8	52 mm	HN-1	8.8	2.5x2.2	+	X	+	X
28mm/2.0	9 - 8	74°	22	9.8in.	-	1 : 5.3	52 mm	HN-1	12.6	2.5x2.7	+	X	+	X
28mm/2.8	8 - 8	74°	22	7.9in.	-	1 : 3.9	52 mm	HN-2	8.8	2.5x2.1	+	X	+	X
35mm/1.4	9 - 7	62°	16	11.8in.	-	1 : 5.5	52 mm	HN-3	14	2.7x2.9	+ *	X	+	X
35mm/2.0	8 - 6	62°	22	11.8in.	-	1 : 5.7	52 mm	HN-3	9.8	2.5x2.3	+	X	+	X
35mm/2.8	5 - 5	62°	22	11.8in.	-	1 : 5.7	52 mm	HN-3	8.4	2.5x2.1	+	X	+	X
Normal														
50mm/1.2	7 - 6	46°	16	19.7in.	-	1 : 7.9	52 mm	HS-12, HR-2	13.3	2.7x2.3	+	X	#	+
50mm/1.4	7 - 6	46°	16	17.7in.	-	1 : 6.8	52 mm	HS-9, HR-1	8.8	2.5x2.0	+	X	+	X
50mm/1.8	5 - 6	46°	22	23.6in.	-	1 : 9.6	52 mm	HR-4	5	2.5x1.4	+	X	+	X

	Elements Groups	Angle of View	Minimum Aperture	Close-Focus Distance	Macro	Max. Repro. Ratio (approx.)	Filter Size/Type	Lenshood	Weight oz.	Size in inches	TC 201	TC 301	TC 14A	TC 14B
Telephoto														
85mm/1.4	7 - 5	28° 30'	16	33.5in.	-	1 : 7.9	72 mm	HN-20	21.7	3.1x2.8	+ *	X	+	X
85mm/2.0	5 - 5	28° 30'	22	33.5in.	-	1 : 8.1	52 mm	HS-10	10.9	2.5x2.4	+	X	+	X
105mm/1.8	5 - 5	28° 20'	22	39.4in.	-	1 : 7.6	62 mm	built-in	20.3	3.1x3.5	+ *	X	+	X
105mm/2.5	5 - 4	23° 20'	22	39.4in.	-	1 : 7.6	52 mm	built-in	15.2	2.5x3.0	+	X	#	X
135mm/2.0	6 - 4	18°	22	4.27ft	-	1 : 7.5	72 mm	built-in	30.1	3.2x4.1	+ *	X	+	X
135mm/2.8	5 - 4	18°	32	4.27ft	-	1 : 7.5	52 mm	built-in	15.1	2.5x3.6	#	X	+	X
135mm/3.5	4 - 4	18°	32	4.27ft	-	1 : 7.5	52 mm	built-in	14	2.6x3.5	+	X	+	+
180mm/2.8 ED	5 - 5	13° 40'	32	5.9ft	-	1 : 7.5	72 mm	built-in	28	3.1x5.4	+ *	X	+	X
200mm/2.0 IF-ED N	10 - 8	12 ° 20'	22	8.2ft	-	1 : 10	Gelatin filter	HE-4	89.3	5.2x9.2	+	X	#	+
200mm/4.0	5 - 5	12° 20'	32	6.6ft	-	1 : 7.5	52 mm	built-in	17.9	2.6x4.9	#	X	+	X
300mm/4.5	6 - 5	8° 10'	32	11.5ft	-	1 : 9	72 mm	built-in	42	3.1x8.0	X	+	#	+
300mm/4.5 IF-ED	7 - 6	8° 10'	32	8.2ft	-	1 : 7.2	72 mm	built-in	37.1	3.2x7.9	X	+	X	+
400mm/2.8 IF-ED	8 - 6	6° 10'	22	13.1ft	-	1 : 8.3	52 mm	HE-3	180.3	6.8x17	#	+	#	+
400mm/3.5 IF-ED	8 - 6	6° 10'	22	14.8ft	-	1 : 9.8	39mm	built-in	98	5.3x12	X	+	#	+
400mm/5.6 IF-ED	7 - 6	6° 10'	32	13.1ft	-	1 : 8.8	72 mm	built-in	42	3.3x10.3	X	+	X	+
500mm/4.0 PIF-ED	8 - 6	5°	22	16.4ft	-	1 : 8.7	39 mm	HK-7	105	5.4x15	X	+	X	+
600mm/4.0 IF-ED N	8 - 6	4° 10'	22	21.3ft	-	1 : 9.5	39 mm	HE-5	197.4	6.8x18.7	X	+	X	+
600mm/5.6 IF-ED N	7 - 6	4° 10'	32	16.4ft	-	1 : 7.3	39mm	HE-4	98	5.2x15.6	X	+	X	+
800mm/5.6 IF-ED	8 - 6	3°	32	26.2ft	-	1 : 12	52mm	HE-3	190.8	6.4x21.8	X	+	X	+
Zoom Lenses														
28-85mm/3.5-4.5	15 - 11	74° - 28° 30'	22	2.6ft	0.23 m	1 : 3.4	62 mm	HK-16	17.9	2.6x3.8	+	X	+	X
35-70mm/3.5-4.5	8 - 7	62° - 34° 20'	22	19.7ft	0.35 m	1 : 4.4	52 mm	HN-22	8.9	2.5x2.7	+	X	+	X
35-105mm/3.5-4.5	16-12	62° - 23° 20'	22	4.6ft	0.27 m	1 : 4	52 mm	HK-11	17.9	2.5x3.7	+	X	+	X
35-135mm/3.5-4.5	15 - 14	62° - 18°	22	4.9ft	0.4 m	1 : 3.8	62 mm	HN-22	21	2.7x4.4	+	X	+	X
35-200mm/3.5-4.5	17 - 13	62° - 12° 20'	22	4.3ft	0.3 m	1 : 3.5	62 mm	HK-15	25.9	2.8x5	+	X	+	X

	Elements Groups	Angle of View	Minimum Aperture	Close-Focus Distance	Macro	Max. Repro. Ratio (approx.)	Filter Size/Type	Lenshood	Weight oz.	Size in inches	TC 201	TC 301	TC 14A	TC 14B
50-135mm/3.5	16 - 13	46° - 18°	32	4.3ft	0.6 m	1 : 9.3	62 mm	HK-10	24.5	2.8x5.2	+	**X**	+	**X**
50-300/4.5 ED	15 - 11	46° - 8° 10'	32	8.2ft	-	?	95 mm	HK-5	68.3	3.9x9.7	+	**X**	+	**X**
80-200mm/4.0	13 - 9	30° 10'-12° 20'	32	3.9ft	-	?	62 mm	HN-23	28.4	2.9x6.4	+	**X**	#	**X**
100-300mm/4.0 ED	14 - 10	24° 20'-8° 10'	32	6.6ft	0.71 m	1 : 4.4	62 mm	HN-24	32.6	2.9x7.8	+	**X**	+	**X**
180-600mm/8.0 ED	18 - 11	13° 40' - 4° 10'	32	8.2ft	-	?	95 mm	HN-16	113.8	4.1x15.8	**X**	+	**X**	+
Special Lenses														
28mm/3.5 PC	9 - 8	74°	22	11.8ft	-	1 : 6.9	72 mm	HN - 9	13.3	3.1x2.7		**X**		**X**
35mm/2.8 PC	7 - 7	62°	32	11.8ft	-	1 : 5.3	52 mm	HN - 1	11.2	2.4x2.6		**X**		**X**
55mm/2.8 Micro	6 - 5	43°	32	9.8ft	-	1 : 1.9	52 mm	HN - 3	10.2	2.5x2.8	+	**X**	+	**X**
105mm/2.8 Micro	10 - 9	23° 20'	32	16.1ft	-	1 : 2	52 mm	built-in	18	2.6x3.6	+	**X**	+	+
120mm/4.0 Medical	9 - 6	20° 30'	32	10.2ft	-	1 : 1 (2:1 w/close-up)	49 mm	-	31.2	3.9x5.9	+	+		
200mm/4.0 Micro IF	9 - 6	12° 20'	32	28in.	-	1 : 2	52 mm	built-in	28	2.6x7.1	**X**	+	#	+
105mm/4.5 UV	6 - 6	23° 20'	32	17.7in.	-	1 : 2	52 mm	built-in	18.4	2.7x4.6	+ (1)	**X**	+ (1)	**X**
58mm/1.2 Noct.	7 - 6	40° 50'	16	19.7in	-	1 : 6.7	52 mm	HS-7, HR-2	16.3	2.9x2.5	+	**X**	+	**X**
500mm/8 Reflex N	6 - 6	5°	-	4.9ft	-	1 : 2.5	39 mm	HN-27	29.4	3.5x4.6	+	**X**	+	**X**
1000mm/11.0 Reflex	5 - 5	2° 30'	-	26.2ft	-	1 : 7.4	39 mm	built-in	66.5	4.7x9.5	#	**Y**	#	**Y**

+ Fully suitable.
- Not available, not recommended.
\# Can be used but inferior results or vignetting possible.
X Unsuitable.
Y Can be used without filters only.
(1) Cannot be used for UV photography.
* Uneven exposure if used at apertures smaller than f/11.
** AF focusing only with F4, all other cameras require manual focusing but will work in all exposure modes.

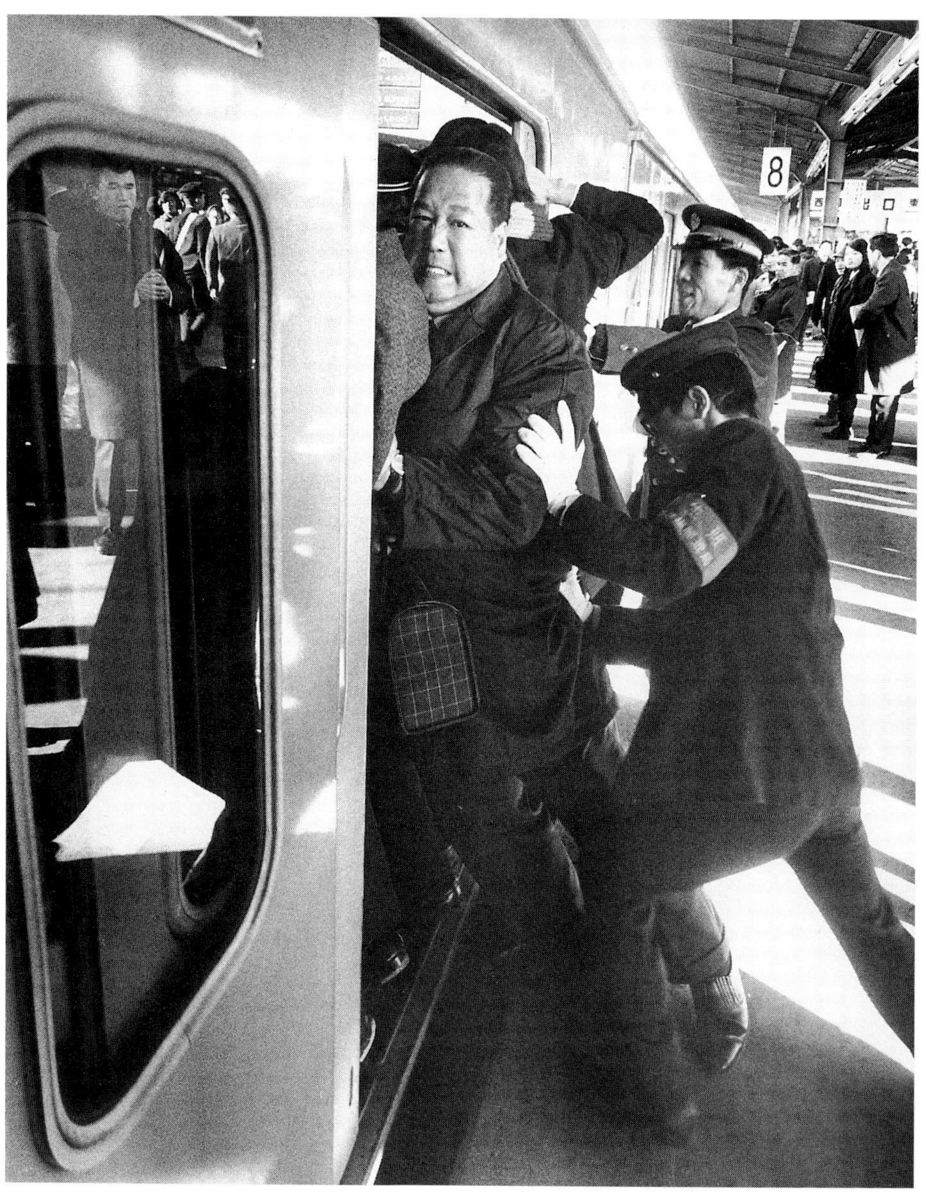

As photojournalists can attest, sometimes a scene will have a critical moment when all of the visual elements come together to produce an exceptional photograph. Under these conditions, the photographer and the equipment must be ready to grab the shot as illustrated here by a "moment" captured in the Tokyo subway system. This often means relying on a modern camera's automated exposure and focusing system. Photo: Rudolf Dietrich

Close-up Lenses and Accessories

Those who wish to photograph small objects or detailed areas of larger subjects should become familiar with the wide range of specialized close-up equipment offered within the Nikon system. This specialized form of photography has important applications in many fields including the biological, medical and physical sciences, as well as nature photography, in law enforcement, and in hobbies such as coin and stamp collecting. In spite of these many applications and the generally high level of interest in the types of photographs produced by macro equipment, most photographers have only a limited knowledge of macrophotography and little of the specific equipment that makes this form of photography easier.

Definitions and Scope

Close-up photography, as the name implies, means getting closer to the subject in order to concentrate on a specific area. In fact, this form of photography is really about magnification of the subject's image on film. Thus, people working in this area use the ratios between the real size of the subject relative to how large it appears on film in order to have a common point of reference. Most lenses, for example, have a close focus distance that limits them to magnification ratios of between 1:6 and 1:10, which is just barely within what is usually thought of as close-up photography. That is, they cannot get any closer to magnify the on-film image greater than between one-sixth and one-tenth of the object's real size. That means, for example, an object of 1.2ft. (36cm) in length will barely fill the 36mm length of a small format film at a magnification ratio of 1:10. Furthermore, zoom lenses are usually more limited, particularly if their close focus distance, and hence their magnification ratio, is based on the shorter end of the zoom range. Some offer an additional macro setting of about 1:4, but this is usually for the widest focal length in the zoom's range.

Definition of the Term Macro

When taken literally, the term "macro" refers specifically to an image whose magnification ratio is 1:1. Images in the range of 1:10 to 1:2 are then simply close-ups, while shots from 2:1 to 10:1 are extreme close-ups, sometimes called loupe images. These differences have, however, become blurred with modern usage. All images from about 1:4 down to 1:1 now seem to be lumped together under the term "macro." In order to avoid confusion then when doing "macro" or close-up work, it is probably best to quote the magnification ratio.

Scale and Image Sizes: There is frequently confusion about what magnification ratios actually mean. As has been said, the magnification ratio gives the relationship between the image size and the subject. Thus, the 1:10 ratio cited earlier means that the object is 10 times larger than the picture. A 24 x 36cm object would therefore be reproduced by filling the small format 24 x 36mm frame completely. In order to determine the image size from the object size, multiply the height and width by the ratio. At a ratio of 1:2, for example, a 1.2 x 1.8cm .5in. x 7in. subject would appear on a 6 x 9mm image field and at a ratio of 2:1 on a 24 x 36mm field.

In addition to concerns about how much larger a subject appears on film, there is also the point that all lenses intended for normal distance photography are designed to offer their best performance at or near infinity focus. This does not mean that macro lenses are corrected only for the closer focusing distances,

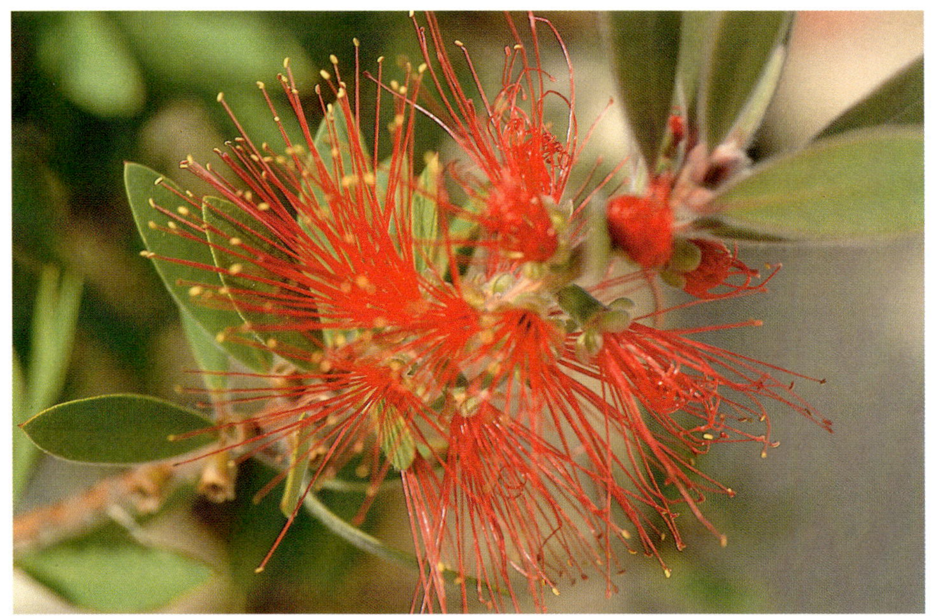

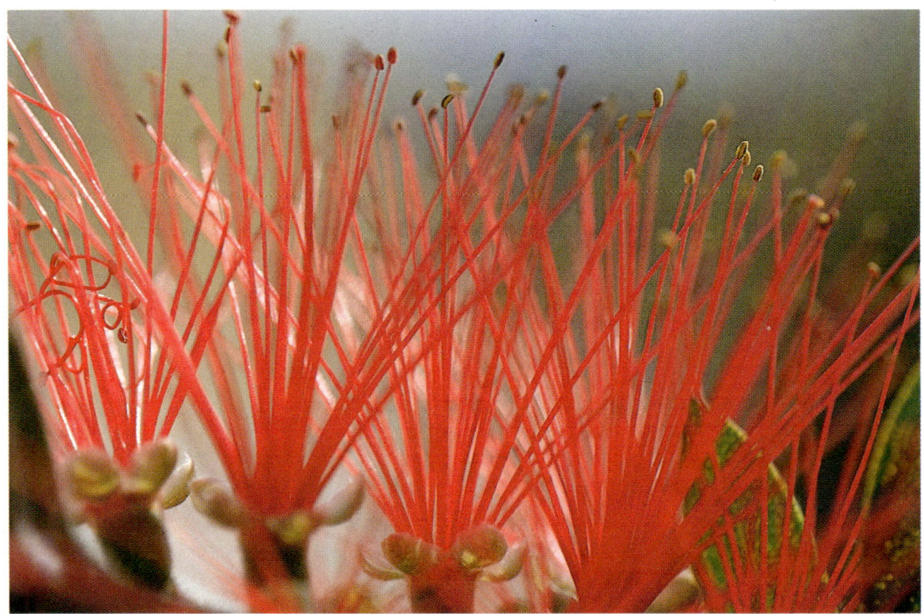

Macro photography: Reproduction ratio 1:2 top and 1:1 bottom. These images were taken hand-held with a slight breeze using autofocus at f/8 and 1/250. Greater sharpness and depth of field could have been attained had there been no wind and by using a tripod. The images illustrate the superb qualities of the AF Micro Nikkors or AF Nikkors with close-up adapters for macro photography.

giving only average performance at infinity. On the contrary, the modern Nikon macro lenses, (called Micro Nikkors) are optimized for the close-up range from 1:10 to 1:1. This "optimization" includes, in most cases, the additional characteristic of a "flat field" correction in which the usual differences in sharpness and contrast between the center of the field and the edges is much less than with a typical conventional lens. This is particularly important for flat subjects as on a copy stand or in a slide duplicator. But in addition, because of floating elements used in the construction and other design features, Nikon's Micro/macro lenses also have excellent correction to infinity. The Micro Nikkors are, therefore, applicable to both close-up and normal distance applications and, consequently, many photographers use them as all-round lenses. It is because of this fact that they have been included within the general lens section within the Lenses Chapter as well. (Nikon's close focusing lenses should really be called Macro Nikkors, but Nikon uses the term Micro, reserving the name "macro" for their specialized loupe lenses with even higher magnification ratios such as 40:1).

Macro Lenses

Advantages of longer focal lengths in macro photography: as a lens increases in its magnifying power by coming closer to the subject, the issue of working distance becomes increasingly important. This is generally the distance between point of focus and the front of the lens that is largely a function of differences in focal length; i.e., longer focal length lenses have greater working distances. The particular picture taking situation will dictate how critical this characteristic is and, therefore, which focal length to use. Thus, when working on a copy stand, which has only a limited amount of room between the subject and the top of the camera rail, a 50-60mm lens is the only real choice because longer focal lengths have too narrow a field of view to take in general copy stand subject matter. So here, a larger working distance actually works against the application. Working under field conditions in a typical nature setting, however, will often require a longer focal length in order to avoid shadows being cast over the subject, or in order to be able to "reach down" into some foliage to capture a flower blossom as well as staying back far enough to avoid scarring a living subject, such as a dragon fly on its perch. The difference in working distances among focal lengths is substantial. For example, at a ratio of 1:1, where the size of the subject and its on-film image are the same, the working distance is 4in. (10cm) with a 50mm lens, and 8in. (20cm) with a 100mm lens. In other words, each doubling of the focal length doubles the working distance. The use of 100mm or 200mm Micro Nikkors is therefore recommended whenever there is a need to remain at a longer, non-interfering distance.

Advantages and disadvantages of macro lenses: The main advantages of all the Micro Nikkors over other forms of macro adaptations, such as close-up lenses and extension tubes, are their ability to focus continuously from the maximum magnification ratio to infinity with a high level of optical quality throughout. Simply put, no other form of close-up equipment can match the ease of focusing with its automatic metering or AF function intact through the whole near/far range of the macro lens, all with excellent overall image quality throughout. There is also the advantage of being able to use these lenses for general photography as noted earlier. That may raise the question, "why don't all photographers use macro lenses instead of the non-macro designs?" For one thing, Nikon's Micro lenses, like all macros made by other manufacturers, are slower by one to three stops than their non-close focusing counter parts. They are also more expensive and generally larger, and in some cases (i.e. the 100mm f/2.8 micro), somewhat heavier than comparable convention lenses used with extension tubes or close-up filters. These detractions aside, it is certainly worth thinking about purchasing a Micro Nikkor to serve this dual role unless having a large maximum aperture is essential.

AF and Non-AF Micro Nikkors: See "Macro Lenses" page 112.

Macro Photography with Close-Up Filters

How close-up filters work and their applications: close-up filters work as positive lenses that shorten the focal length of the lens, just as a magnifying glass allows our eye to see more of a subject than the eye alone can at the same distance. They accomplish this without any light loss since there is no change in the lens to film distance as happens with both macro lenses and extension tubes as they focus closer. Like many camera manufacturers, Nikon offers two different grades of close-up filters; the less expensive, single element designs designated by strength as in +1, +2, etc., and a corrected (and more expensive) multi-element version with a "T" nomenclature as in 5T or 6T. Depending on the lens and focal length, a magnification ratio of 1:1 (true macro) can be reached, but at the price of acceptable quality in the case of the single element group. Distortion and loss of sharpness, particularly in the border areas, are quite noticeable with the single element optics. The multi-element versions are much better. They excel at all magnifications, extending the range of a micro Nikkor or any lens using an extension tube. The single element filters deliver acceptable results when used in the +1 and +2 strengths and are really unsuitable for critical work where edge to edge quality must be maintained. They work best in shots of three-dimensional objects such as flowers, insects, small animals or portraits, where the subject is usually in the middle of the frame so the edge falloff in quality is less noticeable.

Stop down when using close-up filters: the best advice for using any close-up filter, especially the single element design, is to close down the aperture to the middle range of f/stops on the lens. This will help compensate for the optical faults at work. Fortunately, this is a good procedure to follow in all close-up work because depth of field is minimal as the on film image is magnified.

Using close-up filters with autofocus: Autofocus lenses are particularly well suited to macro work with close-up filters since close-ups can be done quickly and accurately. Automatic focusing, however, is only possible if the lens is positioned such that it is actually possible to achieve focus on that particular subject. That is, the autofocus mechanism only works if you are able to focus manually from the same lens position. Thus, it is a good idea to first find an appropriate distance to the subject by focusing manually and then switch to autofocus mode.

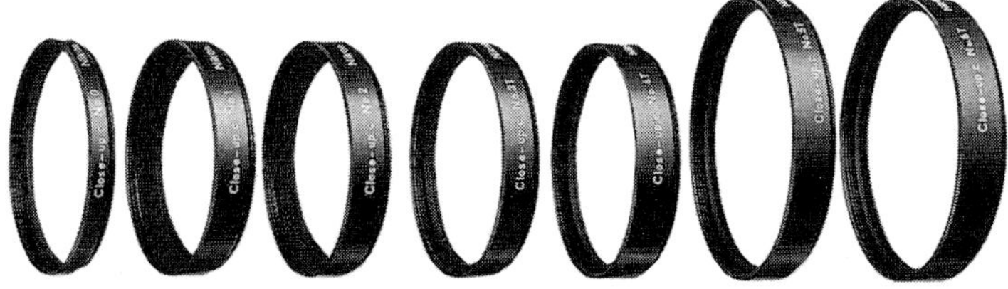

Nikon close-up lenses are the least expensive way of obtaining higher on-film magnifications. The multi-element 5T or 6T models give results superior to the less expensive single element designs.

Reproduction Ratios with Close-up Lenses 0, 1 and 2*

Close-up Lens	0	1	2
Primary Lens			
24mm	1:58 - 1:7.8	1:28 - 1:6.9	1:14 - 1:5.6
28mm	1:49 - 1:3.7	1:24 - 1:3.4	1:12 - 1:3.1
35mm	1:39 - 1:4.9	1:19 - 1:4.4	1:9.4 - 1:3.7
50mm	1:27 - 1:5.3	1:13 - 1:4.7	1:6.6 - 1:3.3

* The accuracy of the ratios depends on the actual lens in use.

Advantages and disadvantages of close-up filters: Taking into consideration the earlier comments concerning optical quality, close-up filters are, nevertheless, the easiest and cheapest way to increase the magnification ratio of any lens. That makes them an ideal accessory to carry around for occasional use without adding any bulk to one's camera bag. The multi-element designs will also deliver very good results when used alone in their lower strengths and as an auxiliary to any high quality existing close-up arrangement. Also, the speed of the lens is not affected (that is, there is no need to compensate for light loss) and the AF exposure metering or exposure modes of the modern AF cameras still work. Disadvantages are the reduction in image quality as noted and the limited range of magnification ratios a given lens covers. In other words, the loss of infinity focus.

The Nikon close-up filter range: There are close-up filters for 52mm diameter threads (a common size among Nikon lenses) in the form of simple lenses, such as Number 0 with +0.7 diopter correction, Number 1 with +1.5 correction, and Number 2 with +3 correction. Those with higher image quality requirements using 52mm, can use two element achromatics "Ts," such as the 3T with +1.5 diopters, and the 4T with +2.9. These are also available for 62mm diameter lenses: the 5T and the 6T respectively. Several filters can be combined, but this is not to be recommended with the single element diopters because of optical quality. With the achromatic multi-element filters, place the stronger lens first on the main

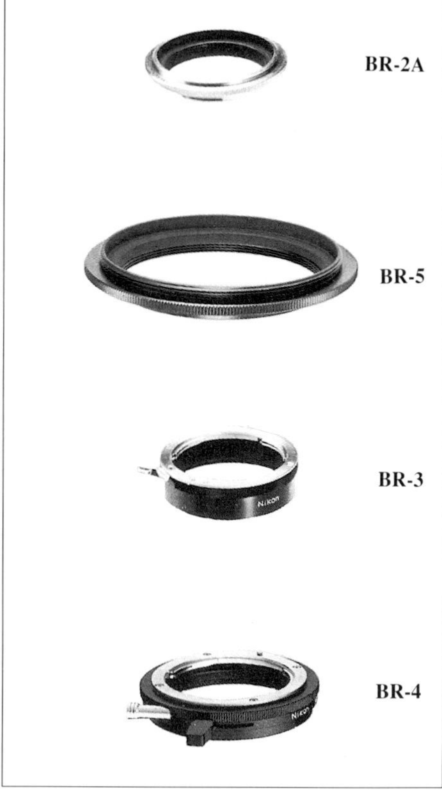

Reproduction Ratios with Nikon Extension Tubes

Extension Tube	PK-11A	PK-12	PK-11A + PK-12	PK-13	PK-11A + PK-13	PK-12 + PK-13	PK-11A + 2 PK-13's
Lens							
20mm/2.8 AF **	1:2.6 - 1:2	1:1.5 - 1:1.2	1.1:1 - 1.2:1	1.3:1 - 1.5:1	1.7:1 - 1.9:1	2:1 - 2.2:1	2.4:1 - 2.5:1
24mm/2.8 N AF **	1:3 - 1:2.3	1:1.7 - 1:1.5	1:1.1 - 1:1	1.1:1 - 1.2:1	1.5:1 - 1.6:1	1.7:1 - 1.8:1	2:1 - 2.1:1
28mm/2.8 N AF **	1:3.6 - 1:2.4	1:2.1 - 1:1.6	1:3 - 1:1.1	1:1 - 1.1:1	1.2:1 - 1.4:1	1.4:1 - 1.6:1	1.7:1 - 1.9:1
35mm/2.0 AF **	1:4.5 - 1:2.5	1:2.6 - 1:1.8	1:1.6 - 1:1.3	1:1.3 - 1:1.1	1:1 - 1.2:1	1.2:1 - 1.3:1	1.4:1 - 1.6:1
50mm/1.8 N AF	1:6.4 - 1:3.3	1:3.7 - 1:2.4	1:2.3 - 1:1.7	1:1.9 - 1:1.5	1:1.5 - 1:1.2	1:1.2 - 1:1.1	1:1 - 1.1:1
60mm/2.8 Micro AF ***	1:7.5 - 1.2:1	1:4.3 - 1.4:1	1:2.7 - 1.5:1	1:2.2 - 1.6:1	1:1.7 - 1.8:1	1:1.4 - 1.9:1	1:1.2 - 2.1:1
85mm/1.8 AF	1:10.6 - 1:4.6	1:6.1 - 1:3.5	1:3.9 - 1:2.6	1:3.1 - 1:2.2	1:2.4 - 1:1.8	1:2 - 1:1.6	1:1.7 - 1:1.4
105mm/2.8 Micro AF ***	1:13.1 - 1.1:1	1:7.5 - 1.2:1	1:4.8 - 1.3:1	1:3.8 - 1.4:1	1:3 - 1.5:1	1:2.5 - 1.6:1	1:2.1 -1.7:1
135mm/2.8	1:16.9 - 1:5.2	1:9.6 - 1:4.2	1:6.1 - 1:3.4	1:4.9 - 1:3	1:3.8 - 1:2.5	1:3.3 - 1:2.3	1:2.7 - 1:2
180mm/2.8 IF N AF	1:22.5 - 1:5	1:12.8 - 1:4.3	1:8.2 - 1:3.6	1:6.5 - 1:3.2	1:5.1 - 1:2.8	1:4.3 - 1:2.6	1:3.6 - 1:2.3
300mm/4.5 IF-ED	1:37.5 - 1:5.9	1:21.4 - 1:5.2	1:13.6 - 1:4.5	1:10.9 - 1:4.1	1:8.4 - 1:3.6	1:7.2 - 1:3.3	1:6.1 - 1:3

* Values are as accurate as possible.

** For better quality images at magnification ratios greater than 1:1, these lenses should be reversed by using a BR-24 reversing ring.

*** Produces best results with extension tubes.

lens. All current Nikon close-up filters are multicoated.

Macro Photography with Extension Tubes

How extension tubes work and their applications: Extension tubes of various sizes can be placed between the lens and camera, thereby increasing the lens' distance to the focus plane of the film and hence increasing the close-focus distance. Increasing the lens-to-film distance causes the "speed" of the lens to drop noticeably due to a light loss. Since conventional lenses are not optimized for close-ups, using extension tubes may bring out any weak-

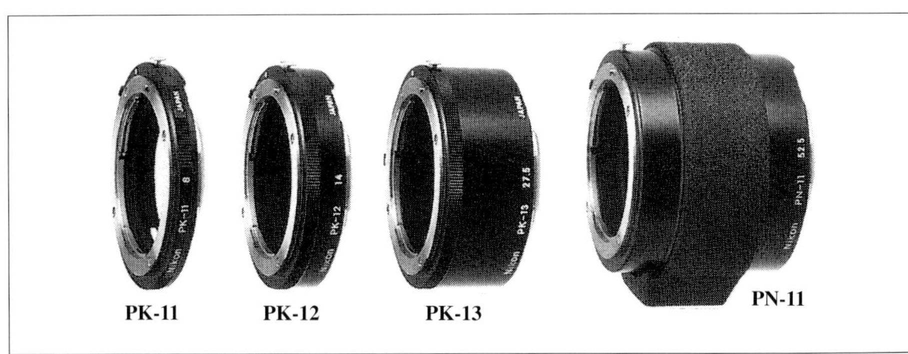

Extension tubes lengthen the distance between the lens and the camera body thus increasing how close the lens can be focused and consequently, the reproduction ratio of the subject on film.

nesses in the lens. By comparison, however, extension tubes are usually a better choice than close-up filters since they do not introduce the effects of a second lens system. Lenses with CRC close-up correction, for example, perform best when their full close-up setting is used in combination with extension tubes. Extension tubes are available in various lengths and can be used in combination to increase the close-up range. Extension tubes can be used with any lens. The more extreme wide-angle lenses, however, should not be used with extension tubes since their wide field of view designed for infinity focus will tend to work against distortion free images. Nikon's special wide-angle macro loupe lenses are specially optimized for close-up work and are, of course, corrected for this close-up function, performing extremely well.

Loss of light: The loss of light with extension tubes can reach several stops, depending on the length of the extension tubes or bellows extension and the lens' focal length. In terms of the AF light minimum levels, the effective aperture can quickly fall below f/5.6 which would render the AF system inoperative, even if AF extension tubes were available.

Important note regarding AF compatibility: *Old (M and M2) Nikon extension tubes* ***cannot*** *be used with AF lenses and/or AF cameras because of the possible danger of damaging electrical lens contacts!* Also, instead of the older PK-11 tube, the PK-11A has to be used on AF cameras.

Restricted auto functions on AF cameras: Unfortunately, there are no Nikon extension tubes available to date that have AF drive transmission capabilities, or the electrical contacts for AF lenses. When using the available manual extension tubes with AF lenses, neither autofocus nor matrix metering, program or shutter priority modes will work. Only aperture priority mode or manual mode can be used.

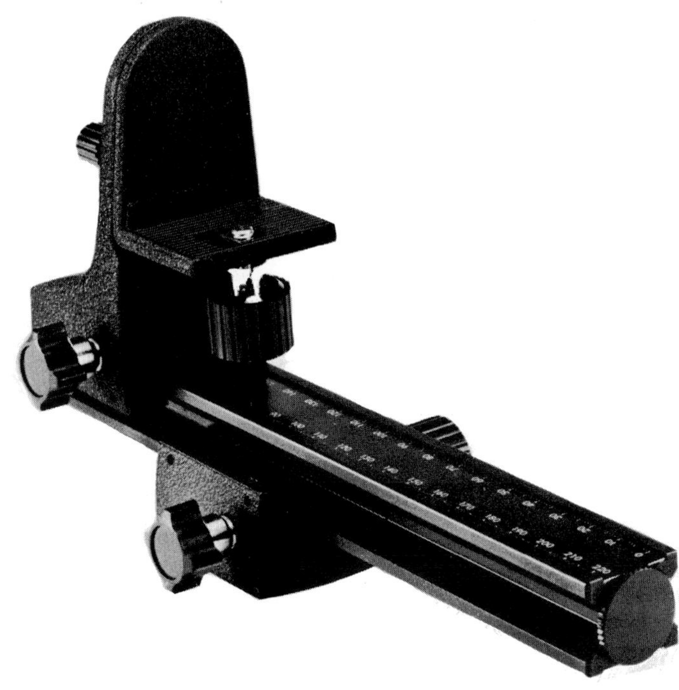

PG-2

Reproduction Ratios with PB-6 Bellows*

	With PB-6 Bellows	PB-6 with PB-6E Extension
Nikkor Lens		
20mm/2.8 AF **	4.5:1 - 11:1	23:1
24mm/2.8 N AF **	3.5:1 - 9:1	19:1
28mm/2.8 N AF **	3.3:1 - 7.5:1	16:1
35mm/2.0 AF **	2.5:1 - 5.5:1	12.5:1
50mm/1.8 N AF	1:1.5 - 4:1	8.5:1
60mm/2.8 Micro AF	upto 3.5:1	7.5:1
85mm/1.8 AF ***	1:2 - 2.5:1	5.3:1
105mm/2.8 Micro AF ***	upto 2:1	4.3 :1
135mm/2.8	1:3 - 1.5:1	3.4:1
200mm/4.0	1:4.5 - 1:1	2.4:1
19mm/2.8 Macro ****	-	40:1
35mm/4.5 Macro ****	-	20:1
65mm/4.5 Macro ****	-	10:1
120mm/6.3 Macro ****	-	4:1

- Not compatible.

* More or less accurate values.

** For reproduction rations 1:1 or larger, these lenses should be reversed. The values in the table are given accordingly.
Lenses with a 52mm filter thread can be reversed without accessories. Lenses with a 62mm thread require a BR-5 reversing ring.

*** These lenses give optimal image quality up to about 2:1.

**** These lenses give optimal image quality from 2:1 and larger.

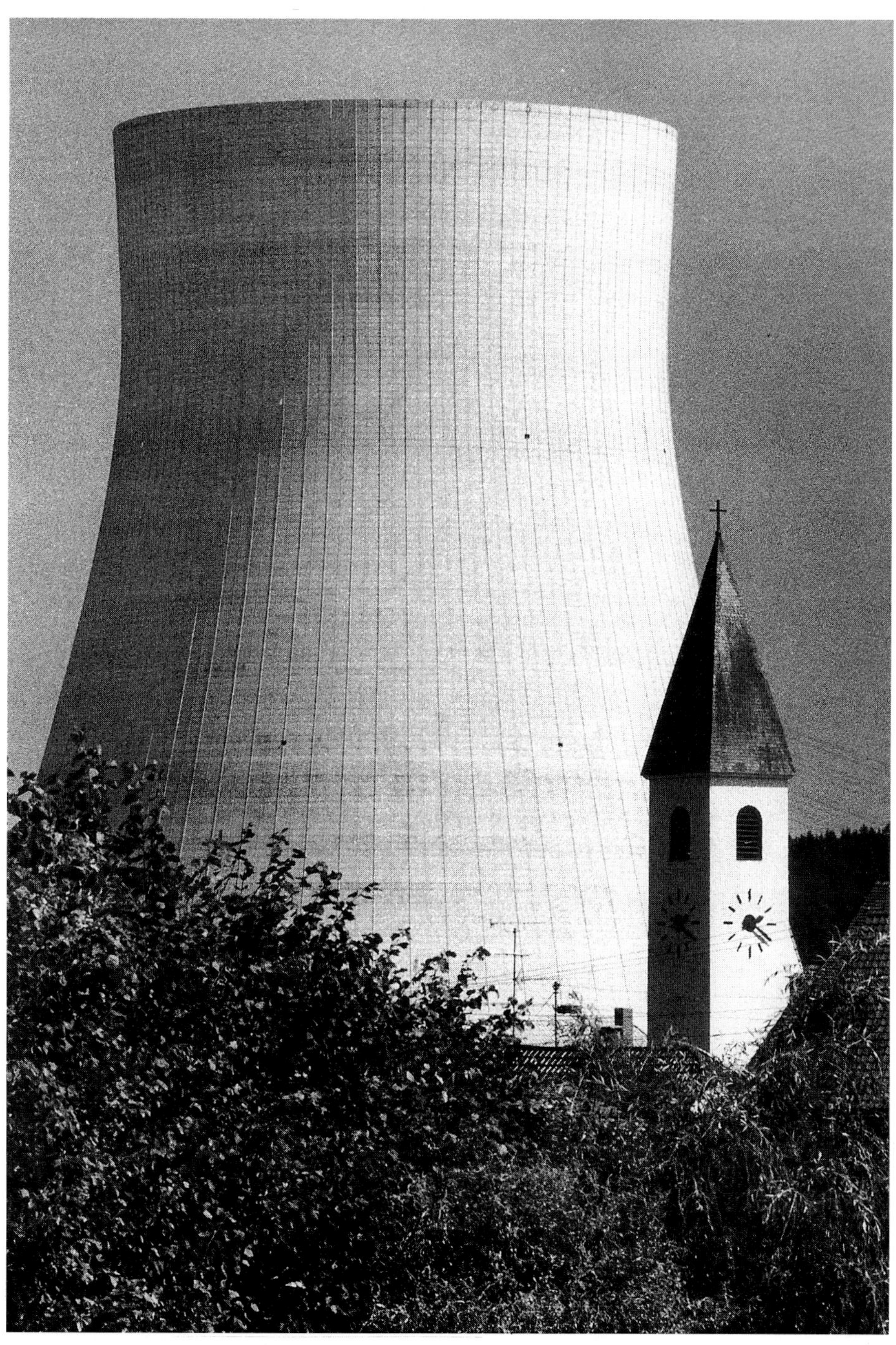

The ability of telephoto lenses to compress subject matter is illustrated here; the atomic plant's cooling shaft appears even closer to the church tower due to the use of a 180mm lens. Photo: Rudolf Dietrich

Reversing rings: For 1:1 and larger magnifications, some consideration should be given to "retro" mounting any lens. "Retro" means that the lens is used backwards (rear element pointing towards the subject, front element towards the camera) via an appropriate adapter or, as it is more commonly known, a reversing ring. The effectiveness of this procedure is based on an interesting optical relationship. The correction of asymmetric lenses is adjusted such that the distance from lens to subject is larger than the distance from lens to camera. At 1.01:1.00 this relationship reverses, which translates to an easy and inexpensive way to have 1:1 range magnifications. Nikon offers four reversing rings compatible with Nikkors. For automatic aperture control, an adapter BR-6 is mounted on the lens' bayonet mount and is closed down when the shutter is fired using an AR-10 double cable release.

PG-2 camera focusing stage: When a predetermined, fixed magnification must be maintained, the PG-2 does the focusing by moving the camera closer or further from the subject. In this way, the lens is not used to focus, thus maintaining magnification.

Advantages and disadvantages of extension tubes: The most important advantage is that extension rings bring out the best optical quality in macro lenses since these lenses are designed for close focusing. The automatic aperture also remains functional in most cases and they are relatively inexpensive when compared to a macro lens. Disadvantages are the loss of light and the loss of continuous focusing to infinity. Furthermore, those who need to make fine adjustments in the magnification ratio or need to work in the larger extension ranges would be better off using macro bellows.

The Nikon extension tube range: There are 4 Nikon extension tubes currently available: PK-11A, 8mm long; PK-12, 14mm; PK-13, 27.5mm; and PN-11 with 52.5mm. These extension tubes transmit both the spring controlled aperture as well as the AI System aperture values.

Macro Photography with Bellows

Principles and applications: The amount extension tubes and close-up filters can change a lens' magnification ratio has certain practical limits in terms of image quality and the ease of making adjustments in the magnification ratios, to say nothing of the unwieldy nature of

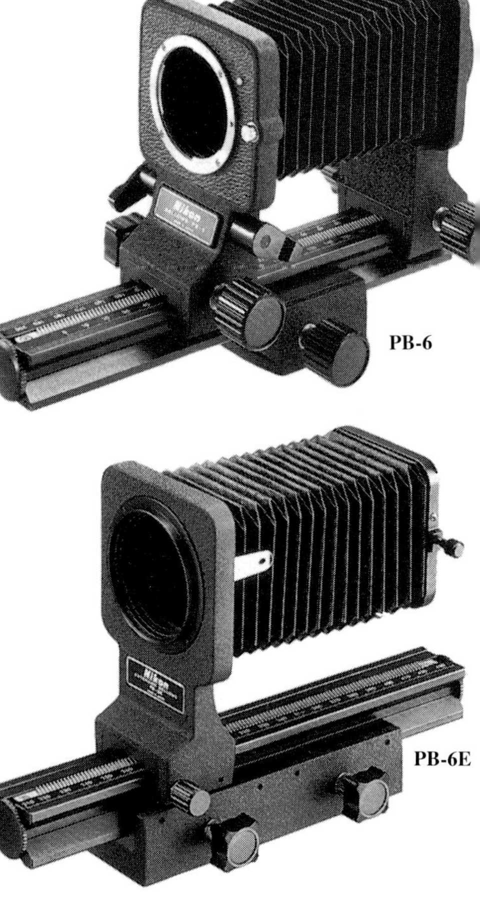

PB-6

PB-6E

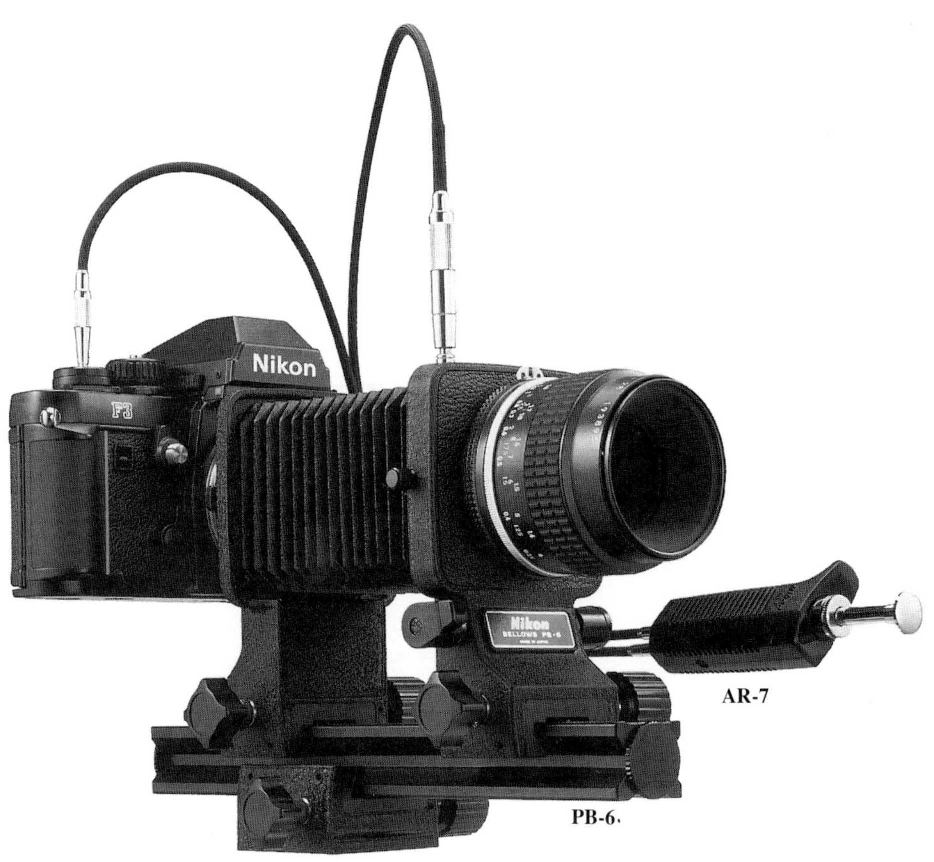

stacking extension tube on extension tube. A macro bellows, such as the Nikon PB-6, allows a stepless selection of magnification ratios over a comparatively larger range of values. The cost is not having a reasonable minimum extension when the bellows is completely contracted to its smallest extension point. For example, the minimum magnification ratio of a 50mm lens becomes 1.5:1, but is stepless up to 4:1 (with the PB-6E Extension Bellows, this maximum magnification reaches 8.6:1).

Which lenses to use on the bellows: In principal, one can use the same lenses as with extension tubes (AF Nikkors, non-AF Nikkors, Micro Nikkors). In addition, there is the option of using enlarging lenses which are specifically designed for close-up work, such as the EL Nikkors (special adapter EI-F required). Other options include Nikon's Macro lenses, AF Nikkors and non-AF Nikkors: with the limitation that these lenses are not optimized for macro and the loss of some auto functions and spring-controlled aperture as described below.

Using Micro Nikkors on a bellows: All Micro Nikkors are appropriate for use with an adjustable bellows, producing high quality results. Up to a ratio of about 3.5:1, they offer the best results. A cable release connector is mounted on the front standard to stop the lens down, while a second cable connection (using a double cable release) fits the camera body thus allowing wide open focusing. The special cable release AR-7 (for F4, F3 and N6006) or the AR-10 (for the F4S, F4E, N8008/F-801

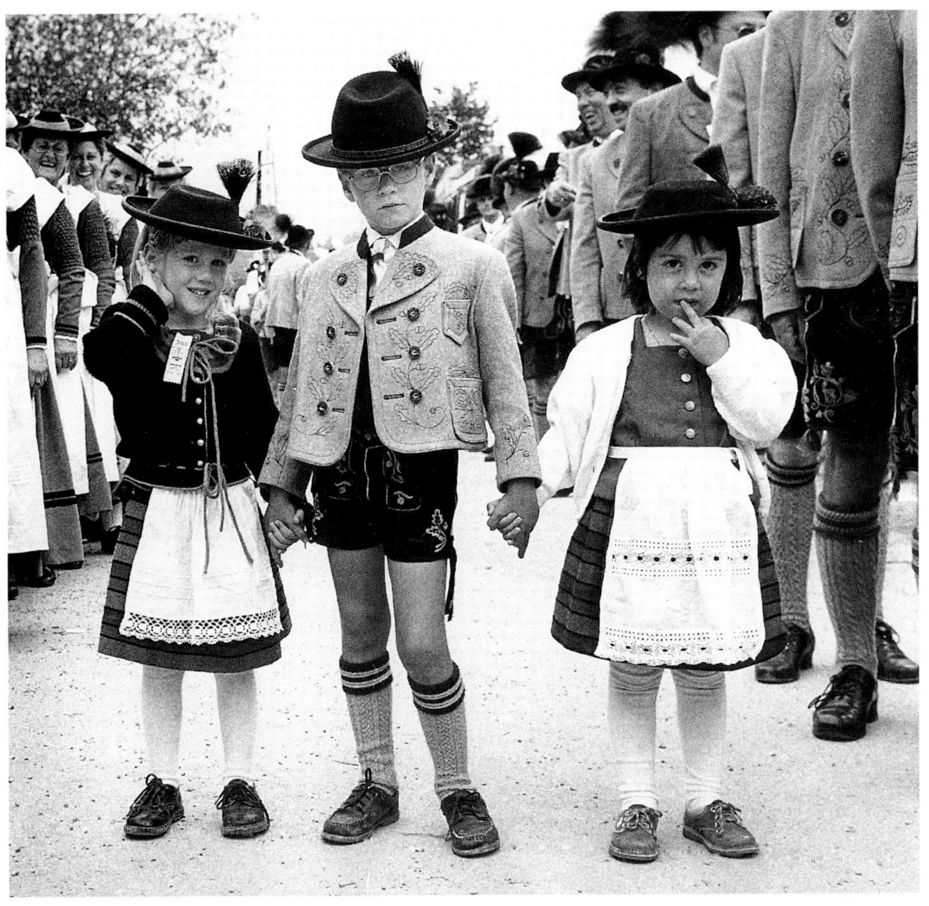

One of the greatest benefits of modern auto-exposure and auto-focus cameras is the ability to capture events and scenes that might otherwise have been missed. Photo: Rudolf Dietrich

and N2000/F-301; N90/F90 with AR-10 and MC-25) closes the aperture shortly before the exposure takes place.

Reduced auto functions with AF cameras: Macro bellows that have motor connections for autofocusing will most likely never be available for many reasons, not the least of which is that the typical reduction in light transmission through the bellows would render the AF mechanism, that depends on f/5.6 as a maximum, ineffective. Furthermore, some sort of flexible "electronic pathway" would have to be perfected to link lens with camera. All this is a lot of trouble to add autofocus to what is essentially an operation easily handled by manual focus. When using AF lenses with the PB-6 bellows, therefore, autofocus, matrix metering and program and shutter priority modes do not work. One can only work manually or in aperture priority mode, but take care: *depending on the camera, displayed exposure values will be wrong or not shown at all.*

Reversing rings and additional adapters for reverse mounting a lens: At magnification ratios around 1:1 and higher, macro lenses should be mounted backwards since this will more likely produce better results. Nikon offers 4 forms of inversion rings that fit Nikkor lenses. To maintain automatic aperture, an additional adapter is mounted on the lens's

Overview of Reproduction Ratios and Focal Lengths

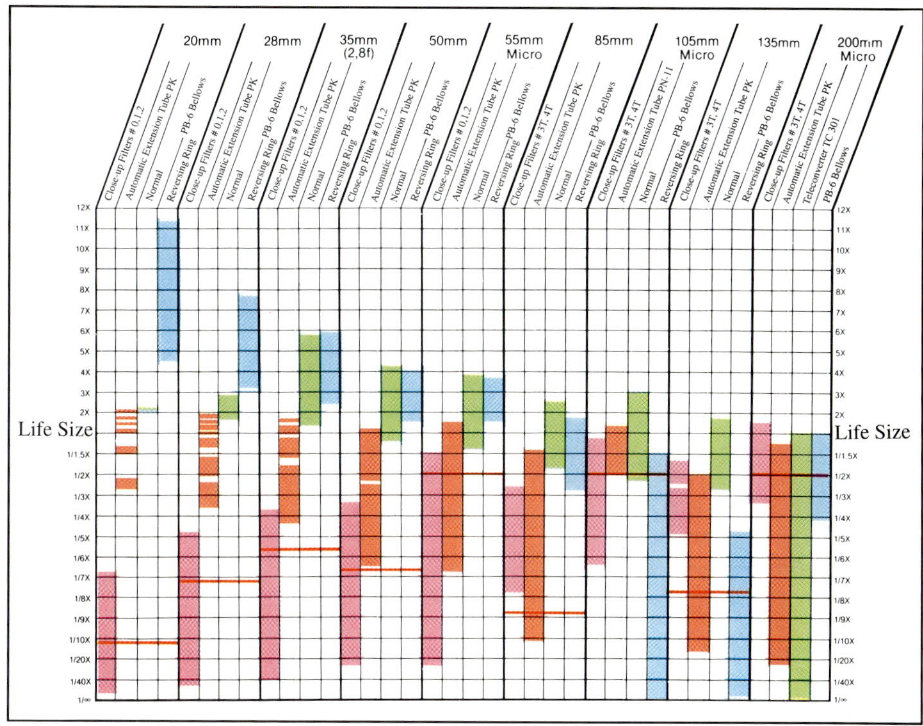

bayonet mount which, in conjunction with the double cable release BR-6, closes the aperture automatically.

Macro photography with EL Nikkor enlarging lenses: High quality enlarging lenses, such as the EL Nikkors, can also be used with an adapter ring. These lenses are optimized for high reproduction ratios. Normally, these lenses have a 39mm threaded mount and therefore require the EL-F adapter. When using enlarging lenses, one has to do without automatic aperture control with f/stop setting being made manually. It should be pointed out that at a ratio of 1:1 the maximum depth of field is about 1mm, which pretty much precludes working with anything else but a static subject, and preferably one that has a relatively flat plane.

Macro Nikkors: For close-up work with larger magnification ratios one can use, for example, the Micro Nikkor AF 60mm f/2.8 (PB-6 bellows + PB-6E extension) for up to about 8:1 with good results. It should be remembered, however, that lenses with ratios greater than 2:1 require highly specialized corrections. Nikon therefore offers through its Instruments Division 4 loupe lenses (Macro Nikkors) with focal lengths of 19mm, 35mm, 65mm and 120mm. They also mount onto the standard 39mm thread and are connected via the EL-F adapter to the PB-6 bellows unit. When shooting with these magnification ratios, there is no real chance whatever for working with moving objects or from a hand-held position. In fact, great care must be taken to insure a parallel relationship is maintained between the film plane and the subject plane to make maximum use of what little depth of field is available (e.g. by using the PF-4 copy stand). At a reproduction ratio of 1:1 at f/22 the depth of field is only about 1mm. At the maximum magnification ratios of these lenses, however, it can shrink to less than the thickness of a hair!

Macro-Nikkor 19mm f/2.8: magnification ratio 15x-40x.
Macro-Nikkor 35mm f/4.5: magnification ratio 8x-20x.
Macro-Nikkor 65mm f/4.5: magnification ratio 3.5x-10x.

Integrated slide rule for focusing using lens distance: In the 1:1 and larger range, the subject's reproduction size is determined first and then the image is focused by changing the distance from the lens to the subject. The PB-6 bellows unit has a 7.1in. (18cm) long slide rule for this purpose built into the bellows rail.

Advantages and disadvantages of the bellows unit: The PB-6 bellows unit is inferior to the Micro-Nikkors up to 1:1 with respect to ease of handling. Even extension tubes combined with certain lenses (especially micro Nikkors) offer results equal to those obtained with the PB-6 and an enlarging lens, and are less expensive and easier to handle. Another disadvantage is the comparatively large minimum extension of the PB-6. This means that there is always a gap in the magnification ratios that can be produced with the lens alone and with the lens and bellows. The major advantage of the bellows, on the other hand, is that it can be used with a wide variety of lenses to produce stepless magnification ratios larger than 1:1.

Aids for viewing in macro photography: Working comfortably in the macro range and beyond without straining the eyes and forcing oneself to take rather uncomfortable positions while working with the standard eye level viewer, requires the use of a number of important close-up accessories. Various viewfinders can be substituted with certain cameras to allow for waist level viewing in the case of a low to the ground shot. These waist level viewers also allow strait-on viewing when working on a copy stand, thus avoiding having to stand on a chair. The F3 owner would use a DW-3 or DW-4, while the F4 photographer has the DW-20 or DW-21. All four permit viewing the ground glass from above at a 90° angle to the normal viewing position. The DW-3 and DW-20 are simple, folding viewfinders with a swinging 5x loupe for critical focusing. DW-4 and DW-21 are magnifying viewfinders that show the image enlarged by 6 times through a rubber eye cup. Diopter correction from +3 to -5 is built into the optical system. These viewfinders have a small disadvantage, however; they invert the image which might be confusing. Owners of other Nikon cameras only have the DG-2 and DR-3 viewfinder as options. These units basically fit on all cameras, but require the appropriate adapter. Viewfinder ground glass screens Type B (matte ground glass with fresnel lens and a finely matted central area) are probably the best for close-up work. The N4004/F-401, N6006/F-601, N8008/F-801 and F4 come standard with this kind of ground glass. A B-type glass can also be used with the F3 and FM-2n. Those who do a great deal of copy work, either on a copy stand or in a slide duplicator, might want to streamline the process of aligning the original in the viewfinder by using a Type E screen. This type is exactly like the Type B, but has an additional grid system etched into it, for use with the F4, F3, F8008/F-801 and FM-2n. When using the F4 with the DW-21 finder, or the F3 with the DW-4, the very bright Type M ground glasses are recommended with the lower level of light typical with a bellows.

Copy Stands in Macro Photography

Those who wish to reproduce flat art or small objects on the exact same plane as the film, should consider purchasing a good copy stand such as the Copy Stand PF-4. This unit is well built with a usable base board of 18.7in. x 13.2in. (47.5cm x 33.5cm) and a 41.4in. (105cm) long column, maximum distance from film plane to base board is 35in.(88.8cm) with a right angle cross section for precise axial alignment. Height adjustments are effortless thanks to a counterweight that runs up and down the column. There is also a separate focusing mechanism for fine focusing. All cameras with and without motors can be used with this unit. To extend the photographic possibilities, the camera can be tilted 45° and 90° left and right respectively. The column can be attached directly to a table (without the base board) using the PC-3 table clamp. This type of unit is only necessary for those users who have to frequently make specialized images with various types of lighting, as in either halogen or flash, or rear lit subjects as in copying large transparencies off of a light box.

Slide Copying Setups

Slide copying is a specialized area of macro photography in which copies of slides are made as "insurance" of those send to publishers, to

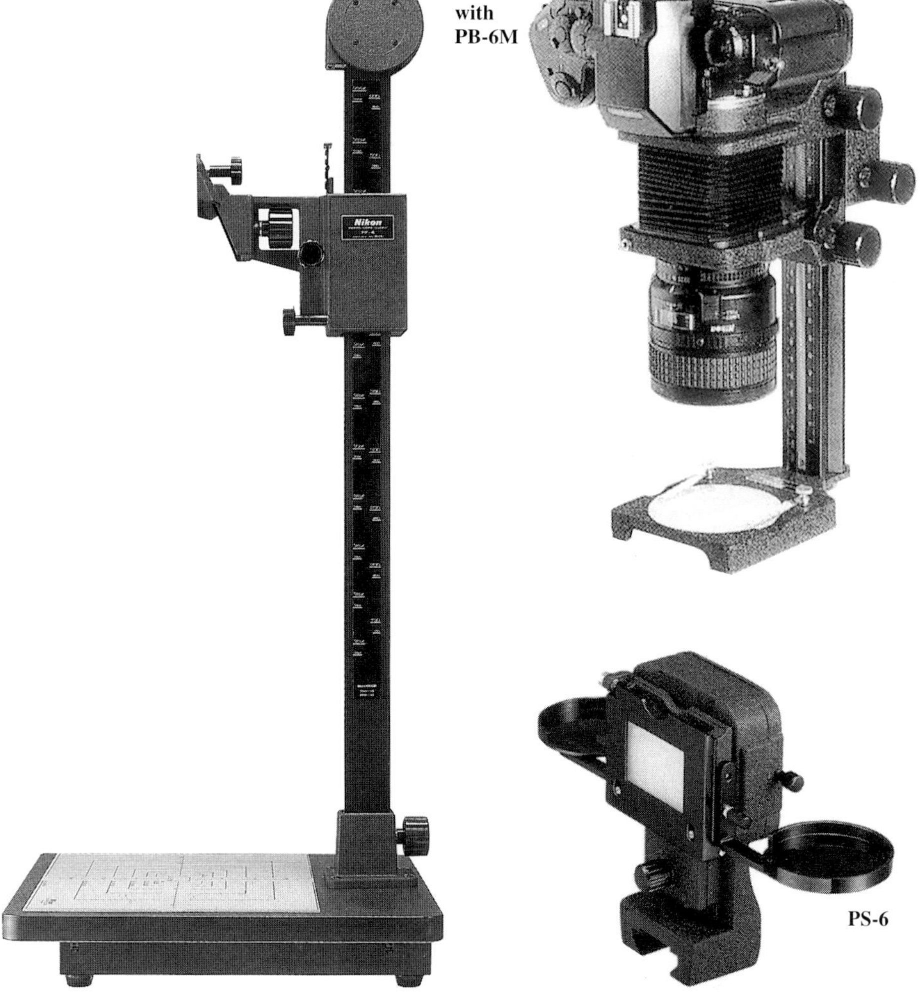

PF-4

PB-6 with PB-6M

PS-6

the lab for printing, to contests, etc. The main disadvantage of conventional slide copiers is that the reproduction size is often slightly larger than 1:1. That is, part of the original is cut off. If you wish to shoot at exactly 1:1 or select larger reproductions steplessly, use a slide copying attachment for the macro bellows.

Slide copying attachment for Macro Bellows: A compatible slide duplicating attachment, the PS-6, for lenses of focal lengths from 20-55mm is available. The unit can be moved 6mm up and down and 9mm from side to side to shoot sections of the image. Enlarging lenses attached to macro bellows are particularly suitable and optimized for close-ups and hence their use in slide duplicating. The PB-6M Macro Copy Stand is for lenses up to 60mm in diameter with an opaque acrylic plate to diffuse the light source. Copying attachments for the 55mm Micro Nikkor for slide dupes at 1:1 magnification with the normal non-AF Micro Nikkor 55mm f/2.8 requires the ES-1 slide copying attachment that screws into the filter ring. The extension tube PK-13 is also necessary.

Macro Photography with Flash

Normal TTL flash units sometimes meet the limits of their control range in macro work which can cause overexposures. Perfect lighting can, however, be obtained after experimentation. A specialized macro flash unit is recommended for photography in the magnification range of 1:2 and higher.

Macro Flash unit SB-21: The Macro flash unit SB-21 (Guide Number - 39 (ft.), 13(m) at ISO 100) was specially designed for macro photography with a light cell that can be attached to a 52mm or 62mm filter ring. At first glance, it is very similar to a ring flash. Actually, it consists of two separate flash tubes, one on the left and one on the right, that can be triggered simultaneously as well as individually. Consequently, both three-dimensional as well as flat lighting can be produced. A modeling lamp, that does not quite approximate its light output, is built in. As well as TTL control, the unit can be set to 1/1(full), 1/4 and 1/16 power manually. The unit comes with a diffuser SW-8 for illumination when the subject distance is less than 1.5in (40mm). The battery and control units are available in two designs, depending on the camera used. The AS-12 is for the F3, and the AS-14 for all other cameras. The power supply comes from either 4 AA batteries or the external battery pack LD-2 from the Medical Nikkor 120mm f/4 which holds 8 batteries. The LA-2 AC adapter makes batteries unnecessary. To mount the SB-21 on lenses that are reversed use a BR-3 (52mm) or BR-5 (62mm). TTL film sensitivity with the F3 and N4004/F-401 is ISO 25 to ISO 400. With the F4, N8008/F-801, N6006/F-601 and N2000/F-301, it is ISO 25 to ISO 1000.

Medical Nikkor 120mm f/4 IF: See chapter "Lenses, Specialized Lenses" in the "Macro Lenses" section page 112.

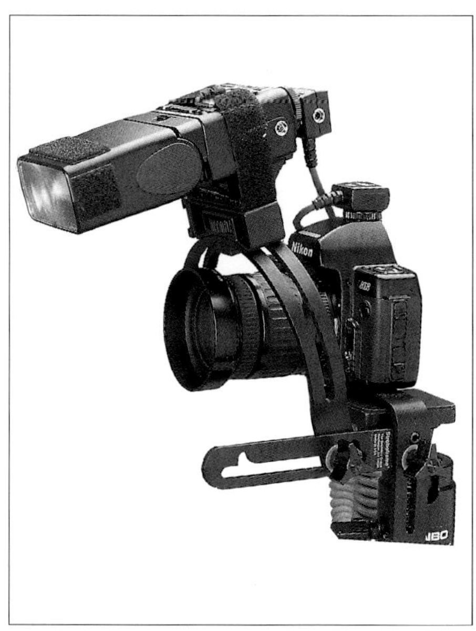

The Stroboframe® LP Macro Bracket: This flash bracket is designed specifically for close-up photography. It permits the flash to be positioned close to the subject for even flash coverage.

Nikon Flash System

The photographer's desire to be less dependent on available light by having access to a portable light source that can be controlled is as old as photography itself. In the early days of photography, when wooden, large format cameras supported by heavy tripods and equipped with slow lenses and films where standard equipment, the photographer had to put his clients' heads into holders so that they would not move during the exposure that typically lasted several minutes. The use of burning magnesium powder in a trough as a light source significantly cut down on exposure times and was seen as a great improvement regardless of its rather combustible nature. The resulting bright light brought exposure times down to seconds. It was only at the end of the 1920s that the flash tube as we know it today came into mass production. Basically, it was a magnesium filament inside a glass tube that was ignited electrically. Considerable amounts of short-lived light could thus be generated, depending on the size of the glass tube or, as it was commonly known, the flash bulb. In this form, it eventually became the cheapest and easiest solution to the illumination problem for the snap shots of amateur photographers.

In the '40s, the first electronic flash units were introduced and came into widespread use by the late 1950s. These flashes used a capacitor to release electric power into a glass tube containing gas to produce a sudden, bright blast of light. This is a consequence of the fact that an electron burst develops in the high voltage field and triggers the gas. Moreover, the release can be reproduced with the same flash tube as soon as the capacitor is recharged; hence, its inherent advantage over the flash bulb. The first electronic flashes were considerably heavier than today's remarkably compact units. Back then, a flash with guide number 30 weighed about 4.5lbs. (10kg) compared to the 12.3oz. (350g) or so for a comparable unit today. Just how far modern flash technology has come in satisfying the needs of professional photographers and a review of Nikon's flash units are the subject of this chapter.

Flash - Not the Be All and End All Light Source

Where there is light, there is also shadow and that, in essence, is the problem with small, powerful light sources. Flash units mounted on top of, or on the side of, a camera do not always result in the desired illumination, primarily because they are a small, concentrated light source that most often produces large black shadow areas and harsh light which often combines to give a less than flattering rendering of a person or product.

Disadvantages of hot shoe and handle type flashes: the lack of subtle detailing by the light itself and intrusive shadows results in a rather contrasty and yet flat look to the subject. That is, it does not bring out the contours of, for example, a face, or the surface structure of a three-dimensional subject. Instead of soft, detail defining shadows that are typical of an indirect or sidelight from such sources as a window or a studio umbrella, direct camera flash creates unsightly, hard shadows with little chance of subtle forms.

Light fall-off in depth: scenes that have depth clearly show the unavoidable falloff of illumination from such a small, narrow- angled light source. For example at a wedding, the overexposed faces in the foreground of a long table versus the individuals in shadows at the other end of the table.

Intrusive reflections: on-camera flash can also create intrusive reflections. Thus, photographing a fine piece of highly polished dark furniture or having a pane of glass (or worse, a mirror) in the picture, often results in a burst of white light from the shiny surface, along with an underexposed image as the automatic mechanism of the flash reacts to what it rightly "sees" as a flood of light.

Lack of atmosphere: direct flash images sometimes have the appearance of being sterile since a scene's atmosphere or mood comes, for the most part, from the diffusion of ambient light. If this mood is blasted away by flash, the subtleties of the scene and, therefore, its real attraction are lost. It is therefore no surprise that many news photographers, who rely heavily on flash, try to shoot whenever possible with available light or use flash in the fill-flash mode.

Tricks of the Trade in Flash Photography

Indirect Flash

If the flash unit is sufficiently strong, it can be changed from a hard, point light source into a larger, softer source by bouncing it off a white wall or ceiling. Yet, the loss of light, depending on the angle of light and the reflective properties of the surface, can be considerable. If there is enough power, however, the effects of reflections, hard shadows, washed out light skin faces, and significant light fall-off from the center to the edge of the scene can be virtually eliminated by this "bounce" technique. The reason is that the light is now falling on the subject from a wide area across the ceiling instead of just from the small flash tube. This is the same principle involved in the design of a studio umbrella. Indirect, or bounce flash requires the photographer to have some experience with this approach in order to precisely calculate the results in advance. In color photography, the slightest deviation of the wall color from pure white results in a color cast in the whole image. Those who want to use their camera as a creative tool or for snap shots (without the intrusion of the harsh look of direct flash) should consider this approach wherever the setting permits.

TTL Multiple Flash

The principle of TTL controlled multiflash: The problem of light falloff in the distance and hard shadows resulting from a single point source of light can also be solved by using several flash units simultaneously. The on-camera flash would, for example, trigger a precisely positioned flash that illuminates the background via a slave circuit. The problem is, of course, how to calculate the effect of both flash units correctly and others if they are added. Nikon offers the option of controlling several flash units simultaneously through its Multiflash System. Several units can be combined and correctly exposed images obtained with this TTL flash control.

Number of flash units that can be combined: The Nikon TTL Multiflash System can control up to five Nikon flashes via compatible cameras. The combined length of the multiflash cable cannot, however, exceed 32.8ft. (10m). With the N4004/F-401, N6006/F-601, N8008/F-801 and F4, the combined power draw of the flashes cannot exceed a certain value. This value is the sum of the identification numbers of the individual flashes. Thus, the SB-24 and SB-25 have 1, SB-16, SB-17 and SB-23 have 4, SB-22 6 and SB-20 9. For example, the F8008/F-801 and F4 have a limit of 20. (The maximum value for the other cameras can be found in their instruction manuals).

Adapters and cords for multiflash: Some Nikon flashes have built-in ports that allow direct connection of the multiflash cable to use a second flash in combination with a camera mounted flash. Otherwise, one needs an adapter cable that slides into the hot shoe to connect the first free flash. The TTL SC-17 cable is used with the N2000/F-301, N6006/F-601, N8008/ F-801 and F4. This cable ends in an adapter that takes the first flash on a hot shoe and has 2 multiflash ports for connecting additional flashes via the multiflash cables SC-18, 5ft. (1.5m) long, or SC-19, 10ft. (3m) long. In order to mount flashes on tripods, use the AS-10 multiflash adapter with tripod-mount hot shoe with Nikon System contacts and 3 multiflash ports for additional flashes. The primary flash for the F3 can be set up for TTL control via the SB-17 or the SB-16A and additional flashes via the SC-18 or SC-19. (TTL controlled multiflash is not possible with the FM-2n).

Selecting the main flash: In order to ensure that TTL controlled multiflash works acceptably, the most powerful flash has to be selected as the main unit. The weaker units can only be used for fill or effect lighting such as illuminating a background. If the scene is limited to illuminating small objects or portraits and a diffuser or some sort of reflector (or reflecting surface such as a ceiling) is used, an experienced photographer can achieve studio-like results with the Multiflash System by applying simple lighting setups normally used with studio flash units. The lack of any modeling lights does, however, leave the result of a multiflash exposure more or less to chance.

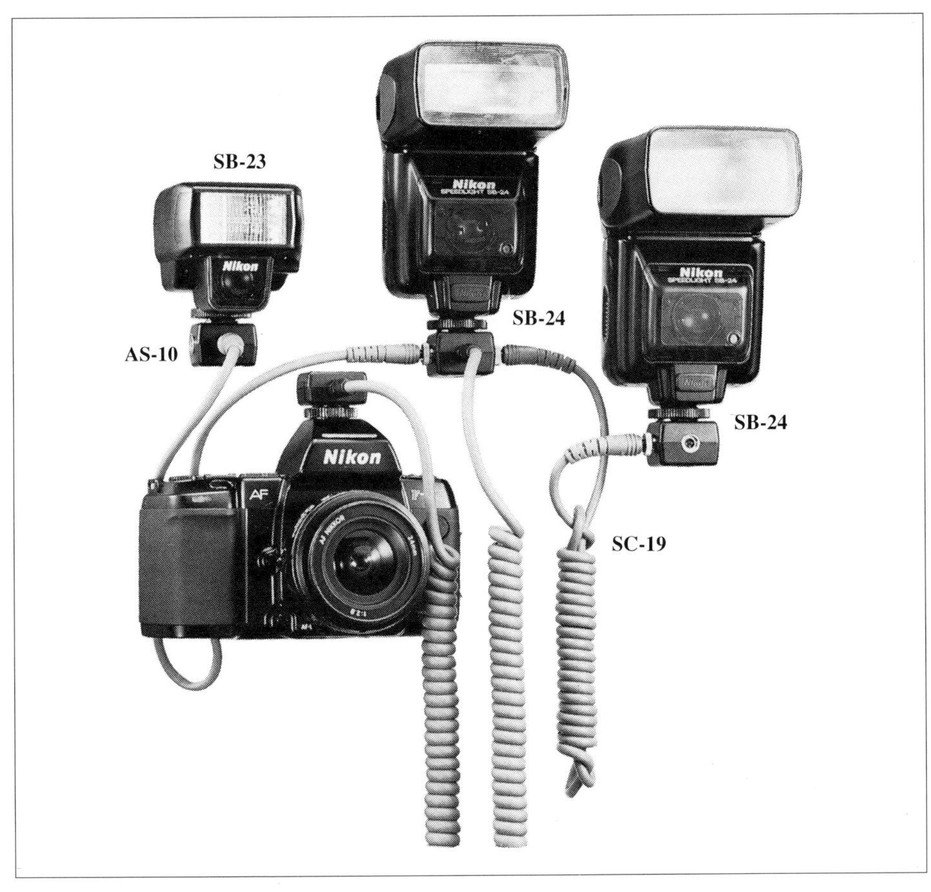

Automatic Fill Flash

When working with automatic flash units: automatic flash units have a sensor built into the flash unit which monitors the amount of light sent out by the flash when they are used as the main light source. But in addition to acting as the sole light source, these units can also be used for fill flash; a situation in which the flash is used at a lower power level than the main light setting in order to "brighten" of "fill" in the shadow areas of an otherwise well lit situation. For example, wedding photographers will use flash to remove the dark shadow areas under the eyes and neck of faces caused by bright sun. Another typical application is when the light source is behind the subject (backlighting) and the idea is to balance the face illumination with that of the backlight for an evenly lit picture. In the case of a fill-flash application, the flash illumination is set on the automatic dial at one to two stops below the ambient light f/stop value. Exactly which ratio of ambient to flash fill light represented by these choices will depend on the amount of fill the photographer likes in the picture. Thus, if the ambient light setting is f/8 at 1/60 second, the flash can be set at f/5.6, for a 2:1 ratio or f/4.0 for a 4:1 ratio as well as settings in between. For every stop of difference, the ratio between the main light and fill light doubles. Thus, one and one half stop difference would equal a 3:1 ratio. For a light balancing situation, such as the back light example, the difference might shrink to a half stop difference or be virtually equal depending on the preference of the photographer. Any of these applications of flash can be accomplished without specialized fill-flash modes.

Fill-flash with conventional TTL flash: fill-flash is possible with the TTL flash arrangements that are built into most of the presently available Nikon cameras. It is based on a sensor located in the camera that meters the light reflected from the film plane during the flash exposure. The camera controls the flash output based only on the light that is coming through the lens to take the picture. Because of this arrangement, the method just described for fill-flash using automatic flash units will not work with TTL since the flash and ambient readings are not independent of one another. Of course, there is still the option to set the flash to manual and calculate exposure (using the guide number) based on distances and apertures. A much more effective method is to use electronic fill flash modes that are based on a TTL measurement.

Matrix controlled fill flash modes: Most modern Nikon AF cameras incorporate a finely tuned TTL fill flash mode that takes surrounding light conditions into consideration in combination with either built-in camera flashes (N4004/F-401 and N6006/F-601), or with hot shoe mounted flash units (SB-16B, SB-20, SB-22, SB-23, SB-24 and SB-25).

TTL multi-sensor fill flash mode: To date, this mode is only possible with the N90/F90 in combination with any AF or AI-P Nikkors and any Nikon TTL flash unit. As with normal matrix-controlled TTL fill flash, aperture and/or shutter speed as well as a pre-selection of flash duration are set based on a measurement of ambient light (and possibly subject contrast) before the exposure takes place. After the shutter is released and the flash is triggered, the TTL control (based on a five-field matrix metering system) takes over. This exposure metering is independent of the mode selected before the exposure takes place. Extreme reflective properties of the subject are thus well corrected.

As shown here, balancing available light with fill flash can be done automatically with a Nikon AF camera and multiple Nikon system flash units. 

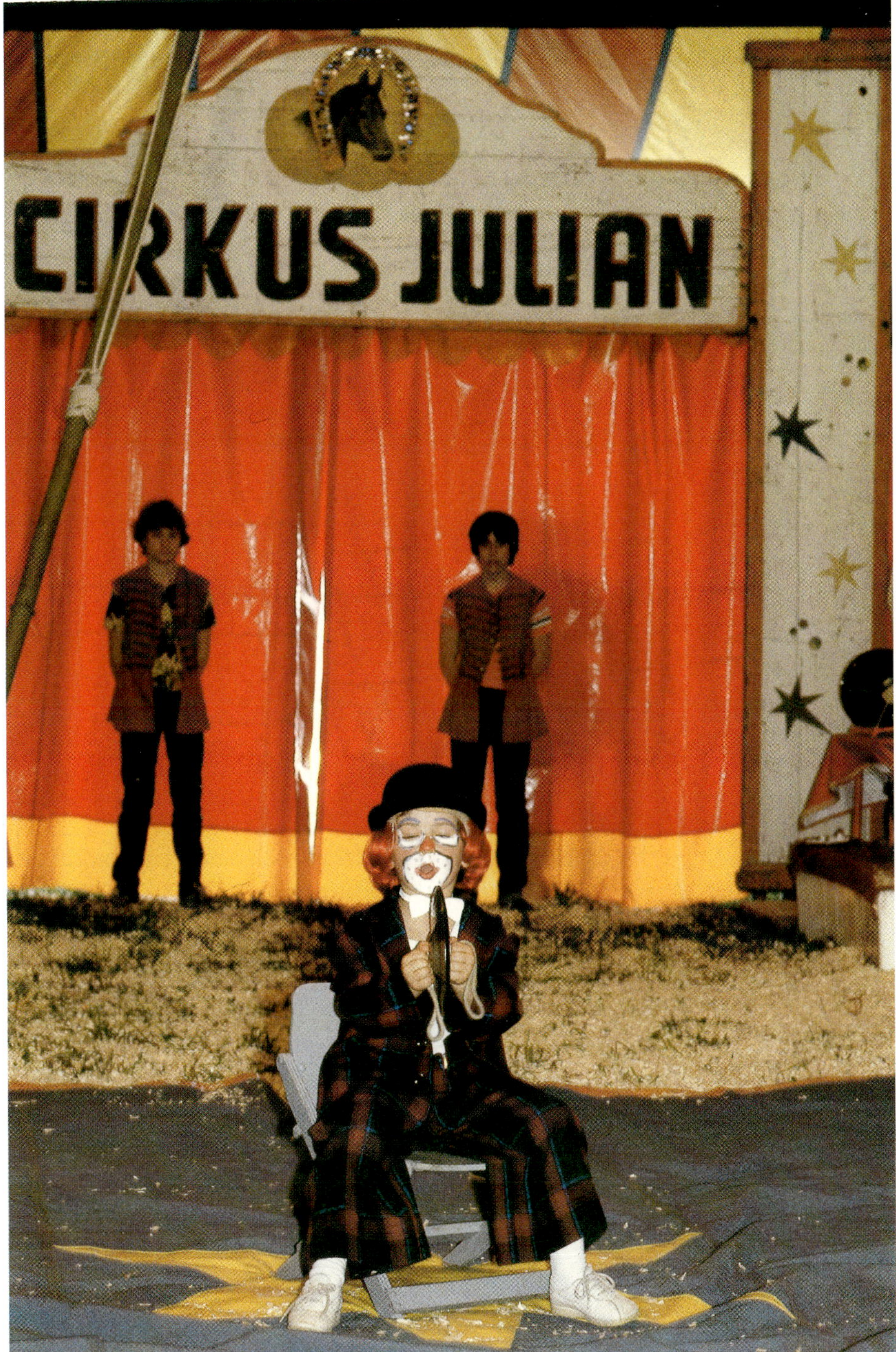
CIRKUS JULIAN

TTL multi-sensor fill flash mode with test flash: to date, only possible with the N90/F90 combined with the SB-25 and any AF or AI-P Nikkor. When the trigger is fully depressed, the SB-25 sends out a series of invisible measuring flashes that are picked up by the multi-sensor and measured by the unit's electronics. This flash control obtains information regarding the spatial distribution of the subject as well as its reflective properties and can, therefore, select an appropriate flash duration correction.

3D matrix-controlled fill flash: to date, only possible with the N90/F90 combined with the SB-25 and any Type D Nikkor. Compared to the above, the distance to the subject is also taken into account by using the Type D lenses. This lends increasing accuracy in identifying off-center subjects and extreme reflective properties.

Guide Number of Nikon System Flash Units
Definition and practical meaning: the highest light output that a flash can produce (corresponding to a flash in manual mode at full power) is given by the so-called guide number. This guide number is cited relative to a film speed, most frequently, ISO 100. When using a faster or slower film, a correspondingly different guide number applies. For example: GN 30 at ISO 100 equals GN 42 at ISO 200, GN 60 at ISO 600 or GN 21 at ISO 50. A flash unit's guide number is a representation of its output in terms of the parameters of distance (range) and aperture.

Guide number	= aperture x distance
Aperture	= guide number / distance
Distance	= guide number / aperture

If one divides the guide number by the flash-to-subject distance, the appropriate aperture is obtained for correct exposure. For a specific aperture, divide the guide number by the aperture and obtain the correct distance for that aperture.

Calculations with GN not necessary in automatic flash modes: When using a flash manually, the flash distance and the appropriate aperture are determined with the help of a dial on the back of the flash unit and then making the recommended settings on the camera. With non-TTL automatic flash units, or a TTL unit in its automatic non-TTL mode, on the other hand, the correct aperture is first set manually on both the camera and the flash unit. The output is then controlled automatically by the sensor in the flash unit. The number of apertures that can be chosen is limited to a small range, depending on the model. More powerful units tend to have more choices. With TTL flash, on the other hand, one can select from a very wide range of apertures to set on the lens. The flash output then occurs automatically via the sensor in the camera.

Flash in the Studio

Studio Methods

Why shoot in the studio and not on location? The justification for shooting in the studio is, on the one hand, independence from the weather within predictable location lighting conditions. On the other hand, work in the studio is very often necessary because of the need to produce exactly what the client wants. This usually requires the use of several high-powered flash units along with a wide range of reflectors and light sources (i.e. hard spotlights or soft, hazy lights) to reproduce everything from brilliant sunshine to the soft light coming from a north-facing window. All this is usually done with such power as to permit the smallest apertures, even with slow film.

Since the flash duration of most studio flashes is at least 1/500 second or shorter, movement can also be frozen and one can shoot hand-held without a tripod. In addition to light sources, the use of reflector boards or diffusers in the studio is commonplace in order to literally shape the light's effect. The lighting can also be previewed because studio flash units have modeling lights that vary their output proportionally to the flash power selected. In this manner, it is possible to have a good idea of the lighting conditions at the time of exposure, unlike the situation with hot shoe flashes that leave you, quite literally, in the dark until the film is back from the lab. It is obvious that any auto-flash mode would not be appropriate in such a precisely arranged multi-flash studio situation. After all, each flash in such a setup would be accorded a different output or purpose, which would be impossible for a camera flash sensor to "understand."

Manual flash exposure metering in a studio arrangement: after all the parameters have been set on the various studio flash units, the camera's aperture is determined through a test flash. To do this, one uses a hand-held flash meter to measure the light falling on the object (incident light reading) facing the direction of the camera. When metering light in this incident method, the light that hits the subject is the point of the measurement and not the light from the subject itself. The reflective properties of the subject are not being measured as would occur with the use of a reflected light meter. It may, therefore, be necessary to adjust the exposure to a subject that has unusual reflective properties as in being very shiny.

Triggering flashes via cables, remotes, etc. in the studio: the flash is triggered by a meter 39.4in. long cable that is plugged into the camera's sync socket. Unfortunately, many otherwise advanced cameras lack this important "studio feature" and thus a sync cable adapter, AS-15, that slides into the hot shoe is required for the N2000/F-301, N4004/F-401, N6006/F-601, N6000/F-601m and N8008/F-801. An alternative is to use a low powered hot shoe flash aimed at the ceiling to trip the slave sensors that are part of most studio strobes. This "trip flash" attached to the camera fires and the others trigger at the same time via their slave circuits. Another way of dealing with firing these flash units is to use an infra-red sensor such as those manufactured by Wein, available as an accessory for cordless infrared triggering via a transmitter that is mounted on the camera's hot shoe and receivers that go on each flash head, or the power pack to which the heads are attached. This is, without doubt, the most elegant solution.

Effect of filters, extension tubes, etc.: most filters and every extension tube in close-up photography requires corresponding aperture corrections or changes in the flash output, if not working TTL. Refer to the instruction sheets that come with these accessories

Studio Flash Exposures with Nikon Cameras

In principle, all Nikon cameras can be used for photography with studio flash units in manual or auto focus mode. In fact, aside from being able to set the shutter speed and aperture in conjunction with meter readings of the studio strobes, the only thing one really needs from the camera is to be able to select the flash sync speed manually and to be able to set the lens aperture manually. It would, however, be useful to have the effective aperture value shown in 1/3 stops on the lens since exposure control in studio settings with transparency films is often on this level. Aside from that, all of the presently available Nikon cameras, with the possible inconvenience of the PC connection noted earlier, work very well under studio conditions.

Nikon Flash Units

The following sections detail the characteristics of the Nikon system flash units. Only those currently available are included.

SB-11 Flash

Compatibility: TTL flash with adapter SC-12 (F3) or with SC-23 (N2000/F-301, N6006/F-601, N8008/F-801, F4, N90/F90); conventional non-TTL auto flash with the FM-2n and all other Nikon cameras via the sensor cable SC-13 and the SU-3 sensor. ***Output and coverage:*** handle-type flash with guide number 118 (ft.) 36 (m) at ISO 100 and coverage corresponding to a 35mm wide angle lens (with diffuser SW-3, the GN drops to 82 (ft.) 25 (m) and coverage increases to a 28mm lens). ***Reflector:*** tiltable. ***Flash modes:*** TTL flash; non-TTL flash; and manual mode. ***Auto range at ISO 100:*** non-TTL autoflash mode at apertures of f/4, f/5.6 and f/8 [23.6in.-29.5ft. (0.6m-9m) at f/4; 23.6in.-21ft. (0.6m-6.4m) at f/5.6; 23.6in.-14.8ft. (0.6m-4.5m) at f/8: each at ISO 100]. TTL auto flash mode, in comparison, has an extended, stepless aperture range. Manual flash: at 1/1 (full) to 1/4 power. ***Film speed range:*** ISO 25-800; TTL mode ISO 25-400. ***Recycle time:*** approximately 8 seconds for full charge with fresh batteries. ***Flash capacity:*** approximately 150 flashes at full power. ***Batteries:*** AA type, 8 total. Capacity can be increased with the external battery packs SD-7 and SD-8. ***Standard accessories:*** wide angle diffuser SW-3; flash rail SK-4; sync cable SC-11; sensor SU-3 with option of 3 computer apertures 4/5.6/8 and 1/1 (full) and 1/4 power in manual. ***Size:*** without rail HxWxD: 10.9 x 4.1 x 4.6in. (276 x 104 x 118mm). ***Weight:*** without batteries and rail 30.3oz. (860g).

SB-14 Flash

Compatibility: TTL flash with adapter SC-12 (F3) or with SC-23 (N2000/F-301, N6006/F-601, N8008/F-801, F4, N90/F90); conventional non-TTL auto flash with the FM-2n and all other Nikon cameras via the sensor cable SC-13 and the SU-3 sensor. ***Output and coverage:*** handle-type flash with guide number 105 (ft.) 32 (m) at ISO 100 and coverage corresponding to a 28mm wide angle lens; with diffuser SW-5, GN drops to 72 (ft.) 22 (m) and coverage extends to a 24mm lens. ***Reflector:*** tiltable and rotatable, additional diffusers can be mounted. ***Flash modes:*** TTL, non-TTL, manual. ***Auto range at ISO 100:*** non-TTL flash mode at apertures of f/4, f/5.6, f/8 [2ft.-26 ft. (0.6m-8m) at f/4; 2ft. - 18.4ft. (0.6m-5.6m) at f/5.6; 2ft.-13.1ft. (0.6m-4m) at f/8; at ISO 100]. TTL flash mode has, in comparison, a wider, stepless range of apertures. ***Manual mode:*** at full and 1/4 power. ***Film speed range:*** ISO 25-800; TTL mode ISO 25-400. ***Recycle time:*** approximately 8 seconds at full power with fresh batteries. ***Flash capacity:*** approximately 270 flashes at full power. ***Power source:*** no built-in battery compartment, instead external battery unit SD-7 which holds 6 AA cells. ***Unique feature:*** external battery unit. ***Standard accessories:*** wide angle diffuser SW-5, flash rail SK-5, sync cable SC-11, sensor unit SU-3. ***Size:*** without rail HxWxD 8.5 x 3.7 x 3.6in. (217 x 94 x 91mm); battery unit SD-7 3.7 x 7.9 x 1.8in. (95 x 200 x 45mm). ***Weight:*** without batteries and rail 18.2oz. (515g); battery unit SD-7 15.5oz. (440g).

SB-140 Special-Purpose Flash

Compatibility: a special version of the SB-14 with the same functions but is intended for UV and infrared photography. TTL flash mode with the SC-12 cable (F3) or the SC-23 (N2000/F-301, N6006/F-601, N8008/F-801, F4, N90/F90); conventional non-TTL flash with all Nikon cameras also with the SC-13 sensor cable and SU-3 sensor unit. ***Output and coverage:*** GN 104 (ft.) 32 (m) with SW-5V and normal ISO 100 film; GN 52 (ft.)16 (m) with SW-5UV and Kodak spectroscopic film 103-0; GN 72 (ft.) 22 (m) with SW-5IR and Kodak high speed infra-red film 2481; coverage corresponding to a 28mm wide angle lens. ***Reflector:*** rotatable and tiltable. ***Mountable band width filters:*** (given with respect to transmitted wavelengths in nm = nanometers):

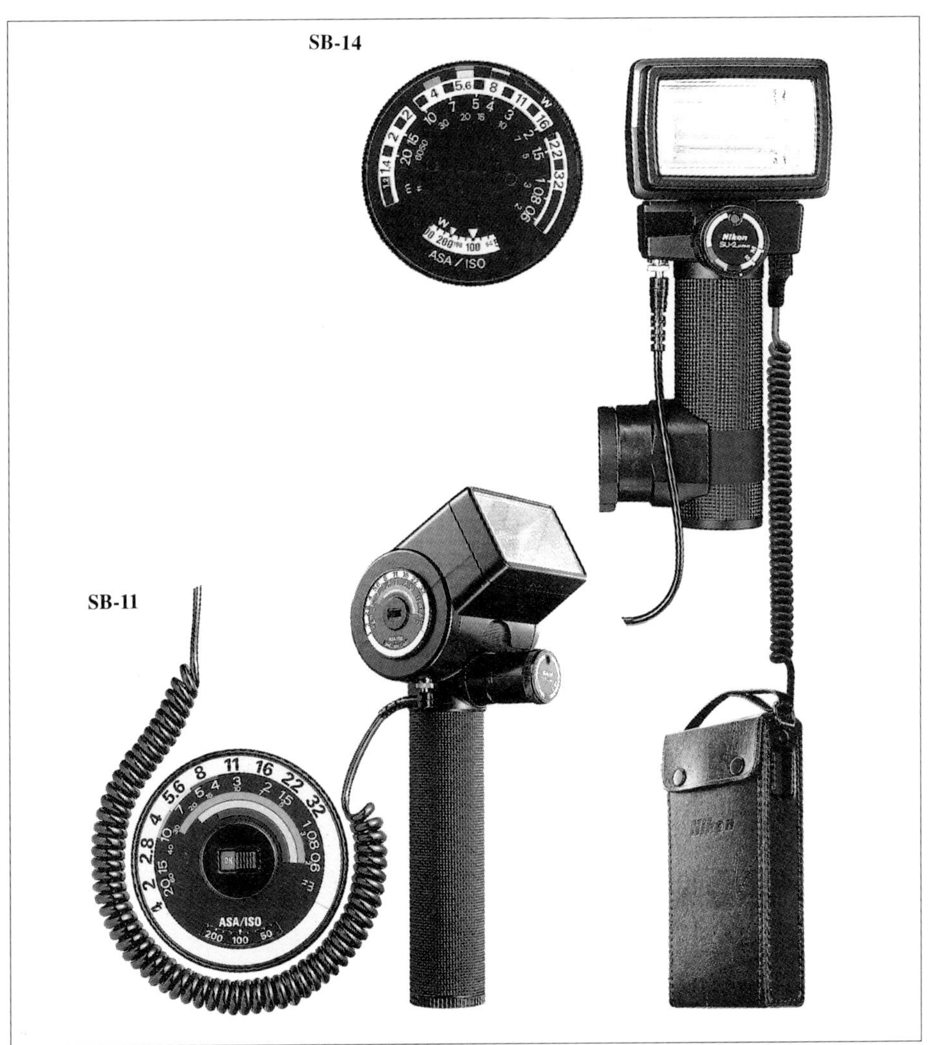

SW-5V = 400-1100nm; SW-5UV = 300-400nm; SW5-IR = 750-1100nm. ***Flash modes:*** without filter, like the SB-14 (only for normal films that are sensitive to the visible spectrum). Automation not possible in the real UV and IR ranges. ***Auto range at ISO 100:*** same as the SB-14 (above). ***Film speed range:*** ISO 12-1600. ***Recycle time:*** approximately 9.5 seconds at full power with fresh batteries. ***Flash capacity:*** approximately 270 flashes at full power. ***Standard accessories:*** band pass filters SW-5V, SW-5UV, SW-5IR; flash rail SK-5; sync cable SC-11; sensor unit SU-3 with settings of 4 computer apertures f/4, f/5.6, f/8 as well as manual full and 1/4 power. Size: without rail HxWxD: 8.5 x 3.7 x 3.6in. (217 x 94 x 91mm); battery unit SD-7, 3.7 x 7.9 x 1.8in. (95 x 200 x 45mm). ***Weight:*** without batteries and rail 18.2oz. (515g); battery unit SD-7, 15.5oz. (440g).

SB-16A/SB-16B Flash

Compatibility: (A-version, TTL with the F3); (B-version with the N2000/F-301, N4004/F-401, N5005, N6006/F-601, N8008/F-801, N90/F90 and F4); all program TTL modes and fill-flash modes that are available on the respective cameras; non-TTL autoflash possible with the unit's built-in sensor when using the FM-2n and all other Nikon cameras; flash shoe in the A-version interchangeable with the AS-8, special shoe for the F3, and in the B-version with the AS-9 for all other Nikon cameras. ***Output and coverage:*** GN 105 (ft.) 32 (m) reflector position 35mm, at ISO 100. ***Reflector:*** tiltable and rotatable zoom reflector with 4 settings (28mm, 35mm, 50mm, 85mm) with an additional diffuser SW-7 (to 24mm); fixed secondary reflector for fill-flash when bouncing the main reflector. ***Flash modes:*** TTL; non-TTL with built-in sensor; manual. Auto range at ISO 100: non-TTL with the fixed apertures of f/4 and f/8. All apertures from f/2 to f/22 can be steplessly selected independent of the film speed and minimum distance. The range is from 23.6in.to 52.5ft. (0.6m to 16m), depending on the aperture. ***Manual flash:*** at full power; with motor drive setting with GN 26 (ft.) 8 (m) at 1/16 output. ***Film speed range:*** ISO 25-1000, TTL ISO 25-400. ***Recycle time:*** approximately 11 seconds at full power with fresh batteries. Flash capacity: approximately 100 flashes at full power. ***Batteries:*** 4 AA type. ***Unique features:*** TTL multiflash port. With TTL cable SC-14, remote flashing (A-version with the F3) possible. ***Standard accessories:*** wide angle dif-

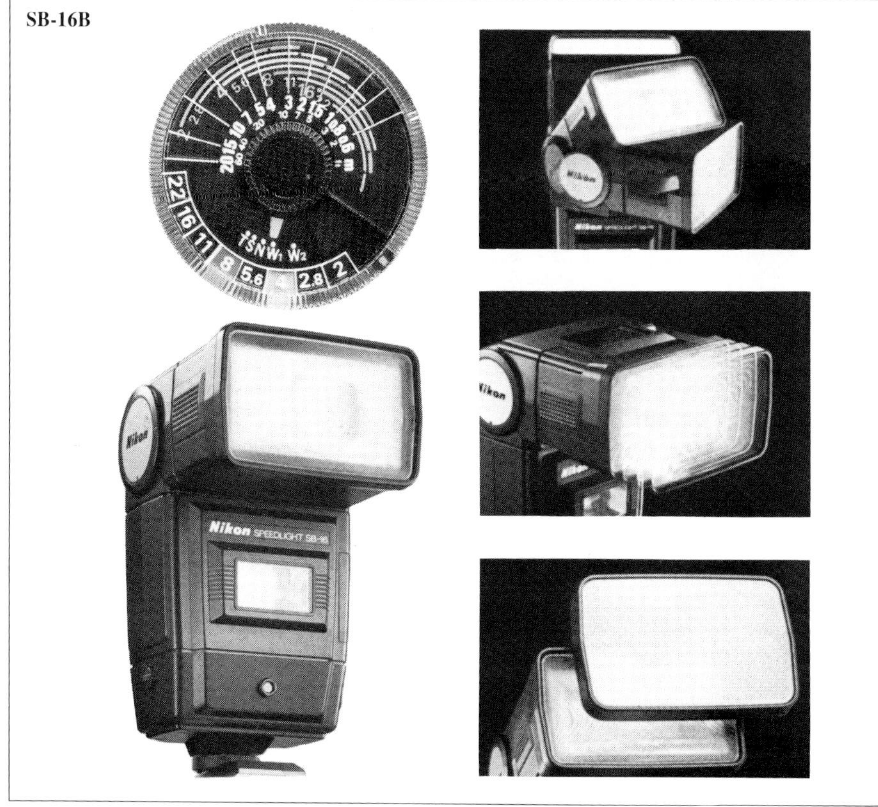

SB-16B

fuser SW-7; soft case SS-16; battery holder MS-5. ***Size:*** HxWxD: SB-16A 6.5 x 3.2 x3 .9in. (166.5 x 82 x100mm); SB-16B 5.7 x 3.2 x 3.9in. (144 x 82 x 100mm). ***Weight:*** without batteries SB-16A 18oz. (510g); SB-16B 16.5oz. (470g).

SB-17 Flash

Compatibility: Specially designed for the F3, the SB-17 is compatible with all other Nikon cameras with the accessory shoe AS-6; TTL mode only with the F3; all other Nikon cameras allow non-TTL auto flash control via the built-in sensor in combination with the AS-6. ***Output and coverage:*** GN 82 (ft.) 25 (m) at ISO 100 (35mm); with the wide angle diffuser SW-6 up to 28mm at GN 59 (ft.)18 (m). ***Reflector:*** rotatable; additional diffuser screen. ***Flash modes:*** TTL mode (see above); non-TTL auto mode; manual. ***Manual mode:*** full power and motor drive setting with 4 sequential flashes (3.5 images/second) at GN 7. ***Auto range at ISO 100:*** non-TTL auto mode with the fixed apertures of f/4 and f/8; 23.6in.-20.4ft. (0.6m-6.2m) at f/4 and 23.6in.-10.2ft. (0.6m-3.1m) at f/8. In TTL mode, all apertures between f/2 and f/22 can be steplessly selected independent of film speed and minimum distance. The range varies between 23.6in. (0.6m) and 41ft. (12.5m) depending on aperture. ***Film speed range:*** ISO 25-1000, TTL 25-400. ***Recycle time:*** approximately 8 seconds at full power with fresh batteries. ***Flash capacity:*** approximately 160 flashes at full power. ***Batteries:*** 4 AA type. ***Unique features:*** TTL multiflash port. ***Standard accessories:*** wide angle diffuser SW-6; soft case SS-17; battery holder MS-6. ***Size:*** without accessory shoe HxWxD 1.7 x 4 x 3.5in. (43 x1 01 x 90mm) ***Weight:*** without batteries 10.6oz. (300g).

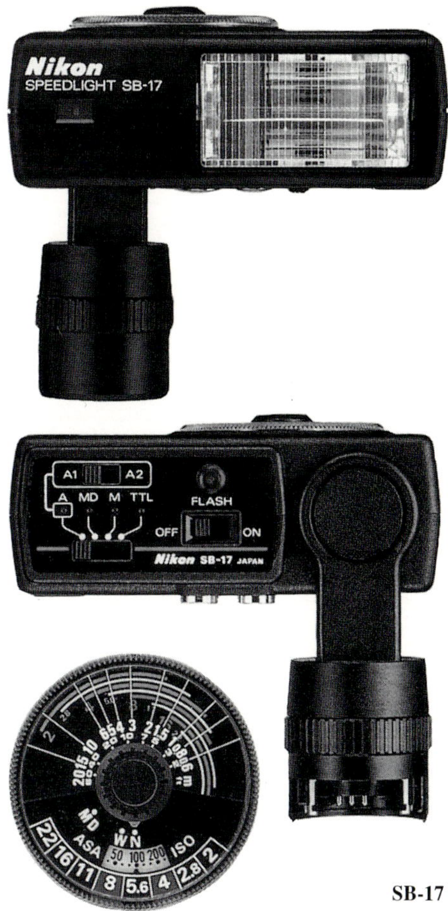

SB-17

SB-20 Flash

Compatibility: TTL mode with N2000/F-301, N4004/F-401, N5005, N6006/F-601, N6000/F-601m, N8008/F-801, N90/F90 and F4; depending on the camera, also TTL program mode and fill flash mode. FM-2n, F3 (only via AS-4 or AS-7 adapters) and all other Nikon cameras allow non-TTL autoflash via the built-in sensor. ***Output and coverage:*** GN 98 (ft.) 30 (m) at ISO 100 (reflector at 35mm). ***Reflector:*** tiltable zoom reflector with 3 settings (28mm, 35mm, 85mm). ***Flash modes:*** TTL auto flash mode; non-TTL flash mode with built-in sensor; manual. Auto range at ISO 100: non-TTL flash mode with fixed apertures of f/2, f/2.8, f/4, f/5.6 and f/8 6.2ft.-49.2ft. (1.9m-15m) at f/2 and 4.3ft.-32.8ft. (1.3m-10m) at f/2.8; 3.3ft.-24.6ft. (1m-7.5m) at f/4; 2.3ft.-17.4ft. (0.7m-5.3m) at f/5.6; 2ft.-12.1ft. (0.6m-3.7m) at f/8, all at reflector setting 35mm. All apertures can be steplessly selected in TTL mode independent of film

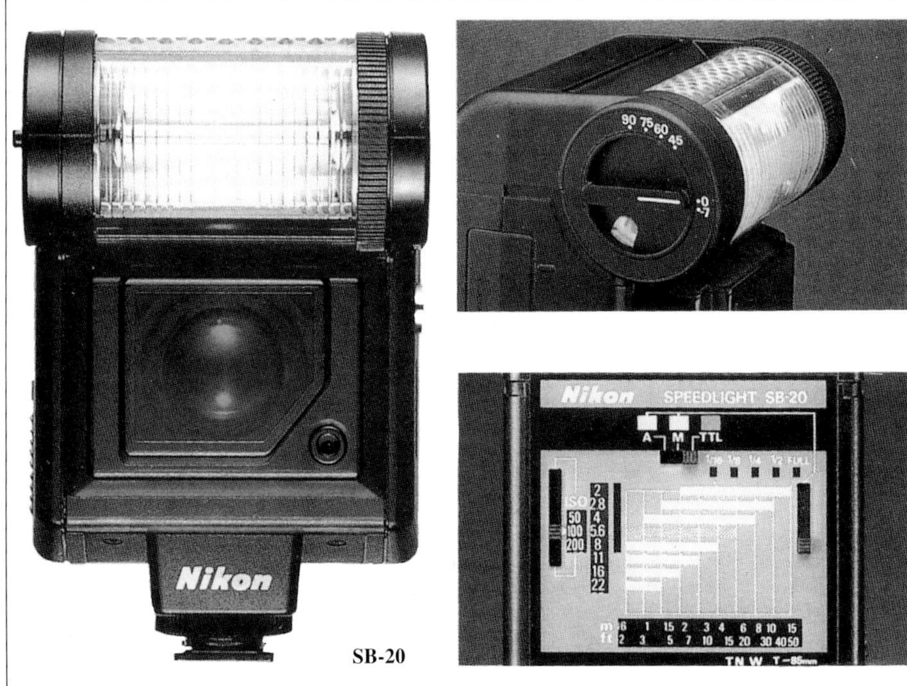

SB-20

speed and minimum distance. The range varies between 1.6ft. and 65.7ft. (0.5m and 20m) depending on aperture. ***Manual flash:*** choice of full power, 1/2, 1/4, 1/8 and 1/16, in the latter case, up to 8 images per second with motor-drive cameras. ***Film speed range:*** ISO 25-1600; in TTL mode ISO 25-1000 with N2000/F-301, N6006/F-601, N6000/F-601m, N8008/F-801 F4 and N90/F90 or ISO 25-400 with the N2000. ***Recycle time:*** approximately 7 seconds at full power with fresh batteries. ***Flash capacity:*** approximately 160 flashes at full power. ***Batteries:*** 4 AA type; external battery units SD-7 or SD-8 can be connected for additional capacity and shortened recycle times. ***AF Illuminator:*** If lighting is insufficient to allow the AF system to focus in "S," sharpness priority mode, the flash emits LED measuring light in the direction of the subject. AF cameras can thus focus in complete darkness. ***Unique features:*** Stand-by setting for self shut-off after 1-2 minutes and reactivation after touching the shutter release of an N2000, N6000 and all AF Nikon cameras; TTL multi-flash port. Remote flash possible with the SC-17 TTL cable on the N2000, N6000 and all Nikon AF cameras. ***Accessories:*** Soft case SS-20 (included); battery holders SD-7 or SD-8. ***Size:*** without accessory shoe HxWxD: 4.3 x 2.7 x 2.8in. (110 x 70 x 71mm) ***Weight:*** without batteries 9.2oz. (260g).

SB-22 Flash

Compatibility: TTL flash mode with N2000/F-301, N4004/F-401, N5005, N6006/F-601, N6000/F-601m, N8008/F-801, N90/F90 and F4; depending on the camera, also TTL program mode and fill flash mode. FM-2n, F3 (only via AS-4 or AS-7 adapters) and all other Nikon cameras allow non-TTL autoflash via the built-in sensor. ***Output and coverage:*** GN 82 (ft.) 25 (m) at ISO 100 and coverage corresponding to a 35mm lens (GN drops to 59 (ft.) 18 (m) and coverage extends to 28mm coverage with wide angle diffuser). ***Reflector:*** tiltable with optional wide angle diffuser. ***Flash modes:*** TTL auto mode; non-TTL auto mode; manual. ***Auto range at ISO 100:*** non-TTL auto mode with built-in sensor for f/4 2.6ft.-20.4ft. (0.8m-6.2m) and f/8 2ft.-14.4ft. (0.6m-4.4m) each at ISO 100. TTL flash mode with stepless selection of apertures from f/2-f/22. The range varies between 2ft. and 65.7ft. (0.6m and 20m) independent of film speed and aperture. ***Manual flash:*** choice of full power and motor drive setting MD for a series of 4 exposures (with up to 5 images per second) with a GN of 8 at ISO 100. With external battery holder MD-7, a series of up to 40 images is possible. ***Film speed range:*** ISO 25-1600; TTL mode ISO 25-1000 with N6006/F-601, N6000/F-601m, N8008/F-801, N90/F90 and F4 (ISO 25-400 with N2000). ***Recycle time:*** approximately 4 seconds at full power with fresh batteries. ***Flash capacity:*** approximately 200 flashes at full power. ***Batteries:*** 4 type AA; the SD-7 or SD-8 battery units for increased flash capacity and reduced recycle time. ***AF Illuminator:*** If lighting is insufficient to allow the AF system to focus in "S" mode, the flash emits measuring light in the direction of the subject. AF cameras can thus focus in complete darkness. ***Unique features:*** stand-by setting for self shut-off after 1-2 minutes and re-activation after touching the trigger of an N2000/F-301, N6000/F-601m and all AF Nikon cameras; TTL multiflash port. Remote flashing possible with the SC-17 TTL cable on the N2000/F-301, N6000/F-601m and all Nikon AF cameras.

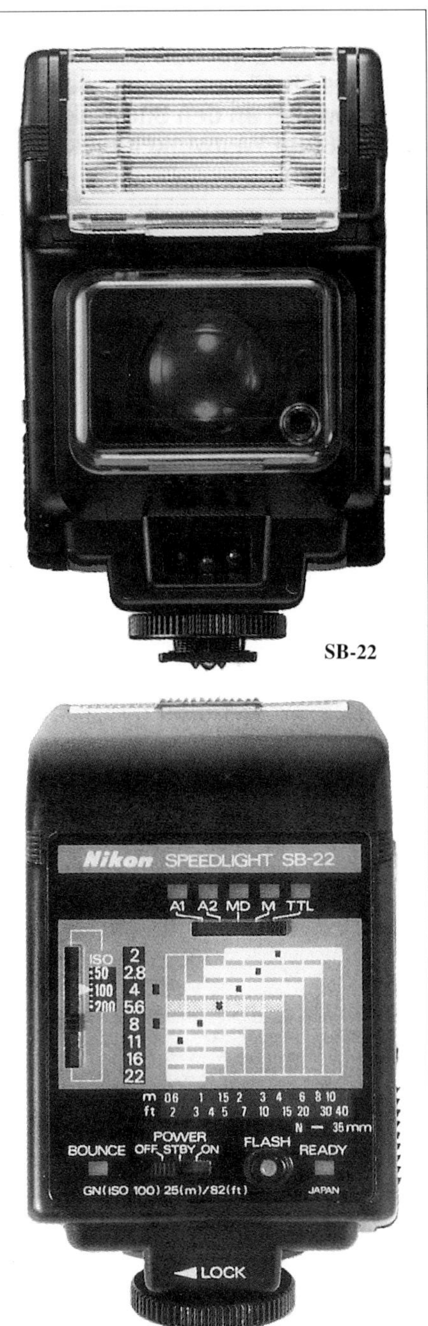

SB-22

Accessories: Soft case SS-22 (included); battery holders SD-7 or SD-8. Size: without accessory shoe HxWxD: 4.1 x 2.7 x 3.1in. (105 x 68 x 80mm) ***Weight:*** without batteries 8.8oz. (250g).

SB-23 Flash

Compatibility: TTL flash mode with N2000/F-301, N4004/F-401, N60006/F-601, N6000/F-601m, N8008/F-801, N90/F90 and F4; depending on the camera, also TTL program mode and fill flash mode. FM-2n, F3 (only via AS-4 or AS-7 adapters) and all other Nikon cameras allow non-TTL auto flash via the built-in sensor. ***Output and coverage:*** GN 20 at ISO 100 and coverage of 35mm. ***Reflector:*** fixed reflector with fixed angle of illumination. ***Flash modes:*** TTL auto mode; manual. ***Auto range at ISO 100:*** 2.3ft.-12ft. (0.7m-3.5m) at f/5.6. Other film speeds as well as all other apertures result in correspondingly different ranges. ***Manual mode:*** only at full power. ***Film speed range:*** ISO 25-1600; TTL mode ISO 25-1000 with N6006/F-601, N6000/F-601m, N8008/F-801, N90/F90 and F4 (ISO 25-400 with N2000). ***Recycle time:*** approximately 2 seconds at full power with fresh batteries. ***Flash capacity:*** approximately 400 flashes at full power. ***Batteries:*** 4 AA type. ***AF Illuminator:*** If lighting is insufficient to allow the AF system to focus in sharpness priority mode, the flash emits LED measuring light in the direction of the subject. AF cameras can thus focus in complete darkness. ***Unique features:*** TTL multiflash port; Remote flashing possible with the SC-17 TTL cable on the N2000, N6006 and all Nikon AF cameras. ***Standard accessories:*** Soft case SS-23. ***Size:*** without accessory shoe, HxWxD: 2.6 x 2.5 x 3.3in. (67 x 64 x 84mm) ***Weight:*** without batteries 4.9oz. (140g).

SB-24 Flash

Compatibility: TTL flash mode with N2000/F-301, N4004/F-401, N6006/F-601, N6000/F-601m, N8008/F-801, N90/F90 and F4; depending on the camera, also TTL program mode and fill flash mode. FM-2n, F3 (only via AS-4 or AS-7 adapters) and all other Nikon cameras allow non-TTL autoflash via the built-in sensor (See special functions). ***Electronics:*** micro-processor controlled thyristor connected in series. ***Flash duration:*** depends on the power level; it lies between about 1/1000 second (at 1/1 power or TTL control at full) and 1/20000 second (at 1/32 or TTL control at minimum). ***Output and coverage:*** the guide number depends on the reflector setting and the film speed. At ISO 100 the following values apply: GN (ft./m) 98/30 at 24mm, 105/32 at 28mm, 118/36 at 35mm, 138/42 at 50mm, 157/48 at 70mm and 164/50 at 85mm. ***Zoom head:*** motor zoom between 24mm and 85mm controlled by buttons. Fully automatic setting with the N8008/F-801, N90/F90 and F4 when using AF lenses. ***Tilt flash head for close-up and bounce:*** with click stops vertically from -7° to +90°, horizontal from -90° to

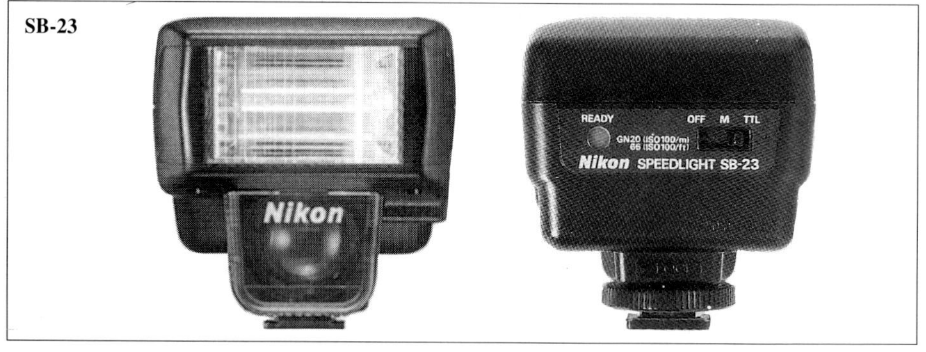

SB-23

+270°. ***Synchronization:*** choice of NORMAL with the front curtain and REAR with rear curtain. Independent of special flash units, the N6006, N6000 and N90/F90 have rear sync with all modern Nikon System flashes. Long-time sync SLOW with all appropriate cameras. ***Flash modes:*** TTL (via the camera's built-in sensor); A (computer flash via the sensor built into the flash); M (fully manual setting of output and aperture appropriate for the distance). Auto range at ISO 100: in non-TTL mode (computer flash), the fixed apertures of f/2, f/2.8, f/4, f/5.6, f/8 and f/11 can be selected. TTL flash mode with stepless selection of apertures from f/1.4 to f/32 independent of film speed and minimum distance. The range varies between 2ft. and 65.7ft. (0.6m and 20m) depending on aperture. ***Manual flash exposure corrections:*** corrections between +1 and -3 EV applying only to the TTL flash automation can be set with the F4 or N8008/F-801. (N2000, N6000 and N90 can do this with other Nikon System flashes as well.) ***Manual flash:*** Power levels of 1/1, 1/2, 1/4, 1/8, 1/16 and 1/32 can be selected in manual mode. At 1/16, short motor-drive series exposures or single images with strobe effects with up to 8 images per second can be created. ***Strobe flash:*** strobe function where time between flashes of 1/10 second to 1 second can be selected as well as number of flashes per frame from 2 to 8.

Film sensitivity range: manual ISO 6-6400; in TTL mode, depending on the camera, from ISO 25-1000 or ISO 25-400. Recycle time and number of flashes: with 4 fresh batteries, approximately 100 flashes at full power with recycle times between approximately 7 and 30 seconds can be produced. ***Batteries, power sources:*** 4 AA type. The SD-7 or SD-8 can also be connected for extended flash capacity and shortened recycle times (i.e. for longer motor-drive series). ***Stand-by:*** approximately 80 seconds after the last flash, the SB-24 turns itself off. It reactivates when the shutter of an N2000/F-301, N6000/F-601m or any AF Nikon camera is touched. ***Flash control:*** The flash unit has a red indicator light that shows if the flash is ready and if the flash output it suf-

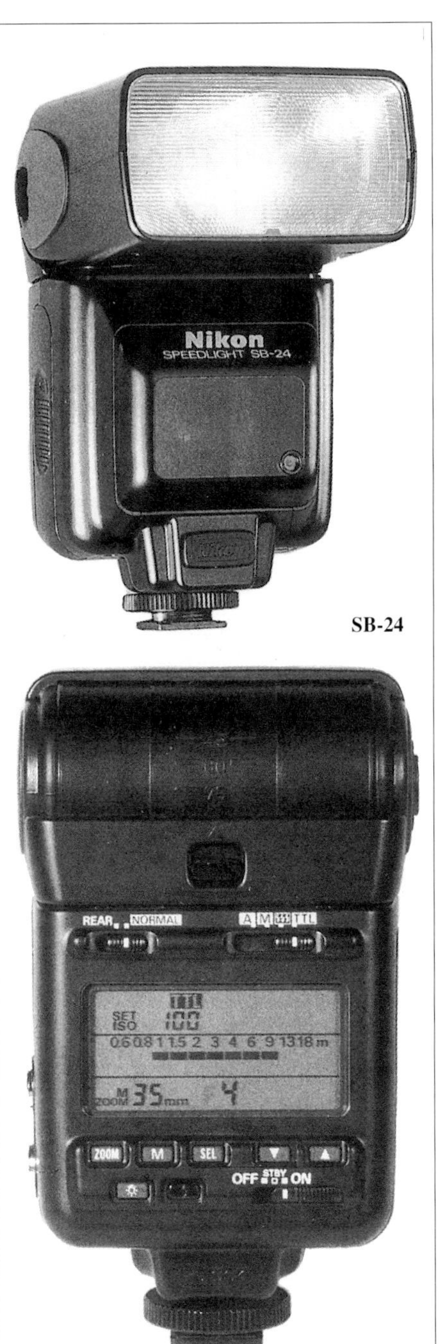

SB-24

ficient. ***Test flash function:*** The indicator light is combined with a manual trigger button. In A and TTL modes, the reflected light is read by a sensor in the flash unit. ***AF Illuminator:*** If lighting is insufficient to allow the AF system to focus in sharpness priority mode, the flash emits LED measuring light in the direction of the subject. AF cameras can thus focus in complete darkness. ***Operation:*** Main functions via main switch, all fine-tuned functions via buttons. All functions and values are displayed on an LCD panel. ***LCD Panel:*** shows all functions and values. ***Display illumination:*** fluorescent illumination activated for approximately 8 seconds. TTL multiflash port: Remote flash is possible with the N2000/F-301 and N6000/F-601m and all AF Nikon Cameras via the SC-17 TTL cable. ***Size:*** without accessory shoe HxWxD: 5.2 x 3.1 x 3.9in. (131 x 80 x 100mm). ***Weight:*** without batteries: 13.7oz. (390g) ***Accessories:*** soft case SS-24 (included), battery units SD-7 and SD-8.

SB-25 Flash

Compatibility: TTL flash mode with N2000/F-301, N4004/F-401, N5005, N6006/F-601, N6000/F-601m, N8008/F-801, N90/F90 and F4; depending on the camera, also TTL program mode and fill flash mode. FM-2n, F3 (only via AS-4 or AS-7 adapters) and all other Nikon cameras allow non-TTL auto flash via the built-in sensor (See special functions). ***Electronics:*** micro-processor controlled flash unit with an Isolated Gate Bipolar Transistor (IGBT). ***Flash duration:*** depends on the output power. It varies between approximately 1/1000 second (at 1/1 or TTL at full) and 1/23000 second (at 1/64 or TTL at minimal). ***Color temperature:*** Approximately 5600 K. ***Output and coverage:*** the Guide Number depends on the reflector setting and the film sensitivity. At ISO 100 the following holds: GN (ft/m) 66/20 at reflector setting 20mm, 98/30 at 24mm, 105/32 at 28mm, 118/36 at 35mm, 138/42 at 50mm, 157/48 at 70mm, 164/50 at 85mm. ***Zoom head:*** motor driven (via buttons) for adjustment between 24mm and 85mm. Fully automatic setting when used in conjunction with the N8008/F-801, F4 and N90/F90 with AF lenses. Built-in, manually engaged diffuser for 20mm. ***Auxiliary reflector:*** When using indirect flash, can be pulled out to produce highlights (i.e. in eyes). ***Tiltable flash head for close-up and bounce:*** click stops from -7° to +90° vertically and from -90° to +270° horizontally. Locks automatically in the normal position. ***Synchronization:*** choice of NORMAL with the front curtain and REAR with rear (2nd) curtain (only with the N8008/F-801 and F4). Independent of special flash units, the N6006/F-601, N6000/F-601m and N90/F90 have rear sync with all modern Nikon System flashes. Long-time sync (slow) with all appropriate cameras; FP continuous discharge of the flash for synchronization at high shutter speeds from 1/250 to 1/4000: only available with the N90/F90 to date. ***Flash modes:*** TTL (via the sensor built into the camera); A (computer flash via the sensor built into the flash); M (fully manual setting of aperture and output appropriate for the subject distance); Auto range at ISO 100: in non-TTL mode, the fixed apertures of f/2, f/2.8, f/4, f/5.6, f/8 and f/11 can be selected. In TTL mode, apertures from f/1.4 to f/16 can be freely selected independent of film speed and minimum distance. The range varies from 2ft. to 65.7ft. (0.6m to 20m) depending on aperture. ***Manual flash exposure corrections:*** corrections between +1 and -3 EV applying only to the TTL flash automation can be set with the F4 or N8008/F-801 (N6006/F-601, N6006/F-601m and N90/F90 can do this with other Nikon System flashes as well). ***Manual flash:*** power levels of 1/1, 1/2, 1/4, 1/8, 1/16, 1/32 and 1/64 can be selected in manual mode. At 1/16-1/64, short motor-drive series exposures or single images with strobe effects with up to 8 images per second can be created. ***Stroboscopic flash:*** Strobe function where time between flashes of 1/50 second to 1 second is dependent on the output power (1/8 to 1/64) can be selected as well as number of flashes per frame from 1 to 160. Exact display of aperture and distance ensure correctly exposed images even in this mode. ***Film sen-***

sitivity range: manual ISO 6-6400; in TTL mode, depending on the camera, from ISO 25-1000 or ISO 25-400. ***Recycle time and number of flashes:*** with 4 fresh batteries, approximately 100 flashes at full power with recycle times between approximately 7 and 30 seconds can be produced. ***Batteries, power sources:*** 4 AA type. Additional external battery units SD-7 and SD-8. ***Stand-by:*** approximately 80 seconds after the last flash, the SB-25 turns itself off. It reactivates when the camera's shutter release button is touched. ***Flash control:*** the flash unit has a red indicator light that shows if the flash is ready and if the flash output it sufficient. Underexposure display in exact values: only with the N90/F90 to -3 EV in steps of 0.5 EV. ***Test flash function:*** the indicator light is combined with a manual trigger button. In A and TTL modes, the reflected light is read by a sensor in the flash unit. ***AF Illuminator:*** If lighting is insufficient to allow the AF system to focus in sharpness priority mode, the flash emits LED measuring light in the direction of the subject. AF cameras can thus focus in complete darkness. ***Operation:*** main functions via main switch, all fine-tuned functions via buttons. All functions and values are displayed on an LCD panel. ***LCD Panel:*** shows all functions and values. ***Display illumination:*** fluorescent illumination activated for approximately 8 seconds. TTL multiflash port: Remote flash is possible with the N2000/F-301 and N6000/F-601m and all AF Nikon Cameras via the SC-17 TTL cable. ***Locking the flash in the hot shoe:*** the N90 has an additional pin in its hot shoe which guarantees that there is good contact between the flash and camera. ***Pre-flash for red-eye prevention:*** only with the N90/F90. ***Measuring flash:*** for fine-tuning the flash automation; only with the N90/F90. ***Range scale switchable:*** meters or feet. ***Size:*** approximately (WxHxD) 3.1 x 5.3 x 4in. (79 x 135 x 101mm). ***Weight:*** approximately 13.4oz. (380g) without batteries. ***Accessories:*** carry case is a standard accessory; battery units SD-7 or SD-8.

SB-25

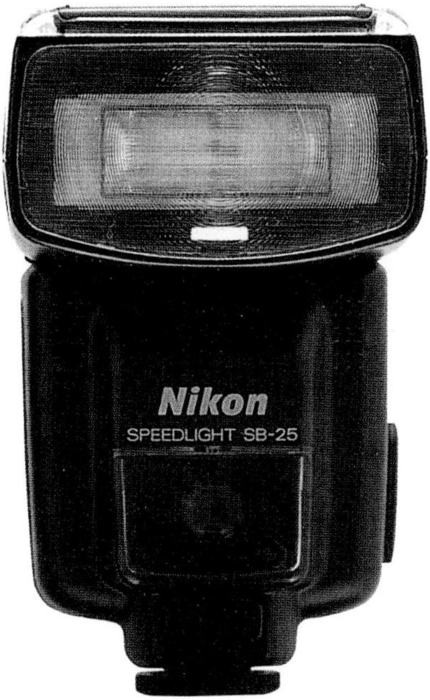

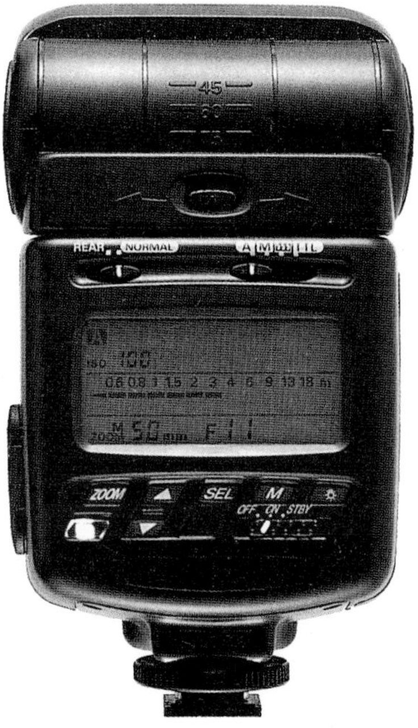

SB-21A/SB-21B. Macro TTL Flash

Application: see also Macro Accessories chapter. The SB-21 is specially designed for close-up photography. It can be mounted on a filter thread of 52mm or 62mm and consists of two individually controlled flash tubes and a modeling light that can be turned on if required. The battery unit is mounted on the camera's hot shoe and connected to the flash via a cable. ***Compatibility:*** TTL compatible (in A version with the F3, in B version with the N2000/F-301, N4004/F-401, N5005, N6006/F-601, N6000/F-601m, N8008/F-801 N90/F90 and F4). The AS-12 battery unit fits into the F3's unique hot shoe. The battery unit AS-14 fits on all other Nikon cameras. The combination of AS-12 and SB-21 is called the SB-21A, while the AS-14 and the SB-21 together are called the SB-21B. ***Output:*** the Guide Number is 43 (ft.) 13 (m) at ISO 100. ***Flash modes:*** with TTL or manual. Auto range at ISO 100: f/2.8 to f/32. ***Manual flash:*** full, 1/4 and 1/16 power can be selected. ***Film speed range:*** with the N8008/F-801,F **N90/F90** and F4 in TTL mode, ISO 25-1000; ISO 25-800 with N2000, N4004, N6006, N6000; ISO 25-400 with F3. ***Recycle time:*** approximately 8 seconds at full power with fresh batteries. With the external battery unit LD-2, the time is shortened to 4 seconds (up to 300 flashes). ***Flash capacity:*** approximately 200 flashes at full power. ***Batteries:*** 4 AA type. The LD-2 battery unit of the Medical Nikkor can also be connected. ***Standard accessories:*** SW-8 diffuser, 52mm adapter ring, 62mm adapter ring, soft case SS-21 for the SB-21, soft case SS-17 for AD-12/14. ***Other accessories:*** SL-1 focus adapter ring for Nikon AF 35-70mm or 35-105mm, focus adapter ring for 28-85mm or 35-135mm lenses, LD-2 external battery unit. ***Size:*** SB-21, HxWxD 4.7 x 5.1 x 0.8in. (120 x1 30 x 21m); AS-12/14, 3.5 x 3.9 x 1.6in. (90 x 100 x 41.6mm) ***Weight:*** SB-21, 5.1oz. (145g), AS-12, 9.9oz. (280g), AS-14, 8.8oz. (250g), each without batteries. See table, Overview of Nikon Flash Units.

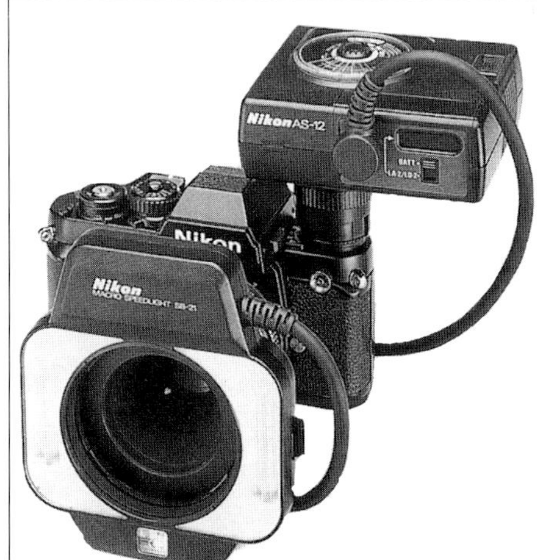

SB-21A, SB-21 with AS-12 Adapter

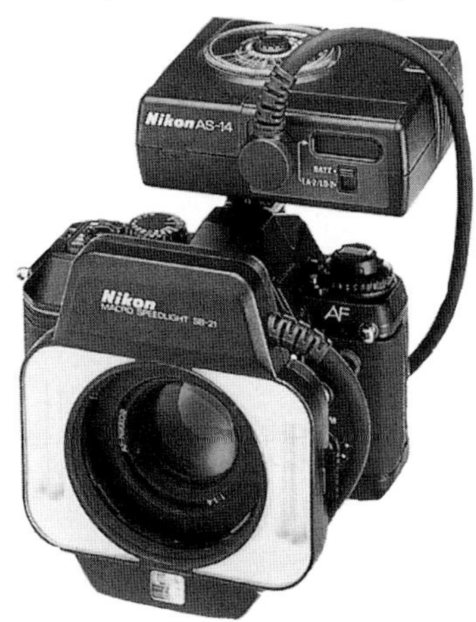

SB-21B, SB-21 with AS-14 Adapter

SW-8 Diffuser

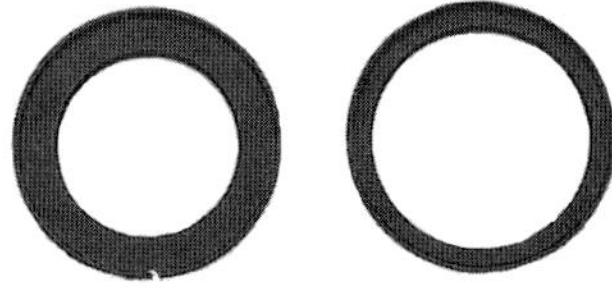

52mm Adapter **62mm Adapter**

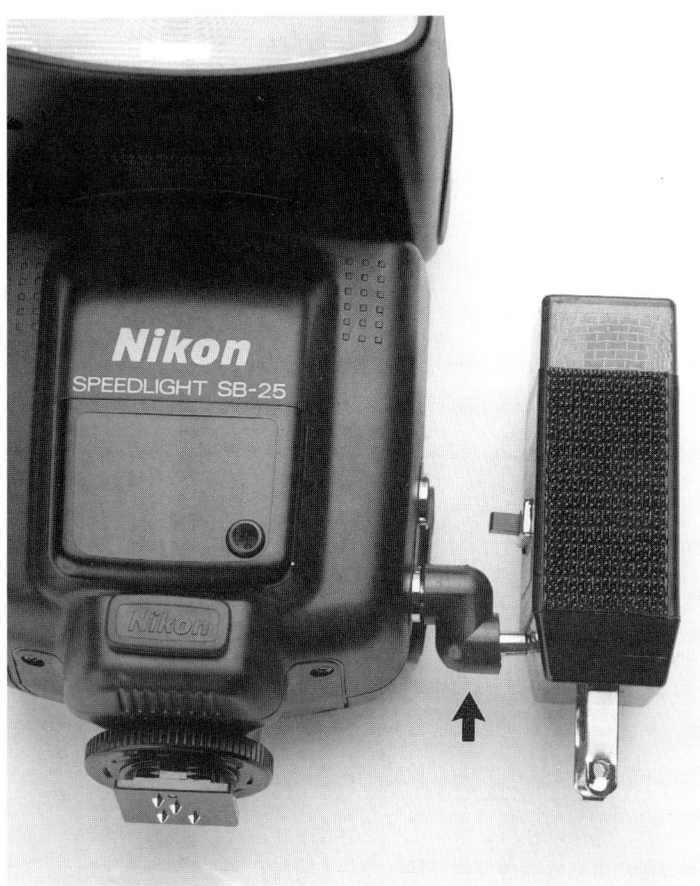

The PCM Adapter (indicated by the arrow) from Wein Products allows for cordless connection of photo slaves and remote control receivers to the SB-25's flash sync contact. In this case the PCM adapter is used to connect a Wein Pro-Sync™ infrared receiver to an SB-25. For further information contact Saunders (address on back cover).

Overview of Nikon System Flash Units

	SB-11	SB-14	SB-140	SB-16A/ SB-16B	SB-17	SB-20	SB-21A/ SB-21B	SB-22	SB-23	SB-24	SB-25	Medical Nikkor
Characteristics*												
Flash Type	S	S	S	K	K	K	K	K	K	K	K	-
Internal Batteries	+	-	-	+	+	+	AS-12 / AS-14	+	+	+	+	-
External Power Pack	SD-7; SD-8	SD-7; SD-8	SD-7; SD-8	-	-	SD-7; SD-8	LD-2	SD-7; SD-8	-	SD-7; SD-8	SD-7; SD-8	LD-2
AC Adapter	-	-	-	-	-	-	-	-	-	-	-	LA-2
Test Flash	+	+	+ **	+	+	+	+	+	+	+	+	***
Aperture in "A" Auto-sensor mode	3	3	3 **	2	2	5	-	2	-	6	6	***
TTL Flash Mode	+	+	+ **	+	+	+	+	+	+	+	+	***
Ready Light in Viewfinder	+	+	+	+	+	+	+	+	+	+	+	+
Flash Head Movement	A	B	B	B	A	A	-	A	-	B	B	-
Focal Lengths Covered	35	28	28	Zoom 28 - 85	35	Zoom 28/35/85	-	35	35	Mot. Zoom 24-85	Mot. Zoom 24-85	-
Wide Angle Adapter	28mm SW-3	24mm SW-5	24 mm SW-5	24mm SW-7	28mm SW-6	-	SW-8	28mm built-in	-	-	20mm built-in	-
Guide no. (feet) 20mm / 35mm / 85mm	- / 118 /-	- / 105 /-	** - / 105 /-	- / 105 / 138	- / 82 / -	- / 98 / 118	(43)	- / 82 / -	- / 65 /-	- / 118 / 164	65 / 118 / 164	52
Guide no. with Motordrive (feet)	-	-	-	28	26.4	-	-	28	-	28	28 - 13	-
PC Plug	+	+	+	+	+	+	+	+	-	+	+	-
TTL Multiflash Plug	-	-	-	+	+	-	+ / -	-	-	+	+	-
Recycle Time (sec.)	8	8	8	1	8	7	8	4	2	7	7	9
Max. Flash Duration (sec.)	1/800	1/800	1/800	1/1250	1/1400	1/1200	1/1600	1/1700	1/2000	1/1000	1/1000	1/500
Min. Flash Duration (sec.)	?	?	?	1/8000	1/10000	1/15000	1/25000	1/8000	?	1/20000	1/23000	?
Manual Power Selction	1/1, 1/4	1/1, 1/4	1/1, 1/4	MD	MD	1/1 - 1/16	1/1 - 1/16	MD	-	1/1 - 1/32	1/1 - 1/64	-
AF-Illuminator	-	-	-	-	-	+		+	+	+	+	-
No. of Flashes per Set of Batteries	150	270	270	100	160	160	200	200	400	100	100	90
Weight (w/o Batteries)	30oz.	18oz.		17/15.5oz.	10.5oz.	9oz.	14.9oz.	8.8oz.	4.9oz.	13.7oz.	13.3oz.	-
HxWxD (in.)	11 x 4.1 x4.6	8.5 x 3.7 x 3.6	8.5 x 3.7 x 3.6	6.5/5.7 x 3.2 x 3.9	1.7 x 4 x 3.5	4.3 x 2.8 x 2.8	4.7 x 5.1 x 0.8	4.1 x 3.1 x 2.7	2.6 x 2.5 x 3.3	5.2 x 3.2 x 3.9	5.2 x 3.1 x 4	-

+ Available or applicable.

- Not available or applicable.

? Not known

K Hot shoe, compact flash.

S Handle-type flash.

A Tilts only.

B Tilts and swivels.

* The extent that the feature can be used is dependent on the camera.

** All auto functions of the IR or UV SB-140 Flash can only be used in visible light with normal sensitivity films.

*** Auto flash results from electronic coupling of focus distance and aperture setting.

Selecting a Nikon Flash Unit

Generally speaking, photographers use camera-mounted flash units out of necessity because of poor lighting. Which flash unit, then, is the best choice? The previous sections described the technical characteristics of the various flash units to help answer that question. The following sections, on the other hand, will summarize their differences with respect to uses.

Handle-type flash SB-11: the handle-type flash became the trademark of the reporter. The main reasons for this, no doubt, lies in the fact that a high output or guide number per battery is required for this purpose which was originally not possible with hot shoe flashes. This type flash has also proved easy to use because of its handle. The location of the light source, slightly away from the optical axis, also results in a more pleasant lighting for portraiture at a distance of about 6.6ft. (2m) than that of a hot shoe mounted flash. In spite of the increased power and variety of hot shoe flashes available today, many photo-journalists still prefer the handle-type flash. The comparatively slow recycle time of the SB-11 is, however, a definite disadvantage in hectic situations. The SB-11 is slightly more powerful than the SB-14 and has a built-in battery holder. Those who find a separate battery unit cumbersome will therefore prefer the SB-11.

Handle-Type flash SB-14: the uses of this unit are similar to those of the SB-11. While the SB-14 has a lower output than the SB-11 and has an external battery unit, it boasts a higher number of flashes per set of batteries. The recycle time, however, is just as unassuming as with the SB-11. The separate battery unit that can be handily tucked into a jacket pocket makes the camera-flash combination lighter and easier to use. The SB-14 is probably the first choice for the reporter or anyone who uses a lot of flash.

IR and UV flash Unit SB-140: for night photography (as an IR flash); for shots with UV light; for documentation in science, technology, research, forensics, etc. The ideal flash if visible light is not permitted or does not produce the desired results. Can be used without the IR or UV filters and is then very similar to the SB-14.

Hot shoe flashes SB-16A and SB-16B: the SB-16 (both A and B) is one of the most powerful and flexible flash units for non-AF photography. It is probably only worth purchasing as a new accessory for the F3 or FM2 if the photographer is not considering switching to autofocus in the foreseeable future.

Hot shoe flash SB-17: easy to use and small and will always find room in a pocket. It is the all-purpose flash for the non-AF occasional photographer with an F3 or FM2.

AF Hot Shoe flash SB-20: the AF equivalent of the SB-16B. Besides the SB-25, it is the most powerful and most flexible AF flash. A good choice for the AF photographer who values higher aperture numbers for greater depth of field, or who wants to flash over larger distances.

AF Hot Shoe flash SB-22: contrary to the SB-20, this unit places less emphasis on output, but more on fast recycle times and higher flash capacity. An all-round flash for use with AF cameras.

AF Hot shoe flash SB-23: the SB-23 is an alternative to the built-in flash units of the N4004/F-401/N5005 and N6006/F-601 because of its one second recycle time. Its power makes it ideal for TTL controlled fill flash with the N6000/F-601m, N8008/F-801 and F4. For the occasional AF photographer, the SB-23 is the ideal multi-purpose flash thanks to its built-in AF illuminator and inexpensive cost. Its light and compact size make it convenient to keep around all the time.

AF Hot shoe flash SB-24: Nikon's first powerful, exciting multitask flash, the SB-24 set the pace for all flash units.

AF Hot Shoe flash SB-25: to date, it is the most versatile hot shoe flash in the Nikon System. Its ease of use and light weight for the number of features it offers are definite advantages, but operationally it can be a little difficult because of its small keys. The design logic is better, however, than with the SB-24. It boasts coverage from 20mm, an aperture range from f/1.4 to f/32 and a power range to 1/64. These features put the SB-25 at the forefront of the entire flash market. On top of this, it offers pre-flash, test flash and an underexposure read-out accurate to 1/3 stop in conjunction with the N90/F90.

Macro TTL flash SB-21A/SB-21B: those who seldom shoot in the macro range can solve their problems with one or two normal flashes on remote (with the TTL adapter SC-17 for example) using tents made of tracing paper or similar setups that will result in fairly even lighting. Those who frequently work in the close-up range will find the SB-21A or SB-21B extremely useful.

Flash Accessories

Information regarding the possibilities of combining the various cameras with the specific flash units given in the preceding discussions, is summarized in the following table. Also included is a description of all cables and adapters that serve as the connectors between the various cameras and flashes. *Important Note Regarding Connection of non-Nikon Flashes:* All modern, fully-electronic Nikon cameras can only hold 12V across their flash contacts. In addition, one has to watch that contact fittings on other flash units might bend when installed, resulting in short circuits (i.e.; all cameras newer than the F3). Nikon does not assume any liability for damages resulting from the use of incompatible non-Nikon flashes. Older flash units, or flashes from other manufacturers, have the triggering voltage right on the ISO contact which can result in damage to the low-voltage electronics of the camera.

Flash Adapters, Couplers, Sync Cords, TTL Cords

AS-15 Adapter: This adapter serves to trigger the flash. It is mounted in any normal Nikon hot shoe and makes contact only with the PC connection (not the Nikon System Contacts). Any normal sync cable (such as the SC-11 or SC-15) can be connected to the ISO port on the adapter (i.e. for studio flash units). It is necessary for all cameras that do not have an ISO port (i.e. N2000/F-301, N4004/F-401, N5005, N6000/F-601m and N8008/F-801). *Important:* To connect cameras and flashes (for example Nikon Handle Type flashes SB-11, SB-14 and SB-140) with System contacts for ready light, TTL control etc., the appropriate Nikon System Adapters and System cables should be used to avoid problems with these very complex electronically based systems.

SC-11 and SC-15 Cords: These accessories basically trigger the flash. Sync cables SC-11 (13.4in., 34cm) or SC-15 (spiral 3.3ft.,1m) connect all cameras with PC ports (without the AS-15) to a flash unit that also has an PC port. The flash could also be connected via the hot shoe and the AS-15 adapter. All hot shoe flashes can thus be used remotely. *Important:* To connect cameras and flashes (for example Nikon Handle Type flashes SB-11, SB-14 and SB-140) with system contacts for ready light, TTL control etc., the appropriate Nikon System Adapters and System cables should be used to avoid electronic problems and possible damage.

Flash Adapter AS-4 for F3: used when flash units with standard ISO shoes, for example the SB-16B, SB-20, SB-22, SB-23, SB-24 or SB-25, are to be mounted on the unique shoe of the F3. *Important:* flash ready status is transmitted, but only auto modes without TTL are possible.

Flash Adapter AS-6: used when Nikon flashes SB-16A and SB-17 with F3 shoes are to be used on Nikon cameras with ISO shoes. *Important:* Flash ready is status transmitted, but only auto modes without TTL are possible.

Overview of Camera/Flash Combinations

	N90/F90	F4, F4S, F4E	N8008, N8008s F801, F801s	N6006, N6000 F601, F601M	N4004/s, N5005 F401/s/x	N2000 F301	Nikon F3	Nikon FM2
SB-25	A, A-TTL, A-3D, A-M, AF	A, A-TTL, AF	A, A-TTL, AF	A, A-TTL, AF	A, A-TTL, AF	A, TTL, P	A (*AS-4, AS-7*)	A
SB-24	A, A-TTL, A-M, AF	A, A-TTL, AF	A, A-TTL, AF	A, A-TTL, AF	A, A-TTL, AF	A, TTL, P	A (*AS-4, AS-7*)	A
SB-23	A-TTL, A-M, AF	A-TTL, AF	A-TTL, AF	A-TTL, AF	A-TTL, AF	TTL, P	M (*AS-4, AS-7*)	M
SB-22	A, A-TTL, A-M, AF	A, A-TTL, AF	A, A-TTL, AF	A, A-TTL, AF	A, A-TTL, AF	A, TTL, P	A (*AS-4, AS-7*)	A
SB-20	A, A-TTL, A-M, AF	A, A-TTL, AF	A, A-TTL, AF	A, A-TTL, AF	A, A-TTL, AF	A, TTL, P	A (*AS-4, AS-7*)	A
SB-17	A (*AS-6*)	A (*AS-6*)	A (*AS-6*)	A (*AS-6*)	A (*AS-6*)	A (*AS-6*)	A, TTL	A (*AS-6*)
SB-16A	A (*AS-6*)	A (*AS-6*)	A (*AS-6*)	A (*AS-6*)	A (*AS-6*)	A (*AS-6*)	A, TTL	A (*AS-6*)
SB-16B	A, A-TTL, A-M	A, A-TTL	A, A-TTL	A, A-TTL	A, A-TTL	A, TTL; P	A (*AS-4, AS-7*)	A
SB-14	A, A-TTL (SC-23), A-M	A, A-TTL (SC-23)	A, A-TTL (SC-23)	A, A-TTL (SC-23)	A, A-TTL (SC-23)	A, TTL, P (SC-23)	A, TTL (*SC-12*)	A
SB-140 (IR, UV)	A, A-TTL (SC-23) *, A-M	A, A-TTL (SC-23)*	A, A-TTL (SC-23)*	A, A-TTL (SC-23)*	A, A-TTL (SC-23)*	A, TTL, P (SC-23)*	A, TTL (*SC-12*) *	A*
SB-11	A, A-TTL (SC-23), A-M	A, A-TTL (SC-23)	A, A-TTL (SC-23)	A, A-TTL (SC-23)	A, A-TTL (SC-23)	A, TTL; P (SC-23)	A, TTL (*SC-12*)	A
SB-21A (Macro)	M (*AS-6*)	M (*AS-6*)	M (*AS-6*)	M (*AS-6*)	M (*AS-6*)	M (*AS-6*)	TTL	M (*AS-6*)
SB-21B (Macro)	A-TTL, A-M	A-TTL	A-TTL	A-TTL	A-TTL	TTL, P	M (*AS-4, AS-7*)	M

A Automatic mode via sensor built into the flash unit. Can be switched to manual mode.

A-TTL TTL flash mode dependent on camera model including matric controlled fill flash mode in shutter prefered, aperture prefered and program modes.

TTL Normal TTL flash mode in aperture prefered mode, no fill flash mode, etc..

A-M TTL control via multi-sensor when using AF lenses.

A-3D 3D matrix controlled flash when using AF-D lenses.

P Program flash mode with automatic aperture selection.

M Only fully manual flash possible.

AF The flash unit has an AF illuminator, allowing the camera to focus automatically even in complete darkness.

( ) The parentheses contain the necessary adapter or adapter cord.

* Auto flash modes work only with normal film sensitivities and visible light.

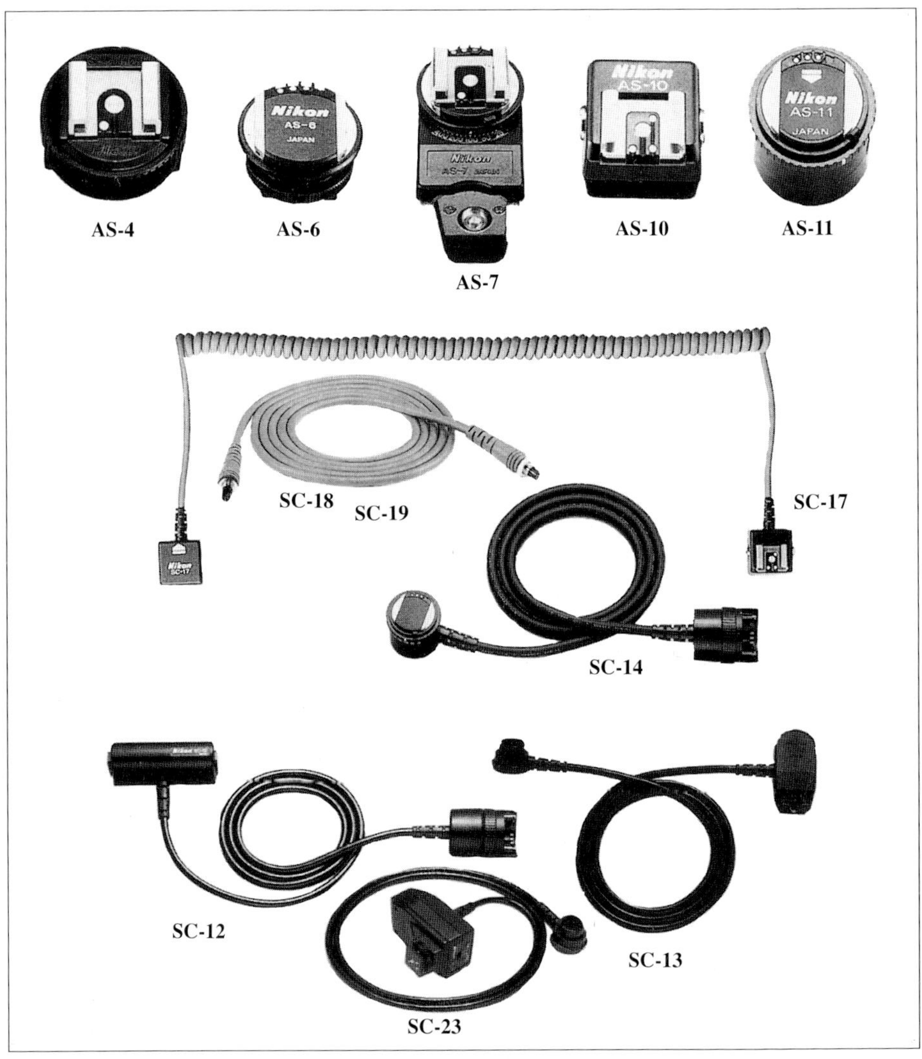

Flash Coupler AS-7 for F3: allows the film to be rewound and the camera back to be opened while a flash is mounted on the camera. TTL mode is maintained with the special F3 flashes (SB-16A or SB-17). A PC port is integrated into the adapter which permits normal flash units to be used, but only with transmission of flash- ready and auto modes without TTL.

Flash Coupler AS-8: the lower portion of the SB-16A consisting of an F3 shoe.

Flash Coupler AS-9: the lower portion of the SB-16B consisting of a normal shoe as well as ISO and system contacts.

TTL Cord SC-12 for F3: allows TTL operation with the F3 and handle-type flashes SB-11, SB-14 and SB-140 (length: 3.3ft.,1m).

TTL Cord SC-14 for F3: this 3ft. (1m) long cord allows remote flashing with the F3 and the SB-16A and SB-17 flash units.

TTL Remote Cord SC-17: one end of the 5ft. (1.5m) long coiled cord is an adapter that fits on all Nikon cameras with Nikon system contacts. It reads all information regarding flash ready, TTL control, etc. The other end has a hot shoe and multiflash port for mounting any Nikon System Flash or for connecting additional flashes via other TTL cables (i.e. SC-18 or SC-19). With the N2000, N4004, N6000, N8008 and F4 and the flashes SB-15, SB-16B, SB-20, SB-22, SB-23 and SB-24, remote TTL flashing maintaining all camera specific functions such as matrix controlled fill flash.

TTL Extension Cord SC-18 and SC-19 (also called TTL multiflash cords): these cords have plugs at both ends that connect to Nikon's multiflash port (i.e. in the TTL adapter cord SC-17, in the multiflash distributor AS-10 and in various Nikon System flash units). They transmit all Nikon system control commands with all camera specific options (i.e. matrix controlled fill flash). The SC-18 is 5ft. (1.5m) long and the SC-19 is 9.8ft. (3m) long. (See also section on Multiflash at the beginning of the Flash Units chapter.)

TTL Multiflash Adapter AS-10:: connects to the flash unit's ISO foot and accepts a TTL cord SC-18 or SC-19. A flash unit can be mounted directly on the adapter's hot shoe. Additional flashes is connected via the three multiflash ports (see also Multiflash section at the beginning of the flash units chapter).

TTL Adapter Cord SC-23 (for handle-type flash units): allows TTL control when using N2000/F-301, N4004/F-401, N5005, N6006/F-601, N8008/F-801, N90/F90 and F4 with the handle-type flashes SB-11, SB-14 and SB-140 (length: 3ft., 1m).

TTL Adapter Cord SC-24 for F4: allows off-camera flash while maintaining all camera specific options with the F4 if the camera has either the DW-20 or DW-21 viewfinder (coiled, 5ft., 1.5m).

"Stroboframe®" Flash Brackets

Nikon does not offer a comparable flash bracket, nevertheless I consider Stroboframe brackets useful for discussion at this point. These innovative flash brackets have been manufactured and successfully marketed for years by The Saunders Group in the United States.

Sturdy, sensible modular design: The basic principle of this particular model is a sturdy, lightweight aircraft aluminum frame with ergonomically molded grips. Electrical or mechanical cable releases may be accessibly mounted in or near the side grip. The top bar of the bracket features a 1/4"-20 screw for attaching dedicated cords or it also accepts standard flash mounts which are modular designed. The flash mount on the SC-17 remote cord may be securely attached with the standard 1/4"-20 screw. At the base of the bracket is a platform which holds the camera securely. Beneath that is an comfortable, ergonomically-shaped palm grip.

Advantages of using a Stroboframe bracket: Many professional photographers prefer to use off-camera flash because it offers better lighting control. Direct, on-camera flash is often harsh and unnatural with heavy, hard-edged shadows. When the flash is too close to the lens, "red-eye" can occur. This is a condition caused by the light from the flash reflecting from the inner eye, resulting in an unattractive, "blood-shot" appearance. One solution is the use of bounce flash, but this technique has its own problems and limitations. Factors such as ceiling height, texture or color can often cause unpredictable results.

A simple way to avoid undesirable results in flash photography is a well-designed bracket such as Stroboframe. Using a bracket raises

Stroboframe Flash Bracket

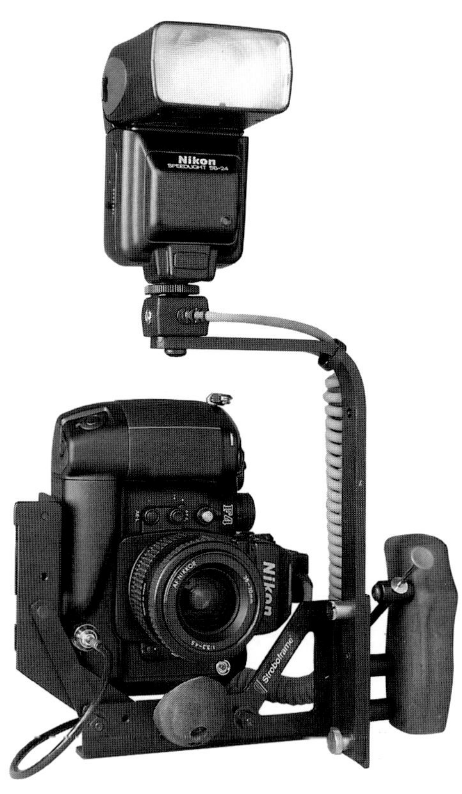

the flash to the correct height for a natural lighting effect. Shadows fall behind and below the subject and harsh edged "ghost shadows" are eliminated, even when the subject is close to the background.

One very interesting benefit of using a Stroboframe bracket is that the camera platform can be rotated quickly and easily between horizontal and vertical formats. The advantage is that the flash remains, at all times, centered above the camera in the same position for high, natural-looking lighting. Even though the SB-25 by itself can be tilted for vertical and horizontal formats, the bracket maintains the ideal high-above-the-lens, flash position. Also, time-consuming, renewed positioning of the flash head is not necessary.

With Stroboframe, the SB-25 also becomes a photojournalist's flash: It used to be that photojournalists would almost exclusively use side-mounted, handle-type flash units. One reason was that the bar-style bracket provided a secure support for the entire flash/camera combination, which is of great advantage when being jostled. Compared with this the combination of say, an N90/F90 or N8008/F-801 camera with the SB-25 mounted directly on the shoe is rather unstable in ones hands. In addition the connection between flash unit and camera is rather rigid so that impact with the flash unit might damage the camera's accessory shoe or the flash unit. A sturdy, well-engineered, Stroboframe Flash Bracket solves this problem. Along with the many lighting advantages listed above, Stroboframe brackets are a distinct advantage for photojournalists as well as many other photographers.

Nikon Photography - The Picture Taking Process

Communicating with Photography

An experienced photographer characteristically is aware of what he wants to say with his photography before putting the camera to his eye. The ability to accomplish this level of picture making is really an example of applied photographic methods aimed at communicating a particular message. The working professional survives because of this skill, while the serious non-professional strives to achieve it and then uses it for his own pleasure. Producing photographs on this level cannot be learned entirely from books. On the contrary, there must be a process of trying out what one has learned and experimenting with it by taking lots and lots of pictures. Taking the time to read and become well informed beforehand, however, makes the hands-on process much more of an efficient experience and provides specific directions in which to concentrate one's energies. Thus, what follows here is a review of those critical points that form much of the foundation of the whole picture taking process which is carried out, to one degree or another, by every knowledgeable photographer.

Composition and Shutter Speed

Blur or Freeze? Photography is based on an illusion in which certain mechanisms, such as the shutter speed, are used to convey information as, for instance, subject movement. Generally we have two choices; to have the subject's motion blur on film or to freeze the action sharply at some point in its development. Thus, the viewer interprets the blur as movement beyond the camera's ability to capture it and the stop action as a stage of motion that has been captured and is not ordinarily seen because it occurs too fast for our eyes. Choosing between these two types of interpretation is a matter of knowing which shutter speed to use under what circumstances. The following table shows shutter speeds that will allow you to capture moving objects fairly sharply with normal focal length lenses. If you want to show the subject more clearly (to freeze the action), you will have to shorten the exposure time. If you want to emphasize movement (as in a blurred effect), you have to expose slightly longer. If you are using a shorter focal length lens at the same subject distance, then exposure times must be longer and for longer focal lengths the times become shorter. So this table represents a starting point for your experimentations which, with a little note taking, will give you a selection of effects to consider for various shutter speeds with your favorite lenses.

When photographing a subject whose movement is along a specific direction, as in a car crossing your view point, there are really three choices of method. Holding the camera still and using a fast shutter speed such as 1/250 second will freeze the action, while a slow shutter speed such as 1/30 second will blur the car and leave the background sharp. But following the car (panning) at 1/30 second will produce a subject reasonably in focus with a blurred background. Thus, the "blur factor" works either on the subject or the background.

Still another option is to use flash as the main light source which will freeze very fast moving subjects; or fire the flash while using a slow shutter speed which will freeze the subject sharp at that moment, but accompanied by the blur of the ambient light. When doing this, calculate the flash exposure at the same aperture value as the available light exposure or 1/2 stop less. This technique gives very unusual effects with slower shutter speeds of between 1/4 and 1 second or more. Some of the more advanced flash units also have second (REAR) curtain flash sync, which will allow you to produce an after image blur that can appear like a streak effect behind the subject as it moves across the field of view.

Composition with Aperture

Aperture controls depth of field as well as what is in and out of focus in the scene. Basically, there are two applications: either the subject, background and foreground are held in focus by using a small aperture opening (e.g. f/11 or f/16) for a large depth of field, the subject remains in focus while throwing the background areas out of focus using a larger aperture (eg f/2.0 of f/1.8) with a narrow depth of field. From a compositional point of view, areas appearing out of focus are less important than those in sharp focus. Thus, the subject would be isolated by an out of focus background. A more complete discussion of controlling depth of field follows below.

Sharpness

If you wish to show the tiniest details clearly as is so important, for example, in architectural photography or in commercial work, you must select the aperture at which the lens is sharpest. All optics represent compromises in design such that some apertures are going to deliver sharper pictures than others. In general, a wide open aperture produces the poorest performance because of aberrations in the optics of the lenses themselves (e.g. spheric and chromatic aberration as well as astigmatism, etc.). By stopping down to the middle of the aperture range, optical performance is generally maximized. Stopping down further to the smallest apertures might result in a loss of quality due to diffraction. (Diffraction can be described as a spreading of light rays as they bounce off the corners of the diaphragm blades; the smaller the aperture, the higher the percentage of light affected). As a generalization then, lenses have optimum optical levels between typical middle settings of f/5.6 and f/11 and it is always recommended that a photographer test their lenses to determine just how much loss of image quality there actually under their typical shooting conditions.

Depth of Field

It is not possible for a lens to capture everything in sharp focus from a 0 point of focus to infinity. The area that is considered as being in focus in front of and behind the point of focus is referred to as the depth of field. There are several conditions that affect the amount of depth of field present.

First rule of thumb: large camera to subject distances with small aperture (e.g. f/11, f/16, f/22) results in a large depth of field. For example, a 50mm lens, 9.8ft. (3m) away from the subject, has a depth of field of 9.5ft.-10.3ft. (2.88m-3.14m) at f/1.2. But at f/5.6 the same lens at the same distance, yields a depth of field of 8.2ft.-12.1ft. (2.5m-3.7m) while at f/22 it has grown to 5.3ft.-49.3ft. (1.6m-15m). Thus, as mentioned earlier, depth of field is controlled by the specific aperture setting. So if the focal length and distance remain unchanged, the area in front of and behind the subject in focus is controlled by the aperture selected only. With architectural work, where a large depth of field is usually required, you would stop down. In portraiture, where a sharp background might be disturbing and distract the viewer from the important subject, a smaller aperture would be preferred.

Depth of field and focus distance: if a 50mm lens is focused at 1.6ft. (0.5m) at f/8, the depth of field covers from 1.6ft.-1.7ft. (0.49m-0.54m). Focused at 9.9ft. (3m), the depth of field becomes 7.2ft.-17ft. (2.2m-5.2m) and at infinity, it becomes 29.5ft. (9m) to infinity. Therefore, the shorter the focus distance, the narrower the depth of field. Correspondingly, depth of field increases with increasing focus distances.

Focal length and reproduction ratio: short focal length lenses deliver a large depth of field, but this is only true if you use different

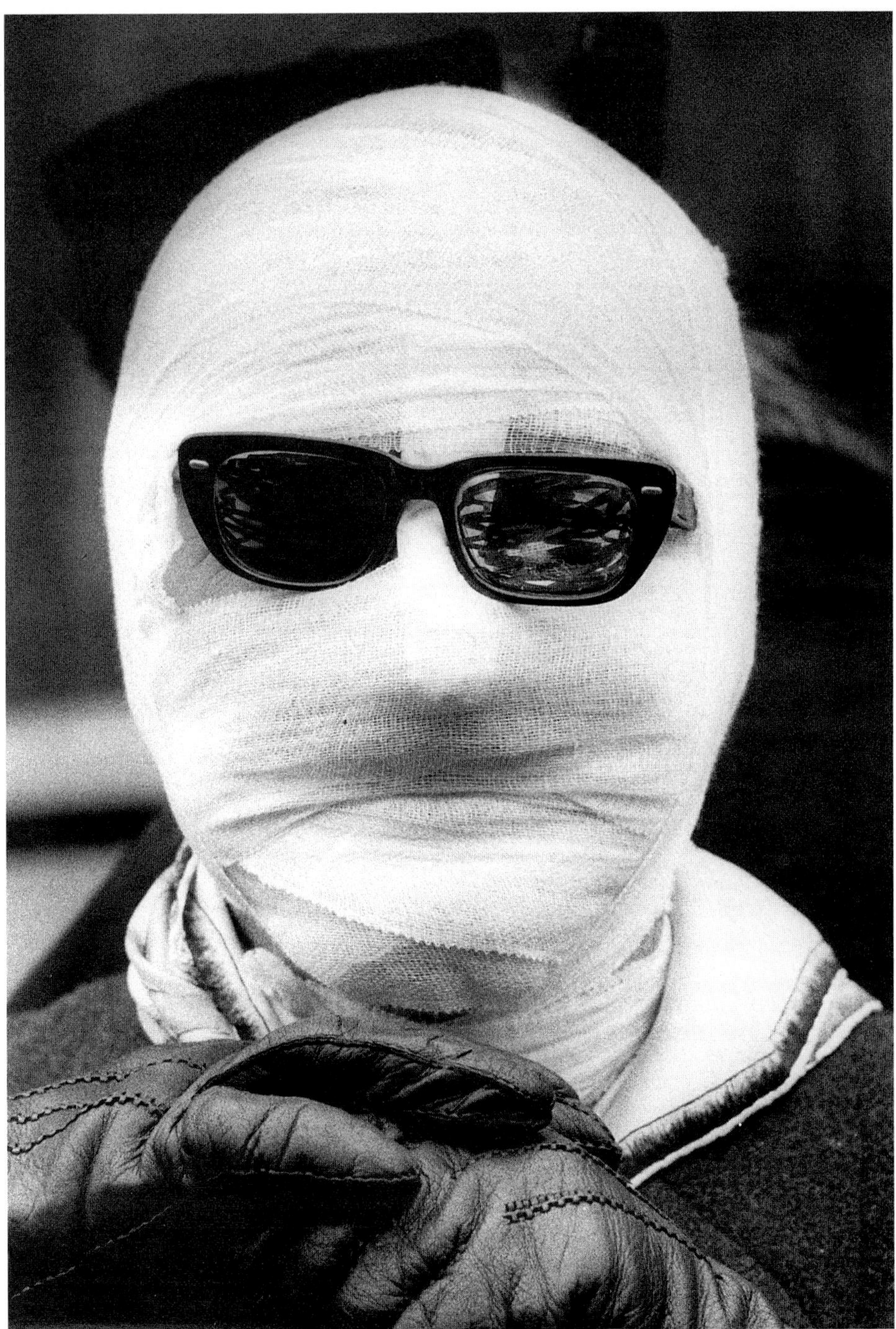

This portrait of a person protesting airport expansion illustrates how telephoto lenses excel at allowing the photographer to stand back from the subject while still getting a closely cropped photograph. Photo: Rudolf Dietrich

focal lengths on the same subject at the same focus distance. For example, if the focus distance is 13.1ft. (4m) and the aperture is f/8, the depth of field will be from 2.6ft. (0.8m) to infinity with a 16mm lens, while with a 50mm lens only from 29.5ft. (9m) to infinity. Since the focus distance (distance from camera to subject) remains constant in our example, the reproduction ratio (the actual size of the subject versus its on film size) increases with increasing focal length. This means that while the depth of field is noticeably greater with the 16mm lens, the subject is reproduced much smaller. Let us look at the situation another way. We will change the focus distance while changing the focal length to keep the subject the same size in the view finder and therefore on film. Since you would have to move a good deal closer with a wide angle lens than with a normal or telephoto, the depth of field will shrink again. The rule of thumb that depth of field increases with shorter focal lengths (and decreases with longer focal lengths) only holds with different image reproduction ratios. At the same reproduction ratio, that is, where the subject appears the same size on film because different lenses have taken the picture at different distances in order to get the same size on film image, the depth of field will be the same for all lenses regardless of focal length.

Practical Tips Regarding Depth of Field

Maximum depth of field: this is obtained by focusing on the most important area of the subject and closing down as much as possible with due respect to the effects of diffraction on image quality mentioned earlier. In other words, you may have to decide between the importance of needing a large depth of field and the possible loss of image quality caused by a small aperture setting (this is where your hands-on experience and familiarity with particular lenses comes in). *Note:* if you are using autofocus, you must frame the most important area of the subject in the AF measuring field.

Narrow depth of field: if you only want a well-defined, narrow section of the image to be sharp, you must open up as much as possible and focus very carefully (or let the AF mechanism focus for you).

Sharp foreground, blurred background: If you want a sharp foreground up to the subject, you have to select a focus point closer to the camera and set the aperture such that the subject just comes into focus. With autofocus, you would focus on a point in front of your subject and then expose the desired image with the stored focus setting. Be sure to press your preview button to see these depth of field changes.

Blurred foreground, sharp background: If you would rather have the foreground blurred and the background with the subject in focus, the same procedure applies as above, just that you focus slightly behind the subject.

Depth of field tables and diagrams: depth of field tables and diagrams that are specific to each lens are particularly helpful when working with precise depth of field requirements. Such information is found on the instruction sheet that comes with Nikon lenses. You can read the range of distances that the depth of field covers at each f-stop. You should definitely refer to these documents if you need to control the depth of field very accurately.

Depth of field preview button: this is a very useful feature which, unfortunately, is not on all Nikon cameras. Pressing the button stops down the aperture so that you can see the effect of a particular aperture; otherwise, all Nikon cameras display the least amount of depth of field since they are designed to have the lens remain wide open until the moment the shutter release button is activated. This stop down approach works best in bright light and it may be difficult, if not impossible, to use in dimmer light, especially when portions of the focusing screen "black out" due to insufficient illumination.

Focal Length and Angle of View for 35mm Format (24mm x 36mm)

Focal Length (mm)	15	20	24	28	35	50	85	200	300	500
Angle of View	110°	94°	84°	74°	62°	46°	28°	12,3°	8,2°	4,2°

Composition and Focal Length

The focal length of a lens has a profound effect on the portrayal of a subject, and on the whole scene in general, by controlling two important image characteristics: the reproduction ratio and the perspective or relative size and distance between all elements in a scene. In short, the long or telephoto lenses increase the reproduction ratio and, therefore, compress the distances between elements, while the shorter or wide-angle lenses lower the ratio and thus increase the distances between elements.

Focal Length, Reproduction Ratio and Perspective

Focal length and angle of view: the angle of view refers to how much of the scene the lens "sees". It can be measured horizontally, vertically or across the film frame's diagonal. However it is measured, the larger the figure, the wider the angle of the view and the smaller the figure, the more narrow or telephoto the view. Logically, the angle of view determines how big subjects will appear on film, which is technically expressed as the reproduction ratio. It should be pointed out that the angle of view is calculated on the basis of the size of the film's format. That explains why a normal 50mm focal length in 35mm photography is considered a moderate wide angle lens in 2-1/4 x 2-1/4 (6 x 6 cm) medium format cameras. In medium format, the 50mm must cover a larger film area. The angles of view of common focal lengths in 35mm photography are given in the table, Focal Lengths and Angles of View for the 24x36mm Format (above).

Focal length, angle of view and reproduction ratio: in summary then, if we consider various focal lengths at the same subject to camera distance, the following holds: with small focal lengths/large angle of view, a great deal of the subject is shown on film and it appears smaller. With long focal lengths, less of the subject is shown on film and it appears larger.

Distance, focal length and reproduction ratio: if the focal length and hence the angle of view are given, the reproduction ratio depends on the distance. The reproduction ratio, V represents how large the subject will be shown on the film (V = image size/subject size). The following holds: the shorter the distance, the larger the reproduction ratio. If the reproduction ratio is given, the focal length is determined by the distance: the shorter the distance, the smaller the focal length necessary for the same reproduction ratio. Let us consider a flat subject, a 15.8ft. x 23.7ft. (4.8m x 7.2m) wall for example, that has to be reproduced at a ratio of 200:1 on 35mm format 24x36mm film. With an 80mm lens (angle of view approximately 30°), we require approximately 44.3ft. (13.5m) distance. With a 50mm lens (angle of view approximately 46°), a distance of 28ft. (8.5m) is required, while with a 21mm focal length (angle of view approximately 90°) the distance is only11.5ft. (3.5m).

Focal length and perspective: since most subjects are not flat but 3-dimensional, some parts of the subject will be further away from the camera than others. Closer parts will be reproduced larger and more distant areas smaller. The amount of difference is dependent on the angle of view or the focal length. The shorter the focal length, the larger the foreground will appear in relation to the background. Therefore, those parts of the subject closer to the camera, as in an outstretched hand, will appear considerably larger and quite out of proportion in the case of a wide angle lens. The different perspectives of the various lenses can be summarized as follows: shorter focal lengths, the so-called wide angles, emphasize the foreground, make the background smaller and deeper, and thus increase the feeling of depth. Long focal lengths, so-called telephoto lenses, bring the background closer, thereby reducing the feeling of depth and giving a feeling of compression of subject matter.

Characteristics of Focal Lengths

Typical characteristics of normal lenses: the so-called, "normal" focal length lies between 40mm and 55mm and corresponds to a 50° angle of view. This angle of view is approximately that of the human eye thus, pictures taken with normal focal length lenses seem very realistic. A normal focal length lens takes natural-looking pictures just about on its own, providing you are not shooting from an unnatural distance. It is not a coincidence that photos taken with 35mm to 55mm lenses have been the standard for successful photojournalism. No other lens will give you the same image quality and speed for the money. The fast speed is not only important for available light photography, but it also works well in drastically reducing depth of field and when it is necessary to isolate a subject. The larger the aperture, the smaller the depth of field and the more a subject can be separated from a blurred background.

Typical characteristics of wide angle lenses: lenses with focal lengths less than 40mm, such as 35mm or 28mm, are called wide angle lenses while focal lengths of 24mm, 20mm or even 16mm are often called super-wide angles. Photos taken at the same distance from the subject with wide angle lenses differ from those taken with normal lenses in the following respects: there is significantly more included in the frame in wide angle pictures due to the noticeably larger angle of view. A consequence of this is reduced reproduction ratios. Even the spatial impression is different than with normal focal lengths. This is demonstrated by getting close to the subject so it appears just as large as it would be with a normal lens. You will not only see more of the subject thanks to the larger angle of view, but the perspective is also unique. The wide angle lens exaggerates the appearance of objects in the foreground causing the background to shrink. In a portrait for example, the nose and chin that are close to the camera will appear unnaturally large while the ears, which are further away from the camera, will seem small. Consequently, a wide angle is very effective in emphasizing a main subject, causing it to stand out from its surroundings.

Converging lines in wide angle photography: these occur most often with wide angle lenses but are sometimes noticeable even in normal lens photography. Converging lines occur when the camera has to be severely tilted. such as when photographing a large building close up, thus exaggerating perspective. The building facade seems to get smaller at the top. In order to prevent this, the film plane and the subject plane must be parallel. Shooting from a position as equal to the mid-point of the subject as possible will decrease this effect but in many cases, this would only be possible with a crane or a helicopter. Converging lines can also be remedied by using longer focal lengths and a larger focus distances. However, the best solution to this problem in 35mm photography is a shift lens or PC Nikkor. By displacing the lens parallel to the film plane, a PC Nikkor controls perspective distortion. Another solution is to turn this problem into a feature by deliberately using converging lines since these lines make the viewer think of majesty and overpowering size.

Typical characteristics of fisheye lenses: although wide angle lenses distort the edge of the image more than longer focal lengths, they still have a central perspective. This means that lines in the direction of view seem to converge at one point, infinity. This is not so with

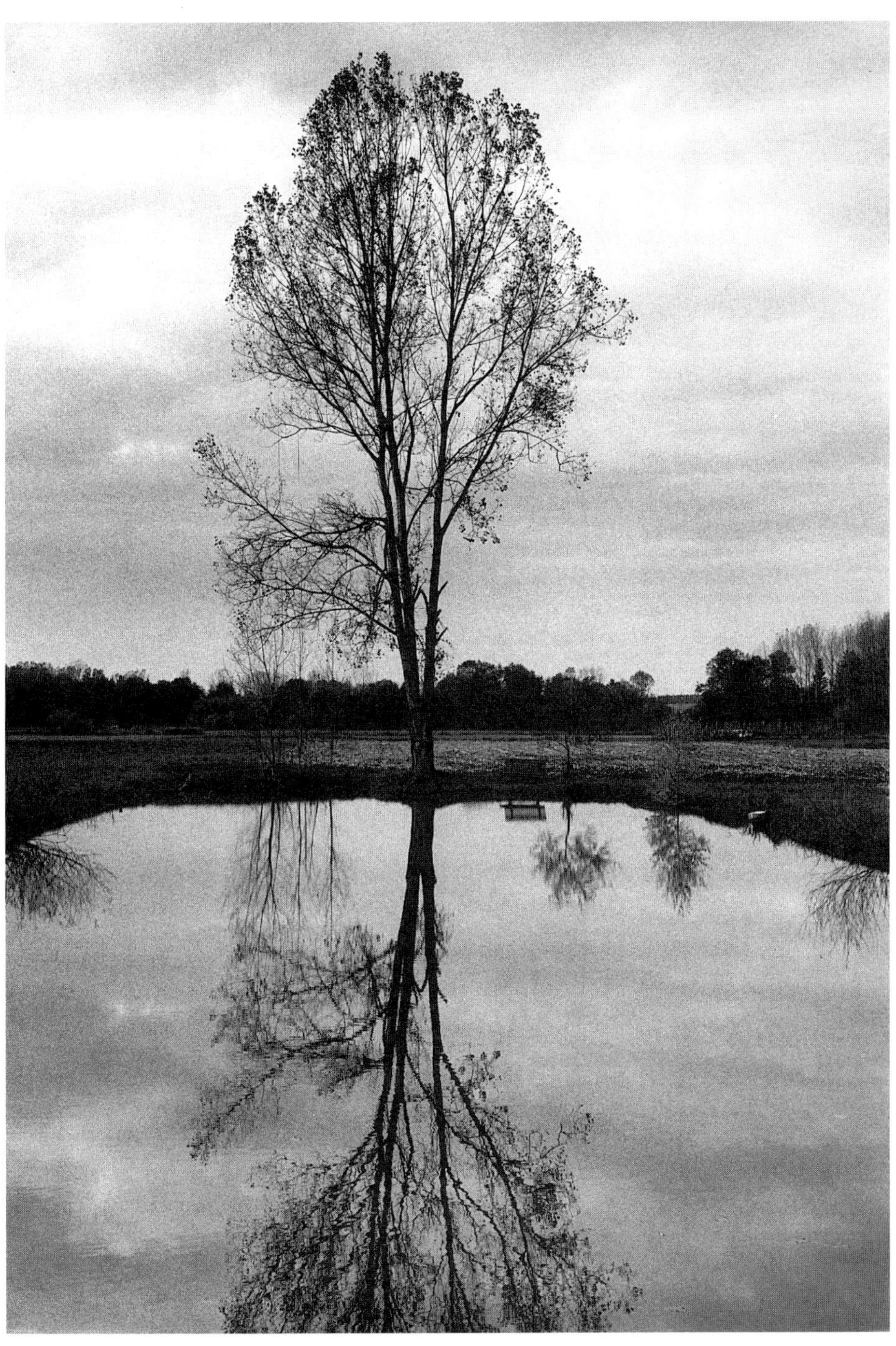

Photographic compositions are often the consequence of a number of elements working together to produce a complete statement as in this combination of reality and reflection. Photo: Rudolf Dietrich.

fisheye lenses which have spherical perspective. Here, only lines passing directly through the center of the image remain straight. All other lines, that would normally be parallel bend around a central point. The angle of view becomes extreme (with the Nikkor 6mm f/2.8, for example, 220°!) and one can get a large portion of the subject in the frame, however, it is badly distorted. With technical pictures, such as satellite photos that are evaluated by a computer, this might not be a problem. Pictures of people, however, are practically impossible. Even in landscape photography the fisheye can be problematic. There is often something disturbing in a landscape such as electrical wires, highway overpasses or even the sun. Aside from that, one has to make sure that one's shoes are not in the frame with a 180-220° angle of view.

Typical characteristics of telephoto lenses: lenses with focal lengths longer than 55mm are considered telephoto lenses. Telephoto shots are characterized by a smaller angle of view and a greater reproduction ratio. These are excellent lenses for concentrating on the subject and are especially useful for photographing people. However, in order to avoid emphasizing every blemish one should use soft lights or a diffusion filter, especially in color photography. A diffuser in front of a remote flash or TTL multi-flash is also advisable. Further information is located in the Portraits section.

Recommendations for Various Subjects

Nudes

Lenses: In figure or nude photography, the same desirable conditions apply as with portraiture; that is, to maintain appropriate proportions of the figure (see that section below). Short telephoto lenses are particularly effective at this because they decrease the size distortion caused by moving a subject or its parts, as in an outstretched hand, closer to the camera. Because of the tendency of wide-angle lenses to exaggerate the size of anything close to the camera, care must be take when using them in shooting the figure. This cautionary note also applies to a normal focal length used at a very close position which can cause a slight overemphasis of near body parts or objects. The bottom line here is that you must definitely watch perspective so that certain parts of the body are not emphasized through an unfortunate selection of position. One technical note; certain stronger soft focus filters, which are popular in both nude and portrait photography, often cannot be used with autofocus cameras.

Film and flash: In general, fine grain films are a popular choice when working with the figure, with many photographers preferring a weak soft filter to diffuse some of the not so flattering skin flaws that are captured in detail by these films. Grainy films are the choice of other photographers who like the soft, texture pattern that they produce, giving a romantic or "old fashion" interpretation, especially when pushed. Direct or undiffused flash will render the subject very sharp and thus emphasize every blemish. For this reason, many photographers favor a diffused or bounce flash technique.

Architecture

Lenses: Since these types of photographs are usually overviews of a building or an interior often taken inside at close range, a wide angle is recommended. If this is going to be a dominant subject in your photography, then the purchase of a PC lens (to deal with converging lines) is highly recommended, as is low to medium sensitivity film to produce good sharpness. There is also the need for careful composition and large depth of field with typical apertures of f/8 to f/16. Consequently, the use of a cable release and tripod is essential.

Film: overview shots of a structure in both color and black and white are typically going to show a lot of detail, making the use of the highest resolution films of low to middle sensitivity a must.

Note on the use of flash: the high power of the SB-24 or SB-25 is excellent when shooting architecture inside in conjunction with a wide-angle setting. That is, since one usually uses wide-angle lenses when shooting at close quarters, the zoom head should be set to wide angle. Their use is limited to moderate to small rooms. The SB-25 with its built-in diffuser adds another advantage of a more pleasing, softer light that does not cast deep shadows. In larger spaces it will be necessary to use additional slave driven flashes to illuminate the scene evenly. But it must be said that shooting interiors with flash is a specialized area which requires specific techniques beyond what is being covered in this section.

Slide Duplication

Dupes of original slides to protect against loss when sending work to agencies, publishers, labs or photo contests, etc. is a common practice among active photographers, especially professionals.

Slide copying apparatus: copying slides is a special area of macro photography which employs a wide range of equipment, from working with a slide dupe attachment on a bellows unit as offered by Nikon, to a sophisticated slide duplicator with its own color balanced light source made by several manufacturers. One important variable with duplication is that the reproduction ratio is often slightly more than 1:1, meaning that some of the original will be cut off. There are two things needed in the Nikon system for obtaining exactly 1:1; an appropriate macro lens (i.e. the AF Micro Nikkor 60mm f/2.8 or a 50mm El Nikkor enlarging lens) and a bellows unit with slide duplicating adapter. Both optics are used to shoot back lit slides, such as from a copy stand, and illuminating the slide from below with flash. Nikon offers the PS-6 adapter as an accessory for the PB-6 bellows unit. This holds the slide at the end of the bellows and a light source, such as an SB flash, is fired at the diffusion glass at the back of the unit holding the slide.

Film: the best option is Slide Duplicating Film, such as that available from Kodak, which is processed in E-6 chemistry. Duplication films characteristically have low contrast emulsions to deal with the buildup of contrast that occurs when regular slide films are used.

Color filtration: Slide duplicating films do not have exactly the same color sensitivity as daylight films. On top of this, they are UV-sensitive, so pay close attention to the filter recommendations on the data sheets that come with the dupe film. Basic settings for slide duplication are in the area of f/8-16 to be assured of enough depth of field which, at 1:1 magnification, is very small. As pointed out earlier, however, the sharpest apertures are a couple of stops below maximum opening and there is always the question of diffraction, so a good compromise is around f/8, provided the light source can be adjusted to this exposure. The flash illumination can now be controlled either through TTL modes, full manual flash operation by various distances from flash unit to slide, or through neutral density filters.

Duping with TTL flash: flash units have made themselves indispensable for slide duplication, but using TTL modes will require some testing and calibration. It would probably be best to make test shots with different ISO settings until a corrected setting is obtained. Ideal for this purpose is setting a correction factor between +1 and +3 EV which only affects the TTL flash, if this is possible with your camera, and the SB-24 or SB-25. If not, the camera's exposure control can be used.

Fully manual flash: Full manual control of the flash output can also produce the necessary results. Use a series of test exposures with various output levels according to the power output control options on the particular unit.

Family Pictures to Preserve Memories
Pictures of a birthday party, school event, cookouts etc., probably represent the most important reason for having a camera in the home. Most of these type shots are taken at a distance of 4.9ft.-13.1ft. (1.5-4m), so with few exceptions, focal lengths between 28mm and 100mm are enough to cover the majority of these situations. Therefore, the most appropriate lens is a "moderate zoom" that covers this range. Its ability to quickly switch between wide angle and telephoto is perhaps the strongest argument for its use on such a camera.

Film: modern ISO 100-200 negative films, with their fine grain and exposure tolerance, are excellent choices and recent advances in film technology now make the newest ISO 400 films another good choice. The same generalization applies to B&W or color slides, where the choice between ISO 100 or ISO 400 films would depend on the specific lighting conditions.

Flash techniques: when using direct flash with low ambient light, you must watch that the subject is not too far away. This sets up a situation where the foreground will be too bright and the background too dark because of the light fall-off of a small, on- camera flash. If you can flash indirectly, i.e. off a white ceiling or by using some of the after market clip-on diffusers, the results are usually far more desirable and easy to control with the TTL flash mode.

Interior Shots
Lenses: wide angle lens is indispensable for interior shots because of the more confined nature of the setting. Typically, in these situations, a normal lens gives too limited a view, making a 35mm or 28mm the lens of choice. Anything wider will bring into play the exaggeration of size associated with extremely wide fields of view and problems in flash coverage.

Children
It is probably fair to say that pictures of children usually look posed. A little bit of small talk during the picture taking session, therefore, will often work wonders. That depends on the photographer having the camera ready to go and not wasting the short attention span of a child while the settings are made. Patience is the key, as any professional will tell you, and having everything ready is essential, right down to removing obtrusive items in the setting to making the child comfortable and at ease, perhaps with their favorite toys. The option to the posed shot under these conditions is unobtrusive photography from a distance which relies on short to medium telephoto focal lengths.

Special note on flash: when working with children, a number of pre-flashes or test shots can serve to lighten the mood. Also, children who are not used to having their picture taken with flash may be startled by direct flash, making a bounce or diffused form more desirable. (See also Portraits and the red-eye effect).

Landscape
Lenses: focal length choices are based on the effect desired in the final image and the contents of the landscape itself. Thus, for large sweeping views, wide-angle lenses, especially the super-wides are the best choices. Remember that these will also make very dramatic presentations of important foregrounds by exaggerating the size when you move in close and yet still have a significant view of the rest of the scene to provide background. Normal lenses will tend to render a scene with natural proportions across a limited view which, accordingly, does not lend itself easily to dramatic presentations. Telephoto lenses will tend to compress sprawling landscapes and allow you to "stack up" or "pull together" separated parts of a scene as well as making it easier to home in on a single subject. Most landscapes look best with sharp focus throughout, so be careful of the more limited depth of field when telephotos are used.

Film: whether color or B&W, high resolution films between ISO 25 to 100 are most appropriate because of the amount of detail, and a solid tripod is always recommended.

Optimal aperture range: if you want to reproduce the finest details, you have to use the aperture at which your lens' image quality is the best. Large depth of field also requires higher aperture numbers (i.e.; smaller openings). One should therefore use manual exposure modes or aperture preferred modes (or the landscape program on the N90) in apertures of f/8-11 (up to f/16 with telephotos) whenever possible.

Close-ups or Macro Photography

The prerequisites for good macro photography are: good subject illumination, precise focusing, as large a depth of field as possible, best optical performance, and a solid tripod that allows the photographer to change position easily.

Lenses: whether the subject is an insect, a coin, stamps, flowers, rocks, jewelry or integrated circuits, its features can only be photographed from close up with large magnification ratios. Any of the Macro lenses offered by Nikon are to be recommended for photography up to 1:1; with choices between focal lengths dependent on the shooting conditions. For ratios larger than 1:1, an adjustable bellows with a normal lens mounted forward or reversed is probably the best all-around combination. Optimal illumination. (See Chapter, Close-up Lenses and Accessories p. 137. *Important:* beware of distracting shadows which are disturbing enough in normal photography, but whose effects are literally magnified in macro photography. Ring flashes, normal flashes with light tents or special cold light sources with fiber optics available from other manufacturers represent different types of lighting options for macro work.

Auto exposure modes: Aperture preferred or fully manual modes can be used and save time when setting up for many shots over the course of a day's shooting. The most important thing to keep in mind beyond having a rock solid tripod, is the limited depth of field which really makes the use of very small aperture openings a necessity. One can use tables to determine the so-called optimum aperture. (A few guidelines: ratio 1:1, f/16, 2:1 f/11, 5:1 f/5.6).

Minimum aperture for flash: Nikon recommends a minimum aperture depending on film sensitivity for TTL controlled flash modes when the subject distance is less than 2ft. (60cm). *Important:* if a larger aperture is selected, the exposure time might be too short for the TTL automatic to determine the correct flash output. Nikon's rule of thumb for this purpose is:

Numerical example: At a distance of 9.9in. (25cm) between flash reflector and subject and a film speed of ISO 100, the aperture should be at least f/16.

Configuration of the flash unit: the SB-24 and SB-25 can be used with subject-lens distances of up to 1.6ft. (50cm) at a bounce head setting of -7°. If the distance is shorter, the full load of the flash will not hit the subject. An option here would be to use a macro bracket such as the *Stroboframe® LP Macro Bracket.* This bracket allows great flexibility in positioning and aiming the flash in order to direct the light where it is needed most.

Aperture = Film Sensitivity Coefficient/Subject Distance (m)

ISO	100 or less	125-400	500 and more
Coefficient	4	8	11

Remote flashes with TTL control: Macro photographs are best done with a remote flash (adapter cable SC-17) in TTL mode. Soft light and reduction in flash output: If the illumination appears too bright or too hard in test shots, the light can be reduced and diffused by using a sheet of tracing paper over the flash. The *Stroboframe® Lepp II Macro Flash Bracket* positions one or two flashes for close-up photography when artistic lighting or modeling effects are desired.

Portraits

Lenses: portraiture demands careful lighting, an understanding of how to poise a subject, and attention to detail. As for focal lengths, moderate telephotos from 80mm to 105mm give the best proportions to the main structures of the face, as well as placing the photographer at a comfortable working distance as compared to using a normal lens. For example, the model's face can fill the frame at a distance of 4.9ft. to 9.8ft. (1.5 to 3m) and still have room to move. On top of this, the perspective of the face appears natural while a 50mm or shorter lens makes a frame-filling face look rather bulbous. The normal lens works better for the full body pose or group shots and in some cases, a moderate wide-angle lens, provided care is taken to not distort the subject by an unusual placement of the camera.

Film: in portrait work the color balance of the film is the most critical factor and your choice should have a color palette that renders the skin tones of a subject as close to natural as possible. Fine grain emulsions are also preferable with ranges of ISO 50 to 100 for both color and monochrome work as the most desirable. B&W film processing and printing should favor a soft treatment in terms of contrast that is typical of warm tone papers and soft working developers.

Appropriate apertures: frequently, the background is better rendered as out of focus in a portrait setting, so a near wide open aperture of f/4 to f/5.6 is often used, although this will depend very much on the position of the camera in relation to the subject and the focal length used. Thus, for a 105mm lens positioned up close, f/8 may be needed to have enough depth of field to record the entire head within the depth of field, while further away, f/4 is a better choice to keep the background "soft." Larger apertures may also have the secondary advantage of making the subject itself also look slightly soft because of the optical quality of the lens.

Focusing: because of the limited depth of field, one usually focuses on the eyes, because eyes that are out of focus are more disturbing than blurry ears, or a nose that is starting to fall out of focus.

Note on flash: a diffuser in front of the flash or indirect bounce flash will help prevent too hard and contrasty a rendering where the highlight areas of the face seem washed out. Again, a piece of tracing paper or any one of the after market diffuser attachments can be very helpful.

Pre-flash to prevent red-eye and unnatural expressions: Pre-flash is possible with the N90/F90 and SB-25. This is not really necessary to prevent red eyes if the flash unit is held off camera (see also, Red-eye).

Groups and Large Subjects

Fully manual flash: in full manual mode, the optimum exposure aperture for flash depends on the distance to the subject. In the case of a large group shot, keep in mind that every person in the group is at a different subject to camera distance, so even light coverage is always a consideration. This is often not much of a problem when the group is close together, but there are times, such as with a receiving line at a wedding, when you will have to pick a setting based on a middle distance between the beginning of the line near you and the end far from your position. This compromise is pretty much the best way to go, especially when you cannot arrange the group. If the light

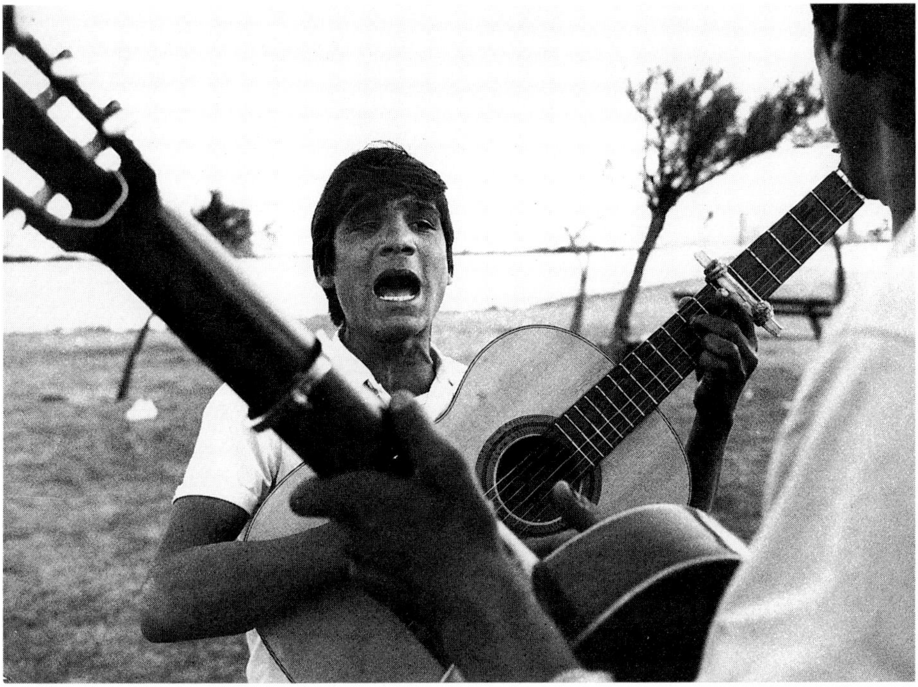

Use of depth of field: The intentionally shallow depth of field in the top photo caused the background to be out of focus. However, the background was consciously included in the image of the flute player in the park (bottom). Photos: Rudolf Dietrich.

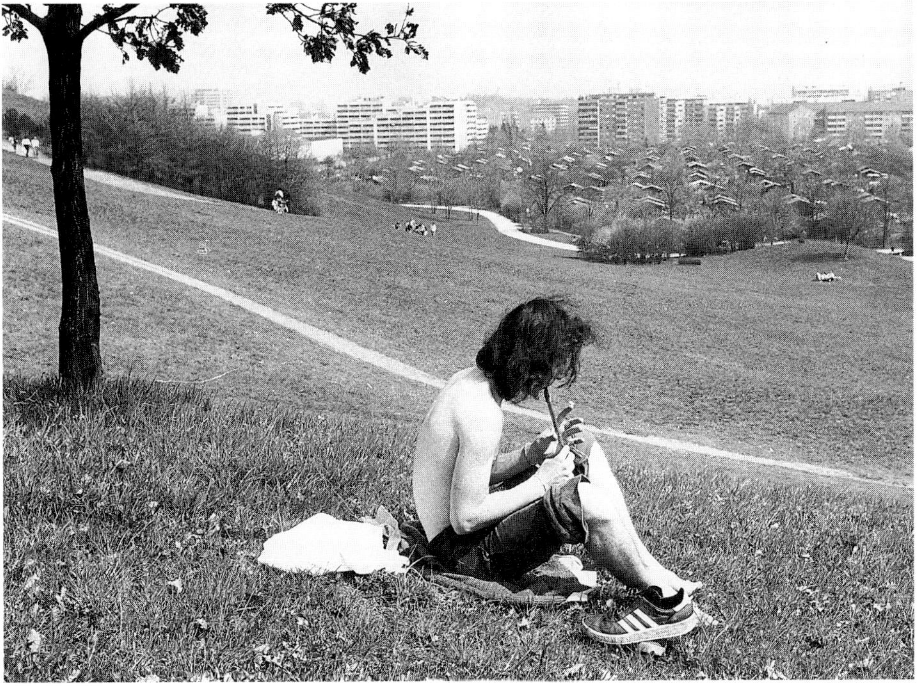

fall-off is greater than one stop at the edges, then a decision should be made to take two pictures of a smaller area of the whole scene that are well lit, versus one that takes in the whole, but has significant shadow areas at the ends of the frame. Another consideration is the position of an important subject, such as the bride. The correct exposure should then be calculated around this person's position. This, then, becomes more a portrait of her on the receiving line as opposed to a group shot of the whole receiving line. One other possible solution is to use bounce flash off a white ceiling in this situation.

TTL flash: in TTL flash mode, the light reflected from the subject is measured even if the light is indirect. If the subjects are grouped close together or a bounce flash is used, TTL is the preferred approach. But if you have to split the difference as mentioned above, TTL will react to the nearest subject and that means having to switch the flash to a manual mode set for the middle point.

Variations in background illumination: since scenes with a lot of depth tend to swallow flash illumination, ambient light can be used to balance the lighting by selecting a slow sync mode, depending on the camera model. In other words, use the flash at an aperture setting as close as possible to the ambient light so as to balance the light. This is only realistic and practical if there is enough ambient light to get within one and a half to two stops of the main flash illumination and without having to resort to very slow shutter speeds which will record the blur of peoples' movement.

Copy Work

Lenses: as in macro photography, lenses that are optimized or appropriate for close-up work should be used when doing copy work. The best optics are those that have a flat field; that is, they are evenly corrected across their entire image area, as opposed to other lenses which are more likely to show a drop off in the center to edge sharpness and contrast.

Copy stand: a good copy stand is vital to keep the camera and the subject perfectly parallel and it is a good idea to use a bubble level to check the alignment of the camera relative to the baseboard when it is mounted.

Positioning light sources: even illumination requires two lamps or flash units of the same power at an angle of 45° to the subject set about 2.6ft. (80cm) away from the subject on the baseboard.

Flash units: it is very important to make sure that both flash units are putting out the same amount of power to give even lighting. The easiest way to do this is to have units with the same power output, or ones whose output can be controlled in stops. It is also recommended that diffusers be used on the flash heads. Triggering can be performed via the TTL cords SC-17, SC-18, SC-19 and AS-10 since these also trigger non-TTL flashes.

Red-eye

Causes: the most common cause of the red-eye problem in flash pictures can be traced to a flash unit mounted directly on the camera's hot shoe. If the flash axis and lens axis are very close, the light reflected from the red lining of the eye is visible. If there is a noticeable difference between these two axes, the red light is reflected out of the view seen by the camera.

Remedies: a good way to prevent red eye is to use a remote flash that is positioned above the lens as is the case with the Stroboframe flash bracket, or to use an indirect flash as in a bounce off the ceiling. Even a diffuser in front of the flash reduces this effect. Of all these choices, a flash bracket offers the most consistent results; indirect flash and diffusers may be least desirable in some circumstances, as in high ceilings or colored walls, which may introduce a color cast. There is less of a problem with red-eye when using the SB-24 and SB-25 since the reflectors of these flash units are relatively far away from the lens axis and are, therefore, less likely to produce red eye.

Pre-flash for relaxed faces: the N90/F90 combined with the SB-25 can trigger a pre-flash which sometimes gets people to relax and not have a stiff, unnatural expression.

Product Photography

Unique requirements: product photography requires a high degree of accurate and precise presentation to depict it as correct as possible. This means, as a rule, good sharpness, large depth of field, and even lighting. Studio product photography therefore requires a great deal of flash power.

Lenses: high quality lenses are very important. The focal length depends on both the desired composition and the required reproduction ratio on film.

Film: High resolution, fine grain films requiring high levels of illumination are necessary.

Auto modes, apertures: Because of the required image quality and usual large depth of field, one would select a relatively large aperture number of f/8 or f/16 in manual or aperture preferred mode.

Illumination: even lighting is required. Harsh shadows and hard lighting are considered undesirable. Dark shadows should only be used as a precise creative tool to support the product.

Note on flash: if studio flash units are not being used, one can get amazingly far with a powerful flash such as the SB-25. The flash can be transformed into a large, soft source, for example, by using it with an umbrella. An additional reflector (cardboard covered in tin foil, for example) beside the subject fills shadows and this setup will work quite well for typical small products. More flash units can be added with three flash units capable of handling virtually any medium size product. An alternative is to use a sheet of tracing paper hung about 1 yard from the flash unit to work as a diffuser for the main light while a second unit can be used to control background illumination or as a bottom light. The third unit could then be used as a fill or as an accent light. The lack of modeling lights can be overcome by the use of 60W lamps with reflectors on clamps at the position of each flash.

Photojournalism

Full auto: a modern AF camera, a good zoom of about 80-200mm and/or moderate zoom of say 28-70mm, mid-speed films around ISO 200, AF sharpness priority mode and program mode with TTL fill flash mode (if necessary) are a good combination for the kinds of action grab shots so common in "on the run" situations faced by reporters.

Sports and Action

Lenses: when the subject is moving, shooting from a close position is often not possible and a good telephoto lens from 180mm to about 400mm is necessary. Whether it is a horseback rider, a good return in tennis, or children at play, the view from a distance has its advantages: even in the most hectic situations, the photographer has a complete overview of the scene from which to pick out specific happenings.

Film: films of ISO 200 are usually required.

Exposure modes: in order to obtain correctly exposed images, one should meter the main subject (a single soccer player, for example) and then select an aperture and shutter speed combination manually that best suits the motion of the scene. Shutter preferred mode is often used, but this can result in differences in brightness with contrasty subjects even in matrix metering mode. The fast shutter speed programs or the multi-program modes that match themselves to the focal length of the lens generally select appropriate time/aperture combinations with high speed films. The same restriction applies as with aperture preferred mode.

Note on flash: at greater distances you should use high speed films with flash because of the

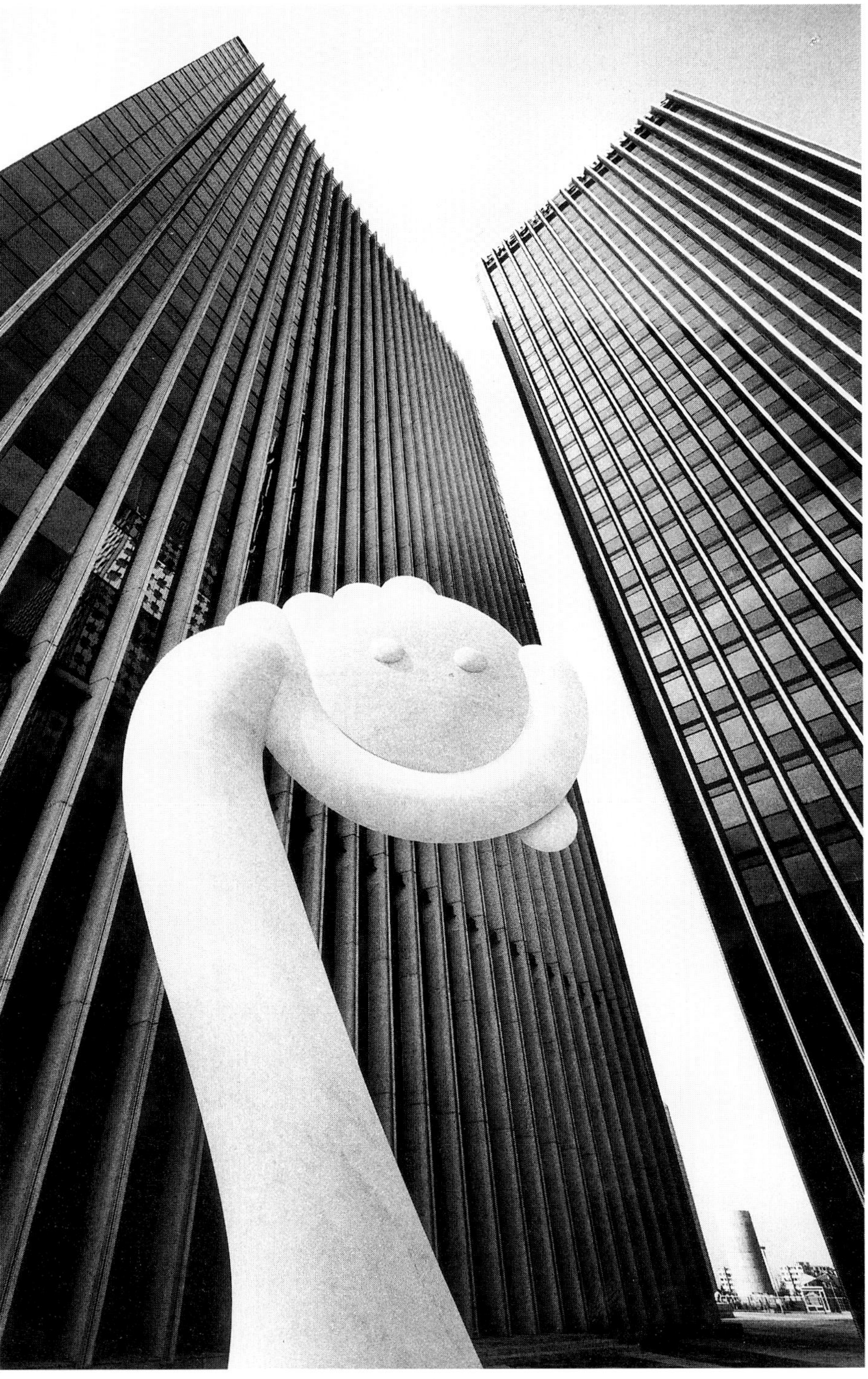

light-fall off from smaller units, such as the SB-24 or SB-25. Nikon's range of products is missing a light concentrating telephoto adapter.

Wildlife

While insects and butterflies can be categorized as subjects for macro photography, larger subjects such as birds and mammals are considered "wildlife" photography. For more detailed information refer to B. "Moose" Peterson's *Nikon Guide to Wildlife Photography* from Silver Pixel Press Division of The Saunders Group (address on rear cover).

Lenses: focal lengths of 400mm, 600mm and higher are part of a wildlife photographer's basic outfit. Fast lenses in this focal length range are heavy, awkward and expensive. But they have become "standard issue" for this type of photography.

Exposure modes: the same applies as for sport and action as above.

Film: ISO 100 films are desirable when possible, but light conditions often call for the use of high speed films of about ISO 400. If shots are done hand held or from a monopod, the faster films are just about indispensable because of subject movement and camera shake.

Tripods: medium sized tripods, monopods, chest supports, etc. prevent fatigue.

Perspective: An ultra wide angle lens was used to capture the high rise complex in Paris (left) in order to include the sculpture in the foreground. Because of this and the noticeable convergence of the lines, the impressive size of the buildings is emphasized.
Motion: The picture of the amusement park (below) is a good example of how motion (as opposed to the people themselves) can be the subject of a picture. Photos: Rudolf Dietrich

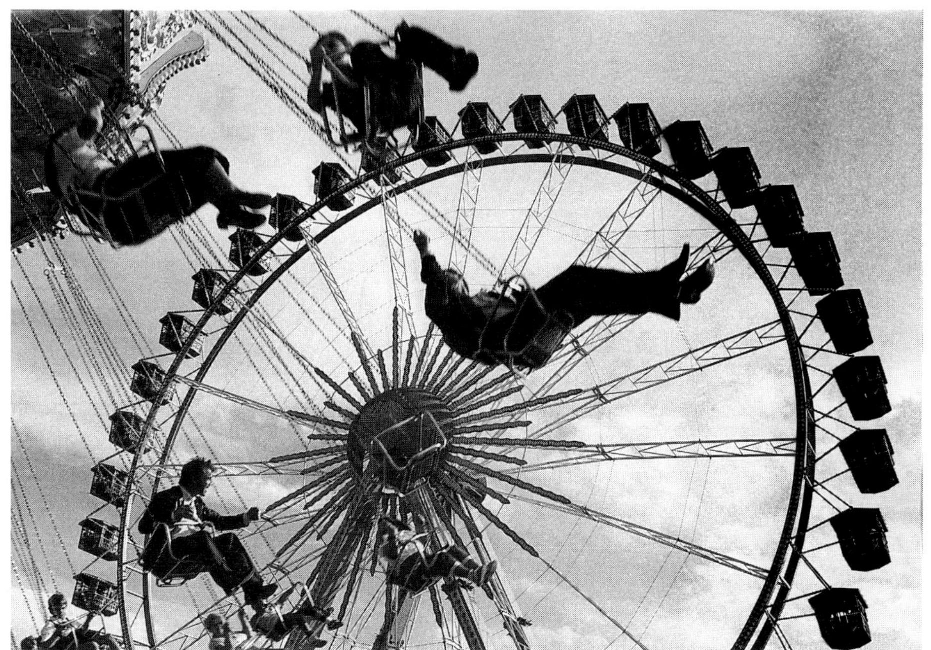

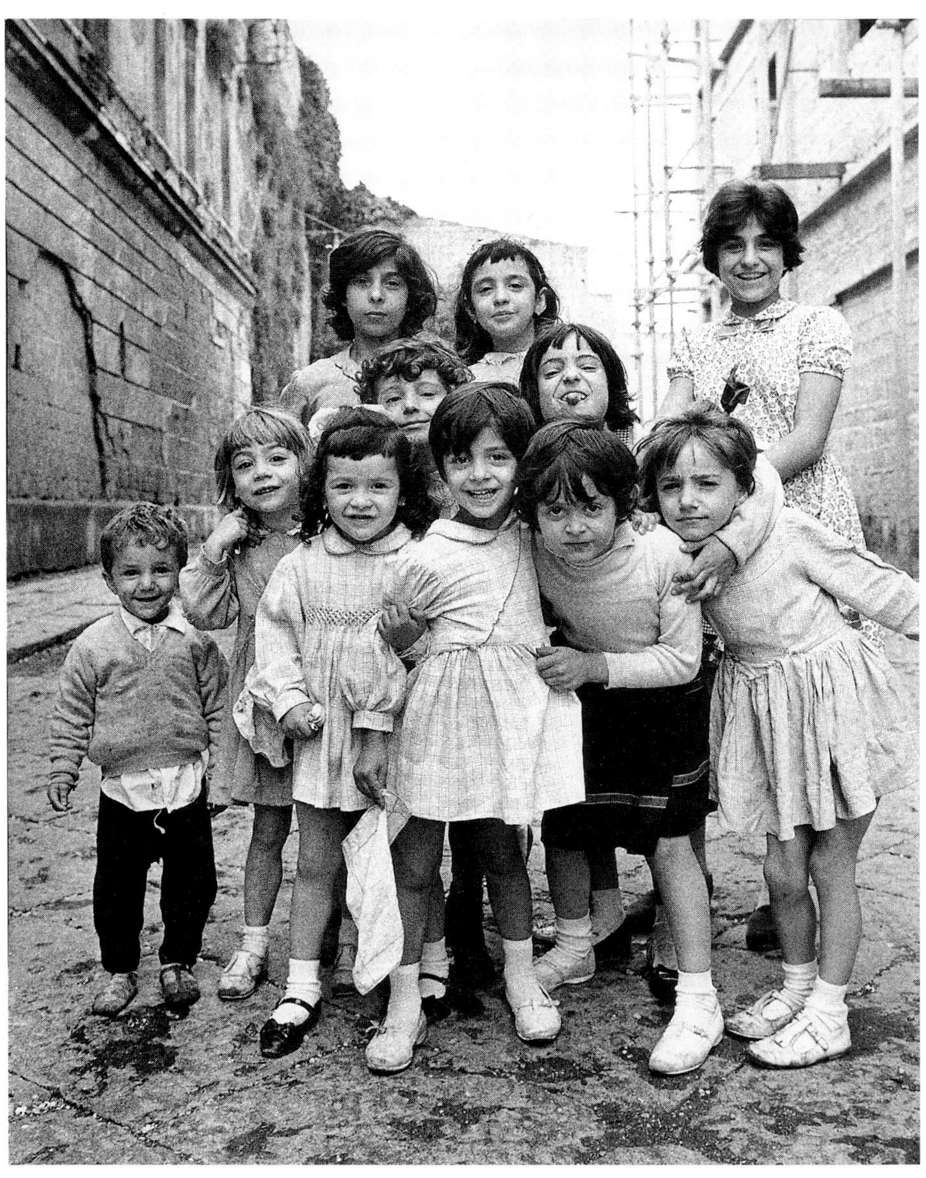

This group of children, who have spontaneously bunched themselves together seem to be challenging to the photographer to take their picture. Such moments demand that the photographer be ready with equipment capable of automatically carrying out the complexities of correct focus and exposure; one of the main reasons for owning Nikon AF equipment. Photo: Rudolf Dietrich.

Nikon Accessories

It is very easy to throw things that you think you will need into a camera bag following the motto "just in case." Unfortunately, that all too often results in carrying around items that are never used, to say nothing of how difficult it makes to find what you need when going through all the clutter in the bag. So, perhaps a better motto is, "as complete as necessary and as little as possible." That also applies as well to the selection of various accessories. There are many of these secondary products that do, indeed, make a difference, but it does take some consideration of their specific purpose and function in relation to your needs in order to determine just what is necessary.

Viewfinder Accessories

Focusing Screens

The camera's focusing screen shows the same image that the camera will capture on negative or slide film. (*Note:* only the F3 and F4 focusing screens show 100% of the image. All other models show a portion reduced up to about 15%.) The image formed by the lens projects onto the SLR mirror which reflects it into the focusing screen. Thus, the viewfinder is the palette on which the photographer composes the image and, as such, its makeup, from the clarity of the view to various visual aids such as grid patterns, can have some effect on the outcome.

Type A (F3): standard focusing screen with split-image indicator, 12mm reference circle for center-weighted metering. It is a fresnel screen which ensures an evenly illuminated image without darkened corners and has universal applications. For longer focal lengths, see type U.

Type B (F4, N8008, N6006, N4004): standard focusing screen without spilt-image or microprism specially designed for AF cameras. It is fresnel ground and has markings for AF measuring field, 12mm reference circle for center-weighted metering and, depending on camera model, a reference circle for spot metering. The matte 12mm circle is very good for manual focusing in close-ups or with fast telephoto lenses. For longer focal lengths from 200mm, the F4 has a type U screen.

Type C: clear focusing screen with cross hairs for aerial images. Specially designed for large reproduction ratios with telescopes (astronomy), but also for macro and micro photography. The cross hairs serve to determine sharpness in the viewfinder. The actual focusing is performed with the microscope, bellows, or telescope on the aerial image.

Type D (F3): completely matte screen that is not fresnel ground and does not have any aids or markings. The so-called classic focusing screen. Good for longer telephoto lenses, close-ups and fish eye lenses.

Type E (FM2, N8008 F3, F4, N90): like type B, but with an additional grid of horizontal and vertical lines. The ideal tool for aligning the camera in copy work, in architectural photography and landscapes with very wide angle lenses. Some photographers prefer the type E as a standard focusing screen.

Type F (F4): like type B., distribution of illumination is specially designed for mirror lenses.

Type G - G1, G2, G3, G4 (F3, F4): particularly bright, clear fresnel screens with a central

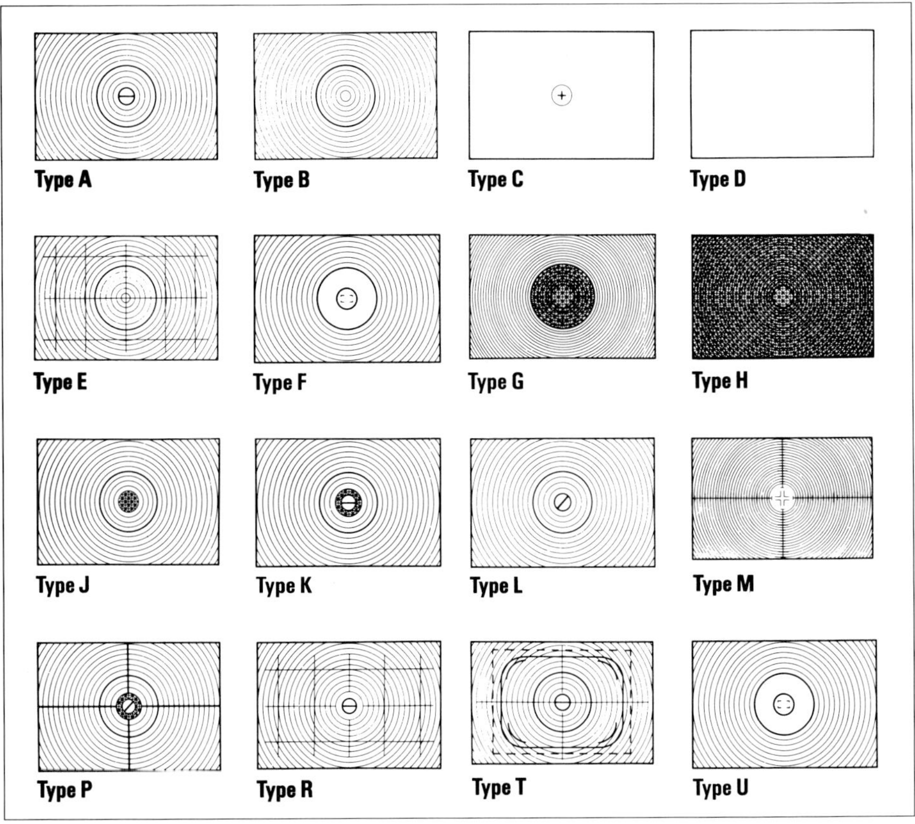

microprism 12mm in diameter which is used for focusing. Microprisms are an excellent focusing aid on the one hand, but certain grinding angles are only good for specific focal lengths and aperture ranges. The type G screen is therefore offered in 4 versions: G1 for fish eye lenses, G2 for focal lengths between 24 and 200mm, G3 for focal lengths between 200 and 300mm, and G4 for focal lengths of 600mm and higher.

Type H - H1, H2, H3, H4 (F3): like type G, but the microprisms cover the entire screen. Portions of the image that are in focus appear clear while the rest of the image seems to flicker. It is specially designed for sports photography and is available in 4 versions which cover the same focal length ranges as those of the type G screen.

Type J (F3, F4): fresnel focusing screen with 12mm reference circle for center-weighted metering and a central microprism area with large prism structure 5mm in diameter. This special microprism design is intended for use with slow zoom lenses.

Type K (FM2, N2000, N6000, F3, F4): the type K screen is the standard focusing screen for modern non-AF Nikon cameras. It is a combination of type A and type J screens. The central split-image indicator is surrounded by a microprism ring. The screen, therefore, offers both of these options for focusing as well as the surrounding matte area for visual control. The brightness of this screen has been improved over the years, resulting in the bright viewing of the N2000 and N6000. The split-image prisms are designed so that they will not darken until f/11 with a wide range of focal lengths.

Type L (F3): like Type A, but the dividing line runs diagonally so that one can focus on both horizontal and vertical lines without turning the camera.

Type M (F3, F4): similar to type C, but optimized for macro photography with marked enlargements. Clear, fresnel glass with double cross hairs and scale lines at a distance of 1mm.

Type P (F3, F4): like type K, but with diagonal split image (as described with Type L) and horizontal and vertical central lines to aid in positioning the camera.

Type R (F3): a combination of Type A and Type E. In comparison to the Type E, the split image distance indicator is an additional aid in focusing on bright subjects.

Type T (F3): like type A but with lines corresponding to a TV screen etched in, along with horizontal and vertical lines passing through the center of the image to aid in positioning the camera. For pictures taken from the TV screen.

Type U (F4): similar to type A or B. The central circle is optimized for manual focusing with telephoto lenses from 200mm.

Eye Cups

Eye cups, made of black rubber, shield the eye at the viewfinder from side and frontal light. The cup also protects the camera's metering system from stray light that enters the viewfinder around the eye which could lead to incorrect exposure readings and hence underexposed images. There are units available that fit the eyepieces of the various Nikon cameras.

Eyepiece Blinds

Metering errors caused by a lamp or the sun shining into the viewfinder when the camera is mounted on a tripod or other fixed mount without an eye at the viewfinder can be substantial. Troublesome stray light can enter during long time exposures with low ambient light conditions as well. There is an eye piece cover available as an accessory for each camera for precisely this reason while most F3 and F4 finders have a built in cover.

High-Eyepoint Viewfinder

People who wear glasses cannot get close enough to the viewfinder to see the entire image. The F3 and F4 have optional HP viewfinders for this reason and, in fact, the HP version has become very popular with most photographers. The N6006/F-601, N8008/F-801 and N90/F90 have HP viewfinders as standard.

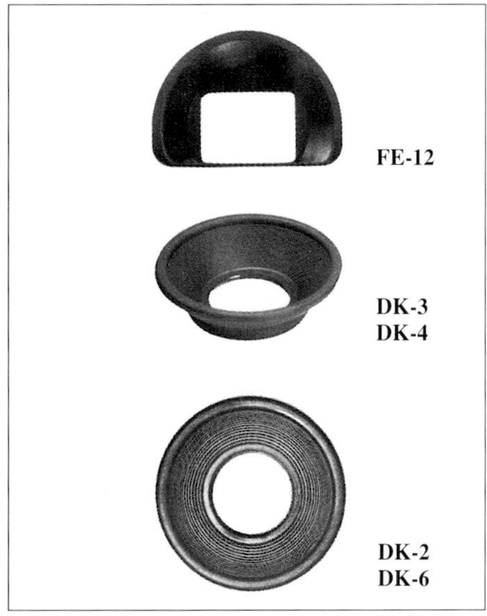

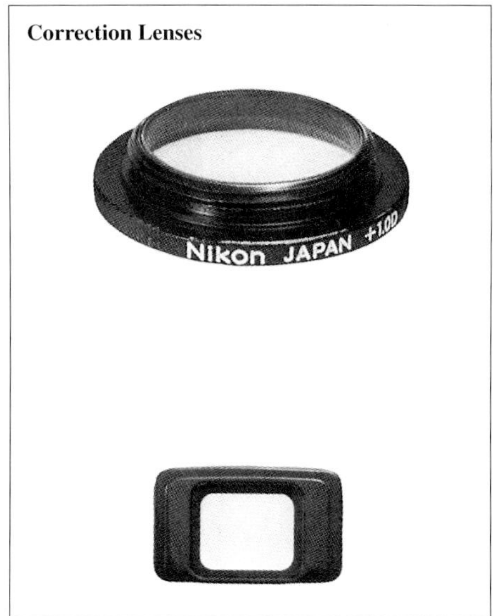

Correction Lenses

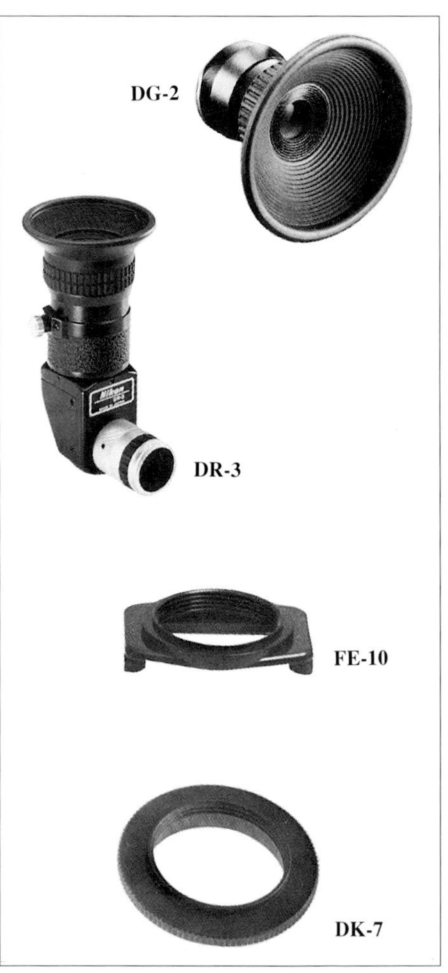

Correction Lenses

Nikon cameras are shipped with a -1 diopter viewer. This lens should allow fatigue-free viewing. For those whose eyesight requires correction, diopters from -5 to +3 in full steps (except for +0.5) are available, either as rectangular or round screw-in types, depending on camera.

User tip: a correction lens should be selected such that it renders optimal sharpness when used in conjunction with the visual aids (-glasses or contact lenses) the photographer usually wears.

Eyepiece Magnifiers and Angle Viewers

The rotatable DG-2 eyepiece magnifier and the DR-3 angle viewer are screwed directly into Nikon cameras with round eye pieces, attached via the DK-1 adapter to high eyepoint viewfinders and via the #2370 adapter to cameras with rectangular viewers. Both have rubber eye cups. The eyepiece magnifier provides a 2x magnification of the center of the image and makes precise focusing easier. Corrections of +1 to -5 diopters are available. The angle viewfinder allows the photographer to view the image at 90° to the optical axis. It is very practical in situations where the camera is mounted such that its own viewfinder is hard or impossible to get at as in a near to the ground arrangement. The angle viewfinder has diopters from +3 to -5. The F3 and F4 also have special viewfinders that show a left-right inverted image.

Optional Viewfinders

The F3 and F4 each have a wide range of interchangeable viewfinders that are optimized for very specialized applications. These finders are described in detail in the corresponding camera chapter.

Instant and Digital Backs

Polaroid Backs

The F2, F3 and F4 can be equipped with an interchangeable Polaroid back. A fiber optic block in the back corrects the image parallax resulting from the shift of the film plane back into the film plane of the Polaroid back. Two 24mmx36mm images can be exposed on a single sheet of Polaroid Professional Pack Film type such as 669 (Color ISO 80/20), or type 664 (B&W ISO 100/21). The usual practice is to dedicate a camera body to this film back, since taking it off and putting it back on results in the loss of a sheet of film (there is no dark slide) and this exchange requires replacing the original back as well. Polaroid backs are an after-market accessory available in the US from NPC Inc.

Digital Imaging Back in the Digital Camera System (DCS) from Kodak

Kodak offers backs with integrated sensors for digital photography for the F3 and N8008/F-801. The quality of the image is sufficient for 7x10cm B&W and similar smaller reproduction in color printing for brochures, magazines etc. This electronic "filmless camera" combination allows the camera to be also used as a film camera when the digital back is removed. It has become popular with desktop publications and catalog shooters, where the image produced on the page is both limited in size and below the very top quality required for a full page illustration in a high quality magazine. These electronic images are intended for transfer into a computer for manipulation and then "dropped into" a page layout using such software as PhotoStyler or PhotoShop.

Applications in actual newspaper reporting: digital images can be transmitted via modem directly to the publisher.

Applications in advertising: even if the actual printed product is produced from classic silver based film, direct transmission of digital images via modem and telephone to the client results in noticeable time savings. After viewing the image on the computer screen, the client can immediately give his OK or request changes which can then be carried out either with the digital camera or a camera with film.

Applications in catalog production: silver based photography has always been a luxury for many catalogs that are printed on inexpensive stock. Images can be taken directly into a computer managed page layout from the DCS system. The whole catalog is produced electronically which represents a dramatic reduction in time. This system also saves photo and litho costs.

POL-A-DAPT-System

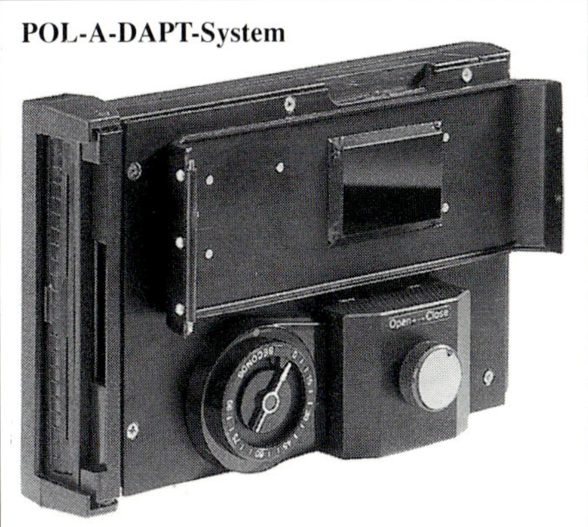

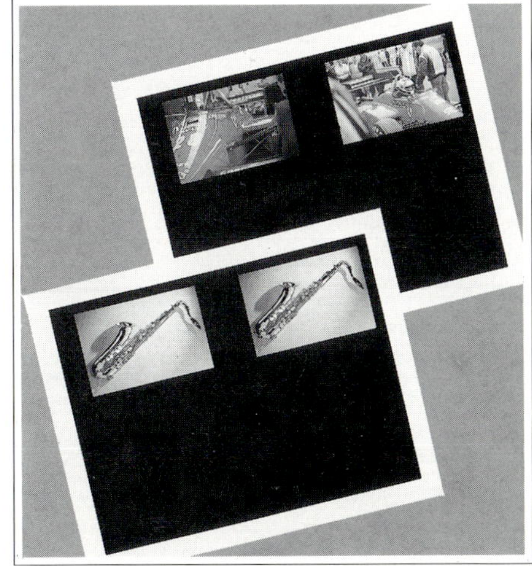

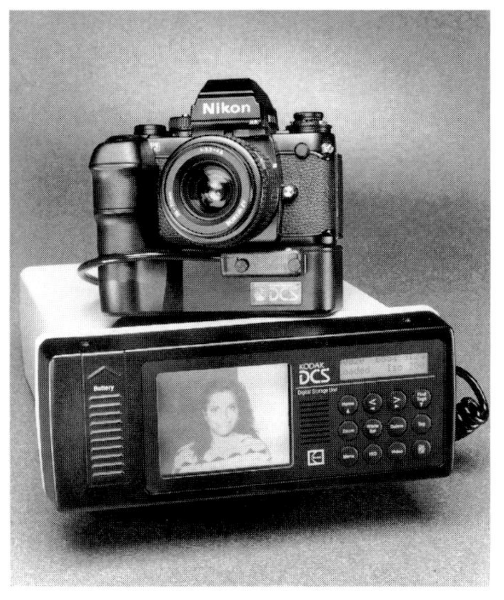

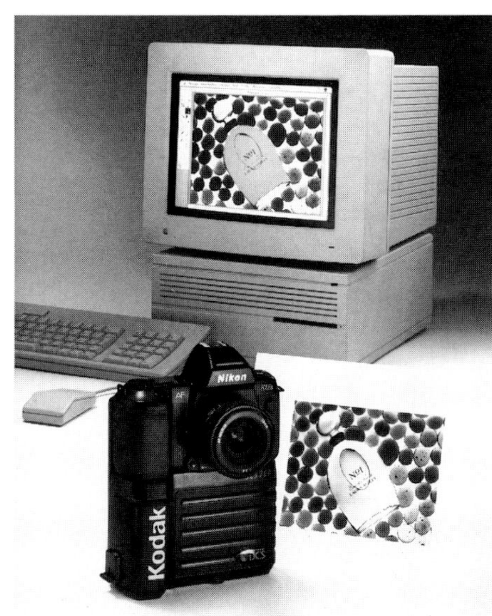

DCS 100 (above) DCS 200 (right)

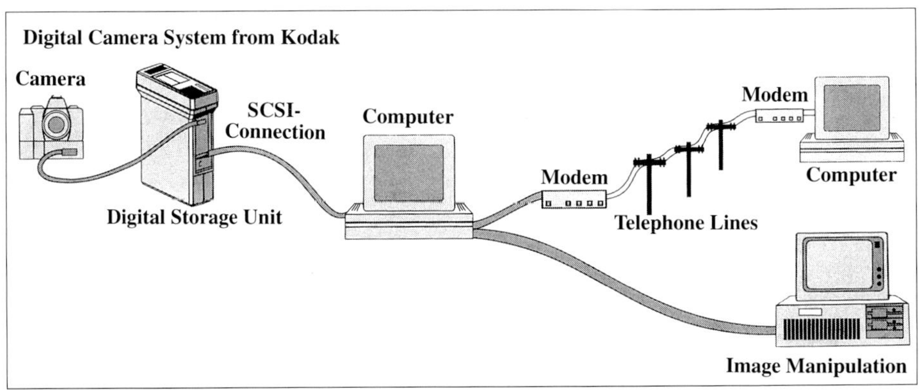

DCS 100 System for the Nikon F3: digital back with a chip whose resolution is 1.3 million pixels. Color sensitivity, ISO 100 to ISO 1600; B&W sensitivity from ISO 200 to ISO 3200. Separate storage unit with hard drive and space for 600 images.

DCS 200 System for the Nikon F8008: digital back with an image sensor that has a resolution of 1.54 million pixels. An 80MB hard drive for approximately 50 images is integrated into the unit. An SCSI interface allows downloading to Macs or IBM compatible computers. With 24 bit color, the image size is 4.5 MB uncompressed (1.5MB B&W).

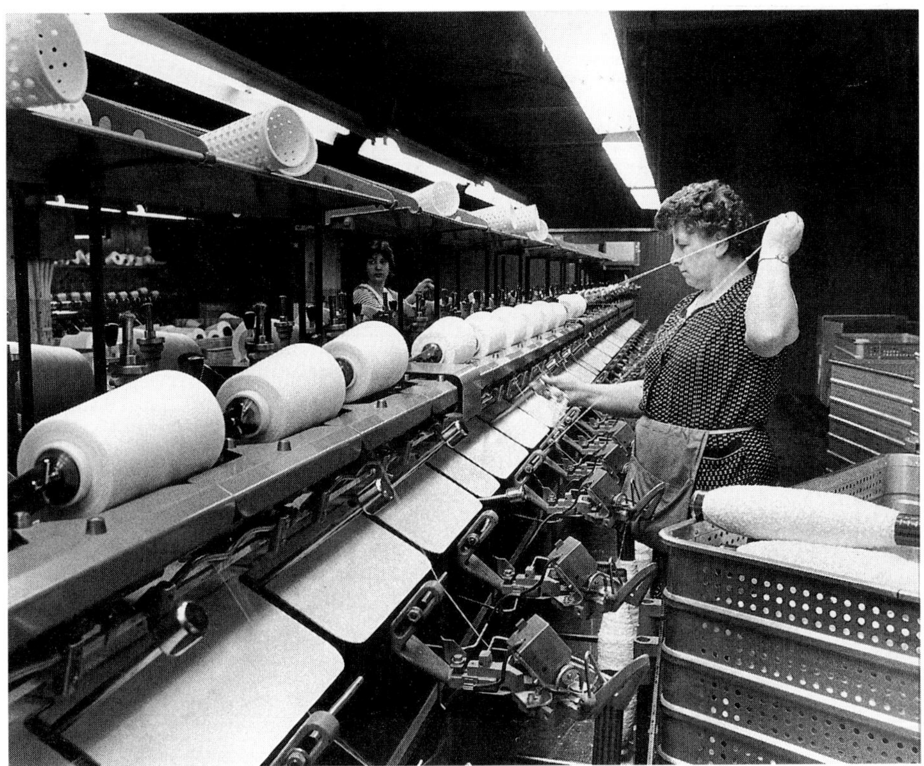

An example of photography for a corporate annual report. Photo: Rudolf Dietrich.

Data and Multi-Function Backs

Databacks have a number of specialized functions, including exposing data, such as time and date, directly onto the film. This is a particularly useful function in the case of documentation applications, as in surveillance and scientific work. The multi-function backs for the N8008 and F4 also contain a whole range of features as listed on the following table that shows compatibility of backs to cameras. Perhaps the most useful function here is the Autobracketing exposure feature. More detailed information can be found in the appropriate camera chapters.

Overview of Data and Multifunction Backs

Backs	Camera	Possibilities	Notes and Specialities
MF-14	F3	*Exposed on the frame:* Date, Time, Number	
MF-16	FM-2n	*Exposed on the frame:* Date, Time, Number	
MF-6/6B	F3 + MD-4	*Leaves film leader out after film is rewound*	
MF-17	F3 + MF-4	*Exposed on the frame:* Date, Time, Number, Notes	Only with 250 Exp *MF-4*
MF-18	F3 + MD-4	*Exposed between frames:* Date, Time, Number- acts like MF-6/6B - leaves out leader	Only with the *MD-4* Motordrive
MF-19	N2000/F-301	*Exposed on the frame:* Date, Time, Number, Notes; *Functions*: Interval timer	
-	N4004/F-401 Quartz Date	*Exposed on the frame:* Date, Time	Special *N4004/F-401* delivered with Data back
-	N6006/F-601 Quartz Date	*Exposed on the frame:* Date, Time	Special *N6006/F-601* delivered with Data back
MF-20	N8008/s/F-801/s	*Exposed on the frame:* Date, Time	
MF-21	N8008/s F-801/s	*Exposed on the frame:* Date, Time, Number Shutter speed/aperture; *Functions:* Interval timer; exposure bracketing; long time exposures, AF-Traps	
MF-22	F4; F4S, F4E	*Exposed on the frame:* Date, Time, Shutter speed/aperture, exposure correction. Can be set to expose between frames.	
MF-23	F4; F4S, F4E	*Exposed on the frame:* Date, Time, Shutter speed/aperture, exposure correction. Can be set to expose between frames. *Functions:* Interval timer, delay, exposure bracketing, film stop during transport, long time exposures, AF-Traps, audible signal	
MF-24	F4; F4S	*Exposed on the frame:* Date, Time, Shutter speed/aperture, exposure correction. Can be set to expose between frames. *Functions:* Interval timer, delay, exposure bracketing, film stop during transport, long time exposures, AF-Traps, audible signal	The MF-24 is a 250 Exposure Back with integrated multifunction data back
MF-25	N90/F90	*Exposed on the frame:* Year, month, day; day, hour, minute or day, month, year (24-hour time. *Functions:* alarm	
MF-26	N90/F90	*Exposed on the frame:* Year, month, day; day, hour, minute (24-hour time); frame number, reference number from 1 to 999999, shutter speed and aperture. *Functions:* among others: series mode, interval timer, long time exposure, multiple exposure, flash exposure correction, flash exposure bracketing, AE/AF storage, AF traps, reset to camera defaults, etc. (See also section on "Special Acessories for the N90"	
-	F90D	See *MF-25*	Special version of the N90/F90, delivered with the MF-25 (available in some markets)
-	F90S	See *MF-26*	Special version of the N90/F90, delivered with the MF-26 (available in some markets)

Overview of Nikon Built-in or Accessory Motordrives

Camera	Motordrive	Operating Modes	Frames/sec.	AC Adapter External Power Pack	Rewind Time	Rolls of Film per Sets of Batteries	Cable Release
F3	optional winder ***MD-4***	S/C	1 / 2 / 3	*MA-4* / -	4.5-8	140	*MC-12A*
FM-2n	optional winder ***MD-12***	S/C	3,5	- / -	M	100	*MC-10/12*
N2002/F-301	built-in	S/C	2,5	- / -	M	60 (*MB-4*), 180 (*MB-3*)	*MC-12A*
N4004/N5005/ F-401/s/x	built-in	S	-	- / -	25	50	-
N6006/F-601	built-in	S/CL/CH	1,2 / 2	- / -	25	75 w/o flash	Cable release
N8008/s/F-801, F-801s	built-in	S/CL/CH	2 / 3,3	- / -	15	120	*MC-12A*
F4	built-in, interchangeable, MB-20	S/CL/CH/CS	3,3 / 4 / 1	- / -	8	30	*AR-3*
F4S	built-in, interchangeable, MB-21	S/CL/CH/CS	3,4 / 5,7 / 1	- / -	8	90	*MC-12A*
F4E	built-in, interchangeable, MB-23	S/CL/CH/CS	3,4 / 5,7 / 1	*MA-4* / -	8	150	*MC-12A*
N90/F90,	built-in	S/CL/CH	2 / 3.6	- / *DB-6*	15	75	*MC-20* / *MC-12A* + *MC-25*

S = Single exposure, **C** = continuous exposure (series), **CL** = slow series, **CH** = fast series, **CS** = quiet series; **M** = manual; **-** = N/A

Motor Drives

Motor drives are indispensable for photographers who are involved in action situations, from shooting sports and fashion to wild life, as well as applications where electronic remote triggering or interval exposures are required. A motor drive is also useful in portraiture because the camera does not have to be taken away from the eye to advance the film, disrupting the flow of the session. As a matter of fact, many photographers like to use a motor drive or the slower motor winder just for the reason that it lets you concentrate on the subject. Other applications include copy stand or macro work since there is no risk of disturbing the camera position when the film is advanced. The "problem" with motor winders and especially motor drives, if you will, is that there is a temptation to take too many pictures; to not wait for the right moment, relying instead on shooting a number of pictures rapidly hoping "to catch" the right poise. The following table gives an overview of the various drives that are available as options, or that are built-in features of various camera models.

Mechanical and Electrical Cable Releases

A cable release is a useful tool in copy work, macro photography or in any long exposure situation because it releases the shutter without shaking the camera. Portraits from a tripod are made easier since they allow the photographer to interact directly with the subject face to face, as opposed to having one's head always behind the camera. If a cable release is not available and the precise time of the exposure is not critical (i.e. with product shots), the self timer can be used as a replacement. All current Nikon cameras, except the N4004/F-401, have some sort of cable release connection. The FM2, N6006/F-601, F3 and F4 have the classic cable release, the N2000 N8008/F-801 and N90/F90 only have an electronic cable release. The F3, FM2, as well as the F4S and F4E, can be electrically triggered via the cable release connector in their motor winders or motor drives. For exposures at a specific time interval, the MT-2 interval timer is available. For real remote triggering, use the ML-3 infrared triggering device for distances of up to 26.2ft., and the MW-2 for distances up to 2300ft. (700m). The ML-2 is discontinued but if you combine the transmitter of the ML-2 with the reciever of the ML-3 it will trigger from distances up to 329ft. (100m).

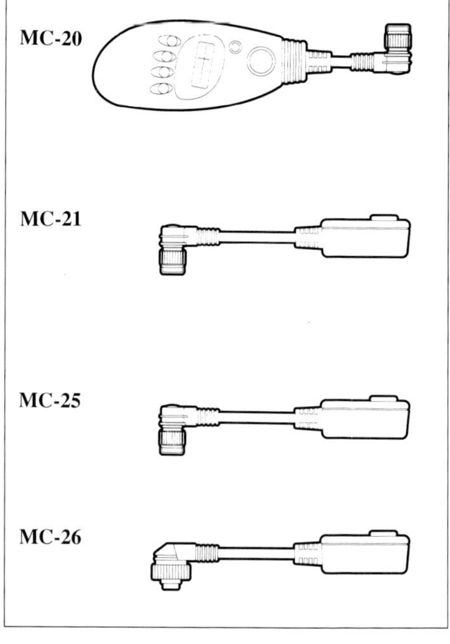

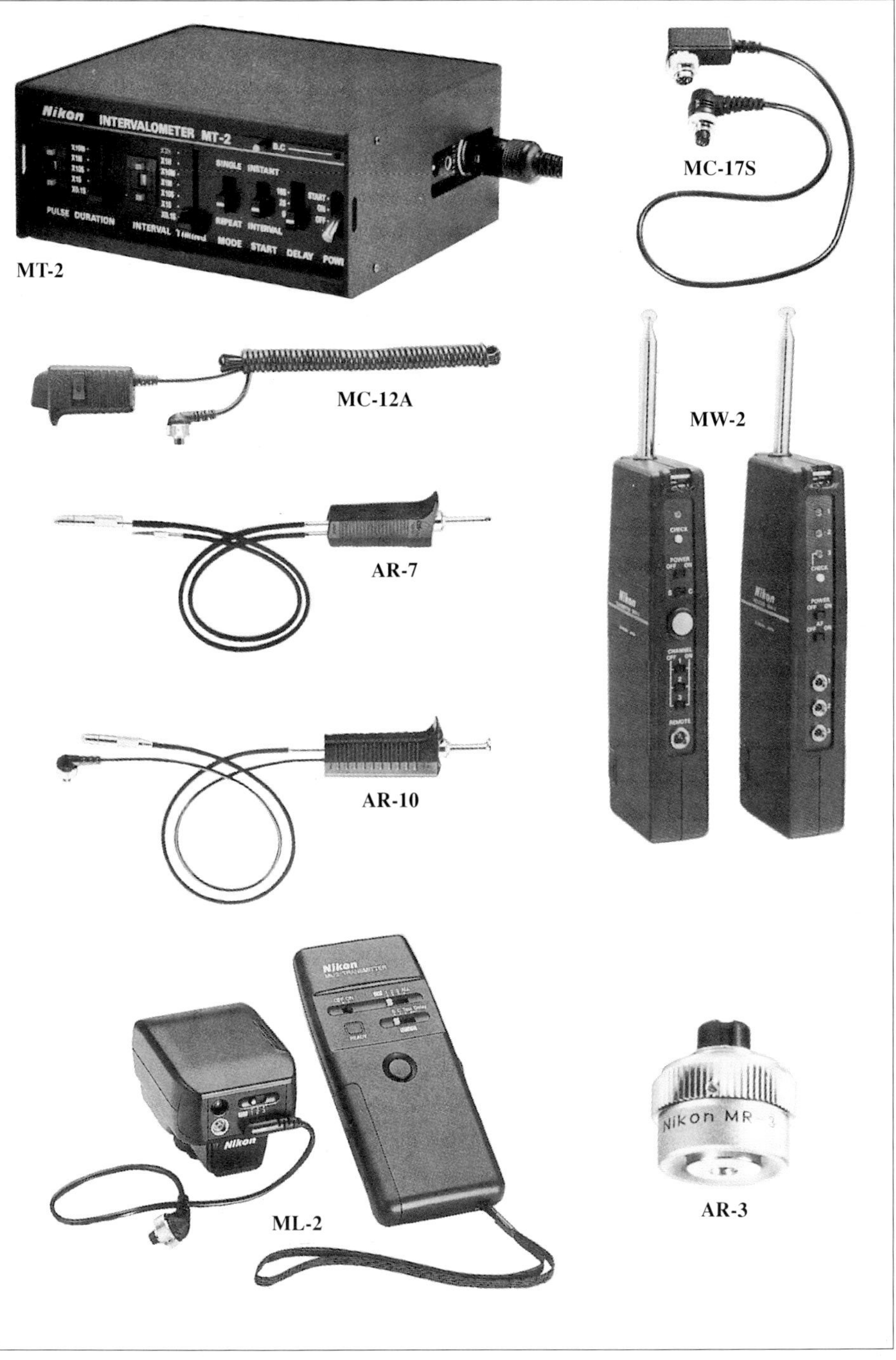

MT-2

MC-17S

MC-12A

MW-2

AR-7

AR-10

ML-2

AR-3

Overview of Cable Releases and Remote Triggering Accessories

Accessory	Description	Compatible Cameras	Notes, Unique Features
AR-3	Cable Release	*FM-2n, F3, N6006/F-601*	same as any standard cable release
MC-12A	Elec. Remote Release	*N8008/F-801, N2000/ F-301, F4S, F4E*	also compatible with F3 and FM-2n with MD-4 or MD-12 motordrives
MC-20	Elec. Remote Release	*N90/F90*	
MC-21	Electronic Extension	*N90/F90*	lengthens *MC-20* by 10ft.
MC-25	Electronic Adapter	*N90/F90*	for use with N90/*F90* and *MC-12A*
MC-26	Electronic Adapter	*N8008/F-801, N2000/ F-301, F4S, F4E*	for using *MC-20* on these cameras
MC-23	Elec. Coupling Cable	*N90/F90*	for simultaneous release of 2- N90/F90
MC-17S	Elec. Coupling Cable	*N8008/F-801, N2000/ F-301, F4S, F4E*	for simultaneous release of 2 cameras/ also with F3, FM-2n w/*MD-4, MD-12*
MR-3	Cable Release Adapter	*N8008/F-801, N2000/ F-301, F4S, F4E*	for using mechanical cable releases on electrical ports
AR-7	Mech. Double Cable Release	*F4, F4S, F4E, N6006/ F-601, F3, FM-2*	for use with *PB-6* bellows
AR-10	Electro-mechanical Double Cable Release	*N8008/F-801, N2000/ F-301, F4S, F4E*	for simultaneous release of 2 cameras/ also with F3, FM-2n w/*MD-4, MD-12*
MT-2 + MC-16A	Intervalometer	*N8008/F-801, N2000/ F-301, F4S, F4E*	also used with *F3, FM-2n* and *MD-4, MD-12*
ML-3	Infrared Remote	*N8008/F-801, N2000/ F-301, F4S, F4E*	also compatible with F3 and FM-2n with *MD-4* or *MD-12* motordrives
MW-2 + MC-17S	Radio Remote	*N8008/F-801, N2000/ F-301, F4S, F4E*	also compatible with F3 and FM-2n with *MD-4* or *MD-12* motordrives, also with N90/F90 using MC-25 Adapter

Bulk Film Magazines

There are situations in which one cannot load a new roll every 36 exposures as when cameras are installed in locations in which they are remotely triggered and it is not practical to reload a 36 exposure roll. For example, in planes, kites, sailboats etc. that have a camera built in. Others are long time security type installations when an interval timer is in use. In all of these cases, a long film magazine represents a real advantage. Some situations such as formal receptions or fast action sports often do not allow time for frequent reloading but in these cases, however, the long film magazine is usually too heavy and cumbersome.

Comparison of 250 Exposure Backs

	Compatible Camera	Capacity	Ex./sec.	Size (in.)	Weight (oz./g)	Features
MF-4	*F3*	250 frames	5.5	12x3.8x3.3	38.5/1100	Databack
MF-24	*F4*	250 frames	5.7	12x3.5x3.6	49/1400	Integrated Multifunction Back

Lens Hoods

A lens hood should be considered a necessary part of any lens since it prevents stray light from entering. Ideally, only the reflected light coming from the subject itself should be allowed to reach the film. Stray light from sources such as the sun characteristically cause flare which may introduce "light marks" reflected off the lens elements and/or an image with lower contrast, less color saturation and unwanted glare. If, however, you are photographing directly into a light source, even a lens hood will not help. Various models and brands are made of metal, plastic, or rubber and Nikon has a specific one for almost all of their lenses. Lens hoods present no special problems with normal and telephoto lenses, but can cause difficulties when used on wide angle-lenses, especially the super-wide models. For example, installing a filter and the hood together may be enough to have the hood intrude slightly on the corners of the picture causing vignetting. This is because of the significantly wide angle of view of these lenses.

Filters

Filters are among the useful accessories because they solve many of the problems that arise between film and the quality of light. Professionals are well aware of their purposes and use them when needed. Certain filters, such as the color type, reduce the amount of total light that reaches the film. As a result, exposure must be increased by a factor (filter factor) expressed as 2X, 3X etc. (see instructions with filter).

UV or Skylight Filters

There is a common practice in photography to always have a UV or skylight filter on the lens. Some photographers object to this practice because they feel that image quality is effected by the two glass/air contact surfaces which could lead to refraction and stray light problems. Just how much this actually occurs to any noticeable degree is a point of disagreement that varies significantly with the lens being used, the lighting conditions, and the picture-taking technique of the photographer.

What is not controversial is that UV filters not only provide the front element with protection against fingerprints and scratches, but also cut out harmful UV rays. The UV portion of light can produce a slight loss of sharpness due to a loss of contrast and a blueish tinge, even on today's films. Both the UV and skylight filter UV rays, while the skylight filter also just slightly warms the scene because of its pin color. These are good choices on overcast days, on the beach, in the mountains, or in bright sun. The choice of UV versus skylight filter will depend on the film used. The skylight adds the slight warmth which is only really noticeable with color transparency film. Consider also that a scratched front element, and hence a new lens, is considerably more expensive than the price of a good filter. Besides, if one suspects that there might be a reduction in image quality because of the filter, it can always be taken off. (Some of Nikon's larger telephoto lenses are supplied with a glass plate to protect the front element.)

Filters for Color and Black and White Photography

Conversion filters: filters that match the color temperature sensitivity of color films (5600°K daylight or 3200°K artificial light) to the color temperature of subject illumination are called conversion filters. Matching the light source to proper film is critical with transparency emulsions to prevent color shifts. It is also useful with color print films, but here a correction can be made when a print is exposed and processed. To determine the exact color temperature of the subject illumination, a good color temperature meter (such as those offered by Gossen or Minolta) is recommended.

Filters to increase contrast and to change the tonal range: color filters are used to effect the representation of color in B&W photography. Each filter color makes its color lighter and its complementary color darker. Thus, an orange filter makes grass and leaves noticeably darker while a green filter makes them lighter. Furthermore, all color filters will effect the density of the sky to one degree or another. A yellow filter, for example, will darken the sky slightly and therefore make the clouds more prominent. A red filter reduces mist in black & white photography since it reduces the amount of long wavelength light that passes through the mist.

Polarizers
The polarization filter (polarizer) is useful in reducing glare and reflections as well as reducing mist in long distance shots. Depending on which way the filter is rotated on the lens, it allows light from a certain direction (polarization) to pass through. Since light is polarized by reflecting off most surfaces, the polarizer can be used to reduce this glare from surfaces such as water, varnish, glass, plastic, etc., by blocking it from reaching the film (except in the case of unpainted metals). In landscape photography, the effect of mist can be reduced by the polarizer, making the colors more saturated, and the blue of a clear sky becomes noticeably more saturated to various degrees depending on the relationship between the location of the camera and the sun. Since polarizers absorb a great deal of light, longer exposures are necessary. In principle, cameras with TTL metering automatically adjust for this. There are two types of polarizers: circular and linear and circular polarizers are required for all AF cameras. The less expensive linear versions are unfortunately not appropriate, since this design interferes with the AF focusing and autofocus mechanisms.

Special Effect and Creative Filters
These filters represent a broad cross section of effects, from multi-image prisms to dazzling color effects and unusual distortions. The choice of using such filters is up to the photographer since none of these filters are necessary to correct any of the light's qualities as in correction and conversion filters. Some photographers use them freely while others avoid them altogether. Many of these filters are dependent on the focal length used, the focus distance, the space between the filter and the front element, the aperture, the contrast, etc. etc. In short, the possible applications and variations are endless. It should be noted, however, that these filters may require placing the camera in a manual focus and/or manual exposure mode because of the way they effect these cameras and lens functions.

Overview of Nikon Filters

	Type	Filter Factor		Filter Thread Size (mm)									Bayonet
		Daylight	Artificial	39	46	52	62	72	77	95	122	160	
Skylight	L1BC	1	1	x		x	x	x					x
Ultraviolet	L37	1	1		x	x							
	L37C	1	1	x		x	x	x	x	x	x	x	
	L39	1	1							x	x		
Yellow													
Light	Y44	1,5	1			x				x			
Medium	Y48	1,7	1,2	x		x	x	x			x		x
Dark	Y52	2	1,4	x		x							
Orange	056	3,5	2	x		x	x	x		x	x		x
Red	R60	6	5	x		x	x	x		x	x		x
Green													
Light	XO	2	1,7			x							
Dark	X1	5	3,5			x							
Polarizer													
Circular		2-4	2-4			x	x						
Linear		2-4	2-4					x					
Neutral													
Density	ND4	4	4	x		x		x					
	ND8	8	8	x		x							
	ND400	400	400			x							
Amber													
Light	A2	1,2	1,2	x		x	x	x					x
Dark	A12	2	2	x		x	x						
Blue													
Light	B2	1,2	1,2	x		x	x	x					x
Medium	B8	1,6	1,6	x		x							
Dark	B12	2,2	2,2	x		x	x						
Soft Focus	Nr.1				x	x	x						
Soft Focus	Nr.2				x	x	x						

Lens and Camera Protection

Camera bags, camera cases, lens cases, etc.: Nikon offers a wide range of products in these sort of protection accessories. Retailers do not always stock these items, so they usual are ordered from brochures. A wide range of similar products from other manufacturers are available. Here are some guidelines to consider when buying such accessories.

Camera bags the most functional camera bags are designed to make carrying equipment around in a protected manner an easily accessible configuration. If you cannot get at everything easily, then this is really a storage container and you should look for another bag. The photojournalists bag of choice is manufactured of cotton canvas by Domke®. Domke bags are designed for comfortable portability and easy access to all equipment. A good camera bag is an investment that will last for years and become part of your whole approach to photographing your subject.

Camera suitcases: aluminum cases are definitely good protection for camera equipment, but are relatively heavy and cumbersome while not allowing quick access to the equipment. A Domke F-1X is a better choice for storage of a complete camera system.

Tubes and sacks: Lenses are best kept in the camera bag without any other packaging, but in such a way that they do not bang into each other. Lightly padded dividers such as found in Domke bags are therefore crucial. For long telephotos Domke Long Lens Bags offer the best option.

Camera and Lens Caps

Camera body caps: the body cap is indispensable for protection. It should always be on the camera when the body is being stored without a lens mounted. Aside from dust protection, this cap prevents damage to the the mirror or electronic contacts inside the body. Such occurrences could result in serious damage.

Lens rear caps: these are also vital. They should be attached as soon as the lens is taken off the camera body. Otherwise, finger prints and scratches could end up on the rear element. In addition, the contacts at the back of the lens might bend. A front lens cap is necessary when the lens is stored, but unnecessary once the lens is put on the camera (note previous comments concerning the use of a UV or skylight filter on the lens).

Indispensable Items

A dust brush to clean lenses, lens tissue and fluid to remove finger prints are an absolute must. Other helpful items to keep at hand include, a roll of cloth tape, spare batteries for camera and flash, eye piece cover, tripod quick release, a device to pull film out of the cassette, a gray card for exact exposure metering, a small note pad, and a leak proof marker that writes on all surfaces.

Closing Comments

When in doubt about any of the functions of your camera, lens or other Nikon equipment, contact Nikon or an authorized dealer: In countries with Nikon distribution centers, one can obtain detailed information on equipment and accessories from customer service. No do-it-yourself repairs! Nikon customer service is the best place for having equipment repaired, especially in the case of today's electronic based cameras and lenses.

Index